Bronze Age Landscapes
Tradition and Transformation

Edited by Joanna Brück

Oxbow Books 2001

Published by
Oxbow Books, Park End Place, Oxford OX1 1HN

© Oxbow Books, 2001

ISBN 1 84217 062 7

A CIP record for this book is available from the British Library

This book is available direct from:

Oxbow Books, Park End Place, Oxford OX1 1HN
(Phone: 01865-241249; Fax: 01865-794449)

and

The David Brown Book Company
PO Box 511, Oakville, CT06779
(Phone: 860-945-9329; Fax: 860-945-9468)

or

from our website
www.oxbowbooks.com

Cover: Reconstruction of the Later Bronze Age settlement at Barleycroft Farm, Cambridgeshire
(© Joshua Pollard/Cambridge Archaeological Unit)

Printed in Great Britain by
The Short Run Press
Exeter

Contents

Preface

It has given me great pleasure to edit this collection of papers on the British Bronze Age. The volume represents a rich and diverse body of work and illustrates the vibrancy of current research on the period. Viewed by many as a bastion of empirical research methodologies, the British Bronze Age has not, with a few notable exceptions, been a focus for theoretical or interpretative debate since the earlier 1980s, when structural Marxist and neo-Marxist approaches discussed the emergence of social inequality. Throughout the 1990s, research on the Bronze Age has not generally been perceived as lying at the forefront of developments in our understanding of prehistoric societies. Synthetic volumes have appeared relatively regularly over the past twenty years for other periods of British prehistory, but again the Bronze Age has lagged behind in this respect. For some years now, one might argue that there has been a sense of fragmentation and a lack of identity for the period.

It was in response to this in 1998, that Stuart Needham and I decided to consult those with an interest in the British Bronze Age on the need to establish a regular workshop or meeting group. Similar meeting groups have thrived in other specialist areas, whether period- or theme-based. Establishing the Bronze Age Forum, as it has become known, was not an attempt to demarcate research-territory, nor to exclude those interested in thematic rather than period-based issues, nor indeed was it an attempt to bolster the old and rightly-criticised three age system. Rather, the aim was to encourage dialogue and dynamism in research on the Bronze Age, as well as a sense of community and focus for those working in the period. Moreover, despite the problems of the three age system, I would argue that there is particular value in providing a forum for the exploration and interpretation of specific cultural contexts. My own work on Bronze Age settlement has benefited immensely from discussion with those working on other aspects of the period, for example exchange, metalworking and environmental reconstruction, none of which have formed a particular part of my own research to date.

Many of the contributions to this volume were originally presented at a conference held in Cambridge in April 1999, *Place and Space in the British Bronze Age*. This meeting also provided an opportunity for participants to discuss a format for the proposed Bronze Age Forum. The presentations at the conference demonstrated the range and vitality of current Bronze Age research and provided a context for direct contact and discussion between those working in contract archaeology, museums and academia. One could not claim that the meeting was able to define what is special or different about this period of prehistory to others, nor what the specific contribution of those working on the Bronze Age might be to wider issues of archaeological interpretation. Yet, by bringing together a range of research, it became possible to identify questions critical to ongoing and future work, as well as gaps in current knowledge.

While most of the papers in this volume were initially presented at the Cambridge meeting, others were solicited after that date. The volume's theme focuses broadly on British Bronze Age settlement and landscape. However, as many of the papers illustrate, the complexities of the material require that researchers avoid bracketing off these topics from other areas of practice. As a result, the reader will not only find papers here which treat the organisation of domestic space, field systems and cairnfields, and settlement patterns at a regional level, but also metalwork and metallurgy, rock art, funerary rites and other ritual activities. While Bronze Age studies might be said to have focused primarily on artefacts throughout much of their history, and work since the 1980s has largely been site- or landscape-based, current research is beginning to move more confidently between these two levels of analysis, a strength that is very much reflected in this collection of papers.

The volume is not structured into sub-sections, as a series of shared inter-cutting themes weave in and out through many of the contributions. With so much of the synthetic work to date focusing on southern England, it is pleasing to start the volume with surveys of the Bronze Age archaeology of two very different areas of Britain, Ashmore's overview of Scotland and Malim's of Cambridgeshire. Following these, a series of papers explore questions relating to land tenure, territoriality and settlement mobility, with a wider focus on the contrasts between the Earlier and Later Bronze Age. Ashwin and Hinman's papers describe sites of a type characteristic of much of earlier prehistory, including the Early Bronze Age: scatters of pits, postholes and other features, some with deposits of possible ritual significance, which cannot be rationalised into identifiable structures. Garner's contribution in which he reports on a series of Early Bronze Age buildings at Manchester Airport provides an interesting counterpoint to these, suggesting that the kind of variability recently claimed for Neolithic settlement patterns across the British Isles may be characteristic of the Earlier Bronze Age also.

Papers by Field and Yates substantially add to our understanding of Later Bronze Age fieldsystems in southern Britain, and their work helps to underline the long-held sense of difference between the Earlier and Later Bronze Age. On the other hand, Evans and Knight's interpretation of the Barleycroft post-alignments as features central to communal gatherings and ceremonial processions provides a vision of Later Bronze Age land use which is quite different, perhaps even retaining aspects of similarity to earlier 'Neolithic-type' practices. This theme is further elaborated by Johnston and Kitchen, whose contributions challenge the familiar interpretations of land tenure and territoriality in the Later Bronze Age. Like Kitchen, Locock describes patterns of mobility during this period that have to date been largely underexplored.

A change of scale follows, with Brossler, Nowakowski and Brück providing studies of spatial organisation and domestic practice at the level of the individual site. Both Nowakowski and Brück link some of the ritual activities carried out on Later Bronze Age settlements to other areas of contemporary practice, including funerary rites and metalworking. These themes are explored further by Barber, who focuses on the social aspects of metalworking technologies. Pendleton's paper takes a quite different perspective, challenging the recent orthodoxy that seeks to explain all metalwork deposition in social and ideological terms. Timberlake provides a refreshing landscape-scale overview of recent work on metal prospection, mining and extraction. Moving on to the themes of death and memory, Owoc outlines how mortuary practices facilitated both the maintenance and transformation of the social order, while Watson discusses the role of round barrows in structuring the cultural landscape. Jones explores some similar questions in relation to rock art, arguing that this medium allowed the inscription of meaning onto the landscape through reference to the past. Finally, Bradley's Afterword provides an overview of current trends and an evaluation of the kinds of questions that need to form a focus for future research on the Bronze Age. Three of the papers in this collection (Evans and Knight, Johnston, and Owoc) were received after the Afterword was written; hence, Bradley did not have a chance to include these in his commentary.

Many people have contributed to this volume in one way or another. Most particularly, I would like to thank the individual authors for their hard work and support and especially for their patience in awaiting the publication of the book. I am grateful to the other speakers who brought their discussion and ideas to the 1999 conference, but who for one reason or another were unable to contribute to the final volume. Humphrey Case, Niall Sharples, Roger Thomas, Andrew Lawson, Trevor Cowie, Marie-Louise Sørensen and Frances Healy each inspired constructive debate through their measured and thoughtful chairing of sessions at the conference. Since then, a further meeting of the Bronze Age Forum has taken place in Edinburgh in October 2000 and I would like to thank Trevor Cowie and Alison Sheridan for enabling us to continue with these themes and others at that excellent meeting. I am grateful to Josh Pollard and Chris Evans for permission to reproduce the reconstruction drawing of Barleycroft Farm used on the front cover of this volume. Finally, I would like to thank Stuart Needham for his vision and work in bringing the Bronze Age Forum to fruition.

Joanna Brück,
Dublin, July 2001.

List of Contributors

Patrick Ashmore
Historic Scotland
Longmore House
Salisbury Place
Edinburgh
EH9 1SH
ashmore@ednet.co.uk

Trevor Ashwin
38 Cawston Road
Reepham
Norwich
NR10 4LU
trevor@norfarch.netscapeonline.co.uk

Martyn Barber
NMRC
Kemble Drive
Swindon
Wiltshire
SN2 2GZ
martyn.barber@rchme.co.uk

Richard Bradley
Department of Archaeology
University of Reading
Whiteknights
PO Box 218
Reading
RG6 2AA
r.j.bradley@reading.ac.uk

Adam Brossler
Oxford Archaeological Unit
Janus House
Osney Mead
Oxford
OX2 0ES
adam.brossler@oau-oxford.com

Joanna Brück
Department of Archaeology
University College Dublin
Belfield
Dublin 4
Ireland
Joanna.Bruck@ucd.ie

Christopher Evans
Cambridge Archaeological Unit
Department of Archaeology
Downing Street
Cambridge
CB2 3DZ
cje30@cam.ac.uk

David Field
NMRC
Kemble Drive
Swindon
Wiltshire
SN2 2GZ
david.field@rchme.co.uk

Dan Garner
Gifford & Partners
20 Nicholas Street
Chester
CH1 2NX
Dan.Garner@gifford-consulting.co.uk

Mark Hinman
Archaeological Field Unit
Fulbourn Community Centre
Haggis Gap
Fulbourn
Cambridge
CB1 5HD
mark.hinman@virgin.net

Robert Johnston
Department of History and Welsh History
University of Wales
Bangor
Gwynedd
LL57 2DG
r.a.johnston@bangor.ac.uk

Andrew Jones
Department of Archaeology
University of Southampton
Highfield
Southampton
SO17 1BJ
amj@soton.ac.uk

Willy Kitchen
Dearne Valley College
Manvers Park
Wath upon Dearne
Rotherham
South Yorkshire
S63 7EW
willykitchen@supanet.com

Mark Knight
Cambridge Archaeological Unit
Department of Archaeology
Downing Street
Cambridge
CB2 3DZ
mk226@cam.ac.uk

Martin Locock
Glamorgan-Gwent Archaeological Trust
Heathfield House
Heathfield Road
Swansea
SA1 6EL
mlocock@lineone.net

Tim Malim
Archaeological Field Unit
Fulbourn Community Centre
Haggis Gap
Fulbourn
Cambridge
CB1 5HD
Tim.Malim@libraries.camcnty.gov.uk

Jacqueline Nowakowski
Cornwall Archaeological Unit
Corwall County Council
The Kennall Building
Old County Hall
Station Road
Truro
TR1 3AY
jnowakowski@cornwall.gov.uk

Mary Ann Owoc
Department of Anthropology/Archaeology
501 E. 38th Street
Mercyhurst College
Erie
Pennsylvania 16546
USA
mowoc@mercyhurst.edu

Colin Pendleton
Planning Department
Suffolk County Council
Shire Hall
Bury St. Edmunds
Suffolk
IP33 2AR
colin.pendleton@et.suffolk.gov.uk

Simon Timberlake
98 Victoria Road
Cambridge
CB4 3DU
Timberlake@mcmail.com

Aaron Watson
Department of Archaeology
University of Reading
Whiteknights
PO Box 218
Reading
RG6 2AA
a.j.watson@reading.ac.uk

Dave Yates
Department of Archaeology
University of Reading
White Knights
PO Box 218
Reading
RG6 2AA
dtyates@dtyates.freeserve.co.uk

1   Settlement in Scotland during the second millennium BC

Patrick Ashmore

Summary

Work on the Bronze Age of Scotland has been unevenly distributed, and many questions about spatial and chronological distribution remain. Reconstructions of social systems can at best be tentative. Roundhouses and other structures suggest a working hypothesis that there were significant local regional variations, but except perhaps towards the beginning and end of the second millennium BC, there were no great social variations. Objects perhaps suggest an only slightly more stratified society. The evidence and the gaps in it will be reviewed and questions will be asked about what new work and approaches are needed for construction of social models.

Introduction

There is no fully rounded modern account of the second millennium BC in Scotland. Some themes have been summarised recently in Trevor Cowie and Ian Shepherd's contribution on the Bronze Age to 'Scotland: Environment and Archaeology, 8000 BC–AD 1000' (Edwards and Ralston 1997), which also contains overviews on climate, landscape, soils, vegetation and fauna. An anecdotal account, largely based on sites and objects with radiocarbon dates, was provided in my own 'Neolithic and Bronze Age Scotland' (Ashmore 1996). In what follows, I shall take a different approach from both of those syntheses, although I shall focus on what has been scientifically dated to the period, trying to identify problems in the data, and exploring how our understanding can be increased by application of both old and new approaches. My approach is based on the following suppositions. Accounts of what has been discovered are anecdotes – descriptions of what has

been observed, distorted by varying prior assumptions and knowledge. Often the anecdotes are modified in terms of personal experience, through implicit or explicit use of analogies. We group together those modified anecdotes that we think have relevance to each other, based on closeness in character, time and space, to form anthologies. We test the fitness of the groupings and their interpretations by analysis.

I shall rely mostly on sites and objects with radiocarbon dates to describe what happened during the second millennium BC in Scotland, because typology-based chronologies, in areas with low artefact concentrations, can be grossly distorted by heirlooms and other factors. There are no great problems with calibration during the period. Small plateaux in the 1998 calibration curve between 1900 and 1750 BC, 1700 and 1550 BC and 1400 and 1250 BC (Stuiver *et al.* 1998) do not pose problems like the large ambiguities in the Late Neolithic and the Iron Age. They will cause some chronological clumping of sites, but not to an extent prohibiting useful discussion. In what follows, calibrated dates will be expressed as 2-sigma ranges so that there is a 19 out of 20 chance that the true date of the object dated falls in that range.

By 2000 BC, Scotland had been inhabited for at least 6000 years, and farming had been practised for about 2000 years. The people at the mirror image of our turn of the millennium inherited a landscape with arable fields, houses along with dwellings that had been deserted for more than 1500 years, and new and ancient burial places and ceremonial sites. In addition to farmlands, pastures and moor there was still quite extensive woodland cover (Edwards and Whittington 1997, 75) dominated by oak, hazel and elm in the southern half of the Scottish mainland; oak, hazel and birch along the coasts; pine and birch in the mountains; and birch and hazel in the far north and west (Tipping 1994). Barley was the main crop, with wheat grown in a few places; cattle, sheep and pigs were bred.

Around 200 structures and objects have produced radiocarbon dates implying that they more probably than not belong to the second millennium BC. Suitably, two of the earliest dates are from objects associated with bronzes. Wood from the backing of a tubular bronze bead from the Migdale hoard has been dated to between 2300 and 1750 cal. BC (OxA–4659; 3655±75 BP; Sheridan 1996). An ox leather sheath adhering to a copper dagger with a gold-filleted haft has been dated to between 2350 and 1750 cal. BC (OxA–4510; 3690±80 BP; *ibid.*). It was found with a cremation in a pit under a massive cairn at Collessie in Fife, a point I shall return to later. No iron object (apart from iron oxide nodules used as strike-a-lights or for pigment) is associated with dates before 1000 BC and the typologically earliest iron objects are imitations of socketed axes that flourished after that date. The second millennium BC is the core of the Scottish Bronze Age by any definition.

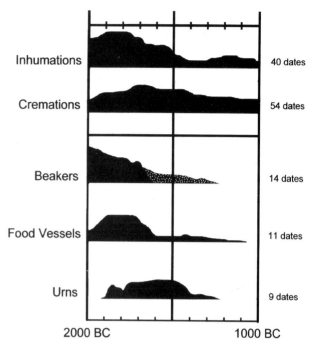

Fig. 1.1 *The chronological distribution of burials and traditional pottery types*

A traditional Bronze Age

Those preliminaries over, I want to start with a sketch of this period in Scotland, with no detail, as if seen from a great distance. During the thousand years, or around 40 generations, between 2000 BC and 1000 BC, well-dated evidence confirms that bone, wood, stone and bronze were used for tools, weapons and ornaments. All of the newly created structures were round, by which I mean circular, oval or pear-shaped, except for field banks and burial cists. They included houses, cairns and small ceremonial sites, the latter along with re-used larger ritual centres. The dated objects are various, including Beakers, Food Vessels, urns and so-called flat-rimmed wares from both domestic and funerary sites, bronze and stone tools, weapons and ornaments, ox yokes and cart wheels, a long bow and a barbed and tanged arrowhead. A comfortingly familiar picture, in fact – when viewed from a distance.

Before discussing settlements, I shall review the evidence for burials and pottery types, using traditional classifications and largely ignoring geographical variation (Fig. 1.1). The reason for doing so is two-fold. Even this, a comparatively rich and geographically well-distributed dataset, has limitations and I want to recite some of the most fundamental of these. I also want to show that most changes during the second millennium BC seem to be gradual, but that this impression may be due to shortcomings in the dating evidence.

Our understanding of burial customs is distorted by biases in information retrieval. Because it was not until recently that it became common to date burials without pots, and since it seems to have become less and less common to include pots with burials as the millennium wore on, both inhumations and cremations of the latter half of the millennium are probably under-represented in Fig. 1.1. However, the summed probability curves suggest that the practice of inhumation in cists, graves and pits (and less formally in middens) had started before 2000 BC and became less popular than cremation after about 1500 BC. Cremation was also used to dispose of mortal remains before 2000 BC and it was probably the most common way of interring the dead from about 1500 BC until after 1000 BC. This is not to say, of course, that either of these methods was necessarily the commonest way of disposing of corpses, given the several methods that leave no detectable traces.

There is a broad geographical variation in general burial preferences. Inhumation (in this small sample) dominates in the east, from Aberdeenshire to the Scottish Borders, in a ratio of 3:2, whereas in the west and north cremation dominates inhumation by over 2:1. There is no convincing evidence that this difference is solely attributable to geological and climatic factors.

A study of well-dated British Beakers suggested to its authors that the use of Beakers began (well) before 2000 cal. BC and that their currency ended about 1800 cal. BC (Kinnes *et al.* 1991, 39), although that carefully phrased conclusion supposes that a tail of dates running to nearly 1500 BC is an artefact of dating inaccuracies and calibration uncertainties (*ibid.*, fig 3). The radiocarbon dates for Beakers in Scotland, summarised in Fig. 1.1, come mostly from graves, but also from ceremonial sites, middens and cultivated soils, and suggest that their use continued to about 1650 cal. BC, possibly until about 1300 cal. BC. Although the three latest dates, from Ashgrove in Fife, Berrybrae in Aberdeenshire and Balbirnie in Fife, were all measured decades ago, and may have been less accurate than modern dates, the Berrybrae and Balbirnie Beakers were both incorporated in special settings in ceremonial sites (Ritchie 1974, 7; Burl 1979, 25–31, 124–125), and it is conceivable that the pots were far older than the contexts in which they were found. The dated Food Vessels from Scotland come from settlements, burials and ceremonial sites. They were first used before 2000 BC and continued in fashion to at least 1600 cal. BC, possibly with some continued use until about 1250 cal. BC, in both east and west Scotland. Cinerary Urns from settlements, burials and ceremonial sites, mostly cordoned, have been dated mainly to between 1900 and 1400 cal. BC, but they were possibly used until about 1250 cal. BC in central, northern and western Scotland at least.

Limitations of the traditional view

However, having provided this sketch, what I want to emphasise is the ridiculously small size of the dated sample. It is small both in absolute and in relative terms and for that reason it cannot be statistically representative of the parent population. Suppose that the average population of Scotland during this period was between 10,000 and 100,000, then at a mortality of six per thousand per year (the mortality rate for Sri Lanka in 1996), 60,000 to 600,000 people died during this period. Between 1 in 600 and 1 in 6000 is represented by the radiocarbon-dated inhumations and cremations.

At best the burial evidence provides a set of conjectures. Much more information will be required before these can be shown either to be fairly accurate or generally wrong. The first conjecture is that the population did not grow markedly during this period (because the burials dated so far are spread fairly evenly over time), and the second is that both inhumation and cremation were used throughout the second millennium in all parts of Scotland. The third conjecture is that most burials were not accompanied by a pot or other inorganic offering (although this conjecture relies on the supposition that there has been a bias towards reporting and dating of burials with artefacts), and the fourth is

that burials with a Beaker or Food Vessel became rare after about 1600 BC. The fifth conjecture is that use of Cinerary Urns (which recent evidence shows were probably slightly fancy forms of domestic pottery) became more popular around 1650 BC; they and accessory vessels were, on present evidence, the most popular kinds of pottery accompanying burials between 1600 and 1400 BC. The sixth conjecture is that inhumation was somewhat more favoured than cremation in the east and that cremation was more favoured in the west and north, despite the lack of solid evidence for or against different survival rates of unburned and cremated bone in different parts of Scotland.

Indeed, the likelihood that all six conjectures are correct is small. However, propositions such as these need to be validated before most social models can be tested. For instance, it would be useful to be able to define the geographical extent of social units, or the degree of variation in social status. There is a hint from the differing emphasis on cremation and inhumation that east and west had weaker social connections between each other than each had internally, and a hint that Food Vessels were the common domestic pot as well as a burial accompaniment in the Inner Hebrides at much the same time as Cinerary Urns were becoming the favoured vessels for both domestic and burial purposes elsewhere in the southern half of Scotland. However, with so little well-dated information, it is not possible to distinguish between almost random local fluctuations in preferences and more consistent differences that might suggest that regional groups expressed a strong sense of identity in their material culture.

A similar problem attaches to our knowledge of ritual and ceremonial. There are very few well dated sites. At Balnuaran of Clava (Bradley 1996; 1997a) and at Newton of Petty (Bradley 1997b), massive cairns surrounded by stone circles were built near the beginning of the second millennium BC. Dates from the complex stone setting at Callanish in the Western Isles (Ashmore 1997) suggest that the site was re-used at about the same time. The recumbent stone circle in Aberdeenshire at Berrybrae (Burl 1979, 25–31, 124–125; Kinnes *et al.* 1991) was reconfigured during this period; it produced radiocarbon dates that when calibrated at 2-sigma indicate a date range in the first half of the second millennium BC. It was also around this time that a cremation burial was set into the collapsed corbels of the chambered cairn at The Ord, Lairg, Sutherland (Sharples 1981). The earlier part of a bimodal distribution of dates from North Mains, Strathallan, Perthshire (Barclay 1983, 259), centres around 1750 cal. BC. This site includes both a henge and a very large mound into which Food Vessels and cremations were set. Taken with the massive burial cairn at Collessie in Fife that I mentioned earlier, these sites of the first quarter of the millennium may reflect traditions that continued on from the Late Neolithic.

Equally interesting is the reuse of ceremonial sites towards the end of the second millennium BC. There was activity at Balnuaran of Clava and Newton of Petty during the last half of the second millennium BC over what seems to have been several generations at least. The same can be said of Temple Wood in Argyll where small kerb cairns were set into the old stone circle (Scott 1989). The latter part of the bimodal distribution of dates at North Mains, Strathallan, referred to above, centres around 1000 cal. BC. In sum, reuse of ancient ceremonial centres in the last few centuries of the second millennium seems to be a fairly widespread phenomenon, perhaps prefiguring the reuse of Neolithic sites during the Iron Age (Hingley 1996).

Thus another conjecture – perhaps something stronger than that – is that people used and re-used impressive ceremonial sites in the first and last quarters of the millennium much more commonly than they did in the middle half, reflecting interests better demonstrated in the Late Neolithic and Iron Age.

Settlements of roundhouses

Roundhouses are distributed throughout Scotland. They are found on marginal land and, mostly as cropmarks, on arable land. Most of them are not truly circular and they range widely in size, wall thickness and height. The largest, in all senses, seem to belong to the Iron Age, although as yet the date of very few roundhouses is known.

Although pioneering work on settlements and field systems has taken place elsewhere in Scotland, for instance on Arran (Barber 1997), in northeast Perthshire (RCAHMS 1990), and in eastern Dumfriesshire (RCAHMS 1998), one of the regions investigated most intensively in recent years is Sutherland. Cowley's recent study of part of the Strath of Kildonan (1998) built on systematic and detailed landscape survey by RCAHMS (*ibid.*, 165), although it did not benefit from recent excavations. Cowley identified three types of grouping of hut circles: isolated houses with no obvious cultivation nearby; small clusters of 2 to 6 houses in areas with small cairns and fragments of field banks; and clusters of 4 to 13 buildings within field systems defined by banks and lynchets. It is worth noting that even in these more coherent systems there were many banks that did not form part of an overall pattern.

Although the distributions of the three types of grouping were not clearcut, they helped to indicate broad variations in intensity of activity across the landscape (*ibid.*, 168, 170). Cowley took into account the destructive effects of later agricultural activity and of chronological variations so far as the evidence allowed, but the information available to him was suitable only for very general conclusions. The larger groupings with obvious field systems were on the better land and the smallest ones on the most marginal land, up-slope and up-river; the latter areas (although perhaps not individual sites) were probably always peripheral.

The need for a combination of landscape survey and excavation with abundant radiocarbon dates has been further emphasised by work in Achany Glen, Lairg (McCullagh and Tipping 1998). Survey of a large strip along a valley side, together with palaeo-environmental work and test-pit excavation at many sites, showed that the area had been cultivated from the Neolithic onward; but most of the upstanding 31 roundhouses in the 60ha intensive survey area probably dated to the second half of the second millennium (*ibid.*, 20, 114, table 4). The field banks did not form coherent large-scale patterns, a point to which I shall return later.

A cluster of houses and field systems, in a cultivated area of about 2ha near Allt na Fearna was the main focus of excavation (*ibid.*, 102). There, two houses belonged to a period between about 1800 and 1600 cal. BC. One of these, House 2, may have been around 10m across internally (GU–3300; 3480±70 BP; *ibid.*, 39–40). This is one of the largest known roundhouses of the earlier half of the millennium in Scotland. The subsequent settlement history of the site was complex, with houses being flattened and their areas cultivated while others were built nearby. The farming landscape changed from unenclosed to enclosed before the middle of the second millennium BC. Around the middle of the millennium the settlement was dominated by a large house, House 4, with smaller houses nearby. Originally almost circular and 11–12m across internally, it produced a date of between 2035 and 1600 BC and another between 1765 and 1515 BC (GU–3158 and GU–3157; 3460±80 BP and 3350±50 BP respectively; *ibid.*, 48). However, there was also much earlier charcoal from the house site and the later of the two dates is probably more to be trusted, since the earlier date may reflect the presence of residual charcoal (cf. Ashmore 1999). The main suite of dates from this house comes from charcoal created during the conflagration of a subsequent phase of building that probably started between about 1600 and 1400 cal. BC (McCullagh and Tipping 1998, 49). In this later form, the house was elliptical (*ibid.*, 103) with a ratio of breadth to length of about 0.87 and a markedly oval internal wear pattern.

After the destruction of House 4 by fire, smaller

houses were built and although occupation continued until near the end of the millennium the structures were of poor quality. The site was reoccupied in the first millennium BC, by which time house-building techniques and agricultural practices seem to have changed significantly with the local introduction of narrow rig cultivation (*ibid.*, 113, 212).

The latest dated structure was House 7 with five Iron Age dates for it and possibly related nearby features ranging from 520–170 cal. BC (GU–3165; 2290±60 BP) to 360 cal. BC–130 cal. AD (GU–3161; 2070±90 BP). The area was sealed by peat at various times between about 560–890 cal. AD (GU–3358; 1340±80 BP) and 1280–1410 cal. AD (GU–3333; 650±50 BP). No later domestic structures were excavated at Allt na Fearna, nor were there obvious candidates, so although the possibility seems to be high that the built landscape elements revealed by archaeology included Iron Age divisions, the likelihood of still later built landscape elements is low.

It is difficult to judge the settlement density in the valley at any one time. There was an average of one hut circle per hectare in the intensively surveyed area, but in the excavated area some houses were clearly the successors of others, and some were not visible before excavation. Over the millennium, the several occupation foci were quite possibly not all occupied at any one time, and thus it is impossible to tell how the overall density of occupation varied. One important conclusion from the excavations at Allt na Fearna, Lairg, was that the morphology of the Bronze and Iron Age roundhouses before excavation did not reflect the original architecture closely (*ibid.*, 112). For instance, although features revealed by excavation, such as the elaborate door of House 4, taken in conjunction with probably contemporary simplification of the nearby House 6, may indicate a social ranking within the cluster of houses (*ibid.*, 114), the details essential to social interpretations were not known before excavation and radiocarbon dating (*ibid.*, 47, fig. 23). All this is bad news for those wishing to construct even provisional social models from field survey evidence alone.

Carn Dubh, Perthshire

A somewhat similar but later settlement sequence has recently been explored in some detail. The earliest excavated house at Carn Dubh, Perthshire, House 3, was built around the end of the second millennium BC (Rideout 1995, 159, 184) in an area where there had been woodland clearance around 2000 cal. BC and permanent settlement from about 1100 BC, give or take a century or so (*ibid.*, 182–183).

The 100ha survey area included about 17 roundhouses (*ibid.*, 145). Most of the houses sat in a zone of short stretches of field bank and small cairns although those on lower ground were not associated with visible field systems. However, the excavator concluded that probably only two or three of the houses of the main grouping were in use at any one time (*ibid.*, 186) and it looks as if this sequence reinforces the impression of a complex succession of use and reuse of house sites seen at Lairg.

Lintshie Gutter and platform settlements

Turning to more southerly parts of Scotland, during the past decade the chronology of platform settlements has come to be seen to cover most of the second millennium BC. Excavations at Green Knowe (Jobey 1980) near Peebles in southeast Scotland revealed roundhouses of the latter half of the millennium. More recent excavations at Lintshie Gutter in the Clyde Valley (Terry 1995) have extended that chronology back near to its beginning.

The putatively Bronze Age settlement pattern in this part of the Clyde valley differs from that in the Kildonan Glen and at Lairg. Almost all the known platform houses belong to clusters or are close to them, with wide spaces between the clusters (Terry 1995, illus. 1). The Clyde in this neighbourhood runs in a narrow flat-bottomed valley between the 250 and 300m contours, and most of the settlements survive at between 300 and 350m above sea level. Perhaps the settlements avoided the flood plain; alternatively, other settlements may have existed nearer to the Clyde but are not archaeologically visible because their houses were not built on platforms or because they have been ploughed flat.

Lintshie Gutter is the largest known settlement in the area. It comprises 30 roughly circular platforms and a roughly circular scoop dug in a hill slope on the west side of the Clyde valley. The size and form of the platforms were related to the angle of the slope into which they were dug. Eight platforms were partially or wholly excavated. Because the area including the platforms had been ploughed, downwash concealed their shapes (*ibid.*, 371) and their down-slope elements had been damaged; none of them returned a complete plan.

Excavation revealed a variety of structures. Five platforms supported ring-groove houses (*ibid.*, 419). They varied in internal diameter between 8m and 13m. Two (on Platforms 5 and 13) had an internal post-ring and were probably timber-framed buildings with conical roofs. Two others had enough internal postholes to suggest they too were roofed. All the houses seem to have had wattle and daub walls, some double-faced and some single-faced.

Although many of the houses showed signs of several phases of building, the radiocarbon dating evidence is ambiguous. There is one third millennium BC radiocarbon date from platform 8, but the charcoal used for it had an isotopic ratio more like that of peat than wood and its status is therefore somewhat ambiguous. Charcoal from the timber-framed oval house on platform 13, which was up to 8m across internally, has been dated to between 2300 and 1500 cal. BC (GU–3198; 3550±130 BP; *ibid.*, 378). A date from the very nearly circular house, about 9m across internally, on Platform 5, of between 1960 and 1510 cal. BC (GU–3200; 3430±90 BP; *ibid.*, 382) is significantly different (T = 5.0 against a 5% probability value of 3.8) from a later date of between 1610 and 1320 cal. BC from an oven in the house (GU–3202; 3200±50; *ibid.*, 384) and either the platform was occupied at times several generations apart or the earlier date was from residual charcoal (cf. Ashmore 1999).

Two platforms (1 and 7 late phase) were markedly different from the others. The structure on Platform 1, which has a very imprecise date between 2000 and 1350 cal. BC (GU–3199; 3360±120 BP; Terry 1995, 380), was probably stone-walled and had no evidence of roofing; it may have been a stock enclosure. That on Platform 7 was small and the structure on it seems to have been used other than as a dwelling place.

Abundant flat-rimmed pots with barrel and bucket shapes, some decorated (*ibid.*, 402), could be described as domestic urn, and those from Platform 5 in particular seem to be similar to Cinerary Urns at a roughly contemporary cairn and small stone setting at Park of Tongland in southwest Scotland (Russell-White *et al.* 1992, 314). Several of the platforms at Lintshie Gutter produced carbonised barley and seeds of cultivation weeds. Bone did not survive in this acid ground.

Although the settlement as a whole was probably occupied at some time or times between about 1900 and 1400 BC, it is not clear how long or how continuously it was in use, nor which houses were contemporary with one another. It seems probable that their general form reflects the nature of the terrain rather than social factors; in other words, there is no impediment to considering them for most purposes in the same way as settlements on flat ground. It is presumed, without any real evidence, that farming took place on the cultivation ridges north of Lintshie Gutter or on the valley bottom. The circumstances here, then, are rather different from those in Sutherland and at Carn Dubh. However, the different sizes of clusters of domestic structures may reflect a difference in the carrying capacity of the land, rather than consciously chosen social differences.

Exploring social hypotheses

What can be done with this sort of evidence? What information can it provide about the way societies worked?

One question is how far was there a common society throughout Scotland? Models of spatially based and of purely relative, or distance-independent, connections between clusters of people provide different answers to questions about the overall degree of connectivity. The crucial question is how far connections were dependent on distance. If the amount of two-way movement between communities was limited by, for instance, political barriers to movement, strong connectivity would have been unlikely. If, on the other hand, distance was not a strong factor, a small number of almost random two-way connections between groups should have led to connections between all groups (Watts 1999, 136–137). These observations can be turned on their head. If there is plentiful connectivity then it can be supposed that there were no political barriers to movement, and vice versa. It seems likely that this period in Scotland saw weak but persistent long distance connectivity, with movements of copper alloy and jet or shale objects over long distances. However, the overall similarity of building and artefact traditions in widely separated areas, and the differing emphases on cremation and inhumation in the east and west, provide different messages. More data with strong chronological controls, and better directed analysis, will be required to explore this and similar questions.

Another question is whether the field evidence can help to characterise other aspects of society. It is intriguing that many of these landscapes are fragmented but have great time depth. The best way forward is to pursue the likelihood that although the evidence available from traditional survey alone allows numerous explanations for the fragmented nature of the landscape, excavation can narrow down the range of possibilities and allow discrimination between different ways of organising society.

This is not a view shared by all; some experienced field-workers believe that these fragmented landscapes are so damaged that their sequences can never be explained at reasonable cost. One frequently advanced hypothesis is that the fragmentary nature of the field systems found in some Scottish groupings of roundhouses and field systems, on what is now marginal land, reflects Medieval and post-Medieval destruction or covering with alluvial or colluvial material. That does not seem likely at Allt na Fearna, Lairg, given the medieval and earlier peat cover. At Carn Dubh, it may be unlikely in the higher part of the area where houses and fragmentary banks survive but likely lower down where there are isolated houses without visible traces of ancient field systems. However, it is likely to be true for the valley bottom below Lintshie Gutter.

A very different conjecture is that the fragmented landscapes reflect a tenurial system in which land was inherited by all those relatives at the same, closest genetic distance from the dead person. In other words, the land was divided up into parcels each of which had about the same amount of pasture, arable and other resources, and those parcels could, where the original holding was not divisible into strips crossing all of the local resources, consist each of several small pieces of land. I am grateful to Alex Woolfe for advancing this suggestion, which he drew from a knowingly loose analogy with Early Medieval land tenure systems. If it is right, we might expect or hope to see smaller and smaller divisions of the land. These would at least occasionally preserve elements of earlier more extensive land divisions. Perhaps this sort of pattern is what Barber found at Machrie North, Arran (1997, figs 35–36), although the resources necessary for adequate chronological control were not available for that exercise, so its utility for testing social hypotheses can only remain speculation until fieldwork of a similar quality but greater extent has been published.

Another conjecture is that the land was not subdivided generation after generation in the way described above. Instead, the land was passed on undivided between new holders. Fragmentation of earlier built landscapes might arise when agriculture on the hillsides of marginal areas such as Allt na Fearna led to soil erosion. If soil tended to pile up against field banks running along the contours, then subsequent farmers might have broken down parts of the field banks by cultivating the thickened soil on and behind them. Successive waves of destruction and re-establishment of field walls would therefore spread the soil down-slope in a punctuated equilibrium pattern. Such a succession of changes should be detectable by excavation in transects running up- and downhill. An important part of such a study would be to identify true lynchets and distinguish them from solifluction lobes and other semi-natural phenomena. Another area of interest in such research would be the relationship between lynchets and earlier embanked field systems.

Any of these ideas, and others, might explain why coherent land division systems do not survive on the landscapes described by Cowley or on those at Lairg and Carn Dubh. However, it does seem that these different explanations should leave different traces behind them. There is a hierarchy of techniques that can be used to explore these questions. The first is traditional survey including aerial survey to map out the more obvious features of the area.

The second is very detailed survey through the recording of all irregularities in the terrain and all vegetation changes, a technique developed by Barber and others in Scotland in the late 1970s and 1980s (Rideout 1995, 141; Barber 1997, 61; McCullagh and Tipping 1998, 20). The third is test-pitting to gain more information about soil depths and the nature of features recorded during the topographical survey. The fourth is detailed environmental investigation through palynological, geomorphological and soil analysis. The fifth is excavation of large areas. The sixth is very abundant radiocarbon dating of several single pieces of unabraded small roundwood charcoal from each important context (Ashmore 1999). Such a programme would not be cheap, but it is necessary if hypotheses such as those described above are to be explored and tested.

References

Ashmore, P. J. 1996. *Neolithic and Bronze Age Scotland.* London: Batsford.

Ashmore, P. J. 1997. Calanais 1, Lewis. *Discovery and Excavation in Scotland* 1997, 116.

Ashmore, P. J. 1999. Radiocarbon dating: avoiding errors by avoiding mixed samples. *Antiquity* 73, 124–128.

Barber, J. (ed.) 1997. *The Archaeological Investigation of a Prehistoric Landscape: Excavations on Arran 1978–1981.* Edinburgh: Scottish Trust for Archaeological Research Monograph 2.

Barclay, G. J. 1983. Sites of the third millennium BC to the first millennium AD at North Mains, Strathallan, Perthshire. *Proceedings of the Society of Antiquaries of Scotland* 113, 112–281.

Bradley, R. J. 1996. Balnuaran of Clava. *Discovery and Excavation in Scotland* 1996, 138–139.

Bradley, R. J. 1997a. Balnuaran of Clava, Inverness. *Discovery and Excavation in Scotland* 1997, 114.

Bradley, R. J. 1997b. Newton of Petty, Inverness. *Discovery and Excavation in Scotland* 1997, 115.

Bronk Ramsey, C. 1995. Radiocarbon calibration and analysis of stratigraphy: the Oxcal program. *Radiocarbon* 37(2), 425–430.

Burl, H. A. W. 1979. *Rings of Stone: the prehistoric stone circles of Britain and Ireland.* London: Frances Lincoln.

Cowie, T. G. and Shepherd, I. A. G. 1997. The Bronze Age. In Edwards, K. J. and Ralston, I. B. M. (eds.) 1997. *Scotland: Environment and Archaeology, 8000 BC–AD 1000*, 151–168. Chichester: John Wiley.

Cowley, D. C. 1998. Identifying marginality in the first and second millennia BC in the Strath of Kildonan, Sutherland. In Mills, C. M. and Coles, G. (eds.) 1998. *Life on the Edge: Human Settlement and Marginality*, 165–171. Oxford: Oxbow Monograph 100.

Edwards, K. J. and Ralston, I. B. M. (eds.) 1997. *Scotland: Environment and Archaeology, 8000 BC–AD 1000.* Chichester: John Wiley.

Edwards, K. J. and Whittington, G. Vegetation change. In Edwards, K. J. and Ralston, I. B. M. (eds.) 1997. *Scotland:*

Environment and Archaeology, 8000 BC–AD 1000, 63–82. Chichester: John Wiley.

Hingley, R. 1996. Ancestors and identity in the later prehistory of Atlantic Scotland: the reuse and reinvention of Neolithic Monuments and material culture. *World Archaeology* 28(2), 231–243.

Jobey, G. 1980. Green Knowe unenclosed platform settlement and Harehope cairn, Peebleshire. *Proceedings of the Society of Antiquaries of Scotland* 110, 72–113.

Kinnes, I., Gibson, A., Ambers, J., Bowman, S., Leese, M. and Boast, R. 1991. Radiocarbon dating and British beakers: the British Museum programme. *Scottish Archaeological Review* 8, 35–68.

McCullagh, R. P. J. and Tipping, R. (eds.) 1998. *The Lairg Project 1988–1996: the Evolution of an Archaeological Landscape in Northern Scotland*. Edinburgh: Scottish Trust for Archaeological Research Monograph 3.

Mills, C. M. and Coles, G. (eds.) 1998. *Life on the Edge: Human Settlement and Marginality*. Oxford: Oxbow Monograph 100.

RCAHMS 1990. *North-East Perth: an Archaeological Landscape*. Edinburgh: HMSO.

RCAHMS 1998. *Eastern Dumfriesshire*. Edinburgh: HMSO.

Rideout, J. S. 1995. Carn Dubh, Moulin, Perthshire: survey and excavation of an archaeological landscape, 1987–90. *Proceedings of the Society of Antiquaries of Scotland* 125, 139–196.

Ritchie, J. N. G. 1974. The excavation of the stone circle and cairn at Balbirnie, Fife. *Archaeological Journal* 131, 1–32.

Russell-White, C. J., Lowe, C. E. and McCullagh, R. P. J. 1992. Excavations at three Early Bronze Age burial monuments in Scotland. *Proceedings of the Prehistoric Society* 58, 285–324.

Scott, J. G. 1989. Excavations at Templewood. *Glasgow Archaeological Journal* 15, 53–124.

Sharples, N. M. 1981. The excavation of a chambered cairn, the Ord North, at Lairg, Sutherland, by J. X. P. Corcoran. *Proceedings of the Society of Antiquaries of Scotland* 111, 21–62.

Sheridan, J. A. 1996. The oldest bow . . . and other objects. *Current Archaeology* 149, 188–190.

Stuiver, M., Reimer, P. J., Bard, E., Beck, J. W., Burr, G. S., Hughen, K. A., Kromer, B., McCormac, G., van der Plicht, J. and Spurk, M. 1998. INTCAL98 radiocarbon age calibration, 24,000–0 cal BP. *Radiocarbon* 40(3), 1041–1084.

Terry, J. 1995. Excavation at Lintshie Gutter unenclosed platform settlement, Crawford, Lanarkshire. *Proceedings of the Society of Antiquaries of Scotland* 125, 369–427.

Tipping, R. 1994. The form and fate of Scotland's woodlands. *Proceedings of the Society of Antiquaries of Scotland* 124, 1–54.

Watts, D. 1999. *Small Worlds: the Dynamics of Networks between Order and Randomness* Princeton: Princeton University Press.

2 Place and space in the Cambridgeshire Bronze Age

Tim Malim

Introduction

This brief overview of Bronze Age Cambridgeshire is the result of a need to give local context to a variety of developer-funded projects undertaken in recent years which have revealed evidence for Bronze Age activity. In order to achieve this, it has been necessary to create a period-specific database and to interface this with a plotting programme that can produce overlays for relevant maps. The database was designed and compiled by Jon Last during 1997–8 and consists of almost 2000 entries grouped into three main categories (settlement, burials, and metalwork), with a series of sub-categories dividing the main groups. The broad subdivision of the period into 'earlier' and 'later' is reasonably easy due to the high visibility of diagnostic flint scatters and burial monuments for the Late Neolithic and Early Bronze Age and of metalwork for the Late Bronze Age. However, the fine dating of all this information has yet to be perfected (in as far as it might be possible) and so the present results are provisional and broad-based.

Cambridgeshire is fortunate in having had the extensive programme of survey and publication of English Heritage's Fenland Project (Hall 1987; 1992; 1996; Hall and Coles 1994; Waller 1994). This has given a detailed environmental background against which to plot material evidence of the period and a valid comparative breadth to the data due to the consistent methodology employed by David Hall in his fieldwalking. In contrast, the data for upland Cambridgeshire derive mainly from the county SMR, the accuracy and completeness of which will require considerable verification. In addition to these main sources, a large amount of excavation has been carried out since the beginning of the 1990s by a variety of organisations, and the main outcomes of these projects have also been included.

Bronze Age Cambridgeshire was already well known before the Fenland Survey and related work, with Cyril Fox undertaking the first overall summary (1923) in which he plotted the distribution of stray finds against the background of a geological map of the area. The value of the region for Bronze Age studies has been demonstrated by some exceptional finds, for example the sheet bronze shields from Chatteris and Coveney, while the hoards at Isleham and Wilburton are nationally important. In addition, several hoards from Grunty Fen contained outstanding gold objects. Early contact with the Rhineland via the Wash and fenland rivers has been suggested on the basis of evidence from barrows. These include the barrow at Barnack, excavated in 1974, which contained a Beaker burial accompanied by a bronze dagger, side-looped pendant of bone and ivory, and greenstone wristguard with sheet-gold domed rivets (Donaldson 1977), and the barrow at Brampton, which contained a maritime Beaker (White 1969). In more recent times, the fieldsystems of Fengate have become one of the best known examples of evidence for Bronze Age agriculture in the country, and preservation of organic remains in parts of the fens has allowed the discovery of the Flag Fen complex. In contrast, the Bronze Age of south Cambridgeshire and Huntingdonshire was largely neglected from the second world war until very recently, although during the nineteenth and the first half of the twentieth century, many barrows were excavated in this area by individuals such as Richard Neville (Lord Braybrooke; whose detailed notes were extensively used by Cyril Fox) and C. S. Leaf. Leaf's excavations included several seasons at Chippenham where he managed to recover some of the very few items of Early Bronze Age metalwork recovered from excavated contexts in the county (Leaf 1936).

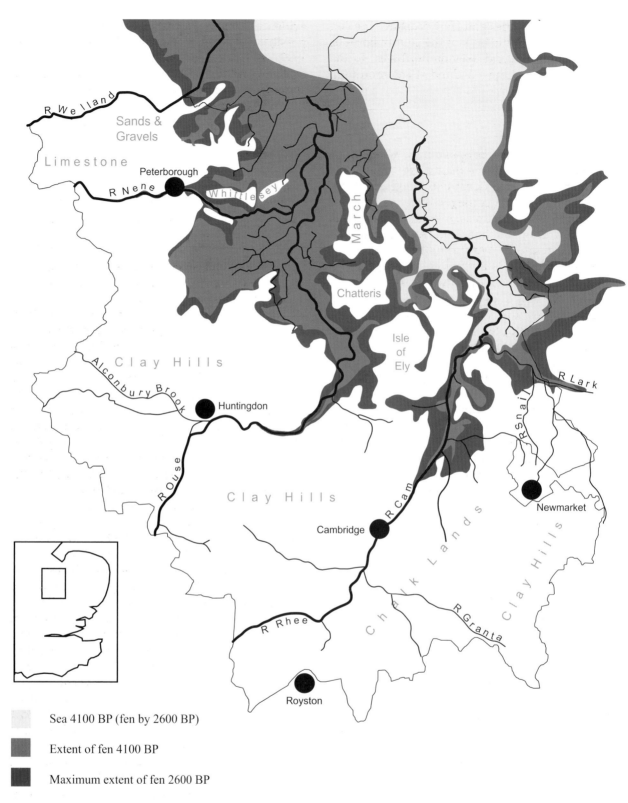

Fig. 2.1 *Topographical background: the Bronze Age fen and drainage pattern, with fen islands named. Rivers, geology and modern towns have also been labelled*

As the first step in interpreting the spatial distribution of finds, the underlying geology and some of the broad topography of the county needs to be sketched out (Fig. 2.1). Clay hills predominate in Huntingdonshire, except where the Great Ouse has cut its way down to gravel terraces. A broad band of chalk composes much of south and east Cambridgeshire, with clay-capped hills in the far south forming the boundary with Essex and Hertfordshire. The Fen and its islands form the bulk of the county north of Cambridge, and fenland extends northwest to the sands and gravels of the mainland at Peterborough.

Communications

Through this landscape, people moved with apparent ease (Fig. 2.2) along the main river valleys (the Welland and Nene, the Great Ouse, and the Rhee-Cam-Granta complex). In the fens, the main rivers, together with other wet areas, provided easy means of communication by boat. In the south of the county, the Icknield Way zone runs west-east through the chalklands as part of the major route between the Thames valley and East Anglia, while routes over the hills in the west of the county can be surmised from the distribution of stone and bronze axes and other evidence; some of these routes have been discussed in detail elsewhere (Fox 1923, 141–158, Malim 2000a). In addition, tracks and droves would have existed to connect settlements along the fen edge. There was a further group of routes that ran north-south through south Cambridgeshire and along the spines of the main fen islands of Ely, Chatteris and March. A series of causeways, trackways and fords also existed in the fens, connecting islands to one another and to the mainland, and dating evidence for these is suggestive of origins in at least the Middle Bronze Age; examples include the site at Little Thetford (Lethbridge 1935). The Roman Fen Causeway, which ran from Fengate to Denver in Norfolk, undoubtedly had its origins as one of these Bronze Age routes, the evidence deriving from its close spatial association with a number of important Bronze Age sites. These include Fengate and Flag Fen at its western (mainland) end, Northey and the Kings Dyke brick pits at the western end of Whittlesey island, and a hoard of axes at Eldernell at the eastern end of Whittlesey island; from these sites, the routeway ran eastwards across the fens to March island and beyond.

Six boats or canoes found within the Cambridgeshire fens have been identified as of possible Late Bronze Age date, but unfortunately little detail was generally recorded of their context or construction. Examples of two at Horsey (Peterborough), and others at Chatteris, Haddenham, Warboys and Whittlesey, are all described as dugout canoes, and part of the V-shaped hull of the Whittlesey example is stored at the National Maritime Museum (Hall 1987, Why A9). Their locations fit well with the pattern of routeways, and the possibility exists that these examples might indicate the former presence of ferries across rivers and particularly wet areas (Fig. 2.2). The county is also exceptional in having evidence for early wheeled transport, with parts of a possible tripartite wheel from Cottenham (Evans 1999, 18–21), and the whole section of another at Flag Fen (*ibid.*, 20). However, radiocarbon dating has shown the Cottenham wheel to be of very late Bronze Age, if not, in fact, Iron Age date (810–400 cal. BC: GU–5731 at 95% confidence) (*ibid.*, 12–13).

Settlement

Evidence in the form of pottery and flint scatters suggests a focus of domestic activity along the southeastern fen edge, especially at Soham, Isleham and Chippenham (Fig. 2.3). However, this distribution is one that reflects a more dispersed pattern than that apparent from the concentrations along the edge of the Suffolk and Norfolk fens (Hall and Coles 1994, fig 39). Elsewhere, occupation sites have been found on fen islands, especially the northern area around Chatteris and Manea (Hall 1992), whereas a blank area exists on the clays in the centre of the Isle of Ely (Hall 1996). Localised areas of settlement have also been discovered during excavation along the Ouse at places such as Huntingdon Race Course (Macaulay in prep.), where hearths and artefact scatters were found in association with fieldsystems, and at Needingworth, where three roundhouses and a rare example of a longhouse all attributed to the Late Bronze Age were associated with an earlier fieldsystem (Evans and Knight 1997, 2).

Closer to Cambridge, Middle Bronze Age structures and a midden have recently been identified at Milton (Connor 1999) and finds scatters, postholes and wells were found at Cottenham (Evans 1999). Fengate and the Welland valley have produced concentrations of settlement in the north, while there is further evidence for settlement at Fordham, Isleham and Wicken in the east of the county. These eastern sites include Dimmocks Cote, Wicken, where a roundhouse, a penannular ditch, alignments of intercutting pits and parts of a fieldsystem (Taylor and Evans 1994) have produced TL dates from pottery spanning the second millennium BC (2285 ± 390 BC–1165± 260 BC: Denham *et al.* 1996). The site also produced Early Neolithic pottery and some Iron Age material. At Landwade Road, Fordham, an enclosure and fieldsystem (Fig. 2.4) have post-Deverel-Rimbury pottery; these are located immediately adjacent to a slightly later settlement with the largest assemblage of Early Iron Age pottery in the region (A. Connor, pers. comm.). At Isleham, a circular post-built structure was found together with intercutting pits, a miniature antler bow and placed deposits of cattle bone (Taylor *et al.* 1995, 174); nearby, pits and wells dated to the Late Bronze Age have also been found, with a further ring-gully of a

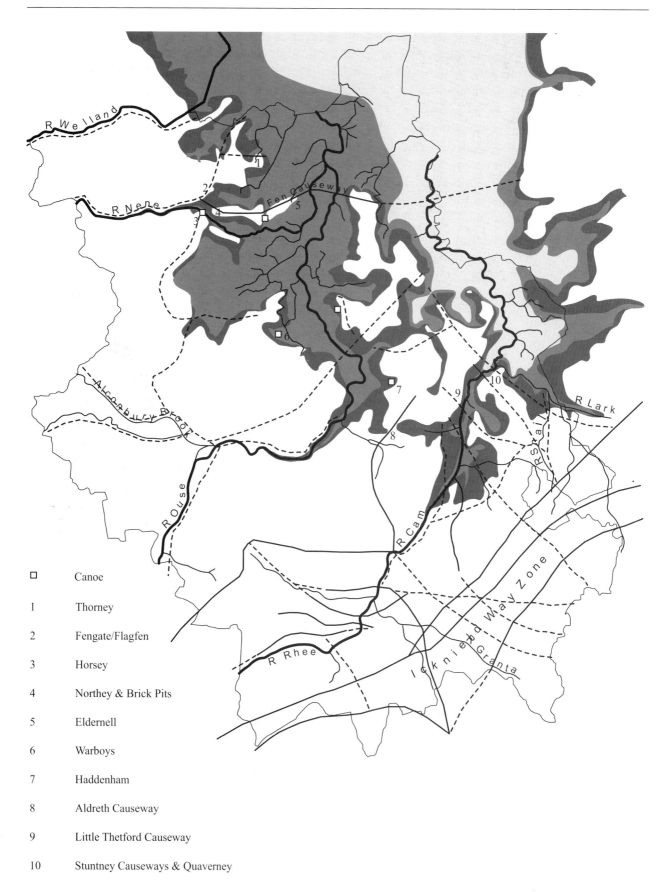

Fig. 2.2 *Communications: major routeways and rivers, with the location of fenland causeways and canoes labelled (Full lines = confident; dashed lines = probable)*

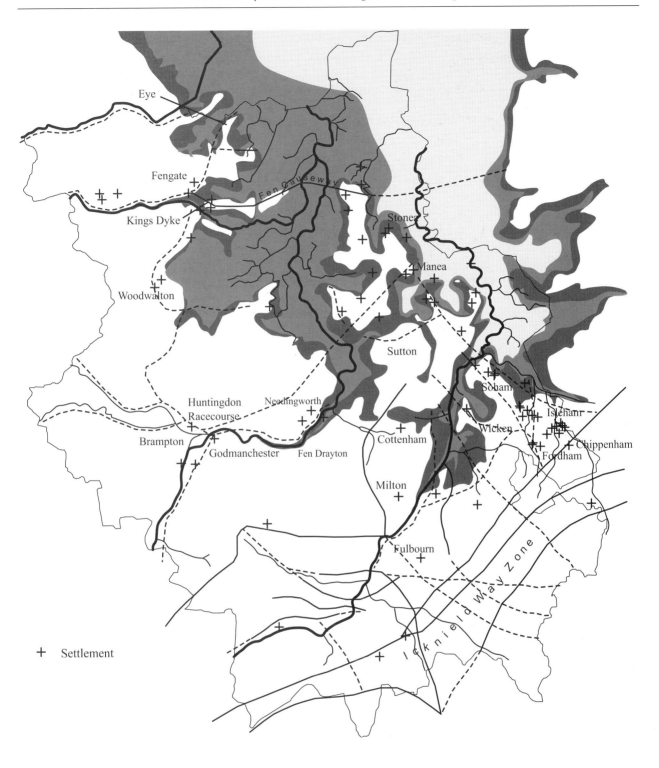

Eye

Fengate

Fen Causeway

Kings Dyke

Stonea

Woodwalton

Manea

Sutton

Huntingdon Racecourse

Needingworth

Soham

Isleham

Wicken

Chippenham

Brampton

Godmanchester

Fen Drayton

Cottenham

Fordham

Milton

Fulbourn

Icknield Way Zone

+ Settlement

Fig. 2.3 *Settlement and field systems, including named sites in the text*

house discovered at another location. Very recent excavations to the northwest of the brick pits at Whittlesey have revealed eight Late Bronze Age structures, mostly roundhouses (M. Knight, pers. comm.). Later Bronze Age structures were also found in the 1970s and 1980s at Godmanchester and Stonea (Green 1977; Jackson and Potter 1996, 68). At The Parks, Godmanchester, a pit containing carbonised six-row hulled barley (radiocarbon dated to 1380–840 cal. BC at 95% confidence: Har–1931) was found with a stakehole structure and West Harling-style pottery, while at Stonea a roundhouse 13m in

A

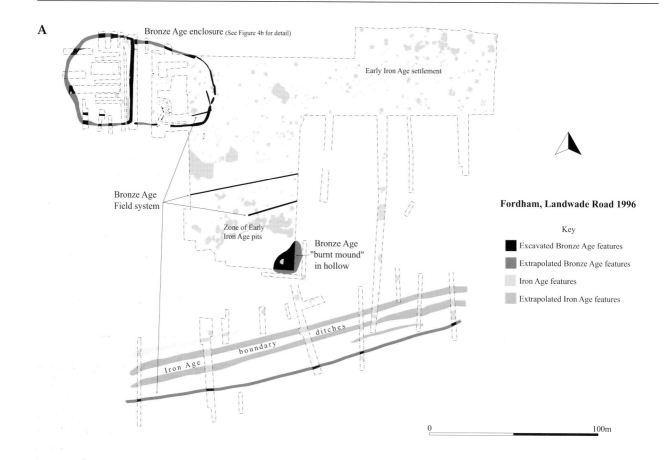

Bronze Age enclosure (See Figure 4b for detail)

Early Iron Age settlement

Bronze Age
Field system

Zone of Early
Iron Age pits

Bronze Age
"burnt mound"
in hollow

Iron Age   boundary   ditches

Fordham, Landwade Road 1996

Key

- Excavated Bronze Age features
- Extrapolated Bronze Age features
- Iron Age features
- Extrapolated Iron Age features

0   100m

B

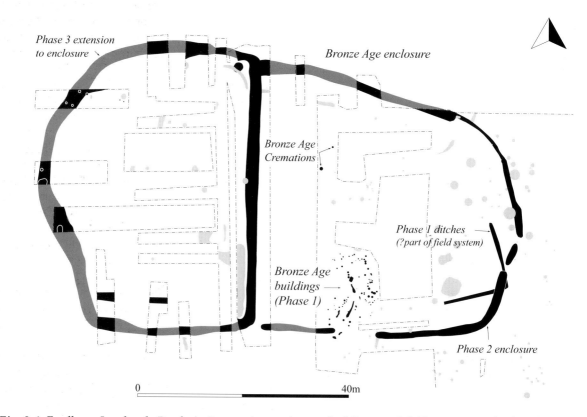

Phase 3 extension
to enclosure

Bronze Age enclosure

Bronze Age
Cremations

Phase 1 ditches
(?part of field system)

Bronze Age
buildings
(Phase 1)

Phase 2 enclosure

0   40m

Fig. 2.4 *Fordham, Landwade Road. A: Bronze Age enclosure, buildings and field system; B: the fine detail of the enclosure shows that it was constructed in several episodes with wide ditches, entranceways, narrow ditches (palisades?) and banks. Recutting of ditches occurred throughout the period*

diameter was found with a mass of postholes and pits, pottery and metalwork dating to the ninth century BC.

Perhaps it is interesting to note from the Fenland Survey data that there appears to be only one site that spans the whole of the period; this site is on the southeastern fen edge at Chippenham (Hall 1996, CHI12, 99). Looking at the material in chronological order, some interesting geographical patterns emerge. Beaker sites occur in three main groups: i) Fengate and the Peterborough fen edge; ii) on the central fenland islands; and iii) on the southeastern fen edge, including settlement activity surviving beneath the Chippenham barrows. Undifferentiated flint sites show a similar pattern to the Beaker settlement but also demonstrate a migration on to higher land, presumably in response to increasing wetness; this is particularly noticeable around Isleham (Hall and Coles 1994, 86). Later Bronze Age flint work and pottery is rare and evidence for settlement has mostly come from excavations at Fordham, Isleham and Wicken in the southeast, and from Cottenham, Needingworth/Bluntisham and Wood Walton in the southern and western fens, as well as more well known examples at Flag Fen, Stonea and the recently found settlement at the Kings Dyke brick pits in Whittlesey.

Fieldsystems

From air photographs, fragments of fieldsystems can be seen along the gravel terraces, the dating for which remains uncertain until excavated sites can be placed in association with them. However, coaxial systems of Middle Bronze Age date and later have been identified at a number of locations through excavation (Fig. 2.3), for example at Eye (Knight, pers. comm.), Fen Drayton (Mortimer 1995), Needingworth (Evans and Knight 1997) and Sutton (Hunn 1992); at these sites, droveways, ditched paddocks, palisade lines and occasional settlement activity form the main features (see also Evans this volume). In addition, other sites with evidence of agricultural activity probably connected with control of livestock have been identified, for example at Fulbourn (Brown and Score 1999). Monuments are also found as parts of these fieldsystems, in some cases acting as nodal points from which alignments were laid out; these are often thought to have already been in existence when the fieldsystem was developed.

However, some sites have provided even earlier dating evidence. For example, recent work at Brampton and Huntingdon Race Course gives an insight into the origins and diversity of activity found within an area previously little known for its Bronze Age remains (Fig. 2.5). A Neolithic ceremonial complex (cursus, henges and long mortuary enclosure) is located on the south side of the Alconbury Brook, with some elements in a cleared landscape to the north, including a sub-rectangular Neolithic enclosure with placed deposits in the ditch (Malim 1999). Continuation of activities into the Bronze Age is demonstrated by pitting and burning in the filled-in ditches of the earlier mortuary enclosure. This has been radiocarbon dated to 2580–2149 cal. BC at 95% confidence (GU–5264) and is paralleled by activity at the spectacular trapezoidal enclosure at Rectory Farm, Godmanchester, 5km down the Ouse (MacAvoy, pers. comm.).

In addition, a palisaded penannular structure with an associated Beaker was excavated at Brampton in the 1960s (White 1969). This structure was buried beneath a later barrow with double ring-ditch and urned cremation. A further isolated pit containing sherds from a number of different Beaker vessels was found as a southern outlier of this landscape at the confluence of two streams (Welsh 1993). On the north side of the Alconbury Brook, a coaxial fieldsystem dating to the *Early* Bronze Age was laid out, interspersed with spreads of domestic activity including a regionally important assemblage of pottery that dates to no later than the earlier second millennium BC. Elements of this fieldsystem were overlain by a round barrow, in the mound of which sherds of Beaker were found, similar to the example across the Alconbury Brook at Brampton (White 1969). Environmental evidence from contemporary palaeochannels (radiocarbon dated to 1910–1740 cal. BC at 95% confidence: OxA–6060 and OxA–6061) have shown that elements of the coaxial fieldsystem run across parts of one in-filled palaeochannel, while flooding from it can be seen to have inundated field ditches that were running back up the gravel terrace (Fig. 2.5). A causeway built across the palaeochannel may date to the same period, and it is interesting to note a possible parallel for this in a recently discovered but more elaborate example at Yarnton in Oxfordshire (G. Hey, pers. comm.).

Larger territorial units might be inferred from other evidence. A series of dykes crossing the Icknield Way in Bedfordshire have been interpreted as Iron Age territorial boundaries (Dyer 1961), and the Mile Ditches near Royston are part of this pattern. Further east, a series of linear ditches and dykes continue this system, dividing up the chalk downlands of the Icknield Way zone at regular intervals. Although in their present massive form their construction has been dated to Anglo-Saxon times (Malim *et al.* 1997), their alignment and their similarity to Bronze Age examples from other parts of Britain may hint at an earlier date. Such practices have been dated to Middle Bronze Age times for parts of Salisbury Plain (see Field this volume) and

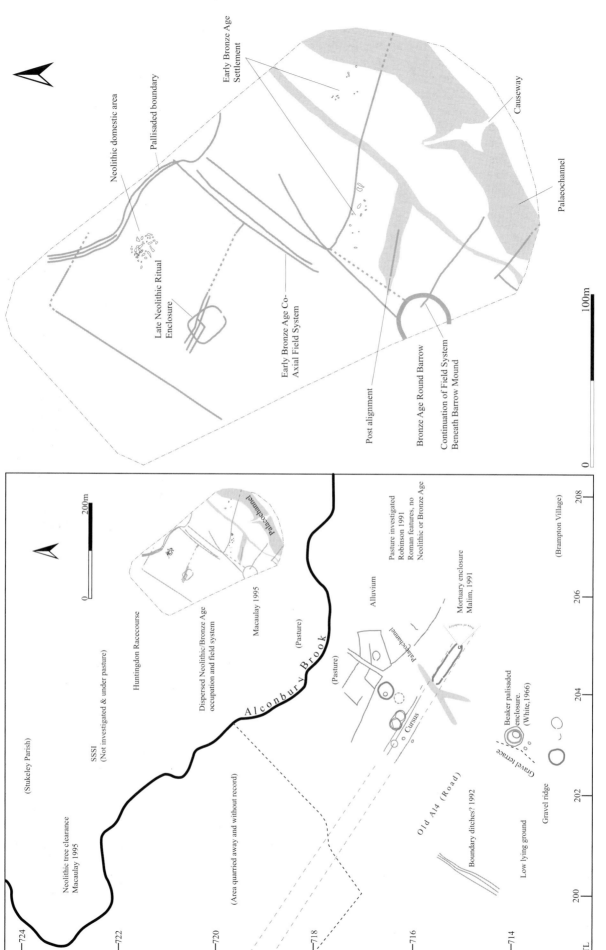

Fig. 2.5 *The Neolithic and Bronze Age landscape at Brampton and Huntingdon Racecourse*

Neolithic domestic area

Pallisaded boundary

Early Bronze Age Settlement

Causeway

Late Neolithic Ritual Enclosure

Palaeochannel

Early Bronze Age Co-Axial Field System

Post alignment

Bronze Age Round Barrow

Continuation of Field System Beneath Barrow Mound

100m

0

(Stukeley Parish)

Neolithic tree clearance Macaulay 1995

SSSI (Not investigated & under pasture)

Huntingdon Racecourse

Dispersed Neolithic/Bronze Age occupation and field system

Macaulay 1995

palaeochannel

200m

0

(Area quarried away and without record)

(Pasture)

Alconbury Brook

(Pasture)

(Pasture)

Pasture investigated Robinson 1991 Roman features, no Neolithic or Bronze Age

Alluvium

palaeochannel

Mortuary enclosure Malim, 1991

(Brampton Village)

Beaker palisaded enclosure. (White, 1966)

Cursus

Old A14 (Road)

Gravel terrace

Boundary ditches? 1992

Gravel ridge

Low lying ground

724

722

720

718

716

714

TL

200

202

204

206

208

for the Dartmoor Reaves (Fleming 1988). The Cambridgeshire Dykes could be part of this phenomenon of early land division; this could, for example, help to explain the association of sites such as the Bronze Age barrow of Mutlow Hill with Fleam Dyke. Furthermore, the distribution of barrows and ring-ditches in south Cambridgeshire (Taylor 1981) clearly shows a zone of affinity with another of the Cambridgeshire Dykes, Bran Ditch, which might indicate its early origin as a territorial boundary. The zone is continued by ring-ditches that follow two tributaries of the Rhee until they meet with the river, after which the number of ring-ditches falls off rapidly (Fig. 2.6).

Burials

Although barrows, ring-ditches and burials seem to occur in similar locations to settlement in the fenland context, by far the majority of burial clusters are in fact found along the valleys of the main rivers or along the chalk moorland in the south of the county (i.e. along the Icknield Way route and away from settlement and water sources at locations such as Therfield and Newmarket Heaths) (Fig. 2.6). The apparent coincidence of settlement evidence with burial seen at the level of a general distribution map perhaps belies a distinction visible at the more detailed level. In spite of the possible hazard from flooding and other factors, the fen edge and islands were attractive areas for settlement because of the large range of resources available from both wetland and dryland environments. It is apparent that the locations chosen for burial sites were in even more marginal land than those used for settlement, and many barrows were thus sealed by peat growth in later centuries, preserving them until very recent times when drainage and desiccation of the fen has brought the land surface back to Bronze Age levels. For example, at Wicken, the land around the investigations undertaken at Dimmocks Cote quarry reveals a mutually exclusive distribution of barrows and settlement, similar to that seen across the whole southern fenland. This is most apparent at Chatteris where the barrow field forms a linear spread along the fen edge skirtland, whereas the lithic scatters representing settlement lie some distance away on slightly higher land (Hall 1992, fig 53).

As part of a survey in 1980, 262 barrows and 1207 ring-ditches were identified in Cambridgeshire (Taylor 1981), and since then others have been added from excavated evidence, fieldwalking, and aerial photography. Although not all of these are of Bronze Age date (for example, a group in the silt fen are in fact the result of Roman or later agricultural activity), the vast majority have been assigned to this period. Little barrow excavation has occurred since the survey was undertaken, and the most prominent burials previously excavated have already been referred to elsewhere in this paper; these include Barnack, Brampton, Mutlow Hill and Chippenham among others. A number of urned and unurned cremations have been receovered, most notably at Haddenham (Evans and Hodder 1994). These are sometimes found in association with other evidence, for example the settlement at Stonea (Jackson and Potter 1996, 68), but are often seemingly of an isolated nature. However, one cremation excavated in the centre of a ring-ditch at Harston was associated with a possible funeral pyre dated to the Early Bronze Age (2020–1540 cal. BC at 95% confidence: OxA–3639), as was charcoal from the postholes of a structure within another barrow (Malim 1994). Perhaps of more interest is the occurrence of inhumations without barrows. For example, at Babraham Road, Cambridge (see Hinman this volume), a skeleton which had been disinterred, partially dismembered, and then reburied was dated to the Early Bronze Age (2205–1895 cal. BC at 95% confidence: Beta–120556). It was found in association with two other burials and pits containing broken-up animal bone suggestive of feasting. Just down the road (literally), a similar skeleton was excavated in the 1970s, but like so many other isolated burials found without grave goods, this burial remained undated. If radiocarbon determination was used as standard practice to date burials of no known period, we could find that far more date back to the Bronze Age than we presently think. The value of such work has been successfully demonstrated along the Norfolk fen edge (Healy and Housley 1992).

Metalwork

As part of the analysis for this paper, all bronze finds have been plotted; firstly altogether, and secondly as three separate groups, so that patterns of distribution for metal axes can be compared with weapons and with hoards. In contrast to the burial evidence, the distribution of bronze axes has a distinct zone along the Rhee/Cam valley route, as well as concentrations at crossing points to the Isle of Ely and along the route of the Fen Causeway. On a wider dispersed level, they occur frequently on the southeastern fen edge and through the fen islands to the edge of the contemporary coast immediately north of March and Littleport (Fig. 2.7). The relative absence of these finds (and of settlement) in the western fen was due to the presence of a large embayment between Chatteris and the western fen edge.

Bronze Age weapons are recorded predominantly

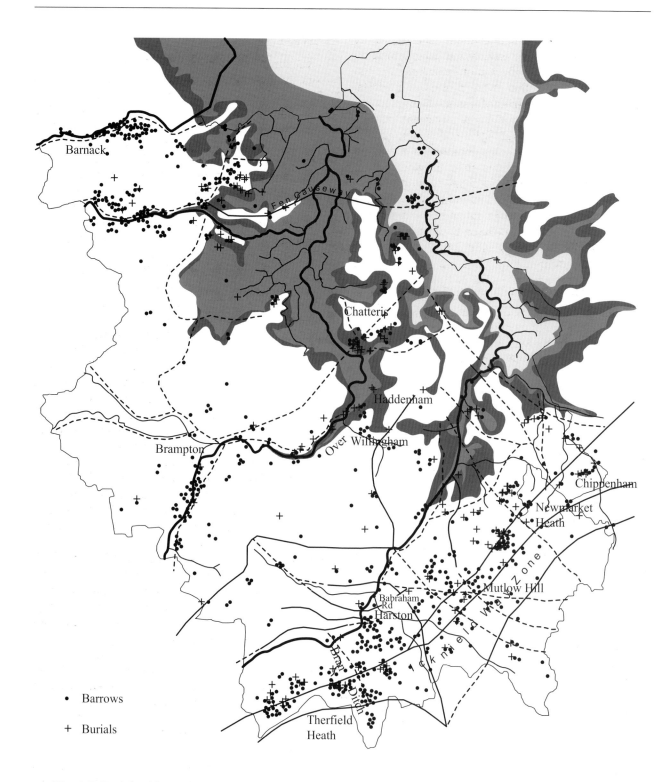

Fig. 2.6 *Burial evidence: barrows/ring-ditches, cremations and other burials, with sites mentioned in the text labelled. Each dot may locate a single example, or it may represent a group of barrows*

from low-lying areas of the county (Fig. 2.7), but whether their deposition actually occurred in wet places rather than on dry land remains to be studied at a more detailed level. Colin Pendleton has found from his studies of the evidence in Suffolk and parts of Norfolk, as well as the Cambridgeshire Fens, that weapons are coincident with other types of metal-work in a variety of geological and topographical locations (Pendleton 1999; this volume). We need to beware the use of spatial analyses from smallscale maps alone, as the picture revealed from largescale plots and contemporary environmental information can show that the distribution of these finds may in fact mirror that of other more mundane artefacts. Furthermore, the degree of association between weapons and Late Bronze Age settlement may be underestimated because of the lack of diagnostic flintwork for this later period that would otherwise help to identify settlement sites. In addition, it should be noted that weapons have been found in dry upland areas within the concentration of settlements at the southeastern fen edge around the boundaries of Soham, Fordham, Burwell and Chippenham, and at a series of sites on the chalk in the south of the county along the Icknield Way zone. Perhaps more surprising still is the single rapier reported as found at Croxton in the heart of otherwise barren claylands, perhaps indicating that a wider distribution of weapons on higher land awaits discovery through extensive fieldwork, and that the present evidence we have for concentrations around fenland could be due to factors of preservation that have given a significant bias to the survival of metalwork from areas with wetter conditions.

Hoards include the famous large collections from Isleham and Wilburton (Evans 1884; Britton 1960), although a number of other smaller sites also exist. These hoards occur mostly around the southeastern fens; few, if any, hoards or isolated metal artefacts have actually been found in areas of deep fen. A detailed study of these hoard sites would be beneficial, and at Isleham proactive work is already taking place. In the winter of 1959–60, over 6500 fragments of bronze were discovered in a pot buried at this site; these have been interpreted as a Late Bronze Age founder's hoard. However, the context of the findspot had been little studied and its exact location was unclear. The first phase of current investigations at Isleham was a magnetometer survey in 1993 to pinpoint a ploughshare that was reputed to have been backfilled into the pit from which the hoard and pot came. Unfortunately, no clear signal was forthcoming, but in 1998 a second phase of survey involved the Ely and District Metal-Detectors' Club who undertook a gridded metal-detecting survey over a wider area and discovered a concentration of Bronze Age metal fragments on the west side of the old course of the river Snail. Further phases of investigation are planned for the near future, as air photographs suggest the presence of an enclosure in the same field; this and flintwork from the field might indicate contemporary settlement. In addition, the hoard itself has been the subject of re-examination in recent years by Peter Northover and David Coombs (pers. comm.).

Discussion

In conclusion, the distributions shown and the recent work touched on demonstrate the value of the data that exist in this county, especially in terms of the variety of new settlement and fieldsystems being found in the south of Cambridgeshire and the Ouse valley. I have only briefly mentioned burial monuments, although I have not discussed the rites associated with them nor described other burials not contained by barrows. Neither have I discussed other kinds of ceremonial complexes, although one possible site deserves mention here. This is the site at Babraham Road which lies at the base of the Gog-Magog hills (see Hinman this volume). The evidence from this location for Early Bronze Age burial, associated with feasting and other activities or features of a probable ritual function, suggests the presence of an atypical monument situated in a location that would have been enhanced by the impressive natural landscape surrounding it; a landscape that contains barrows on the hills above, as well as important ringworks of at least Iron Age antiquity, a major routeway passing close by, and further burials at the ringworks that, although presumed to be Iron Age on present evidence, could, in fact, date from a much earlier time.

The site at Babraham Road demonstrates clear continuity from the Late Neolithic into the Bronze Age, and also shows reuse within the Iron Age. Such evidence for apparent continuity during transitions between periods has also been found at many of the Neolithic ceremonial complexes located at regular intervals along the Ouse (Malim 2000b), at which Bronze Age ritual demonstrably continued the earlier traditions through additions to the monuments and activities such as pitting, placed deposits and burning. Although Iron Age sacred sites are also sometimes found in the same locations (for example a Romano-Celtic temple and square barrows at Diddington and Buckden), this is not necessarily indicative of continuity, as some of these earlier monuments seem to have changed to agricultural use at some point within the Bronze Age. Instead, it is often in fieldsystems and boundaries that continuity from the Bronze Age into the Iron Age and later times is more apparent, through the re-emphasis and additional division of land with coaxial fieldsystems, pit alignments, ditches, fences, droveways and hedges.

The question of ritual deposition as opposed to other causes for the distribution of groups of metalwork is discussed by Pendleton (this volume). It would seem that many different origins can be argued for these finds. Some can be justifiably considered 'votive', whereas others can be seen as promoting social cohesion or can be interpreted as ostentatious deposition in response to economic or

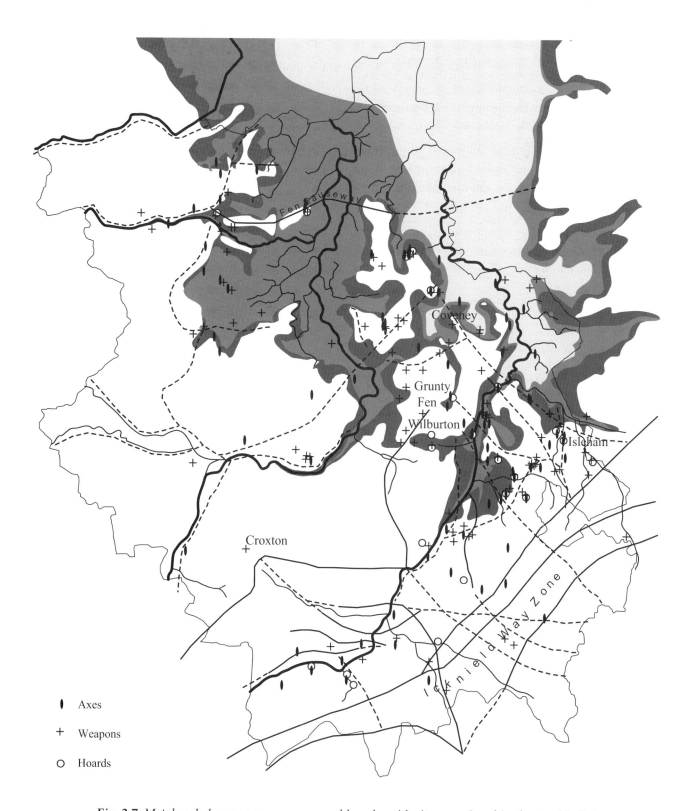

Fig. 2.7 Metalwork: bronze axes, weapons and hoards, with sites mentioned in the text labelled

political pressures. However, the usefulness of applying a 'ritual' interpretation to such finds has been devalued by its application too liberally in the past couple of decades, before this interpretation had been subjected to a more considered discussion of

what the ritual actually involved, its significance for contemporary society, and the detail of its contemporary environmental and settlement context. It is perhaps significant that unlike the Thames, Trent or Witham, the main rivers of Cambridgeshire are not known to have thrown up spectacular finds of artefacts or human skulls.

It is clear that wet parts of the fens and heavy claylands were largely shunned during the Bronze Age, while the rivers and other communication routes were extremely important in linking together the network of settled lands and areas of other activity, both internally and also with communities towards the Thames Valley in one direction, and towards the North Sea zone of continental Europe in the other. Cambridgeshire, then as now, was an important thoroughfare along which new ideas and technologies flowed; no doubt these stimulated development of the local economy. As such, it is important that Bronze Age research in the county develops its own agenda as well as following the national and regional trends that have become current in recent years. As can be seen from the distribution plans, I have shown it is all too easy to plot the use of *space*, but it actually requires the detailed study of the material against the background of the contemporary environment, geology and micro-topography to get a real sense of *place* in the Cambridgeshire Bronze Age.

Acknowledgements

My thanks are due to Jon Last who contributed to the early stages of this survey and who devised and compiled much of the information on the database, and to Aileen Connor and Steve Kemp for manipulating that data into spatial plots for analysis. Jon Cane and Caroline Malim have in turn used the raw plots to produce elegant finished illustrations that set the various distributions against their contemporary environment. Aileen Connor, Mark Hinman, Steve Kemp, Mark Knight and Stephen Macaulay have kindly provided information from a number of their projects. This paper was also helped by production of a parallel contribution for the Cambridgeshire Atlas and my thanks go to Sarah Wroot for prompting me to sort out in my own mind problems with fen edges, rivers, and routeways.

References

Britton, D. 1960. The Isleham hoard, Cambridgeshire. *Antiquity* 34, 279–282.

Brown, R. and Score, D. 1999. A Bronze Age enclosure at Fulbourn Hospital, Fulbourn, Cambridgeshire. *Proceedings of the Cambridge Antiquarian Society* 87, 31–44.

Connor, A. 1999. *Bronze Age, Iron Age and Roman Remains at Butt Lane, Milton, Area A: Summer 1997 Training Excavation*. Cambridge: Cambridgeshire County Council Archaeological Report 145.

Denham, T., Evans, C., Malim, T., and Reynolds, T. 1996. Fieldwork in Cambridgeshire: September 1994–May 1996. *Proceedings of the Cambridge Antiquarian Society* 84, 177–178.

Dyer, J. 1961. Drays Ditches, Bedfordshire, and Early Iron Age territorial boundaries in the Chilterns. *Antiquaries' Journal* 118, 32–43.

Donaldson, P. 1977. The excavation of a multiple round barrow at Barnack, Cambridgeshire, 1974–1976. *Antiquaries' Journal* 57, 197–231.

Evans, C. and Hodder, I. 1994. Excavations at Haddenham. *Fenland Research* 1, 32.

Evans, C. 1999. The Lingwood Wells: waterlogged remains from a first millennium BC settlement at Cottenham, Cambridgeshire. *Proceedings of the Cambridge Antiquarian Society* 87, 11–30.

Evans, C. and Knight, M. 1997. *The Barleycroft Paddocks Excavations, Cambridgeshire*. Cambridge: Cambridge Archaeological Unit Report 218.

Evans, J. 1884. On a hoard of bronze objects found in Wilburton Fen near Ely. *Archaeologia* 48, 106–114.

Fleming, D. 1988. *The Dartmoor Reaves: Investigating Prehistoric Land Divisions*. London: Batsford.

Fox, C. 1923 *The Archaeology of the Cambridge Region*. Cambridge: Cambridge University Press.

Green, H. J. M. 1977. *Godmanchester*. Cambridge: Oleander Press.

Hall, D. N. 1987. *The Fenland Project, No. 2: Cambridgeshire Survey, Peterborough to March*. Chelmsford: East Anglian Archaeology Monograph 35.

Hall, D. N. 1992. *The Fenland Project, No. 6: the South-Western Cambridgeshire Fenlands*. Chelmsford: East Anglian Archaeology Monograph 56.

Hall, D. N. 1996. *The Fenland Project, No. 10: Cambridgeshire Survey, Isle of Ely and Wisbech*. Chelmsford: East Anglian Archaeology Monograph 79.

Hall, D. N. and Coles, J. 1994. *Fenland Survey: an Essay in Landscape and Persistence*. London: English Heritage Monograph 1.

Healy, F. and Housley, R. 1992. Nancy was not alone: human skeletons of the Early Bronze Age from the Norfolk peat fen. *Antiquity* 66, 948–955.

Hunn, J. 1992. *Block Fen A, Mepal, Cambridgeshire*. Oxford: Tempus Reparatum Report 31010 ODF, CAMEBF92.

Jackson, R. and Potter, T. 1996. *Excavations at Stonea, Cambridgeshire, 1980–1985*. London: British Museum Press.

Last, J. 1996. A buried prehistoric landscape at Huntingdon Racecourse, Cambridgeshire. *Council for British Archaeology Mid-Anglia Bulletin* Spring 1996, 30–33.

Leaf, C. S. 1936. Two Bronze Age burials at Chippenham, Cambridgeshire. *Proceedings of the Cambridge Antiquarian Society* 36, 134–155.

Lethbridge, T. C. 1935. Investigation of the ancient causeway in the fen between Fordy and Little Thetford, Cambridgeshire. *Proceedings of the Cambridge Antiquarian Society* 35, 86–89.

Lethbridge, T. C. 1936. Archaeological notes 1: fen causeways. *Proceedings of the Cambridge Antiquarian Society* 36, 161–162.

Macaulay, S. In prep. *Huntingdon Racecourse Archive Report*. Cambridge: Cambridgeshire County Council Archaeological Report.

Malim, T. 1994. An investigation of multi-period crop-marks at Manor Farm, Harston. *Proceedings of the Cambridge Antiquarian Society* 82, 11–54.

Malim, T., Kenn, P., Robinson, B., Wait, G. and Welsh, K. 1997. New evidence on the Cambridgeshire Dykes and Worsted Street Roman Road. *Proceedings of the Cambridge Antiquarian Society* 86, 27–122.

Malim, T. 1999. Cursuses and related monuments of the Cambridgeshire Ouse. In Barclay, A. and Harding, J. (eds) *Pathways and Ceremonies: the Cursus Monuments of Britain and Ireland*, 77–85. Oxford: Oxbow.

Malim, T. 2000a. Prehistoric Trackways. In Kirby, A. and Oosthuizen, S. (eds) *An Atlas of Cambridgeshire and Huntingdonshire History*. Cambridge Centre for Regional Studies. Anglia Polytechnic University.

Malim, T. 2000b. An overview of Neolithic and Bronze Age ceremonial sites along the middle and lower Ouse valley. In Dawson, M. (ed.) *Prehistoric, Roman, and Post-Roman Landscapes of the Great Ouse Valley.* Council for British Archaeology Research Report 119.

Mortimer, R. 1995. *Fen Drayton Quarry.* Cambridge: Cambridge Archaeological Unit Report 156.

Pendleton, C. F. 1999. *Bronze Age Metalwork in Northern East Anglia.* Oxford: British Archaeological Reports, British Series 279.

Pryor, F., French, C., Crowther, D., Gurney, D., Simpson, G. and Taylor, M. 1985. *Fenland Project No. 1: Archaeology and Environment in the Lower Welland Valley.* Chelmsford: East Anglian Archaeology Monograph 27.

Taylor, A. 1981. The barrows of Cambridgeshire. In Lawson, A. J., Martin, E. A. and Priddy, D. 1981. *The Barrows of East Anglia*, 108–120. Chelmsford: East Anglian Archaeology Monograph 12.

Taylor, A. and Evans, C. 1994. Fieldwork in Cambridgeshire: January 1993–September 1993. *Proceedings of the Cambridge Antiquarian Society* 82 , 167.

Taylor, A., Malim, T. and Evans, C. 1995. Field-work in Cambridgeshire: October 1993–September 1994. *Proceedings of the Cambridge Antiquarian Society* 83, 174.

Waller, M. 1994. *The Fenland Project No. 9: Flandrian Environmental Change in Fenland.* Chelmsford: East Anglian Archaeology Monograph 70.

Welsh, K. 1993. *A Beaker pit at Park Road, Brampton.* Cambridge: Cambridgeshire County Council Archaeological Report A21.

White, D. 1969. Excavations at Brampton, Huntingdonshire, 1966. *Proceedings of the Cambridge Antiquarian Society* 62, 1–20.

3   Exploring Bronze Age Norfolk: Longham and Bittering

Trevor Ashwin

Introduction

The wealth and diversity of Neolithic and Bronze Age evidence from Norfolk extends beyond nationally celebrated sites such as the Arminghall henge (Clark 1936) and Grime's Graves (Mercer 1981). The county's many barrows and ring-ditches, most numerous on the highland areas of west and north Norfolk and in the east Norfolk river valleys, have seen several major publications (Lawson *et al.* 1981; Lawson 1986; Wymer 1996; Ashwin and Bates 2000). The vast amount of material from the Norfolk Fens – both 'domestic' and of possible ritual significance – is well known (Bamford 1982; Healy 1991; 1996; Hall and Coles 1994) and the subject of continuing debate (Pendleton this volume). The body of lithic material collected in the Brecklands of west Norfolk and Suffolk, notably in the early years of the twentieth century, is a great asset of lasting value to scholars today (Healy 1998). However, occupation sites of the third and second millennia BC that have seen excavation on any scale are rare throughout East Anglia and beyond (Brown and Murphy 1997). Despite comprehensive publication of sites at Spong Hill (Healy 1988; 1995a), Witton (Lawson 1983) and Redgate Hill, Hunstanton (Healy *et al.* 1993), Norfolk is no exception to this pattern. Excavated 'domestic' remains are at a premium, certainly by contrast with a growing number of excavated barrows and ring-ditches. Future research must try to redress this imbalance between the study of monumental and relatively visible funerary remains and the slighter traces of 'domestic' sites.

Intermittent work by the Norfolk Archaeological Unit (NAU) over the past 20 years at Longham and Bittering in mid-Norfolk, carried out in advance of quarrying, is significant for two reasons. First, a number of Late Neolithic/Early Bronze Age pit groups, lying in proximity to a natural mound seemingly appropriated for ritual purposes, have been recorded and characterised. Secondly, this work has taken place within the heart of northern East Anglia's central till plain, a region dominated by Boulder Clays and poor stony soils. This major landscape zone has seen relatively very few prehistoric discoveries and the intensity and nature of prehistoric land use within it is poorly understood.

Longham and Bittering

The parishes of Longham and Bittering lie in west-central Norfolk, 5km northwest of Dereham and 10km south of Fakenham. They are located on the central Norfolk watershed, which separates the drainage systems of the east-flowing Rivers Yare and Wensum from those of the Nar and Wissey discharging westwards into the Great Ouse and the Wash (Fig. 3.1). The study area coincides with an inclusion of outwash sands and gravels surrounded by extensive Boulder Clay and stony tills. This has seen wholesale gravel extraction in recent decades, and the discoveries considered here were made during and in advance of this work since 1978.

The excavation sites lie atop a low, eastward-protruding spur at an elevation of *c.* 60m OD. Two important later features cross the area. The course of the Launditch, a north-to-south aligned bank and ditch, may be traced over a distance of *c.* 6km. Although regarded for many years as an Anglo-Saxon phenomenon (Lewis 1957; Wade-Martins 1974), an Iron Age date is also possible (Ashwin and Flitcroft 1999). Davies (1996) has suggested that the Launditch formed part of a major series of north-to-south aligned linear earthworks dividing central and west Norfolk in the Iron Age. The modern east-to-west road, Salter's Lane, perpetuates the line of Norfolk's main east-to-west Roman road (Margary

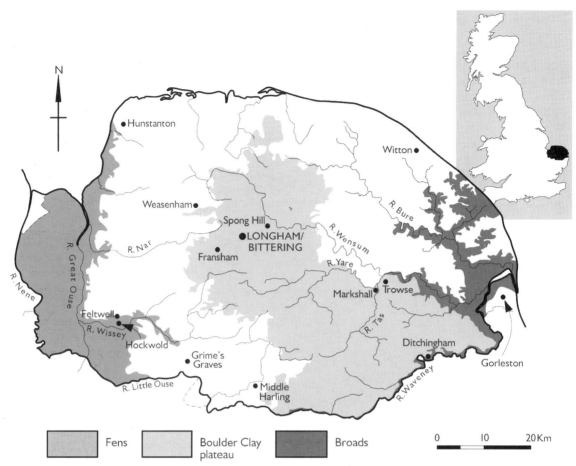

Fig. 3.1 *Map of Norfolk, showing extent of central Norfolk Boulder Clay plateau (light tone) and location of sites mentioned in the text (drawn by David Dobson)*

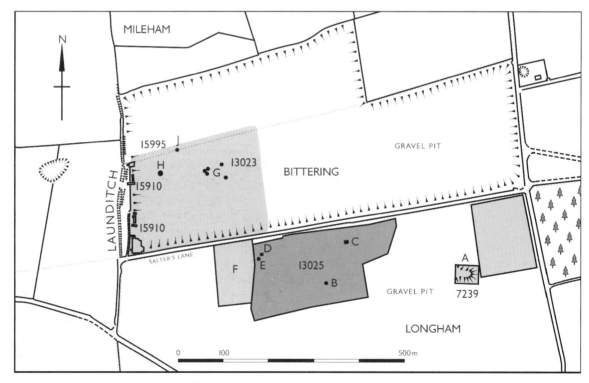

Fig. 3.2 *Longham and Bittering: the study area, showing extents of watching briefs (light tone) and formal excavations (dark tone) and locations of recorded Neolithic and Bronze Age feature groups (drawn by David Dobson)*

1967) which ran from the defended Romano-British settlement at Brampton all the way to the Norfolk Fen edge at Denver. Archaeological monitoring of the quarrying here in 1978 began mainly in response to destruction of the Launditch environs, and therefore the prehistoric landscape described in this paper is largely a chance discovery. To the north of Salter's Lane, the entire area to the west of the Launditch has now been quarried away, while quarrying further to the south is likely to encroach westwards in coming years.

Later Neolithic/Bronze Age features and finds at Longham and Bittering

Full reports on all of the main Neolithic and Bronze Age features have now been published (Wymer and Healy 1996; Ashwin 1998). A number of groups of Iron Age, and possible Iron Age, features from the study area are described by Ashwin and Flitcroft (1999), who also discuss the Launditch's possible date. The Norfolk Museums Service holds all finds and archives. Pre-Iron Age features and groups are located on Fig. 3.2.

The 'Longham mound'

A low plough-spread mound (SMR Site 7239: A), first identified as a possible barrow in 1951, was excavated by John Wymer in 1984 in advance of gravel extraction (Wymer and Healy 1996, 28–35). At the time of excavation, the mound, although distinctly visible from the south and east, was no longer circular (if it ever had been) and was only *c.* 0.8m high. Nine cuttings showed that the feature was a periglacial sandhill composed of a brown silty sand with a very irregular interface with the underlying natural gravel. One pit cutting the mound was of Iron Age date, but at least three complete or partially complete Beakers, two of Case's Middle style and another of Late type (Case 1977), were buried close to the centre. The edges of the features within which they lay were indistinct. No bone fragments or other finds suggestive of either burial or occupation were found. Charcoal from a pit cutting a pit with Middle Beaker produced a radiocarbon determination of 3870±70 BP (HAR–8520; 2550–2060 cal. BC).

Pit groups

Longham Site 13025

An area of *c.* 4ha was stripped of overburden under NAU supervision in 1990 and recorded by a team directed by Heather Wallis (Ashwin 1998). Earlier Neolithic occupation was represented by a single large pit (B) that produced sherds of plain bowl pottery.

Although features were sparse, three groups of Late Neolithic/Early Bronze Age pits were recorded. The most easterly of these, C, consisted of nine sub-circular or ovate pits, some of them very close together and two of them intersecting (Figs 3.3 and 3.4). A total of 344 sherds of Beaker pottery represented at least 96 vessels, nearly all of Case's Late pattern. 203 struck flints were also found, the only retouched objects being scrapers (there were 25 of these). Pieces of burnt flint and/or burnt quartzite occurred in three of the pits. Flotation and plant macrofossil analysis revealed abundant hazelnut shell and smaller quantities of cereal grains along with wood charcoal.

Approximately 15m further to the west was a group of three similar pits. No more Beaker was found but a large lithic assemblage, including 14 more scrapers, was collected from one of them. To the west of these, four subcircular pits (D), lying close to each other and resembling the Beaker pits already described, lay *c.* 1m to the west of a possible hearth. One of the pits contained 46 Bronze Age sherds, apparently of Collared Urn, along with 29 struck flints. Approximately 12m further to the west lay a larger round pit (E) that contained numerous Middle style Beaker sherds along with struck flint and fired clay.

Topsoil stripping of a further area immediately to the west was monitored by the NAU in 1998 (F). Numerous features, most of them small pits, were recorded (Bates 1999). These yielded both Bronze Age and Iron Age pottery, the former including fragments of both Beaker and Collared Urn, but relatively few features were positively datable and little significant patterning could be observed.

Bittering Site 13023

Numerous subsoil features were recorded in this area (G) during a watching brief in 1978. Most of these were pits of Iron Age date (Ashwin and Flitcroft 1999). However, three pits containing flint and Beaker- and Bronze Age-type sherds were considered pre-Iron Age (Wymer and Healy 1996, 38–40). Another feature was a very small ovate 'ring-gully'.

Bittering Site 15995

Several features were excavated and recorded in 1978–9 during a watching brief on topsoil stripping (Wymer and Healy 1996, 36–40). A compact group of seven or eight small features (H) lay *c.* 100m east of the later Launditch. Four pits contained abundant 'Late' Beaker pottery along with struck flint, burnt flint and charcoal; one feature may have been a posthole. Radiocarbon determinations of 3540±70 BP

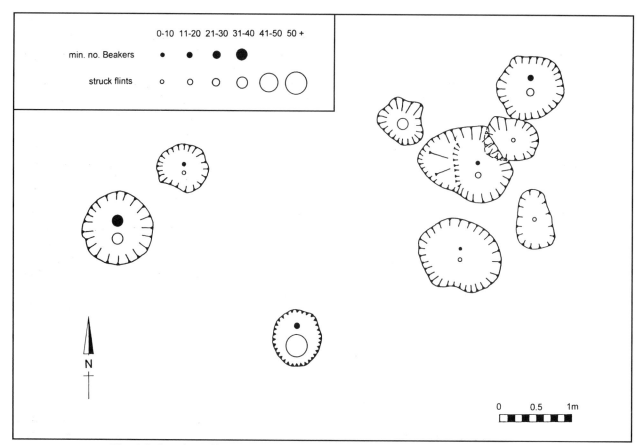

Fig. 3.3 Longham Site 13025: plan of pit group C (drawn by Andrew Crowson)

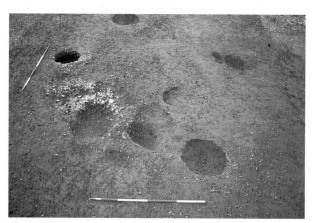

*Fig. 3.4 Longham Site 13025: pit group C looking west
(photo by Michael Hurn)*

(HAR–4636; 2130–1690 cal. BC) and 3790±80 BP (HAR–4637; 2460–1970 cal. BC) were made on charcoal from two pits. Approximately 60m further to the north lay a single pit (J) containing Middle Beaker pottery, flint and charcoal.

Future work

Quarrying will doubtless continue, particularly in the area to the south of Salter's Lane and east of the

Launditch, and this may lead to further discoveries. Ultimately the remains of the Launditch itself, a Scheduled Ancient Monument, may be all that survives these encroachments.

Later Neolithic/Early Bronze Age occupation: recent excavation and research in Norfolk

Work by the NAU has led to the excavation of Late Neolithic/Bronze Age pits similar to those at Longham and Bittering at a number of other sites during the 1990s. Since the interpretative issues raised by sites of this kind are one of the main subjects of this paper, these discoveries are worth summarising in brief.

A47 Norwich Southern Bypass (1989–91)

Major excavations took place around the confluence of the Rivers Tas and Yare, to the southeast of modern Norwich and close to the Arminghall henge and the Roman *civitas* capital of Venta Icenorum (Caistor St Edmund). Their main subject was a series of eight cropmark barrow ring-ditches (Ashwin and Bates 2000). Whereas Neolithic and Bronze Age 'domestic' evidence was sparse, pit groups dating to the third and earlier second millennia BC were excavated at two sites (*ibid.*).

A major gravel extraction area located on a hilltop at Trowse with Newton (SMR Site 9589), *c.* 0.5km east of the Arminghall Henge, saw full archaeological excavation but only after the overburden had been removed by contractors, largely without archaeological supervision. The work was prompted by a series of cropmark 'ring-ditches' that proved – embarrassingly – to be World War II air defence features. Extensive evidence for Iron Age occupation and land division dominated the results. Late Neolithic/Bronze Age activity was represented largely by unstratified flint and a small quantity of pottery, but an isolated group of three pits containing 'Late' Beaker was recorded. The pottery was concentrated in one of the pits, which also contained abundant struck flint including twelve scrapers and a bifacially worked adze. Plant remains retrieved were mostly hazelnut shell, with smaller quantities of cereal grains.

Another pit group was recorded nearby during excavations at Markshall (SMR Site 9584) in advance of gravel extraction in the Tas valley close to the possible site of a deserted medieval village. Several ring-ditches lay nearby, including a very large double-ringed example only *c.* 100m further to the north overlooking the Tas-Yare confluence itself. An isolated group of 14 small pits atop a low sand hill were half-sectioned. Most of these had sterile fills and yielded no finds but one steep-sided round feature, indistinguishable from many of the others in size and form, was filled with black charcoal-rich soil containing numerous sherds from a Grooved Ware vessel of the Durrington Walls substyle. Worked flint recovered included 11 side- and end-scrapers (some of them heavily worn), an oblique arrowhead, cores and retouched flakes. Plant macrofossils recovered included hazelnut shell and sloe fruitstone fragments.

Wood Farm, Gorleston (1999)

During February and March 1999 an NAU team led by Stephen Timms monitored the stripping of a series of access roads and drains forming the infrastructure of a major business park development (SMR Site 11787: Timms and Ashwin 1999). The site itself lies on sandy soil in the centre of the former 'island' of Lothingland. The present coastline lies only *c.* 1.5km further to the east; dry land to the west would have been delimited by the estuary of the River Waveney (echoed by the present outline of the Broads: Fig. 3.1), which was very much more extensive in prehistoric and Roman times than today.

Although features were sparse, a group of five pits containing Beaker and worked flint was found.

Interestingly, these lay 50m outside a major Bronze Age lithic scatter recorded during previous work by the Cambridge Archaeological Unit, which had been targeted by earlier evaluation trenching. The pits were steep-sided and similar to each other; two of them appeared to intersect, although no relationship could be determined between them. All five pits contained Beaker sherds bearing comb-impressed and incised motifs characteristic of Case's Late style, although most of the pottery was concentrated in three of the pits. The 100 sherds recovered represented at least five different vessels. Joining base sherds from two of the pits show signs of ancient weathering, suggesting that these features had been filled simultaneously with material that was not freshly broken or discarded. An assemblage of over 400 pieces of struck flint included numerous fresh flakes, scrapers, a piercer and fragments of two bifacially flaked axes, one of which was polished.

Discussion

Chronology and dating

Beaker pottery was current in the approximate period *c.* 2600–1800 cal. BC (Kinnes *et al.* 1991; Healy 1996, table 13). This is corroborated by the two-sigma ranges of the radiocarbon determinations associated with the pottery from the Longham mound and Bittering Site 15995, indicating the presence of Beaker-using people here during the broad span 2500–1700 cal. BC. Although determination HAR–8520, from the Longham mound itself, appears consistent with the traditionally accepted range of Middle Beaker currency in the later third millennium BC, the results of the British Museum radiocarbon dating program (Kinnes *et al.* 1991) have cast doubt upon the value of Case's (and other) Beaker typologies as dating tools.

Collared Urn appears to have been current in East Anglia *c.* 2000–1400 cal. BC (Healy 1996, table 13). Although no radiocarbon dates are available for the Longham pit group containing this pottery, they probably post-date those producing Beaker. Despite this, the Beaker and 'Early Bronze Age' pit groups are morphologically strikingly similar.

The Longham and Bittering evidence probably reflects numerous discrete episodes of activity over a period of several hundred years. The 'Middle' Beaker pits do not necessarily predate the 'Late' examples (Kinnes *et al.* 1991). Yet the manner in which the two pottery types avoid direct association suggests that these stylistic divisions have some real significance, even if they are not useful as sensitive chronological indicators. The discrepancy between determinations HAR–4636 and HAR–4637 (Bittering

Site 15995) raises the possibility that the various discrete pit groups were added to over an extended period rather than representing short-lived episodes of activity. However, Healy has argued that these two deposits were contemporary on account of their ceramic similarity and physical proximity (Wymer and Healy 1996, 52).

Whittle (1997), with reference to the Neolithic period, has charted the manner in which prehistoric settlement in mainland Britain has increasingly been viewed as a migratory, rather than a sedentary phenomenon. Certainly, it seems likely that the activity represented by the Longham and Bittering pits was episodic, representing repeated visits to this watershed location during the third and earlier second millennia BC rather than continuous occupation. The low densities of features and the extended date range indicated by the associated ceramics both suggest this. Healy (1995a) has suggested that the pit group evidence at Spong Hill points to a similar interpretation and (on the basis of ceramic typology) that this applied to the earlier Neolithic pit groups of the fourth millennium BC there as well.

The pit groups

Despite increasing acceptance that Neolithic and Bronze Age settlement patterns were characterised by a high degree of mobility (Topping 1997), many fundamental questions remain. Notable among them is the extent to which patterns and preferences in human movement may have been dictated by factors of custom, belief and social order rather than agricultural or environmental determinism. The fact that the Longham and Bittering sites lay within a localised area of 'favourable' lighter soil surrounded by less tractable clays should not detract from the possible role played by cultural factors in determining this location's significance. The difficulty involved in making clear distinctions between 'ritual' and 'mundane' behaviour by Neolithic, Bronze Age or Iron Age people persists. Numerous studies (e.g. Cleal 1984; Barrett 1994) have discussed the manner in which ritual and cosmological observances and habits may have penetrated all aspects of prehistoric life, rather than existing within a religious domain set apart from less significant activities. Brück (1999) has gone further, suggesting that the spatially and functionally distinct Bronze Age 'domestic sites' sought by archaeologists over many decades need not necessarily have existed at all. Starting with a critique of the difficulties involved in explaining the lack of Bronze Age sites featuring unequivocal evidence of dwelling structures and domestic activities, she argued that a highly mobile population and a lack of functional

exclusivity between different types of site might account for many of the difficulties in identifying the 'settlements' that archaeologists have hoped and expected to find.

Earlier Neolithic occupation landscapes examined in Norfolk at Broome Heath, Ditchingham (Wainwright 1972), and in Suffolk at Hurst Fen, Mildenhall (Clark *et al.* 1960), although few in number, feature numerous substantial pits that are often rich in artefacts and ecofacts. By contrast, evidence for Late Neolithic and Bronze Age occupation more often takes the form of 'spreads' of material with fewer significant subsoil features (Ashwin 1996; Brown and Murphy 1997). This contrast was emphasised by Healy (1988; 1995a) in her study of Neolithic/Bronze Age occupation remains from the Early Saxon cemetery at Spong Hill, only 6km distant from Longham. At Spong Hill, most of the Peterborough Ware, Grooved Ware and Beaker pottery, as well as the lithic types associated with these wares, came from ploughsoil contexts rather than feature fills. Although later third millennium and second millennium pit groups have been recorded at a number of Norfolk locations, some other 'domestic' sites of the era seem to be represented only by unstratified artefacts (Ashwin 1996, 52–53).

This contrast between Earlier and Later Neolithic remains may reflect significant changes in human behaviour during the third millennium BC, an end to the excavation of deep pits perhaps being combined with increasing surface disposal of waste. Both at Spong Hill (Healy 1988) and at Tattershall Thorpe, Lincolnshire (Chowne *et al.* 1993), substantial Earlier Neolithic features were sealed by a ploughsoil within which Later Neolithic and Early Bronze Age artefacts predominated (Healy 1988, 109). Unfortunately, most of the work at Longham and Bittering could only take place after stripping of overburden by contractors, and neither systematic fieldwalking nor hand-collection of artefacts from the ploughsoil base was possible. Considering the importance of unstratified objects to interpreting Late Neolithic and Early Bronze Age sites, it is unfortunate that the excavated features cannot be viewed within the context of recorded artefact spreads.

The Longham/Bittering and Gorleston pit groups resemble those from the area of the Saxon barrow cemetery at Sutton Hoo (Hummler 1993), also associated with Late Beaker pottery. Although small pits are easily regarded as the main – or only – subsoil feature characteristic of Late Neolithic/Early Bronze Age occupation sites, they were not necessarily a component of all such sites. In fact, the deposition of quantities of pottery and other material within them might represent some kind of unusual or exceptional activity, rather than 'casual' waste disposal within rubbish pits or redundant pits excavated for some other purpose. Although much of the material can be interpreted as occupation refuse, some assemblages at least (for example, the diverse collection of pottery and lithics recovered from the pit at Markshall described above) may have included or been composed of selected artefacts. Very conspicuously fresh flint items, perhaps carefully selected or even specially made, have been recovered at Gorleston (above) and at Spong Hill (Healy 1988, 106). Striking concentrations of objects, including Grooved Ware, flint, stone, charred plant remains and mussel shell, recorded within the fills of individual Late Neolithic pits at Regdate Hill, Hunstanton (Healy *et al.* 1993, 8), are suggestive of careful handling and deposition.

Although some pits might have been furnished with now-invisible organic linings, their small size and the manner in which they frequently cluster can make them hard to explain functionally. Perhaps some had been excavated especially to inter artefactual 'special deposits' for religious or other cultural reasons. In the context of shifting or cyclic settlement patterns that may have persisted for millennia, these could have marked or commemorated specific moments (for example the end or maybe the beginning) within particular episodes of occupation. If this interpretation carries any weight, then the Earlier Neolithic pitting at Spong Hill and Broome Heath, which apparently spanned a lengthy period at both sites, may indicate that practices of this kind were very long-lived in this region.

A lack of clear evidence for associated structures at these sites need not mean that they were absent. Shallowly-founded structures whose remains were mostly confined to the prehistoric topsoil would have left no trace whatever at Longham and Bittering. 'Buildings' of this nature need not have been primitive or unsophisticated, and would fit well with other indications of settlement mobility.

The Longham mound

Wymer's conclusions (1996) that the feature was natural, that there was no clear evidence for burial, and that the Beaker pit deposits reflect a 'mystic motivation' seem incontrovertible. Examples of the 're-use' of pre-existing landscape features for burial in this era have been recorded in the southwest Norfolk Fens at two locations in Feltwell parish. As well as the Late Neolithic/Bronze Age burials excavated by the late Frank Curtis from a natural hillock in Hill Close (Healy 1996, 30–35), excavation of an Early Bronze Age burnt mound in 1992 exposed a secondary Beaker-associated burial with a radiocarbon date of 2140–1880 cal. BC (Bates and Wiltshire 2000). However, it is less certain that the Longham ice mound saw any explicitly funerary activity.

The Longham mound and Feltwell burial are intriguing, considering the small numbers of recorded ceremonial monuments (such as causewayed enclosures and henges) from Norfolk and Suffolk, despite excellent air-photographic coverage over many years. This is true even of areas like the Fen edge where there is evidence for prolonged and intensive occupation (Bamford 1982; Healy 1996). A lack of archaeologically visible ceremonial enclosures might reflect a regional habit of using suitable 'ready-made' topographical features for gatherings or for ceremonial and ritual purposes (Hall and Coles 1994, 62–63). The fact that periglacial features (for obvious reasons!) are seldom deliberately targeted by archaeologists does not help general appraisal of the mound's significance. However, in the millennia prior to agricultural improvement, when many mounds of this kind would have been conspicuous landscape features, it is conceivable that others were put to similar uses.

Brück's critique (1999) of attempts at separating 'domestic' from 'ritual' feature- and site-types is relevant here. Although the Longham and Bittering pit groups contained no entire vessels of the kind inserted into the Longham mound, the possibility that they too were dug especially to receive 'special deposits' has already been considered. This elevated spur of land may even have had significance as a special location or monument, being visited and revisited as such over a lengthy timespan; if so, the range of activities represented might blur any clear dichotomy between the 'domestic' pit groups and the 'ritual' mound deposits. A similar interpretation was suggested by Healy (1995a, 174) for the hilltop site (admittedly a more striking one) at Spong Hill. Echoing Longham, with its 'mound', the Late Neolithic/Bronze Age landscape at Spong Hill includes three barrow ring-ditches (currently unexcavated: Healy 1998, fig. 3), as well as the series of pit groups.

Beaker and Collared Urn

The clear spatial separation between the Beaker deposits of Case's Middle and Late types reinforces the likely distinction between the uses, or the users, of these wares. Although the contrast is no longer thought to be of chronological significance (Kinnes *et al.* 1991), it may reflect either social division or specialised activities. At Longham/Bittering, it is also interesting to observe that the Late-style Beaker pottery occurs in clusters of small pits, unlike the Middle Beaker ceramics which came from single larger features at Sites 13025 and 15995.

The recovery of Collared Urn-type pottery represents one of few discoveries of these wares from non-funerary contexts in the region other than from sites around the Norfolk and Suffolk Fen edge.

Healy (1995a) has argued that Food Vessel, Collared Urn and other Early Bronze Age wares may have been widespread on living sites and yet be un- or under-represented, especially in surface collections, due to their fragility. Suggestions that the abundance of Beaker from Norfolk indicates largescale expansion by Beaker-using communities during the third and earlier second millennium BC must be treated with caution in view of the relative durability and the highly distinctive nature of Beaker sherds.

Finding occupation sites

Although the 'Longham mound' was well known prior to excavation, the Late Neolithic and Bronze Age pit groups at Longham and Bittering were recorded during archaeological monitoring arising from the presence of other more prominent features (i.e. the Launditch and the Roman road). The problems involved in locating and excavating Neolithic and Bronze Age occupation sites – despite the region's wealth of barrows, ring-ditches and artefact finds – have already been discussed above. Not only have very few pre-Iron Age settlement sites been excavated, but those that have been studied have usually been found accidentally by people looking for something else. Heavy dependence on cropmarks in detecting prehistoric sites in a landscape reshaped dramatically by centuries of intensive agriculture is part of this problem, features with deep pits and ditches being characteristic of funerary and ceremonial monuments rather than occupation remains.

Bold suggestions that settlement sites of this period might be sought out by future programmes of research and field survey (e.g. Ashwin 1996, 58) should be tempered by Brück's view (1999) that substantial or heavily characterised 'domestic' sites *per se* did not necessarily exist at all in this period. Yet few important prehistoric occupation sites from the county have been found save by chance. Rescue excavation at Broome Heath, Ditchingham (Wainwright 1972), which led to the examination of numerous Neolithic pits and their contents, had targeted a prominent 'c'-shaped earthwork. The Neolithic and Bronze Age occupation at Spong Hill (Healy 1988) was recorded during excavation of the Anglo-Saxon cemetery there. Pit groups yielding Grooved Ware, Peterborough Ware and struck flint were encountered at a Saxon and medieval site at Middle Harling in 1983 (Healy 1995b). Spreads of 'domestic' material have been found during the excavation of barrows and ring-ditches (e.g. Weasenham: Petersen and Healy 1986). The isolated Beaker and Grooved Ware pit groups recorded by the Norwich Southern Bypass project were found during work in the vicinity of other much more conspicuous

features, in one case a cropmark 'ring-ditch' that proved to date to World War 2! Although trench evaluation at Wood Farm, Gorleston, arose from the site's known prehistoric potential, this work was confined to the area of the Bronze Age flint scatters; the Beaker pits were recorded during subsequent monitoring outside these areas.

It is clear that Bronze Age 'flat' sites still pose challenges to site prospection and evaluation strategies. The fact that the Spong Hill and Gorleston pit groups did not coincide with topsoil flint scatters illustrates the dangers of an over-literal reliance upon the results of fieldwalking alone. The results of comprehensive landscape evaluations of the kind practised, for example, at Willingham/Over, Cambridgeshire (Evans 1999; this volume), are of great relevance.

Settlement, drainage and topography

The Longham/Bittering study area's 'upland' location within the central Norfolk boulder clay region poses further questions about the development and intensity of prehistoric settlement in this under-studied landscape tract. Future research must try to explain the sparseness of recorded Neolithic and Bronze Age sites here (Ashwin 1996, 59). Below average numbers of barrows and ring-ditches are accompanied by very few discoveries of occupation sites like those at Longham and Bittering, and there are few of the major surface collections of objects that are such a prominent feature of Norfolk's prehistoric archaeology. Such negative evidence might indicate that this landscape remained agriculturally marginal and was not heavily frequented prior to the Iron Age (Davies 1996). However, the real picture may be more complex. Low intensities of modern development and mineral extraction in this predominantly rural tract have reduced archaeologists' opportunities to undertake systematic survey and fieldwork, while the dominance of heavy soils unconducive to cropmark formation may account for the low numbers of barrow ring-ditches (Lawson 1986, 117).

No pollen data has been collected to date from any of the Longham/Bittering sites. However, large tracts of the till plain would have been heavily wooded, and remained so in post-Roman times (Williamson 1993). The Longham/Bittering complex may represent numerous episodes of activity within a wooded landscape over a period of several hundred years, reflecting a low density of population and shifting or cyclic occupation of temporary clearings rather than extensive or permanent clearance. Yet it is difficult to use the evidence from these particular sites to generalise about prehistoric occupation on the surrounding claylands because they occupy a localised area of sands and gravel, giving rise to the quarrying that led to the discoveries themselves. These sands and gravels may have supported prehistoric landuse of a different kind to that seen on the heavy boulder clays to the south and the stony tills that dominate to the north.

Prehistorians generalising about the central Norfolk boulder clay region as an undifferentiated marginal unit (e.g. Ashwin 1996) may prove misguided. Local variations in soil type, topography and aspect may have created a mosaic of different habitats within it, some frequented by humans throughout prehistory. The relatively small number of pre-Iron Age artefacts recorded during intensive field survey in the Boulder Clay parish of Fransham, a short distance to the southwest of Longham, appeared concentrated in isolated areas of lighter sandy soil (Rogerson 1995). Conversely, Rogerson noted a complete absence of flint on some of the heaviest clay soils. The site at Spong Hill, which saw intermittent occupation dating back to the fourth millennium BC, is also situated on a gravel knoll largely surrounded by Boulder Clay.

The localised and superficial sandy deposits within which Longham and Bittering lie, the so-called Hungry Hill Gravels (Wymer and Healy 1996), form part of an east-to-west band of sandy soil crossing the mid-Norfolk watershed at this point. This might have been both a focus of population and a natural routeway since early prehistoric times. It is clearly visible in the distribution of recorded Neolithic/Bronze Age barrows and ring-ditches (Ashwin 1996, fig. 5); intriguingly, it is also followed by the main east-to-west Roman road traversing upland Norfolk at this point (Margary 1967; Wymer and Healy 1996).

Conclusions

A popular view of East Anglia as uniformly 'wet' and/or 'flat' cannot do justice to the subtle diversity of its geology and soil regions. Northern East Anglia is a large and varied landscape tract within which to study prehistoric activity. Nowhere more than in 'High' Norfolk and Suffolk, the predominantly clayey upland terrain of the region's central watershed, is there a greater need to improve understanding of the nature and intensity of Neolithic and Bronze Age settlement.

This essay has described a series of unexceptional features in an unremarkable landscape context, and has emphasised numerous problems and ambiguities. Project circumstances have not been ideal: the lack of formal surface collection data from most sites and of opportunities to conduct palynological research are both losses. Yet the results highlight many current research themes regarding Neolithic and Bronze Age occupation sites, of which the issues surrounding mobility and seasonality are only two. Studies of this kind may help to formulate specific questions to be addressed by future research within a local, as well as a broader regional, context.

Acknowledgements

The NAU is grateful for the support of Tarmac Roadstone, Pontylue Gravels, Ennemix Ltd, Redland Lafarge Ltd, the Manpower Services Commission and English Heritage during work at Longham and Bittering. Fieldwork on the Norwich Southern Bypass was funded by English Heritage, Wyatt of Snetterton Ltd. and May Gurney Construction; that at Gorleston was funded by Great Yarmouth Borough Council.

Over the past 20 years, fieldwork at Longham and Bittering has been carried out by, or under the supervision of Frances Healy, Andrew Rogerson, John Wymer, Heather Wallis and Sarah Bates. Helen Bamford (ceramics), Val Fryer and Peter Murphy (plant macrofossils) and Peter Robins (lithics) have also made major contributions during post-excavation analysis. With reference to the other sites considered here, I would particularly like to thank John Ames, Sarah Bates, Peter Robins and Steve Timms.

The paper's conclusions have drawn freely upon the ideas, comments and criticisms of others. Frances Healy and John Wymer kindly read an early version, and my debt to them will be clear to all readers familiar with their work.

References

Ashwin, T. M. 1996. Neolithic and Bronze Age Norfolk. *Proceedings of the Prehistoric Society* 62, 41–62.

Ashwin, T. M. 1998. Excavations at Salter's Lane, Longham, 1990: Neolithic and Bronze Age features and finds. *Norfolk Archaeology* 43(1), 1–29.

Ashwin, T. M. and Bates, S. J. 2000. *Excavations on the Norwich Southern Bypass, 1989–91. Part I: Excavations at Bixley, Caistor St Edmund and Trowse*. Dereham: East Anglian Archaeology Monograph 91.

Ashwin, T. M. and Flitcroft, M. E. 1999. The Launditch and its setting: excavations at the Launditch, Beeston with Bittering, and Iron Age features and finds from its vicinity. *Norfolk Archaeology* 43(2), 217–56.

Barrett, J. C. 1994. *Fragments from Antiquity: an Archaeology of Social Life in Britain, 2900–1200 BC*. Oxford: Blackwell.

Bamford, H. M. 1982. *Beaker Domestic Sites in the Fen Edge and East Anglia*. Dereham: East Anglian Archaeology Monograph 16

Bates, S. J. 1999. *Report on Excavations at Redland Quarry Extension, Salter's Lane, Longham*. Norfolk Archaeological Unit Report 396 (unpublished).

Bates, S. J. and Wiltshire, P. E. J. 2000. Excavation of a burnt mound at Feltwell Anchor, Norfolk. *Norfolk Archaeology* 43(3), 389–414.

Brown, N. R and Murphy, P. L. 1997. Neolithic and Bronze Age. In Glazebrook, J. M. (ed.) *Research and Archaeology: a Framework for the Eastern Counties. 1: Resource Assessment*. Dereham: East Anglian Archaeology Occasional Paper 3, 12–22.

Brück, J. 1999. What's in a settlement? Domestic practice and residential mobility in Early Bronze Age southern England. In Brück, J. and Goodman, M. (eds) *Making places in the prehistoric world: themes in settlement archaeology*, 52–75. London: UCL Press.

Case, H. J. 1977. The Beaker Culture in Britain and Ireland. In Mercer, R. J. (ed.) *Beakers in Britain and Europe: Four Studies*, 77–101. Oxford: British Archaeological Reports, International Series 26.

Chowne, P., Healy, F. and Bradley, R. 1993. The excavation of a Neolithic settlement at Tattershall Thorpe, Lincolnshire. In Bradley, R. *et al. Excavations on Redgate Hill, Hunstanton, Norfolk and at Tattershall Thorpe, Lincolnshire*, 79–117. Dereham: East Anglian Archaeology Monograph 57.

Clark, J. D. G. 1936. The timber monument at Arminghall and its affinities. *Proceedings of the Prehistoric Society* 2, 1–51.

Clark, J. G. D., Higgs, E. S. and Longworth, I. H. 1960. Excavations at the Neolithic site at Hurst Fen, Mildenhall, Suffolk. *Proceedings of the Prehistoric Society* 26, 202–45

Cleal, R. M. J. 1984. The Later Neolithic in Eastern England. In Bradley, R. J. and Gardiner, J. P. (eds) *Neolithic Studies: a Review of some Current Research*, 135–58. Oxford: British Archaeological Reports, British Series 133.

Davies, J. A. 1996. Where eagles dare: the Iron Age of Norfolk. *Proceedings of the Prehistoric Society* 62, 63–92.

Evans, C. 1999. *Mobility and Tenure: the Barleycroft/Over Landscape*. Paper presented at the conference 'Place and Space in the British Bronze Age', Cambridge, April 1999.

Hall, D and Coles, J. 1994. *The Fenland Survey: an Essay in Landscape and Persistence*. London: English Heritage Archaeological Report 1.

Healy, F. 1988. *The Anglo-Saxon Cemetery at Spong Hill, North Elmham, Part VI: Occupation during the Seventh-Second Millennia BC*. Dereham: East Anglian Archaeology Monograph 39.

Healy, F. 1991. Appendix 1: lithics and pre-Iron Age pottery. In Silvester, R. J. *The Fenland Project No. 4: the Wissey Embayment and the Fen Causeway*, 116–139. Dereham: East Anglian Archaeology Monograph 52.

Healy, F. 1995a. Pots, pits and peat: ceramics and settlement in East Anglia. In Kinnes, I. and Varndell, G. (eds) *Unbaked Urns of Rudely Shape: Essays on British and Irish Pottery for Ian Longworth*, 173–84. Oxford: Oxbow Monograph 55.

Healy, F. 1995b. Prehistoric material. In Rogerson, A. *A Late Neolithic, Saxon and Medieval Site at Middle Harling, Norfolk*, 32–46. Dereham: East Anglian Archaeology Monograph 74.

Healy, F. 1996. *The Fenland Project No.11: the Wissey Embayment. Evidence for pre-Iron Age Occupation*. Dereham: East Anglian Archaeology Monograph 78.

Healy, F. 1998. The surface of the Breckland. In Ashton, N., Healy, F. and Pettitt, P. (eds) *Stone Age Archaeology: Essays in Honour of John Wymer*, 225–235. Oxford: Oxbow Monograph 102/Lithic Studies Society Occasional Paper 6.

Healy, F., Cleal, R. M. J. and Kinnes, I. A. 1993. Excavations on Redgate Hill, Hunstanton, 1970 and 1971. In Bradley, R. *et. al. Excavations on Redgate Hill, Hunstanton, Norfolk and at Tattershall Thorpe, Lincolnshire*, 1–80. Dereham: East Anglian Archaeology Monograph 57.

Hummler, M. 1993. The prehistoric settlement: an interim report. *Bulletin of the Sutton Hoo Research Committee* 8, 20–5.

Kinnes, I. A., Gibson, A., Ambers, B., Bowman, S., Leese, M. and Boast, R. 1991. Radiocarbon dating and British Beakers: the British Museum programme. *Scottish Archaeological Review* 8, 35–68.

Lawson, A. J. 1983. *The Archaeology of Witton, near North Walsham*. Dereham: East Anglian Archaeology Monograph 18.

Lawson, A. J. 1986. *Barrow Excavations in Norfolk, 1950–82*. Dereham: East Anglian Archaeology Monograph 29.

Lawson, A. J., Martin, E. A. and Priddy, D. 1981. *The Barrows of East Anglia*. Dereham: East Anglian Archaeology Monograph 12.

Lewis, J. M. 1957. The Launditch: a Norfolk linear earthwork. *Norfolk Archaeology* 31, 419–26.

Margary, I. D. 1967. *Roman Roads in Britain*. London: John Baker.

Mercer, R. 1981. *Grime's Graves, Norfolk, Excavations 1971–72, Vol. 1*. London: Dept of the Environment Archaeological Report 11.

Petersen, F. F. and Healy, F. 1986. The excavation of two round barrows and a ditched enclosure on Weasenham Lyngs, 1972. In Lawson, A. J. *Barrow Excavations in Norfolk, 1950–82*, 70–103. Dereham: East Anglian Archaeology Monograph 29.

Rogerson, A. 1995. *Fransham: an Archaeological and Historical Study of a Parish on the Norfolk Boulder Clay*. Unpublished Ph.D. thesis, University of East Anglia.

Timms, S., and Ashwin, T. M. 1999. *Report on Archaeological Excavations at the South Gorleston Development Area: Construction Phase 1*. Norfolk Archaeological Unit Report 428 (unpublished).

Topping, P. (ed.). 1997. *Neolithic Landscapes: Neolithic Studies Group Seminar Papers 2*. Oxford: Oxbow Monograph 86.

Wade-Martins, P. 1974. The linear earthworks of west Norfolk. *Norfolk Archaeology* 34(1), 23–38.

Wainwright, G. J. 1972. The excavation of a Neolithic settlement on Broome Heath, Ditchingham, Norfolk. *Proceedings of the Prehistoric Society* 38, 1–97.

Whittle, A. 1997. Moving on and moving around: Neolithic settlement mobility. In Topping, P. (ed.) *Neolithic Landscapes: Neolithic Studies Group Seminar Papers 2*, 15–22. Oxford: Oxbow Monograph 86.

Williamson, T. 1993. *The origins of Norfolk*. Manchester: Manchester University Press.

Wymer, J. J. (ed.) 1996. *Barrow Excavations in Norfolk, 1984–88*, 28–53. Dereham: East Anglian Archaeology Monograph 77.

Wymer, J. J. and Healy, F. 1996. Neolithic and Bronze Age activity and settlement at Longham and Beeston with Bittering, Norfolk. In Wymer, J. J. (ed.) *Barrow Excavations in Norfolk, 1984–88*, 28–53. Dereham: East Anglian Archaeology Monograph 77.

4 Ritual activity at the foot of the Gog Magog Hills, Cambridge

Mark Hinman

Background

The following paper seeks to outline the findings of the 1998 Babraham Road excavation undertaken in advance of the planned construction of a new park and ride facility for the City of Cambridge. From an archaeological perspective, the siting of this new development was fortuitous (Fig. 4.1), presenting a rare opportunity to examine a unique and potentially important part of the prehistoric landscape at

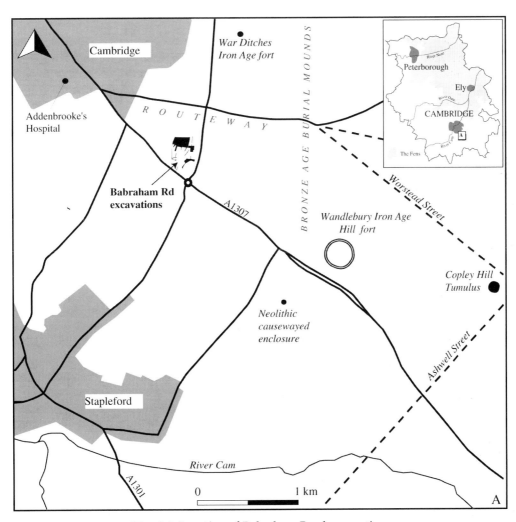

Fig. 4.1 *Location of Babraham Road excavations*

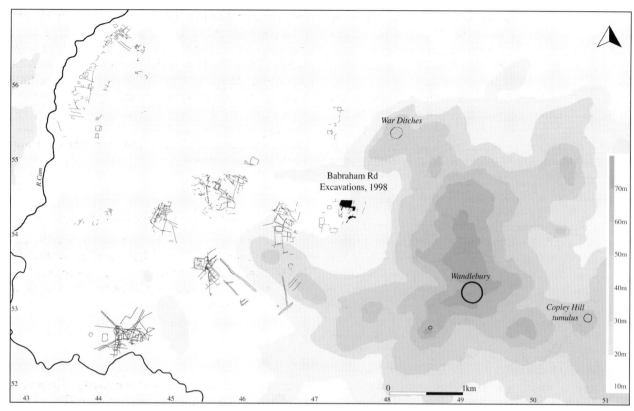

Fig. 4.2 *Site location in relation to local topography, monuments and cropmarks*

the foot of the Gog Magog Hills, wherein the wealth and variety of remains have attracted interest from archaeologists for over 100 years.

Excavation produced evidence for a series of activities spanning more than 2000 years concluding, at the end of the Iron Age, with the apparent reaffirmation of the special nature of this place.

I would first like to outline a sense of place gained during excavation and reinforced through subsequent fieldwork. In order to provide a context within which to interpret the excavation results, a consideration of the surrounding 'space' is required. I will therefore begin with a brief examination of the local landscape as defined by certain of the physical attributes that characterise this area today.

The underlying geology of the area consists predominantly of chalk interspersed with chalky drift. The local landscape owes its current appearance to events at the end of the last Ice Age. The excavation area was located within a depression formed by the thawing of a shallow ice lake *c*. 12,000 BP. The melt waters from this lake exited through a newly formed break in the encircling hills, creating a broad but shallow linear depression or erosion channel, aligned east-west and terminating perpendicular to the current course of the river Cam (Fig. 4.2). As a result of this thaw, the aquifer at the base of the middle chalk was exposed, forming

springs at intervals around the base of the Gog Magog Hills. A number of these springs remain active today, the best known being located at Nine Wells, at the tip of the southern crescent of enclosing hills, adjacent to the naturally formed 'holloway' to the Cam.

Although Cambridgeshire is not generally noted for marked changes in topography, the impression here is of a wide avenue exiting eastwards from the Cam passing through a gap in the hills adjacent to the springs at Nine Wells before entering a broad, naturally formed amphitheatre beyond.

Geographically, the excavation area lies towards the eastern end of this naturally formed bowl enclosed by the western limits of the Gog Magog Hills (Fig. 4.2). On these hills to the southeast stands Wandlebury, a circular ring monument, and immediately to the north the equally enigmatic 'War Ditches', the site of which has now been almost entirely destroyed by chalk extraction. Although these two monuments have been interpreted as Iron Age forts, limited excavation of both sites since the 1890s has indicated significant levels of earlier activity.

The derivation of the name War Ditches is uncertain but may be coincidental with the discovery of numerous human skeletons during quarrying activities there during the latter half of the nineteenth century. Subsequent excavations (Hughes 1898–1903; Lethbridge 1948; White 1963–1964) traced the course of a large circular enclosure of *c.* 150m diameter. The layout of War Ditches is reminiscent of Wandlebury and other monuments of the region, with ditches 5m wide, cut to in excess of 4m in depth, and with probable entrances on both the eastern and western sides. During excavation, human remains were repeatedly discovered within the later fills, some of which had been deliberately inhumed, although the majority, predominantly women and children, were thrown into the ditch. Although unequivocal evidence for activity and settlement has been recorded on the site for the Iron Age and Romano-British periods, this has always been recovered from the upper fills of the ditch or from other features on this site. It is the earliest ditch fills that are primarily of interest here. The basal fills consisted of fine chalky silt deposits of at least 1m in depth sealed by a buried soil horizon indicative of a past land surface. Artefacts recovered from these early fills were exclusively pre-Iron Age and led both Hughes and Lethbridge to conclude that the site had its origins in the Bronze Age. The range of artefacts and the types of animal bones recovered appear to accord well with the Bronze Age assemblages from Babraham Road, although a re-examination of this previously collected material, particularly the ceramics, is desirable.

Wandlebury is notable for its almost perfectly circular plan and also, with an overall diameter of 315m, for its size. The development of Wandlebury clearly has several phases (Hartley 1957; reassessed by Cunliffe 1974). Only recently, however, has the role of this monument as a hillfort been called into question (Evans 1991; 1992). As Evans observes, the siting of the monument away from the crest of a relatively steep slope makes little sense if defence was a primary concern. The recent identification of a possible entrance on the southwestern side of the monument (Pattison and Oswald 1995) increases the parallels with War Ditches.

In addition, a possible causewayed enclosure lies on Littletrees Hill, the hilltop to the south of Wandlebury. A number of barrows run along the ridge between these monuments and a series of prehistoric routeways run through the general area. An extensive Iron Age settlement was located to the west of the site, on ground currently occupied by Addenbrooke's Hospital (Cra'ster 1969).

The site

The activity revealed through excavation can be attributed to three broad periods. Period 1 consisted primarily of pits (including two 'shafts') and human burials, dateable to the Late Neolithic-Early Bronze Age period. Period 2 consisted of a pair of large ditches with v-shaped profiles. These ditches were infilled in the Early-Middle Bronze Age and may be associated with a monument within the immediate vicinity. The final period of activity is represented by a series of enigmatic, rectilinear cut features that are aligned either east-west or north-south and contain fragments of Late Iron Age ('Belgic') and Early Roman pottery.

The Late Neolithic-Early Bronze Age

Features attributable to this period were primarily pits, although two larger shafts and three human burials were also found. Many of these features appeared to form distinct groups in terms of type, content and spatial distribution.

Pits

Although all of these features are subtly different in terms of form and content, the majority of the artefacts recovered point to deposition dates within the Late Neolithic-Early Bronze Age period. The types of artefacts recovered include fragments of Grooved Ware pottery, animal bone (including apparently selected elements of aurochs, red deer, pig, sheep/goat, beaver, pine marten and dog), bone awls and flint tools.

The faunal assemblage as a whole from this period indicates either the presence of, or direct access to a predominantly wooded environment; this conclusion is supported by the results of environmental and molluscan analysis (Fryer 1998; Baxter forthcoming; Meyrick forthcoming). Very young animals appear to be present (Baxter forthcoming), particularly piglets, which may be an indicator of seasonal deposition. Naturally shed antler was also found, including two from red deer of different ages (shed in the autumn) placed at the base of one of the pits; these may be seen as evidence for some form of seasonal ritualistic activity.

The type of flintwork (Bishop forthcoming) appears to be quite specific, with scrapers (used for tasks such as cleaning hides) predominating and also a few arrowheads. In terms of the deposition of lithic material, the pits fall into four main groups: 1) pits with no flint work; 2) pits containing small mixed assemblages of struck or burnt material; 3) pits with finds representative of the complete knapping sequence, including many very small chips, trimming flakes and flake fragments, but with a relative absence of cores, retouched implements and utilised flakes; 4) pits producing the debris from all stages of knapping along with a relatively high retouched component.

Deposition of a range of ceramic, lithic and faunal material within specific features appears to have been both highly selective and at times visibly structured. Lithics were sometimes sorted and deposited by flake size or tool type, while bone awls were often found in association with concentrations of scrapers. The bones of the pine martin (highly sought after for its fur) occurred exclusively within a single pit group in association with bone awls and the greatest concentration of Grooved Ware pottery from the excavation. The range of artefact types suggests that only specific tasks were being carried out at the site or that these particular activities were chosen to be represented symbolically through selective deposition.

Shafts

Excavation has also shown that even features devoid of artefactual remains can provide valuable evidence for human activities. Towards the eastern limit of Area 1 is a large circular pit or shaft 1.9m in diameter with a depth in excess of 1.8m. This feature was completely artefactually sterile and had been infilled with chalk, presumably the same material generated during the process of excavation. Four circular chalk-filled pits approximately 20m to the east of the shaft were also found to be devoid of any artefactual material. The complete absence of artefacts indicates a degree of care at the time of infilling and a seemingly intentional desire to avoid the 'contamination' of the fills of these features. Contrasting with this artefactual sterility, the clearest evidence for selective and structured deposition came from two triple pit groups immediately to the south of this shaft and its satellite features.

A second shaft of similar dimensions was present towards the southern limit of the site, excavation of which produced a complete aurochs vertebra and several fragments of aurochs and domestic cattle bone from towards the base of the cut.

Human remains

Three human burials and a cluster of shallow pits sealed by a deliberately collected layer of flint cobbles and cattle bones characterised the southernmost part of the site. This zone was not subject to open area excavation and the potential exists for the presence of additional human burials in the immediate vicinity.

The burials included the tightly flexed inhumation of a young adult male, the partially-articulated skeleton of a second adult male, and the poorly preserved partial skeleton of a child of roughly five years of age (Duhig 1998).

The partially-articulated skeleton was revealed within a large circular pit. This individual had been interred in a semi-decomposed state and had possibly been decapitated. The grave had subsequently been re-opened, leaving only a fragment of the skull in its original position. The body appeared to have been removed while it was still decomposing, the intent seemingly being to further mutilate the corpse prior to reburial. The skeleton was only 40% complete. The largest recognisable portion within the re-cut pit consisted of the ribs from the right-hand side of the body with the arm still attached, although the hand had been removed and was not present within the burial pit. Prior to reburial, the lower jaw had been moved from the top of the body and placed on top of a pile of partially-articulated foot bones directly below the pelvis. This skeleton has been radiocarbon dated to 2205–1895 cal. BC at 95% probability (Beta–120556).

A child of roughly five years of age was found in a small rectangular pit or grave adjacent to the partially-articulated adult burial. Although the condition of the bones was extremely poor, the position of the surviving limb bones suggests that the body was mutilated or dismembered with only the limbs and skull being placed into the ground.

Despite the proximity of the two bodies, we cannot be sure that the adult and child burials are linked in any way, although a close parallel can be drawn with similar graves found within Wandlebury Ring that are currently considered to be Iron Age in origin.

These two burials lay adjacent to a discrete spread of flint cobbles and animal bone that sealed a series of what proved to be artefactually sterile pits. The faunal assemblage was dominated by cattle bones, perhaps the remains of feasting. At least two aurochs, three domestic cattle, one sheep and one pig were represented; these animals could have provided enough meat to feed over 600 people (Baxter forthcoming, after Legge and Rowley-Conwy 1988).

The third burial, an adult male of roughly 25 years of age, was buried within an irregular-shaped pit, initially identified as a tree root hole. The body was placed in a tightly flexed position, and lay on its left side with the head to the southeast.

The Early to Middle Bronze Age

Evidence from this period consisted of a pair of large steep-sided ditches, aligned east-west. These were over 2.5m wide and 1.2m in depth and were separated by an entranceway of roughly 5m in width (Fig.

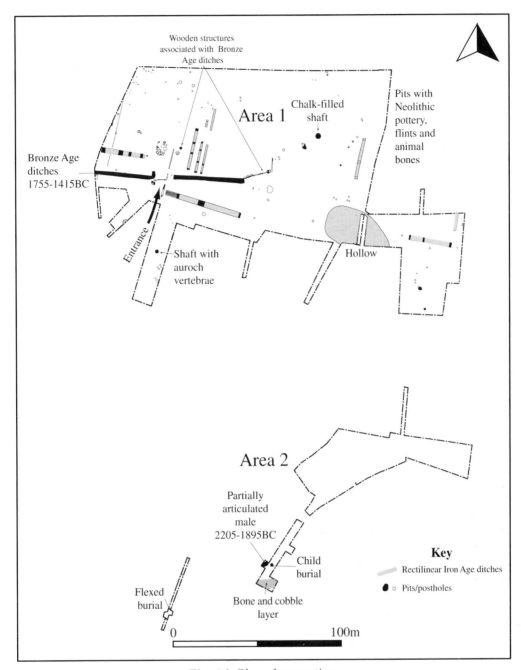

Fig. 4.3 *Plan of excavations*

4.3). The easternmost ditch was 44m long, underlining the scale of these features. They were positioned along the top of a naturally-occurring chalk ridge, rising almost 1m above the landscape to the south. Within the entranceway, a linked series of shallow beam-slots indicated the presence of a wooden structure. The structure had been erected when the ditches were newly excavated and had clearly been removed prior to the accumulation of primary silts within the western terminal. Faint traces of wear survived on the chalk that suggested the passage of foot traffic from the south, turning west into the wooden structure before turning

northwards towards the limit of excavation. The positioning of the ditches on the slight rise in the ground strongly suggests that control of movement and visibility were crucial considerations to the design of this phase of the site. The desire to control movement and visibility seemed to be emphasised by the presence of a further beam-slot extending 7m from the eastern end of the ditch line before turning to the north (Fig. 4.3).

Recent and extensive evaluation trenching of the local landscape (Hinman 1999; Hatton 2000; Kenney 2000) has served to emphasise the unusual nature of these features. The size of the ditches, their position on the top of a naturally formed ridge and the structures within the wide entranceway and ditch end when considered together suggest that these features cannot be interpreted as field boundaries or enclosures.

Two distinct types of use are indicated for these ditches. In their newly constructed form, they were associated with a contemporary wooden structure partially blocking or obscuring the entranceway and perhaps the fence or screen at the end of the ditch line. The ditch cuts were clean, being cut into white chalk. No evidence for associated earthworks was present although it is assumed that the upcast from these features was retained, thus forming a bank.

Infilling appears to have followed the removal of the wooden structure. The basal fills were arte-factually sterile, accumulating through natural processes, with the notable exception of an inverted cattle cranium recovered from the terminal end of the westernmost of the two ditches. These layers probably accumulated through natural processes. Molluscan analysis revealed that open grassland was predominant in the local area at this time (Meyrick forthcoming).

Above the basal fills, three artefact-rich deposits were present within the infilling sequence of these ditches, each separated by a series of sterile silting episodes. Faunal remains form the bulk of the material; these were predominantly cattle, although sheep, pig and the partially-articulated skeleton of a dog were also present. Radiocarbon dating of the latest of these fills has shown that these bones were deposited between 1755–1415 cal. BC (Beta–119801 calibrated at 95% probability). In contrast to the earlier pits, the faunal assemblage from these ditches is clearly dominated by domestic species and contains the only horse bones from the site. The condition of the bones was of insufficient quality to preserve evidence for butchery and gnawing marks.

The deposition of considerable quantities of faunal remains marks a change in use for the site and may be indicative of butchery and/or feasting (Baxter forthcoming). The partially-articulated dog skeleton should not necessarily be seen as a 'special' deposit as dismemberment could have been due to scavenging animals. The separation of these deposits by sterile silting episodes suggests episodic, perhaps seasonal activity. The presence of Late Iron Age ceramics within the latest ditch fills indicates that these features would still have been visible as depressions in the landscape at that time.

The Late Iron Age

Perhaps the most visually striking aspect of the site during this period is the apparent care with which

Fig. 4.4 Looking east towards Wandlebury along one of the Late Iron Age linear features

the area as a whole seems to have been delineated by the cutting of a series of shallow square-ended linear features aligned either east-west or north-south (Figs 4.3 and 4.4). Although the distance between each feature was variable, the dimensions of the individual cuts were remarkably consistent, each having an overall length of *c.* 26m. The fills of these chalk-cut features were quite uniform, the sides vertical and the bases flat. They showed little trace of weathering, indicating that backfilling occurred quite soon after excavation.

These enigmatic features may be seen as compart-mentalising the landscape and are quite distinct from the many enclosure and field-ditches dateable to the Iron Age and Romano-British periods that are known to exist throughout the local area. These features *seem* to respect the earlier phases of pre-historic activity and in particular highlight the position of the Bronze Age entranceway (Fig. 4.3). The base of the earliest of these cuts was not flat but scored by a series of parallel grooves, reminiscent of plough marks, that terminated in line with and south of the earlier entranceway.

Conclusions

The topographical position of the site, sheltered below a west-facing crescent of the Gog Magog Hills, the features present and the artefactual assemblages recovered from those features through excavation, when combined, highlight the presence of a site of great significance for our continuing study of prehistory from the latter part of the Neolithic period through to the end of the Iron Age in Cambridgeshire. The identification of placed deposits, including Grooved Ware pottery and selected tool types within pits, indications of feasting and other seasonal activities, human burials, the use of ditches and associated structures to control movement and visibility, and the unique method of compartmentalising this special area at the end of the Iron Age all suggest that we are looking at an integral part of a broader ceremonial landscape. The physical characteristics of the local landscape from the Gog Magog Hills westwards to the Cam would appear to recall the layout of cursus monuments. Most aspects of the site, if examined in isolation, have strong parallels with features and activities identified at monuments whose origins in many cases date back to the Neolithic period. Such features and activities in these locations are increasingly seen as evidence for aspects of symbolic or ritual behaviour.

The apparent absence of 'domestic' activity throughout the history of use of the site requires clarification. Since the completion of the Babraham Road excavation, the author has been involved in the excavation of in excess of 10km of trial trenching, extending westwards from the site towards the river Cam. This work is revealing an extensive Neolithic, Bronze Age, Iron Age and later presence, with agriculture and settlement predominating in the later prehistoric periods. The recovery of a range of artefacts including socketed axe heads and a rapier after dredging provides new evidence for the importance, in symbolic terms, of the river itself, at least as early as the Bronze Age. These results serve to emphasise the differences in the types of activity between the Babraham Road site and the surrounding landscape of which it was a distinct but integral part.

If, as our current interpretation of the evidence suggests, the site retains a special significance for the population of the area from the Neolithic period to the Iron Age, what are the implications of this discovery? Questions of continuity and change are being applied increasingly to the study of the broader landscape. However, where particular research issues are highlighted, Later Bronze Age and Iron Age themes concentrate on the suggested move away from the symbolic monuments of the Neolithic towards a more functional perception and use of the landscape. Themes concerning aspects of continuity and change in the ritual/symbolic landscape have yet to be explicitly defined as topics for future research. This is not an indication that such topics are seen as a low priority but is simply a function of the present rarity of known sites of Later Bronze Age or Iron Age date presenting such characteristics. An example of the continuing respect for ancient ceremonial sites and a re-emphasis of their status is perhaps best illustrated within Cambridgeshire by the ongoing English Heritage project on the Godmanchester trapezoidal enclosure and associated cursus (McAvoy forthcoming), a monument established in the Neolithic period, but revisited and remodified for ceremonial or religious use at least until the Late Romano-British period.

Despite considerable attempts to seek parallels, the Late Iron Age features of the Babraham Road site appear, to date, unique (Fig. 4.4). There is a degree of doubt concerning the popular view that the nearby earthworks at War Ditches and Wandlebury were constructed primarily as defensive hillforts; that this activity took place initially during the Later Iron Age is also open to further scrutiny. That considerable activity was taking place on these hilltops towards the end of the Iron Age is beyond doubt. Although a thorough re-assessment of the variety of data from previous work in the area is unfortunately beyond the scope and resources of this current project, it is obviously important to see the site within this broader context and not simply to view our results in isolation.

If the Late Iron Age rectilinear features discovered at Babraham Road are partial evidence for the monumental restatement of an earlier symbolic landscape, how will this affect our current understanding of contemporary activity on the surrounding hills? Perhaps this could lead to a reinforcement of the view that these earthworks' primary role was symbolic, part of the process of re-emphasising the importance of an ancient landscape; such a viewpoint should stimulate a re-examination of their origins and of the development of a sense of place within this landscape.

Acknowledgements

The author would like to thank all members of the post-excavation specialist team for their contributions to the project and this paper, Rog Palmer of Air Photo Services for much of the original detail now incorporated into Fig. 4.2, Jon Cane for producing the illustrations, Tim Malim and the AFU for providing the support necessary for the production of this paper and to Jo Brück for constructive and helpful advice.

References

Baxter, I. Forthcoming. Report on the animal bones from Babraham Road, Cambridge. In Hinman, M. Forthcoming. *Prehistoric Activity and Inhumations on Land Adjacent to Babraham Road, Cambridge*. Cambridge: Cambridgeshire County Council Field Archaeological Unit Report.

Bishop, B. Forthcoming. Analysis of the lithic material from Babraham Road, Cambridge. In Hinman, M. Forthcoming. *Prehistoric Activity and Inhumations on Land Adjacent to Babraham Road, Cambridge*. Cambridge: Cambridgeshire County Council Field Archaeological Unit Report.

Cra'ster, M. D. 1969. New Addenbrooke's Iron Age site, Long Road, Cambridge. *Proceedings of the Cambridgeshire Antiquarian Society* 62, 21–28.

Cunliffe, B. W. 1974. *Iron Age Communities in Britain: an Account of England, Scotland and Wales from the Seventh Century BC until the Roman Conquest*. London: Routledge and Kegan Paul.

Duhig, C. 1999. Human remains from Babraham Road, Cambridge. In Hinman, M. *Prehistoric Activity and Inhumations on Land Adjacent to Babraham Road, Cambridge: Post Excavation Assessment of Evaluation and Excavation*, Appendix 4, 64–65. Cambridge: Cambridgeshire County Council Field Archaeological Unit Report PXA 10.

Evans, C. 1991. *Archaeological Investigations at Arbury Camp, 1990*. Cambridge: Cambridge Archaeological Unit Report.

Evans, C. 1992. Commanding gestures in lowlands: the investigation of two Iron Age ringworks. *Fenland Research* 7, 16–26.

Fryer, V. 1999. Molluscan and other remains from Babraham Road Cambridge: an assessment. In Hinman, M. *Prehistoric Activity and Inhumations on Land Adjacent to Babraham Road, Cambridge: Post Excavation Assessment of Evaluation and Excavation*, Appendix V, 66–69. Cambridge: Cambridgeshire County Council Field Archaeological Unit Report PXA 10.

Hartley, B. R. 1957. The Wandlebury Iron Age hill-fort: excavations of 1955–6. *Proceedings of the Cambridgeshire Antiquarian Society* 50, 1–27.

Hatton, B. 2000. *Prehistoric Remains on the New Waitrose Site, Hauxton Road, Cambridge: an Archaeological Evaluation*. Cambridge: Cambridgeshire County Council Field Archaeological Unit Report A156.

Hinman, M. 1999. *Prehistoric Activity and Inhumations on Land Adjacent to Babraham Road, Cambridge: Post Excavation Assessment of Evaluation and Excavation*. Cambridge: Cambridgeshire County Council Field Archaeological Unit Report PXA 10.

Hughes, T. 1898–1903. The War Ditches, near Cherry Hinton, Cambridge. *Proceedings of the Cambridgeshire Antiquarian Society* 4, 1–58.

Kenney, S. 2000. *Iron Age Settlement at Plant Breeding International, Hauxton Road, Cambridge: an Archaeological Evaluation*. Cambridge: Cambridgeshire County Council Field Archaeological Unit Report.

Legge, A. J. and Rowley Conwy, P. A. 1988. *Star Carr Revisited: a Re-analysis of the Large Mammals*. London: Birkbeck College.

Lethbridge, T. C. 1948. Further excavations at the War Ditches, Cherry Hinton, 1939. *Proceedings of the Cambridgeshire Antiquarian Society* 42, 117–127.

McAvoy, F. Forthcoming. *Excavations at Rectory Farm, Godmanchester, 1989–1990*. London: English Heritage.

Meyrick, R. Forthcoming. Molluscan Analysis from Babraham Road, Cambridge. In Hinman, M. Forthcoming. *Prehistoric Activity and Inhumations on Land Adjacent to Babraham Road, Cambridge*. Cambridge: Cambridgeshire County Council Field Archaeological Unit Report.

Pattison, P. and Oswald, A. 1995. *Archaeological Field Survey Report, Wandlebury Hillfort, Cambridgeshire*. London: Royal Commission on Historical Monuments of England.

White, D. A. 1963–1964. Excavations at the War Ditches, Cherry Hinton, 1961 – 1962. *Proceedings of the Cambridgeshire Antiquarian Society* 56/57, 9–29.

5   The Bronze Age of Manchester Airport: Runway 2

Dan Garner

Introduction

A recent archaeological excavation at the site of the Manchester Airport second runway was the culmination of a systematic programme of fieldwork designed and implemented by Gifford and Partners on behalf of Manchester Airport plc. A full account of the work at the multi-period site will soon be published (Garner forthcoming) and this paper is presented as an overview, with some detailed discussion of the Bronze Age evidence recovered from three specific areas: the Sugar Brook, the River Bollin and Oversley Farm.

Topography and geology (Figs 5.1 and 5.2)

Oversley Farm lies on the edge of a natural escarpment overlooking a section of the River Bollin valley (NGR SJ 8156 8338) that effectively marks the boundary between the flat, low-lying Cheshire Plain to the south and west, and the foothills of the Pennines to the north and east. The steeply sloping sides of the Bollin valley provide a natural boundary for the Oversley Farm site to the south and east, while Manchester Airport's first runway has removed the original contours of the landscape to the north and west. Immediately to the south of Oversley Farm, modern landscaping, in the form of a deep cutting made during the construction of the new Wilmslow road (A538) in the 1980s, and prior to this a brick works (later used as a viewing park by the airport), has also adversely affected the original topography.

The site of Oversley Ford is situated on a meander of the River Bollin, 500m to the south of Oversley Farm; although first documented in a charter of AD 1215 (Dodgson 1970, 156), its use as a fording point is probably much older. The crossing point at

Oversley Ford would have provided a route across the significant barrier of the River Bollin, allowing access to the Cheshire Plain and important sites such as Lindow Moss (2km to the south), a wetland area rich in food resources, and Alderley Edge (5km to the southeast), which was exploited for its copper ore during the Early Bronze Age (S. Timberlake pers. comm.). The Bollin valley appears to have been a favoured area in the Bronze Age for both burial and settlement; urned cremations have been found at Wilmslow (Harris and Thacker 1987, 86), an unurned cremation at Fairy Brow, Little Bollington (Tindall and Faulkner 1989), and an enclosed settlement at Heath Farm, Arthill (Nevell 1988). The Manchester Airport excavations have shown that Oversley Farm was the focus for a domestic presence from the Early Neolithic, through the Early Bronze Age and onwards to the present day.

The geology of the area is dominated by a glacial drift of boulder clay, overlying a solid geology of Mercian mudstone. Along the edges of the Bollin valley, isolated patches of glacial sands and gravels overlie the boulder clays. Oversley Farm is located on such a deposit, whereas occupation at the Sugar Brook was located amid the more widespread glacial tills of boulder clay.

Radiocarbon dates

All dates referred to in the text are expressed as a two sigma calibration, unless expressly stated. The fuller details of the dated samples are contained in Table 5.1.

The phasing

Erosion as a result of ploughing prevented the

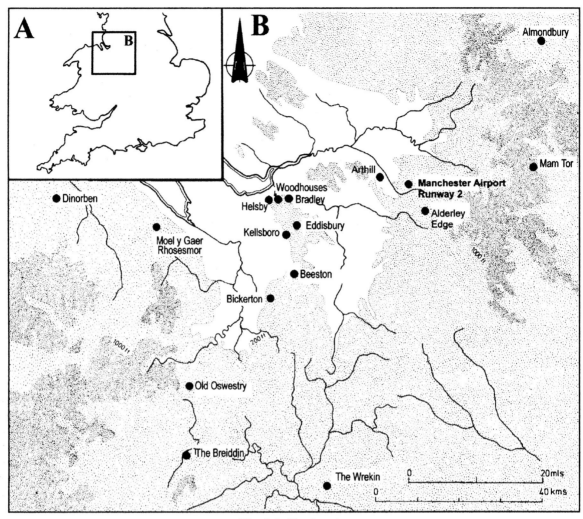

Fig. 5.1 Site location

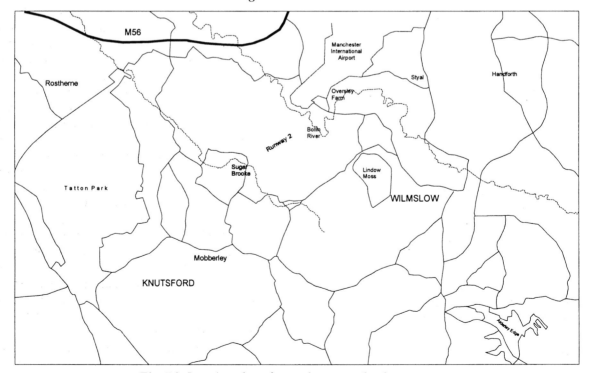

Fig. 5.2 Location plan of second runway development area

establishment of a stratified framework for the Oversley Farm site. Deposits and features were therefore grouped together on the basis of their artefactual contents, or their implied radiocarbon age, rather than by their stratigraphic relationship. For the Bronze Age, the weight of the archaeological evidence starts with phase 2A and continues until the end of phase 2C; the radiocarbon samples suggest a date range for this activity of 2330–1635 cal. BC. On one level, all of this activity can be viewed as belonging to the Early Bronze Age period, but the complex stratigraphy in one part of the Oversley Farm site, the hollow way, necessitated the subdivision of the activity into three separate subphases. This was further complicated by the framework chronology put forward by Needham (1996), which identified the time slot of 2500–2100 BC as the Late Neolithic (copper phase). In the Manchester Airport report, phase 2A has been labelled as the Late Neolithic/Early Bronze Age transition, and the temptation to identify a specifically Beaker phase to the site has been avoided despite the presence of Beaker pottery in some contexts.

The criteria for Neolithic and Early Bronze Age settlement

Within recent studies of the British Neolithic and Early Bronze Age, there has developed a growing avoidance of the word 'settlement'. Instead, alternative explanations for the formation of pit and midden deposits, together with the ephemeral timber structures with which they are sometimes associated, appear to be in vogue. Thomas's *Rethinking the Neolithic* (1991) is probably the most frequently cited text on this subject. In essence, this sees the life of a Neolithic clan or family group as transitory within the wider landscape. Occupation sites are interpreted as temporary or seasonal camps, and the features often associated with them are thought to be the product of ritual rather than economic activity. It is argued, for example, that the most common type of pit-fill deposits, characterised by their affinities to fire (often containing charcoal, fire cracked stone, and pottery – the material of domestic life), have the ritualistic purpose of fixing a site within the landscape (*ibid.*, 76). The association of prestigious items with such deposits and related structures has often led to the conclusion that the site was of ritual significance and in some way exceptional to the typical domestic set-up. For example, the Neolithic building from Fengate has been regarded as a mortuary house on the grounds that it lacked a hearth and had several unusual objects inside it that are not typical of a domestic assemblage (Holgate 1988, 25).

When reviewing the evidence for settlement in Britain during the Beaker period, Bewley (1994, 66) has remarked that negative evidence has led to the conclusion that 'we cannot find the [settlement] sites so they must have lived in temporary settlements which could be easily moved'. He went on to admit that we do not know what the settlement system was and that any society that had such organised burial practices is likely to have had a similarly sophisticated settlement organisation. Bewley concluded that there are two reasons why Beaker settlements are hard to find: firstly, current archaeological techniques are not good enough; and secondly, post-depositional factors may have rendered these sites lost or obscured (*ibid.*). One exception to this is the Beaker settlement at Belle Tout (Bradley 1970), which comprised two overlapping rectangular enclosures within which was evidence for oval and rectangular timber structures and middens containing locally produced pottery. The excavator, Richard Bradley, concluded that the site was not seasonal but continuously occupied. He argued that it was possible to discern a pattern of 'settlement drift', with the settlement nucleus shifting along the valley floor from generation to generation (*ibid.*, 360). Bradley made reference to work by David Clarke (1969, 57) on sites in the Netherlands and Britain demonstrating a similar pattern of shift; Clarke suggested that this was the result of contaminated pits, eroding fields and rotting house foundations. Another study, conducted by Bamford on the Beaker domestic sites of East Anglia, concludes that 'The precise duration of any occupation by a single community must remain a matter of conjecture at present' (Bamford 1982, 54). Bamford (*ibid.*) argues that even continuously occupied settlements would probably have moved from time to time due to the exhaustion of arable or grazing land and that loosely organised farmsteads may have followed a shifting pattern of existence within a circumscribed area.

Early Bronze Age and Beaker sites were probably quite similar in character. Most general works on the subject locate the beginnings of land division in the period from 2100–1500 BC, with settlements represented by clusters of roundhouses forming both enclosed and unenclosed rural farms or hamlets (Parker Pearson 1993, 103). The Dartmoor reaves (Fleming 1988) and the cairnfields of Derbyshire (Barnatt 1994) may demonstrate examples of this change in landscape usage at this time. This pattern is followed and proliferates during the subsequent Middle Bronze Age period when evidence for settlement becomes more convincing and the examples far more numerous.

The purpose of this brief résumé is to place the evidence from Oversley Farm into a wider context and to set some precedents for the interpretation of

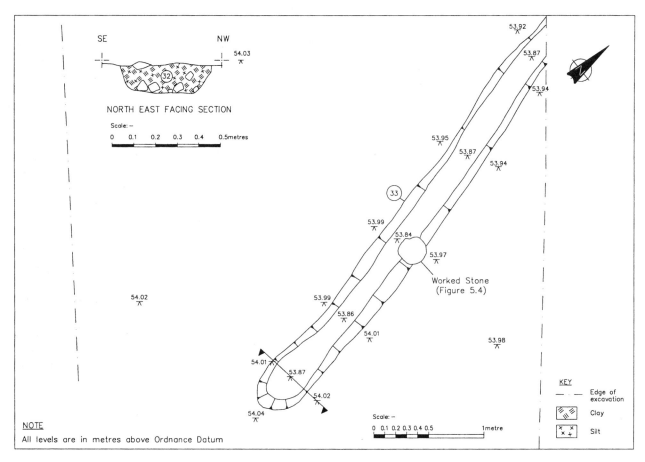

Fig. 5.3 *Plan of the Sugar Brook site*

the various features and deposits encountered. The terms 'domestic site' and 'settlement' seem synonymous, but the criteria for what may be considered permanent, as opposed to temporary or seasonal, seems to be a matter for great debate. Bradley (1970, 360) considered that the settlement at Belle Tout was permanent because of the locally produced pottery, the evidence for permanent structures (but see Bradley's subsequent reinterpretation: 1982) and the presence of four and six-row barley, indicative of both spring and autumn sowing respectively. When examining a Neolithic enclosure at Plasketlands (Cumbria), Bewley used site catchment analysis to argue that the site was a settlement on the grounds of its proximity to the sea, the sandy soils, and the fertile (high and dry) position (Bewley 1994, 48–49). To this equation must be added the factor of post-depositional processes, and when considering a site where erosion can be demonstrated either by natural agents or by the effects of ploughing, too little must not be made of the ephemeral traces of partially surviving structural evidence.

Several of the above criteria apply to the Oversley Farm site regardless of the period under discussion:
1 It is located on the edge of a major river valley that would have been able to provide access by boat to the Mersey Basin and ultimately to the Irish Sea.
2 The site is confined to a glacial deposit of free draining sandy soils.
3 The site occupies a fertile high and dry position within the surrounding landscape.
4 There is evidence that a large proportion of the site has been subjected to severe erosion through long term ploughing.

The remaining criteria used in the consideration of each phase of activity on the site have included:
5 The presence of locally manufactured pottery – given that pottery manufacture may be considered as a 'settled' activity.
6 The presence of 'permanent' structures.
7 The presence of evidence for crop cultivation of more than one variety.

Some of the deposits and features at Oversley Farm demonstrate patterns of deposition that defy a practical explanation and echo findings of ritual deposition in evidence at other sites. However, it would be wrong to identify elements of ritualism as the only process in the formation of significant deposits or structures, with studies of the sites at Skara Brae and Barnhouse on the Orkneys demonstrating the inextricable connection between

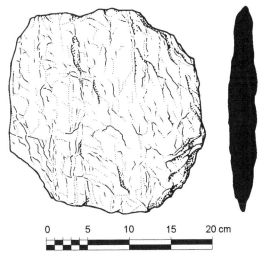

Fig. 5.4 *Stone disc*

domestic and ritual activity (Bewley 1994, 60; Parker Pearson and Richards 1994, 41–47). For this reason, the presence of ritual activities in several phases at Oversley Farm has not led to the preclusion of domestic settlement as the primary function of the site.

The Sugar Brook

This site was located at the southeastern end of the second runway development (Fig. 5.1) on an expansive area of boulder clay. The Bronze Age activity was confined to the truncated remains of a linear feature that had been severely eroded by subsequent cultivation, evidenced by extant ridge and furrow of Late Medieval date.

The feature comprised a linear gully aligned roughly north-south for a length of *c*. 6m (Fig. 5.3), the southern end having a rounded terminus and the northern end simply petering out as the feature became more and more shallow. At the southern end of the feature, where the survival was best, the slot was 0.4m wide and 0.3m deep, the fill comprising a light brown charcoal-flecked clay with a high percentage of heat-fractured stone and several sherds of Bronze Age pottery. A single flint flake was found to the south of this feature, but the most interesting artefact recovered from the gully was a crudely shaped stone disc laid on edge against the side of the cut. This object (Fig. 5.4) was interpreted as a pot lid.

The evidence from Sugar Brook is scant but the linear gully may be a wall slot related to a rectangular structure, the rest of which has been removed by ploughing. No environmental evidence was recovered from samples of the gully fill, but the material seems to be indicative of a domestic site broadly comparable to the occupation at Oversley Farm (see below).

The River Bollin

The area of the Bollin Valley affected by river diversion works was located 0.5km to the southeast of Oversley Farm and 0.5km upstream of the Oversley Ford site (Fig. 5.1). Work in this area concentrated on palaeo-environmental sampling of buried river silts within the old flood plain of the river and during this work several flint artefacts were recovered from the river silts. The flints included fragments of two barbed-and-tanged arrowheads and a complete knife blade of Early Bronze Age type (Wenban-Smith 1998).

The results of the environmental sampling produced an insight into the environment of the late prehistoric river. A sample dated cal. BC 370–5 AD (BETA–112650) produced evidence of a marginal fen vegetation including reeds and horsetails, indicative of a wide stable river channel, the slopes of which were populated with hazel and ash (Shimwell and Downhill 1998). The implication is that by the Iron Age, the Bollin was a rich source for wild fruits and game and that this had probably been the case during the Bronze Age, as indicated by the stray flint finds suggestive of hunting activity.

Oversley Farm (Fig. 5.5)

The Neolithic

One rectangular structure on a north-south alignment was identified in the Neolithic phases of the site. Associated with the structure were several pits containing pottery, lithics, heat-fractured stone and charred material, including cereal (naked barley) grains. It is considered likely that the linear feature referred to below as the 'hollow way' came into existence during the Neolithic period.

The Neolithic/Early Bronze Age transition – phase 2A (Fig. 5.6)

The hollow way (contexts 378 and 578)
The hollow way comprised a shallow linear depression, *c*. 7.5m wide and 0.5m deep, that ran on an approximate north-to-south alignment for the entire length (some 300m) of the western edge of the excavation area. The feature survived to varying degrees along its length with several areas completely eroded by ploughing. Survival was best towards the middle and northern half of the site, where an uninterrupted length of some 75m was recorded. In this area, a patchy metalled surface covered by primary silting deposits was identified. This was cut in several places by pits of varying size and function.

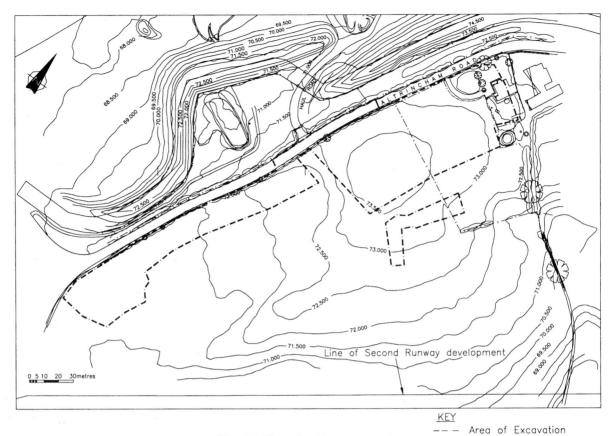

Fig. 5.5 *Oversley Farm excavation*

KEY

– – – Area of Excavation

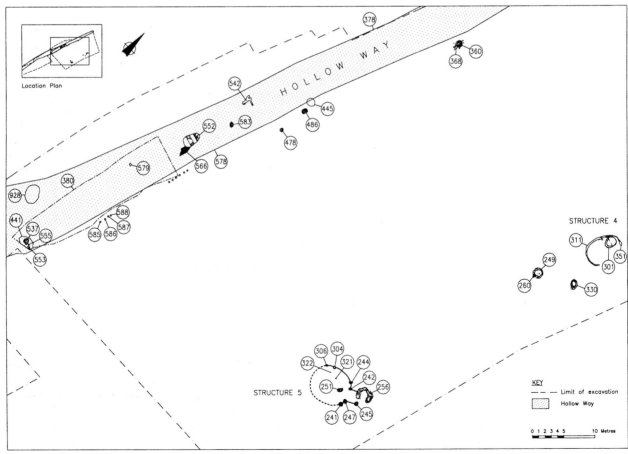

Fig. 5.6 *Phase 2A*

The linear hollow, where it survived best, exhibited a profile of gently sloping concave sides and a flat base. The primary silting of the feature was a pale grey silt-sand containing a small percentage of water worn pebbles that were probably derived from the localised natural gravel deposits. Small amounts of charcoal and heat-fractured stone were also present in this deposit, which had formed in places to a depth of 0.3m. In this phase, in addition to the structures and features described below, the evidence includes a possible fence line along part of the eastern edge of the hollow, the accumulation of fire related deposits such as context 542 (standard radiometric date of 2330–1935 cal. BC: BETA–133370), and the cutting of several enigmatic pits, including pit 360 (standard radiometric date of 2195–1885 cal. BC: BETA–133367).

Midden (contexts 380 and 441)
A deposit of light grey sand (context 380) containing numerous inclusions of heat-fractured stone and water-worn pebbles overlay the primary silts within the linear hollow. This sand had formed to a thickness of 0.12m, and contained occasional charcoal flecks, lithic artefacts and sherds of Beaker domestic pottery (Allen 1998). Deposit 441 lay above 380 in a discrete area 2m x 1.2m and was 0.1m thick. It comprised a dark grey sand-silt containing small pebbles, heat-fractured stone, abundant charcoal and artefacts including Beaker domestic pottery and an exquisite barbed-and-tanged flint arrowhead.

Structure 4
Structure 4 was located on the northeastern edge of the site *c.* 6m to the north of the Neolithic structures. As with those features, structure 4 had suffered from severe plough damage to the extent that no associated surface levels or even a complete building plan survived. The structure comprised a shallow curvilinear slot 0.3m wide and 0.2m deep. This enclosed an oval-shaped area, 6m long and 4m wide. There was a break on the eastern portion of its circuit, possibly implying an entrance. Associated with this structure were several pits, of which internal pit 301 had evidence for an organic lining, probably of leather or wood, that may have been designed to retain water. External pit 249 had been lined with small pebbles, possibly with the intention of creating a working surface for an activity such as the threshing of corn. External pit 330 may have functioned as a storage facility as its backfill 331 produced *c.* 30 sherds of Beaker pottery (Allen 1998).

Structure 5
This oval-shaped building was located *c.* 40m to the south of structure 4 and had no associated surfaces remaining due to extensive erosion from ploughing.

Its complete ground plan could not be ascertained due to the later cutting of a Medieval field boundary ditch that removed *c.* 30 per cent of the projected building plan area. The building was identified through a broken line of six post holes (standard radiometric date of 2135–1745 cal. BC: BETA–133361), suggesting an enclosed area 6.5m long and 5.5m wide. There were two stake holes within the circumference that hint at an internal partition. A possible hearth (context 251: see below) located towards the eastern side of the building could have sat within the entrance, while a further two post holes to the east may represent a porch-type structure, although radiocarbon dating evidence makes the association of these features questionable (standard radiometric date of 1705–1390 cal BC: BETA–127173).

The later date for the possible porch structure may indicate that it was not associated with structure 5, although the possibility that the porch post holes were subsequently contaminated by animal burrowing cannot be ruled out. Interestingly, the latest date for the post settings of structure 5 (1745 cal. BC) and the earliest date for the possible porch (1705 cal. BC) are separated by a time span of 40 years, which is an acceptable lifespan for a timber building of this type.

Hearth 251
The possible hearth 251 comprised an oval-shaped pit aligned on a northeast to southwest alignment, being equidistant from post holes 242 and 247 by *c.* 0.9m. The profile suggests a stepped cut with steep sides and a concave base 0.9m long, 0.5m wide and 0.3m deep. The primary fill 254 (standard radiometric date of 2130–1765 cal. BC: BETA–133366) comprised a dark brown sand-silt, 0.15m thick. This contained a broken fragment of a saddle quern placed on end against the side of the pit, a flat cup-marked stone placed face down on the base of the pit and a rim sherd from a small cup (Fig. 5.7). This deposit was sealed by a lens of clean yellow clay (253) 0.05m thick that in turn was covered by a dark grey charcoal-rich silt-sand (124/252) containing heat-fractured stone.

Discussion of Phase 2A

Activity in the hollow way on the western side of the site appears to begin with evidence for fire settings, patches of metalling and pitting, possibly designed for temporary storage purposes. Although the earliest radiocarbon date from this area is calibrated to 2330–1935 BC (BETA–133370), the hollow way must have formed prior to this date given that it would have taken the passage of a considerable amount of traffic to create it. The

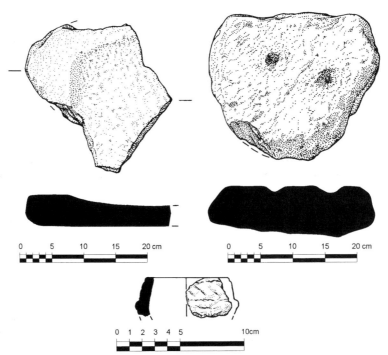

Fig. 5.7 Associated artefacts from pit 251

hollow way may therefore have earlier origins, serving as a track or droveway for the movement of livestock to a crossing point on the Bollin River, possibly at Oversley Ford (which the site overlooks). In fact, the hollow way could well be one of the earliest features on the site, with its north-to-south alignment forming the orientation for the structural elements of the subsequent Early Bronze Age activity. The accumulation of pottery and lithic artefacts in what may be described as a midden-type deposit within the hollow way during phase 2A is a practice repeated in phases 2B and 2C.

Phase 2A is dominated by the appearance of two oval or sub-circular structures along the eastern edge of the excavation, each of which was some 40m to the east of the hollow way. Interestingly, structures 4 and 5 were also *c.* 40m apart suggesting some intended symmetry to the layout of the site during this phase, which is further supported by the apparent preference for easterly-aligned entranceways. Notably, this alignment appears to respect the hollow way, providing further evidence for its early origins. In satisfying the criteria for settlement, it can be noted that this phase contained evidence of permanent structures, locally made pottery and two varieties of cereal crop (naked barley and emmer wheat). To this can be added the presence of a saddle quern fragment indicative of grain processing.

The constructional techniques employed for structures 4 and 5 appear to differ in several ways. Firstly, structure 4 (6m x 4m) is slightly narrower and of smaller dimensions than structure 5 (7m x

6m). Secondly, structure 4 had a continuous wall-slot probably designed to hold a wall of upright planks, whereas structure 5 relied on a series of ground-set upright posts, presumably infilled with wattle and daub panels. Thirdly, structure 4 had its long axis aligned north to south with the entrance-way on the eastern side wall, whereas structure 5 had its long axis on an east to west alignment, with the entrance in the eastern end wall. Finally, the entranceway to structure 5 was 1.6m wide and possibly had an additional porch area (1.5m x 1.5m square) in front of it to the east, and an internal hearth inset 1.2m to the west. In contrast, structure 4 may have had an entranceway up to 4m wide, with no porch-like embellishments and no evidence for internal hearth settings. It is also noteworthy that structure 4 has a cluster of pits associated with it, implying that various craft-type activities were being undertaken in its vicinity.

Elements of ritualism may be associated with structure 5, in the form of a collection of three deliberately-placed unusual objects from the primary fill (254) of possible hearth 251. The objects comprise a quern fragment that could have been deliberately broken or may have been reused (as it resembles crude Early Bronze Age stone hammers found at Alderley Edge that are associated with copper mining activity); a flat blue-green volcanic stone sourced to the Lake District, with two cup-marks pecked into it, that had been placed face down to conceal the decoration; and a decorated rim sherd from an unusual small cordoned cup (Fig. 5.7). The intention for concealment of these objects is further implied by the capping of 254 with a deposit of clean yellow clay (253), effectively creating a false bottom to pit 251.

There are few comparisons for structural elements in domestic sites of this period. Some possible examples exist at Belle Tout (on the south coast near Beachy Head), which the excavator, Richard Bradley, suggested was a continuously occupied Beaker settlement (Bradley 1970). This site had evidence for several possible structures, only two of which (structures 1 and 5, an oval and a trapezoidal building respectively) are now thought to be convincing (Bradley 1982). More recently, small post-built roundhouses have been identified in an Early Bronze Age context (dated by ceramics) at Yarnton in Oxfordshire (Hey 2001). These structures were sometimes located in groups of three to four, but were more often individually scattered buildings (*ibid.*, 220).

Other examples of structures in a Beaker context include a possible oval house of comparable shape and dimensions to Oversley structure 5, excavated at Flamborough, East Yorkshire (Moore 1964, 196), and two circular huts excavated at Gwithian, Cornwall (Thomas 1958), with diameters of 4.5m and 3.6m respectively, each of which had evidence for an entrance porch and central hearth. The Cornish examples represented two phases of occupation at the same site, were associated with pottery and saddle quern fragments, and may have been contemporary with an adjacent field system. A site at Northton on the Isle of Harris (Hebrides) produced evidence of two oval structures, the better-preserved of which was 8.5m long and 4.2m wide; it was suggested by the excavator, Derek Simpson (1976), that the structure may originally have been covered by a tent or upturned boat. From these examples, it would appear that there are certain recurring themes to Beaker period buildings, namely the oval shape and their relatively small dimensions; the suggestion that the covering to such structures may have been an upturned boat or tent might account for these factors. This theory gains some credence from the fact that all of the above examples are located in coastal positions where boats would have been an important feature of everyday life. Oversley Farm being an inland site is an exception to this, although the River Bollin may have made the need for boats equally valid. Alternatively, the oval structures may be part of a structural tradition designed to mimic the shape of a boat, or based on the same constructional technology as boat building.

As an hypothesis, it has been suggested that a standard Bronze Age farming household consisted of two houses, the main one for domestic occupation and the other subsidiary house reserved for cooking and craft-type activities, such as textile production (Ellison 1981). This prognosis may apply to the phase 2A occupation at Oversley Farm with structure 5 comprising the domestic dwelling and structure 4 the workshop.

Early Bronze Age – phase 2B (Fig. 5.8)

Phase 2B probably represents the high point of the Bronze Age evidence from Oversley Farm, not only due to the wealth of artefactual material, but also because of the well-stratified structural features, the availability of radiocarbon dates, and the detailed palaeo-environmental information. The activity in this phase is centred on the hollow way, further highlighting its importance to the community occupying the site. No evidence for stock enclosures or fieldsystems was recovered and the pollen diagram indicates a predominantly open heath-type environment conducive to free-range grazing. Presumably, areas set aside for the growth of crops would need to be delimited and protected by barriers, and fences or hedges seem the most likely agents for this at Oversley Farm as they would leave little trace in the archaeological record. As with phase 2A, there would appear to be two main house-type buildings, one a round structure associated with a midden deposit and the other a rectangular structure with occupation layers and evidence for an internal floor. The additional evidence for two smaller subsidiary structures may be due to better preservation in this area of the excavation.

Structure 6

Structure 6 was located towards the centre of the western limit of excavation and immediately to the west of the hollow way. It differed from the earlier structures in that some stratigraphy survived above and below the structural elements of the building, albeit truncated by later activity associated with the construction of a Roman road. Only half of the building plan was recorded within the area of excavation and further investigation to the west would have been fruitless, as it had been demonstrated during evaluation work that archaeological deposits here had been removed during the first runway development. The structure comprised an interrupted slot 901 (standard radiometric date 1975–1635 cal. BC: BETA–133371) with an internal diameter of 12.5m, inside of which had been deposited a low bank of sand, the top of which was punctuated by various post settings marking a timber wall line. Enclosed by this slot and bank perimeter was a floor surface, 10m in diameter, towards the centre of which was one large pit/post setting, possibly representing a hearth or the location of a timber post designed to support the roof. The

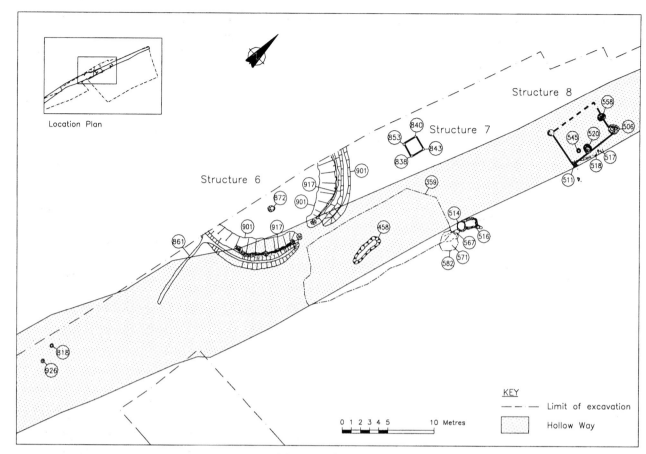

Fig. 5.8 *Phase 2B*

gap that existed in the eastern section of the wall-line may indicate the location of an entranceway, and a shallow channel running away to the south, may represent a gully/drain for the eaves drip.

Structure 7
Structure 7 was located 5m to the north of structure 6 and immediately west of the hollow way. A square four-post structure with dimensions of 1.4m x 1.4m, this building may have functioned as a small granary. Alternatively, the small size of the structural timbers (0.2m in diameter maximum) and the dimensions of the structure plan may argue for this being a free-standing frame for the treatment of animal hides or to support a weaving loom.

Another building may be represented by two postholes (contexts 818 and 926) located 60m to the south of structure 7. The spacing of the posts could suggest a square four-post structure 2.2m x 2.2m. Postholes 818 and 926 were each 0.4m in diameter and 0.3m deep, having steep sides and a flat base. The fill of 818 also contained large angular stones, possibly representing packing material, that included a saddle quern fragment laid flat on the base of the cut. The quern fragment may have been a ritual deposit, possibly a foundation offering to protect the overlying superstructure, and the object may hint at a granary function for the structure.

Structure 8
Structure 8 was a rectangular building, *c.* 5m x 6m, located within the hollow way 12.5m to the northeast of structure 7. The structure was defined to the north, south and east by a group of five substantial postholes (with an average diameter of *c.* 1m and depth of *c.* 0.5m). However, the western edge of the structure could not be traced due to severe water-logging on the site during the excavation. An internal sand and gravel floor surface (standard radiometric date of 1890–1680 cal. BC: BETA–133368) was preserved on the eastern side of the structure, together with an associated internal pit (context 545) that may have served as a hearth or storage area.

The hollow way
During phase 2B, the linear hollow accumulated a complex sequence of deposits highlighted by the construction of structure 8 within it. A spread of midden-type material was deposited to the east of structure 7 and produced a large assemblage of Early Bronze Age pottery and lithics. Pollen from this deposit gives a valuable insight into the environment of the site.

Midden-type deposit (contexts 359, 425, 455, and 475)
Located 2m to the east of structure 6 within the hollow way (378/578) was a layer of black charcoal-rich sand-silt (359/425/455/475) covering an area 19m x 7m. The upper horizon of deposit 359 produced the standard radiometric date of 1965–1630 cal. BC (BETA–127180), while the lower horizon produced the standard radiometric date of 1985–1660 cal. BC (BETA–127181). This layer was *c.* 0.2m thick and contained a high percentage of heat-fractured stone, pottery, lithics, fired clay and burnt animal bone. Charred seeds recovered included naked barley and emmer wheat, as well as ten varieties of crop weed species, suggesting that crop cultivation was being undertaken on or near the site. The occurrence of seeds from the streamside plant meadowsweet would suggest its use as a strewing herb, possibly on the floor of structure 6, or for some domestic purpose, such as the flavouring of mead.

Discussion of Phase 2B

Activities during this phase of the site were focused on the central portion of the hollow way where three distinct structures could be discerned. The largest of these was structure 6, a roughly circular building, that would have had walls made of wattlework. This building is of a type that can be paralleled on later prehistoric sites such as Danebury; it is particularly similar to Cunliffe's house type 2, epitomised by building CS20 (Cunliffe 1993, 60–62). A possibly more relevant comparison can be seen in the Early Bronze Age house at Gwithian, Cornwall, which had a floor area in excess of 100 sq. m and a doorway that faced to the south (Parker Pearson 1993, 10). The most interesting aspect of structure 6 is its close association with the midden area 359 within the hollow way; the midden layers produced radiocarbon dates with a similar range to that from slot fill 900. The fact that the midden was directly in front of the postulated eastern entrance of structure 6 implies that the deposit and the structure are closely related and it is noteworthy that despite the survival of internal deposits within structure 6, no domestic debris was recovered from the building.

Comparisons can be seen at Belle Tout where the pattern that emerged was that the interiors of the structures contained little or no refuse, while the associated debris occupied a midden outside (Bradley 1970, 333). The largest midden at Belle Tout was positioned just outside the entrance to the enclosure surrounding the settlement, leading Bradley to conclude that the domestic rubbish could thus be taken out to be spread on the arable fields located to the east (*ibid.*, 362). At Oversley Farm, the midden was sited on a long-established track or droveway, and environmental evidence suggests its close proximity to arable fields, so a similar explanation of the stock-piling of rubbish for use in manuring could be postulated. If this midden material was being intermittently removed to the fields and subsequently fresh waste was being deposited, this could explain the fragmentary state of the pottery assemblage where very few sherds from any one vessel are represented. It would also explain the range of possibilities offered for the radiocarbon dating for layer 359, as vestiges of any one midden deposit would probably linger after the bulk of the material had been removed for manuring, and would subsequently be subsumed by a new midden deposit.

Structure 8 was the second largest building in the group and was rectangular in shape, being constructed from earth-fast timber posts and sited over the hollow way. Within this building was evidence for a sand and gravel floor surface, above which had accumulated occupation layers mainly characterised by high percentages of charcoal and containing small amounts of domestic rubbish. The main internal feature of structure 8 was a pit that had been backfilled with domestic rubbish and was probably originally intended as a storage pit. The small size would suggest a low capacity for bulk storage of material such as grain and it possibly supported an upstanding wicker basket, as implied by some of the charcoal samples analysed from the site. Belle Tout structure 5 offers a good comparison for this building (Bradley 1970, 328) and a domestic function seems to be inferred.

The smallest building in this phase was structure 7, a small four-post building for which many analogies exist. These structures are often interpreted as granary buildings designed so that the floor is raised off the ground on the four corner posts in order to keep the grain dry and well-ventilated. The small size of structure 7 may be indicative of the relatively low yields of cereals from the site, although an alternative function may have seen it serve as a frame for the treatment of hides or textile manufacture. Certainly, its position between structures 6 and 8 would suggest communal usage. A second similar structure may have existed to the south, associated with a quern fragment, and as this second building is of larger dimensions, it may be a more likely contender for a granary.

With reference to the criteria for settlement, phase 2B produced evidence for permanent structures, locally produced pottery and two varieties of cereal crop (naked barley and emmer wheat). However, to this may be added a wealth of additional environmental information recovered from midden deposit 359; this deposit produced a good pollen count, with associated charred seeds and macro-remains. The combined data suggest that an open landscape

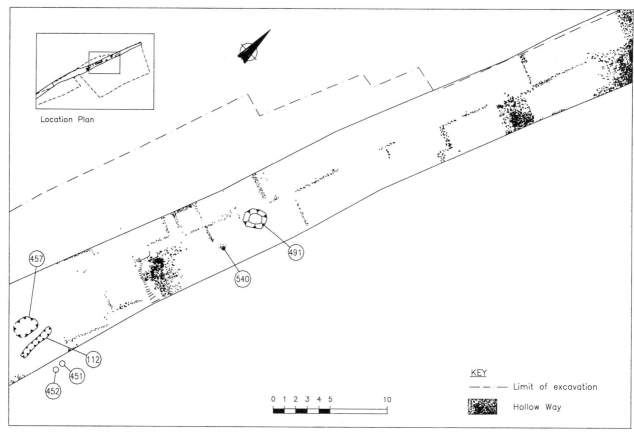

Fig. 5.9 Phase 2C

prevailed around Oversley Farm during this phase, the natural vegetation being a hazel/alder/birch scrub, with a marked absence of primeval or modified woodland. Elevated counts for grasses, heaths, bracken and cereals are strong indicators of open pastoral and arable conditions in the immediate vicinity, and this is supported by the relatively restricted number of weed species, indicating a reduction of diversity through human occupation. The added presence and dominance of plantains can also be seen as a clear indicator of trampled and disturbed ground. The combined evidence would argue strongly in favour of the phase 2B site being a permanently occupied and agriculturally based settlement/farmstead.

Early Bronze Age – phase 2C (Fig. 5.9)

This was the final phase of Early Bronze Age activity on the site and it is highlighted by a paucity of structural evidence. The main feature of this phase was the construction of a compact area of metalling in the base of the hollow way, which ran for a significant length as an uninterrupted surface. Isolated deposits formed above this surface, while intermittent and patchy resurfacing appears to have been undertaken randomly thereafter.

Discussion of Phase 2C

The activity identified in phase 2C would appear to be a continuation of that seen in the previous Early Bronze Age phases with activity concentrated around the hollow way, characterised by pitting, burnt deposits and a build-up of domestic waste. However, two main departures are apparent in the lack of structural evidence and the first clear evidence for a deliberately laid metalled surface within the hollow way (this would presumably have required a significant investment of time and people). To this may be added the unfortunate lack of environmental evidence for this phase of the site, resulting in only one of the criteria for settlement being met (locally produced pottery). This raises the interesting question of whether a lack of criteria indicates a lack of settlement. The area to the west of the site (now the first runway development) could have held evidence of the missing criteria.

The Middle Bronze Age 1500–1150 BC – Phase 3A (Fig. 5.10)

This phase is represented by two isolated pits, 357 (standard radiometric date of 1420–1020 cal. BC: BETA–127177) and 525, neither of which could be

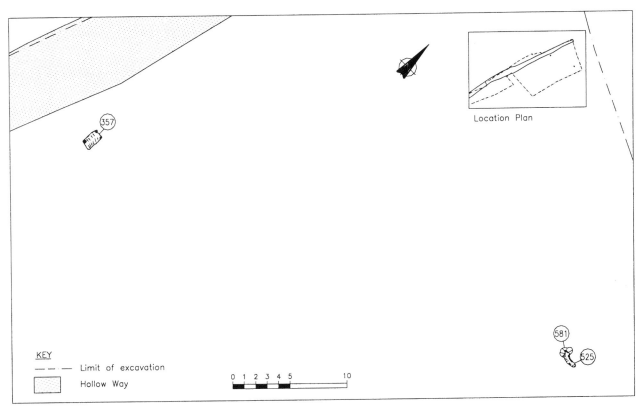

Fig. 5.10 *Phase 3A (Middle Bronze Age 1500-1150 BC)*

linked to any structural features in the excavation area. As such, they serve to demonstrate a continued use of the site during this period, although it is hard to speculate about status or function beyond identifying that elements of domestic life were present. If a pattern of settlement shift was occurring at Oversley Farm from generation to generation, being confined to the natural outcrop of sand/gravel subsoil and the focus of the hollow way, then it may be reasonable to assume that a domestic settlement or farmstead was present, even though no positive trace was recovered.

The Late Bronze Age 1150–750 BC – Phase 3B (Fig. 5.11)

The evidence for this phase of the site is again limited to a couple of pits (standard radiometric date of 910–760 cal. BC: BETA-127178) concentrated along the eastern edge of the hollow way, and some very tentative structural remains that, as with the Middle Bronze Age evidence, serve merely to demonstrate the continued occupation of the site. Artefactual evidence recovered from the pits included a complete saddle quern with accompanying grinding stone (Fig. 5.12), which would again seem to indicate a domestic presence.

Structure 9

This structure was located towards the northern end of the hollow way on the western side of the excavation and lay in the vicinity of pits 355, 594 and 598. The existence of this structure can only be tentatively suggested as the area had been badly eroded by subsequent ploughing and the surviving elements were probably the most substantial components of the building. The structure consisted of four postholes that possibly sat on the line of a circle with a diameter of 10m, at the centre of which lay pits 594 and 598. This could represent the remains of a roundhouse; structures of a comparable size and posthole construction have previously been recorded in Cheshire at Beeston Castle (Ellis 1993, fig. 23) and Tatton Park (Higham 1999, 33) in a Later Iron Age context.

Conclusions

It has been suggested that Early Bronze Age settlement patterns may have followed a cycle of settlement drift (Bradley 1970, 360) and that this may have been confined to a circumscribed area (Bamford 1982, 54). At Oversley Farm, it would seem that the space reserved for structures tended to drift within an area defined by the limits of the sand and gravel terrace, and that the planned layout could vary from a well-spaced symmetrical arrangement to a more nucleated *ad hoc* pattern. However, the location of the hollow way remained a constant, and as such, it

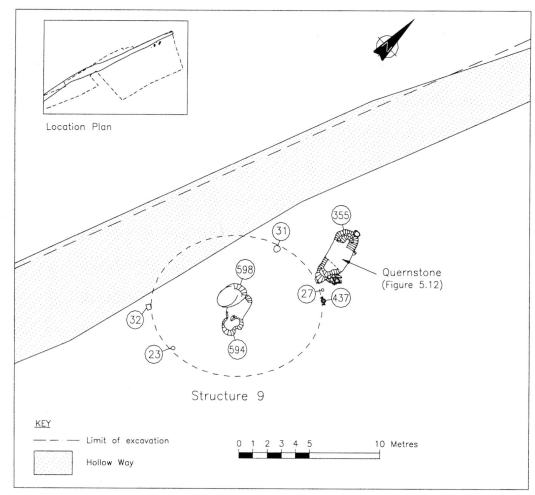

Fig. 5.11 *Phase 3B (Late Bronze Age 1150-750 BC)*

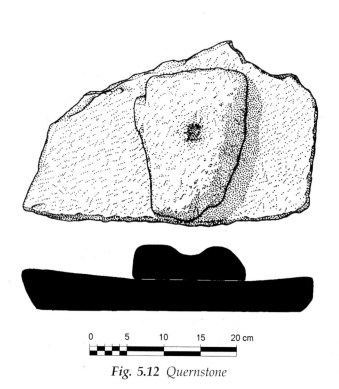

Fig. 5.12 *Quernstone*

repeatedly became the focus for deposition of what may be seen as the elements of domestic life.

Recently, the issue of refuse and midden formation has been the subject of some scrutiny, leading to the suggestion that 'midden sites' were connected with specialised activities such as craft production, feasting or the burial of special deposits. Enhanced refuse generation has been suggested to be linked to the centralised storage of agricultural produce/livestock or the regular introduction of materials to the site by visitors from neighbouring sites of similar status. 'Midden sites' could therefore suggest nodal settlements in terms of the settlement hierarchy, and the ease of access afforded by the proximity to the communication network (rivers or trackways) may have been vital to this success (Needham and Spence 1997, 88). If this argument is valid, then it is certainly pertinent to Oversley Farm, where the trackway itself became the focus of the midden formation.

Whether the site at Oversley Farm is seen as a temporary seasonal camp or a more permanent arrangement, it seems clear that its location was important enough to prompt its regular reuse throughout the Bronze Age (and beyond). This would either imply that the criteria for settlement remained constant throughout the period or that certain factors peculiar to the site acted as a draw to the local populace; this may have been nothing more mysterious than the location of a fording point on the River Bollin. However, when compared to the relatively scant evidence for occupation in the area of the Sugar Brook located on the lower-lying clay-rich soils to the south, a more complex range of factors would seem more likely.

Table 1 Radio-Carbon Sample Details

Context No.	Lab No.	Conventional C-14 Age	Calibrated 2 Sigma	Calibrated 1 Sigma	Calibration Curve Intercept Age
110	Beta-127171	3610 ± 60 BP	Cal BC 2135–1770	Cal BC 2030–1895	Cal BC 1955
43	Beta-127172	4870 ± 80 BP	Cal BC 3795–3510 and Cal BC 3410–3395	Cal BC 3715–3630	Cal BC 3655
119	Beta-127173	3260 ± 80 BP	Cal BC 1705–1390	Cal BC 1620–1430	Cal BC 1515
93	Beta-127174	4210 ± 90 BP	Cal BC 3015–2985 and Cal BC 2935–2560 and Cal BC 2525–2500	Cal BC 2900–2845 and Cal BC 2830–2620	Cal BC 2875
303	Beta-127175	5040 ± 70 BP	Cal BC 3975–3675	Cal BC 3950–3760	Cal BC 3800
316	Beta-127176	1520 ± 60 BP	Cal AD 420–650	Cal AD 465–475 and Cal AD 515–620	Cal AD 560
232	Beta-127177	3020 ± 70 BP	Cal BC 1420–1020	Cal BC 1385–1135	Cal BC 1265
19	Beta-127178	2640 ± 70 BP	Cal BC 910–760 and Cal BC 635–560	Cal BC 830–790	Cal BC 805
470	Beta-127179	2150 ± 60 BP	Cal BC 375–20	Cal BC 345–310 and Cal BC 210–75	Cal BC 180
359 (TOP)	Beta-127180	3490 ± 70 BP	Cal BC 1965–1630	Cal BC 1895–1705	Cal BC 1765
359 (BOTTOM)	Beta-127181	3510 ± 70 BP	Cal BC 1985–1660	Cal BC 1910–1735	Cal BC 1870 and Cal BC 1830 and Cal BC 1780
21	Beta-133364	4570 ± 80 BP	Cal BC 3520–3025	Cal BC 3490–3465 and Cal BC 3375–3315 and Cal BC 3230–3110	Cal BC 3355
92	Beta-133362	5020 ± 90 BP	Cal BC 3985–3645	Cal BC 3950–3695	Cal BC 3790
122	Beta-133361	3590 ± 70 BP	Cal BC 2135–1745	Cal BC 2025–1880	Cal BC 1935
137	Beta-133363	940 ± 70 BP	Cal AD 980–1250	Cal AD 1015–1185	Cal AD 1040
142	Beta-133365	1510 ± 50 BP	Cal AD 430–645	Cal AD 530–615	Cal AD 560
254	Beta-133366	3600 ± 60 BP	Cal BC 2130–1765	Cal BC 2025–1890	Cal BC 1945
360	Beta-133367	3650 ± 60 BP	Cal BC 2195–1885	Cal BC 2125–2075 and Cal BC 2055–1935	Cal BC 2020
464	Beta-133368	3460 ± 40 BP	Cal BC 1890–1680	Cal BC 1865–1835 and Cal BC 1780–1725	Cal BC 1750

501	Beta-133369	3500 ± 60 BP	Cal BC 1965–1680	Cal BC 1900–1740	Cal BC 1865 and Cal BC 1835 and Cal BC 1780
542	Beta-133370	3730 ± 70 BP	Cal BC 2330–1935	Cal BC 2210–2025	Cal BC 2135
900	Beta-133371	3490 ± 70 BP	Cal BC 1975–1635	Cal BC 1900–1725	Cal BC 1770
929	Beta-133372	3610 ± 70 BP	Cal BC 2145–1760	Cal BC 2035–1890	Cal BC 1955
1204	Beta-113151	3400 ± 60 BP	Cal BC 1875–1805 and Cal BC 1795–1525	Cal BC 1750–1620	Cal BC 1685

References

Allen, C. S. M. 1998. *Assessment Report on Bronze Age Pottery from Oversley Farm, Manchester Airport Second Runway.* Chester: Gifford and Partners unpublished report.

Bamford, H. 1982. *Beaker Domestic Sites in the Fen Edge and East Anglia.* Chelmsford: East Anglian Archaeology Monograph 16.

Barnatt, J. 1994. Excavations of a Bronze Age unenclosed cemetery, cairns and field boundaries at Eaglestone Flat, Curbar, Derbyshire, 1984, 1989–90. *Proceedings of the Prehistoric Society* **60**, 287–370.

Bewley, R. 1994. *Prehistoric Settlement.* London: English Heritage/Batsford.

Bradley, R. 1970. The Excavation of a Beaker Settlement at Belle Tout, East Sussex, England. *Proceedings of the Prehistoric Society* 36, 312–379.

Bradley, R. 1982. Belle Tout: revision and reassessment. In Drewett, P. (ed.) *The Archaeology of Bullock Down, Eastbourne, Sussex: the Development of a Landscape*, 62–71. Lewes: Sussex Archaeological Society Monograph 1.

Clarke, D. L. 1969. *Beaker Pottery of Great Britain and Ireland.* Cambridge: Cambridge University Press.

Cunliffe, B. 1993. *Danebury.* London: English Heritage/Batsford.

Darvill, T. 1990. *Prehistoric Britain.* London: Batsford.

Dodgson, J. McN. 1970. *The Place Names of Cheshire*, vol. 1. Cambridge: Cambridge University Press.

Ellis, P. (ed.) 1993. *Beeston Castle.* London: English Heritage Archaeological Report 23.

Ellison, A. 1981. Towards a socioeconomic model for the Middle Bronze Age in southern England. In Hodder, I., Isaac, G., and Hammond, N.(eds) *Pattern of the Past: Studies in Honour of David Clarke*, 413–438. Cambridge: Cambridge University Press.

Fleming, A. 1988. *The Dartmoor Reaves: Investigating Prehistoric Land Divisions.* London: Batsford.

Garner, D. Forthcoming. *Manchester Airport Second Runway: the Excavations at Oversley Farm.* Oxford: Oxbow Books.

Harris, B. E. and Thacker, A. T. (eds) 1987. *Victoria County History of Cheshire*, vol. 1. Oxford: Oxford University Press.

Hey, G. 2001. Yarnton. *Current Archaeology* 173, 216–225.

Higham, N. and Cane, T. 1999. The Tatton Park Project, part 1: prehistoric to sub-Roman settlement and land use. *Journal of the Cheshire Archaeological Society* 74, 1–62.

Holgate, R 1988. *Neolithic Settlement of the Thames Basin.* Oxford British Archaeological Reports, British Series 194.

Moore, J. W. 1964. Excavations at Beacon Hill, Flamborough Head, East Yorkshire. *Yorkshire Archaeological Journal* 51, 191–202.

Needham, S. 1996. Chronology and periodisation of the British Bronze Age. *Acta Archaeologica* 67, 121–140.

Needham, S. and Spence T. 1997. Refuse and formation of middens. *Antiquity* 71, 77–90.

Nevell, M. 1988. Arthill, Heath Farm. *South Trafford Archaeological Society Newsletter*, 103–117.

Parker Pearson, M. 1993. *Bronze Age Britain.* London: English Heritage/Batsford.

Parker Pearson, M. and Richards, C. 1994. Architecture and order: spatial representation and archaeology. In Parker Pearson, M. and Richards, C.(eds) *Architecture and Order: Approaches to Social Space*, 38–72. London: Routledge.

Shimwell, D. and Downhill, S. B. 1998. *The Evaluation of the Environmental Archaeological Potential of Selected Contexts from the Runway Two Development at Manchester Airport.* Chester: Gifford and Partners unpublished report.

Simpson, D. D. A. 1976. The Later Neolithic and Beaker settlement site of Northton, Isle of Harris. In Burgess, C. and Miket, R. (eds) *Settlement and Economy in the third and second millennia BC*, 221–231. Oxford: British Archaeological Reports, British Series 33.

Thomas, C. 1958. Gwithian: ten years' work (1949–1958). Camborne.

Thomas, J. 1991. *Rethinking the Neolithic.* Cambridge: Cambridge University Press.

Tindall, A. S. and Faulkner, P. 1989. Fairy Brow: an Early Bronze Age Cremation Burial at Little Bollington, Cheshire. *South Trafford Archaeological Society Newsletter*, 88–102.

Wenban-Smith, F. F. 1998. *Lithic Assessment Report and Post-Excavation Project Design for an Archaeological Excavation at Oversley farm, Manchester Airport.* Chester: Gifford and Partners unpublished report.

6 Place and memory in Bronze Age Wessex

David Field

Summary

Many visitors to the chalk downlands of Wessex are struck by the extensive open spaces within the landscape. Although this openness is the result of several millennia of human activity, environmental factors indicate that it was perhaps almost as spacious during the Early Bronze Age and was likely to have been maintained by at least an element of pastoralism. To nomadic pastoralists, 'place' moves with the herd, everything else being 'space', although natural features within the landscape that might be important for shelter or water may over time acquire the status of permanent 'places' through memory of past visits. Recognition of the traces of earlier activities might also acquire importance and either attract or repel visitors.

With the creation of co-axial field systems, effectively boundaries to movement, perception of space is likely to have changed. In terms of the old beliefs, the presence of boundaries meant that space was no longer accessible. In contrast, the investment of effort and the development of intimate knowledge of a piece of land is likely to have resulted in individual fields being considered as place. Thus the humanly-created landscape subsumed natural features and an adjustment in perception was necessary. However, the importance of former places may have become of greater significance, partly in order to retain a link with the past but also perhaps to legitimise the present. Thus camps, settlements and enclosures were created close to or on the site of earlier activity, even where this could only have been recognised by surface scatters of flint or different vegetation.

Despite a period of change encapsulated by the extensive use of linear ditches during the Later Bronze Age, almost all the visible landscape may have become place, either as the result of experience and memory, or as a result of the mythology of past encounters. Space moved beyond the horizon. It may be that this lack of space, of feeling hemmed in, led increasingly to competition and conflict during the first millennium BC.

Introduction

The nature of vegetation appears to be crucial in the search for *place* as it has a major impact on how inhabitants perceive the landscape. Forest dwellers, for example, will see little of the horizon and therefore have a completely different conception of *space* to that of farmers living in open country.

The storms of 1989 threw trees that revealed that at least some of the round barrows on King Barrow Ridge near Stonehenge were constructed of turf (Cleal and Allen 1994, 82), while excavations carried out during the 1950s demonstrated that examples on Snail Down were of similar construction (Thomas 1960, 224). Exactly how many of the 700 barrows in the 10km between these two examples were so constructed is uncertain, but together with mollusc profiles from the Stonehenge area (Cleal *et al.* 1995, 484), this evidence provides an indication that large tracts of the landscape were open grassland regularly grazed by herbivores. How extensive this grassland was and how it was maintained is another matter, but it is clear that herding of one form or another was necessary to maintain that type of environment. The intriguing question is whether the pastoral element was the main component of subsistence or whether it depended on other activities not reflected in the mollusc profile, or taking place elsewhere in the landscape. Although the clusters of burial monuments are ubiquitous, there is no trace of settlement. Given the lengthy sequence of construction and the intensity of ceremonial activity at

Stonehenge, it is not surprising that there are scatters of flint in the vicinity of the monument, but by themselves these need not represent typical domestic activity. With the evidence available, we are left to assume that this open grassland came about as a result of a pastoral economy, perhaps transhumant, less likely nomadic.

Pastoralists are likely to *perceive* the landscape differently to dwellers in permanent settlements. In a recent influential volume edited by Hirsh and O'Hanlon on the *Anthropology of Landscape,* an essay by Caroline Humphreys (1997) graphically illustrated the world of pastoralists on the Mongolian grasslands. For them, *place* is wherever they happen to be. It moves weekly. It is wherever they decide to pitch their tent. Their world is perceived as a shifting dome with a new horizon at every move. Humphreys graphically describes how observation of the spiralling smoke from the campfire demonstrates that it is a 3-D world and *space* lies above as well as around.

Transhumants, on the other hand, are likely to utilise a semi-permanent dwelling for part of the year and return to it annually. For them, *place* may be bi-nodal. Which, if any of these, applied during the Early Bronze Age is uncertain, and in any case the situation will not be that simple as patterns are likely to change through time at different rates in each area.

The impression that visitors to the Wessex chalk immediately obtain today is of space. The open downland with its lack of obvious boundaries allows the eye to wander unhindered from horizon to distant horizon. The natural landscape features, the hills and dramatic escarpments, provide a vertical scale in the landscape. They encourage curiosity. It is possible to ascend them and find a level with the birds, or investigate where the spiral of smoke might disappear to. They might provide an interface with the sky or spirit world. From them, it is possible to observe the landscape below in plan view and form a mental image or map of the relationship of *places* to *space*.

In contrast to these high points, the deeply incised coombes and re-entrant valleys provide shelter from the elements. Additionally, before the extraction of large quantities of water by the military, many would have held streams; springs, perhaps the most symbolic of landscape features, may have issued from the head of some. Water is an essential component to successful existence on the permeable chalk, and such water holes may have been revisited on numerous occasions, developing ever more powerful mythologies on each subsequent visit. It is no wonder that barrow cemeteries often cluster in these locations.

Barrows

Snail Down, Wiltshire, is one such example (Mc-Omish *et al.* forthcoming). Here, some 26 round barrows are situated on the slope close to the head of a narrow re-entrant valley. From the gravel spread on the valley floor, and from the evidence of early maps, the valley almost certainly once held water with a spring issuing from close by the position of the cemetery. None of the barrows lie on the ultimate ridge top, or the ultimate narrow valley floor, although in each case they come within 20m of it. Instead, they are ranged along the whole of the slope in the form of a crescent. To all intents and purposes, the cemetery is hidden in the valley and can only be seen as an entity from the opposing valley slope or from the summit of the massive, imposing Sidbury Hill about 1km to the south. No trace of contemporary settlement is apparent,[1] although as the cemetery must have accumulated over a number of generations, one would expect any evidence of adjacent settlement to be firmly engraved on the landscape.

Passing through this landscape punctuated with burial monuments must have emphasised human as well as ancestral presence. The increasing size of barrow cemeteries not only highlighted the fact that others had been there before and had a stake in the land, but also indicated that space was declining. Knowledge about, and myths attached to some of these landscape features may have resulted in certain areas being identified that were inhabited by spirits or were dangerous to visit and therefore taboo.

Fields

In terms of *space*, the laying out of extensive coaxial field systems towards the end of the Early Bronze Age or beginning of the Middle Bronze Age was a revolutionary event, even if such systems were not all in fact absolutely contemporary. The genesis of these vast field systems is unclear. Chris Gingell (1992, 155–156) noted that the lowest levels of a lynchet on Rockley Down near Marlborough produced Beaker pottery. In contrast, at West Overton nearby, Peter Fowler suggested that 'Celtic' fields were marked out with small stone walls around the middle of the first millennium BC (1975, pl. 8b). At Ebbesbourne Wake, in south Wiltshire, fields had become lyncheted and perhaps gone out of use by the time that an Ornament Horizon hoard was deposited within a field (Shortt 1949, 105). Elsewhere, there is some evidence to suggest that such fields were in use during the currency of Deverel-Rimbury pottery, and indeed fieldwork on Salisbury

Plain indicates that they are consistently slighted by linear earthworks, themselves usually thought of as Late Bronze Age (below).

It is evident from both ground and air survey that these 'Celtic' field systems were laid out in a coaxial manner across large areas, running right across much of the higher downland (McOmish *et al.* forthcoming). Although there is a degree of uncertainty because of the fragmentary nature of the evidence, there is little to indicate the existence of large tracts of open downland outside of the field systems; much of the higher chalkland landscape appears to have been laid out in fields. Individual field systems usually seem to cover a continuous area of the order of *c.* 4km length by *c.* 2–4km width. They comprise brickwork or building block patterns, with the prominent axis aligned to the northeast or less often to the north. Although the layout often seems to have respected burial sites, it automatically swept aside any traditional rights, ignoring claims and beliefs about land-use, and would have debarred open-access grazing regimes.

The layout of these fields over many hectares must have been a considerable task and needed some knowledge of elementary surveying practices. The northeasterly baseline, varying a few degrees either side of 28°, is curious. The alignment appears to have no agricultural advantage, and is retained across the topography. The orientation is likely to have had significant meaning beyond simply being a convenient backsight marker for surveyors, and there is just a hint here of some kind of cosmological order to the Bronze Age landscape. Whether influenced by prevailing wind or celestial event, the alignment conceivably provided a deliberate structural link between the constructed and natural landscape, in order to help legitimise the construction of barriers (Snead and Preucel 1999, 172).

The layout, oblivious of the terrain, demanded some central co-operative agreement and control, and speaks of investment in and control of the landscape as much as respect of it. The construction of boundaries not only kept animals out, but pastoralists too, and thus there must have been a major shift in perception of both places and space.

It is not at all clear from where these fields were farmed. Most of the excavated downland settlements seem to postdate the genesis and main period of use of the field systems, while the relationship of artefact scatters to the field systems is often unclear. It has been argued that the coaxials were constructed around existing houses and it was pure chance that the boundaries always avoided houses and yards; hence the lack of archaeological evidence for contemporaneity. Although this may be possible in the case of an occasional single dwelling, the massive field systems must have supported many more units.

After all, these are the descendants of the people who constructed Stonehenge. It seems more likely that settlement existed elsewhere at the time of layout, perhaps at the limits of the system or in the river valleys. On Orcheston Down, Wiltshire, we can observe the junction of two coaxial systems (McOmish *et al.* forthcoming). There is no apparent chronological separation and the two appear to be broadly contemporary. No special boundary features mark the limit of the system and elements of each system simply adjoin the next. Here, as in other cases, the field layout appears to bear no relationship to the position of a single settlement; it is not laid out around a settlement, and has not sprung organically from it. Despite the excellent earthwork survival, there appears to be no settlement present; at least, it does not figure in terms of earthworks or obstructions to the regularity of the field boundaries. Certainly once established, and given increasing population pressure, or family or group friction, it was possible for new farms to be introduced within the system by utilising 'green field' sites, although this may have posed problems for the organisation of the field system as a whole.

Elsewhere, aggregated fields, which appear to be later than the coaxials, may have been constructed over earlier settlement. Alternatively, we can follow Bob Smith's (1985) view of settlement in valleys becoming increasingly permanent in upstream areas through time according to the economic pressures brought to bear on them. The location of round barrows alongside rivers reinforces this and indicates that settlements might have been predominantly riverine, certainly during the early part of the period but perhaps also as the Bronze Age progressed. The orthodoxy of the first half of the twentieth century that prehistoric settlement in Wessex was confined to the inhospitable hilltops, as the river valleys constituted impenetrable 'jungle' and swamp, cannot now be accepted. The 'tangled, marshy, impenetrable morass' of the Vale of Pewsey, for example, has since produced numerous flint scatters, a henge at Wilsford North, a round barrow cemetery at Charlton, and some 35 Bronze Age and Iron Age surface sites (Gingell 1992; RCHME archive), in addition to the well known henge at Marden (Wainwright 1971), all demonstrating that on the contrary the Vale was densely occupied.

With greater investment in the land, *place* became static. There must have been less need or less desire to move distances. Even if a field system was utilised in its entirety, which might seem unlikely, the daily experience was perhaps restricted to its limits. However, the fields themselves should not be seen as *space*. To their users, they would probably have been intimately known, and they may even have had place names. Whether used for folding sheep, or a favourite horse, or cultivation, left fallow, or just retained as property; the drainage, the soils, the aspect would have been extremely familiar. Just as fields are *places* to modern farmers, they are likely to have been perceived as *places* in the Bronze Age. The coaxials effectively civilised *space*; they organised and tamed it.

However, layout of the field system did incorporate earlier sites, many of those places familiar to earlier inhabitants of the landscape. Some of these may have been recognisable because of the presence of earthworks; for instance, there are many examples of field boundaries aligned on round barrows and long barrows. However, it is also likely that earlier flint scatters or vegetation differences masking the site of earlier settlements or gardens were recognised. Today, the position of nineteenth century farmsteads on the military ranges can be recognised by different vegetation even when all traces of buildings have been removed. Not only is the ground flora different, but apple, plum and other fruit trees survive where they once formed part of kitchen gardens. It may be that in prehistory, the presence of ancestral sites so recognised added weight to claims of land rights. Alternatively, it could be that such areas were taboo and were avoided for fear of upsetting the spirits that dwelt there.

Certainly it appears to have been rare at this time to despoil barrows. On Orcheston Down, Wiltshire, the small barrow cemetery was surrounded by 'Celtic' field system, so that the ditch of one prominent barrow was obscured by a field lynchet (McOmish *et al.* forthcoming). Similarly, on Snail Down, Wiltshire, a system of small rectangular fields was placed up and around an earlier extensive and well known barrow cemetery (*ibid.*). The fields themselves are part of a much more extensive coaxial system that covers many hectares, but that has been largely obscured by cultivation of the historic period from the nearby village of Everleigh.

Whatever these fields were used for, and however long the period of introduction, creation of such extensive systems marked a break with any preceding attempts at agriculture or of bounding the landscape. The degree to which it was imposed is by no means clear, but it marks a major change in the *perception of the landscape*. The fields formed barriers in an economic sense, perhaps to keep things in or out, and if they were hedged or fenced this may have been quite practical, but they also formed social boundaries, perhaps related to ownership by groups or individuals. More importantly, they provided a barrier within the natural world quite at odds with the belief systems usually attributed to transhumant or nomadic ways of life, and in this respect may have represented a marked and more significant break with the past.

It may be that it was this apparent lack of *space*, or an inability to react to social pressures, that ultimately proved frustrating, and coupled with changing climate led to the abandonment of coaxial systems, for with the construction of defensive enclosures, signs of stress begin to appear in the record.

Linear Boundaries

There is some evidence for a new order. A system of linear ditches, quite monumental in places, carved up the landscape into units, invariably focussing on river valleys, but extending on to the higher downland. The available dating evidence from Richard Bradley's Linear Ditch Project would place the earliest a little before 1000 BC (Bradley *et al.* 1994) and there are phases of recutting and reorganisation from the eighth to the fifth centuries BC. These herald further change. Whatever they mean, the fact that they consistently slighted 'Celtic' fields indicates that the agricultural regime was no longer adhered to in quite the same way, and it may have been abandoned altogether. On Orcheston Down, for example, a linear ditch, aligned on an earlier barrow, cut across the 'Celtic' field system, effectively putting at least some of it out of use; it respected the barrow, however, and continued across the hillside before being obscured by later use of the field system. Similarly, on Snail Down, a system of linear ditches cut through the fields but respected and enclosed the barrow cemetery. This was a dramatic development. If there were houses among the fields, the event might have been considered akin to the highland clearances. What had been *place* was now essentially *space*, although old fields would still have been recognisable. Initially, hedges and fences may have survived, although after a while they may have been visible only as earthworks or differences in vegetation. However, such features may still have retained affiliations and perhaps fond memories for much of the population for generations.

Although there are variations, the linear earthworks, which can extend for over 3km, invariably comprise a simple ditch with the earth thrown up beside it to form a bank. Rarely are they positioned at arbitrary points within the landscape, or on ridgetops or valley floors. Instead, they often lay along false crests and appear to be of particular importance when viewed from a certain direction. A number appear to function as spines that run across the higher downland and that separate land associated with the main river valleys from the higher downland in the interior of Salisbury Plain; subsidiary ditches emanate from these at right angles and run down into the valleys. Although on no occasion is a full circuit completed, the impression is one of the creation of small territories or farming units. Many appear to divide up the valley areas in the same way that tithings did in the Medieval period, and indeed the similarity to such units particularly in the Bourne Valley was observed by Hawkes (1939). If this is indeed so, and given the difficulty of ensuring water supply on the chalk, we might expect prehistoric settlements to occupy similar positions to the modern settlements situated on the lower valley slopes. Elsewhere on the higher downland, occasional examples of almost complete parcels of enclosed land can be discerned. In these cases, it might be expected that settlement, a farmstead perhaps, lay central to each territory. Despite excellent potential for survival, no such remains have come to light.

Long ago, Hawkes and others suggested that at least some of the land divisions might be something to do with cattle ranching (Hawkes 1939; Piggott 1973, 403). Colin Bowen came to similar conclusions, and this is particularly the case at Snail Down where the area around the barrow group can have been used for little else (Bowen 1978). Indeed, lack of other extant archaeological features close by or within these areas suggests that the only interpretation consistent with this is that the Downs were used for pastoral purposes, and that the co-operative control implied by the coaxial fields had undergone a transformation. The construction of linear ditches must have also been a co-operative venture, but it reflects different social needs and perhaps also a degree of competition. Boundaries have suddenly become important.

On the higher ground, many of these ditches appear to radiate from hillforts, for example Whitsbury (Bowen 1975, 54), Quarley (Hawkes 1939), Sidbury (Bradley *et al.* 1994), East Chisenbury (Brown *et al.* forthcoming), Casterley (McOmish *et al.* forthcoming) and perhaps now Battlesbury (M. Rawlings, pers. comm.), but as Hawkes suggested, the linears appear to predate them, suggesting that these hills were already important focal points within the landscape. The double linear approaching Sidbury from the north is monumental in scale, forming a massive internal agger that Colt Hoare mistook for a Roman road (Colt Hoare 1812, 181). The alignment here is of some importance, for unlike other linears that respect barrow mounds, the Sidbury double linear slices through a disc barrow in order to pursue its course. It may be that it provides a formal approach to the hilltop, an avenue or processional way. A triple linear approaches the enclosure at Suddern Farm (Palmer 1984, 112), while recent excavations by Reading University indicate that among the linears focussing on a midden at East Chisenbury was a double row of posts (Brown *et al.* forthcoming).

Casterley itself is univallate but the rampart surrounding it appears to lack strength, being no more than waist-high in places, and with the entrance situated at a low point within a coombe that leads into the interior of the higher downland. So indefensible is it, in fact, that it seems unlikely to have been constructed as a fort. The so-called 'ramparts' almost appear as a group of linear ditches placed together to form an enclosure. In fact, one side appears to be incomplete. A similar hillfort of large capacity and straight ephemeral defences occurs at Martinsell on the Marlborough Downs; Balksbury, Hampshire, might be another (M. Rawlings, pers. comm.), while a further system of linears that underlies Wansdyke and forms an incomplete enclosure around the prominent Tan Hill on the Marlborough Downs may also come into this category. Like Casterley, this too encompasses a steep coombe as part of its course, in the same manner as some of the larger post-Medieval sheep pens, such as the example on Upavon Down where the coombe itself provides a funnel into the entrance. It is conceivable that these represent early stock enclosures and meeting places. Gingell (1992, 157) has suggested that Burdurop Down may be the site of a Late Bronze Age market, but enclosed sites such as Tan Hill and Yarnbury, both of which were the sites of Medieval and post-Medieval sheep fairs pose an interesting alternative. These are very different *places*, designed for large numbers of people, or animals, or both. Casterley incorporates earlier sites, and in turn later sites were constructed within it (Cunnington and Cunnington 1913). This constant link with the past may have helped justify its role in the present.

Small rectangular enclosures, the typical Middle Bronze Age farmstead, are invariably constructed over 'Celtic' fields. South Lodge (Barrett *et al.* 1991) is perhaps the best known, but field evidence points to others on Salisbury Plain (McOmish *et al.* forthcoming). The fauna from excavated examples was considered to be predominantly cattle but analysis of fauna at Down Farm, Dorset, indicates that sheep may have played a much greater role than formerly anticipated (Legge 1991, 79). All this points to a return to pastoralism at least on the higher Downs. Whether these rectangular enclosures are typical of settlement remains to be seen. Increasingly, there is evidence of open settlement on valley slopes that goes unrecognised on the surface. Scatters of flint and Deverel-Rimbury pottery were frequently recorded among the 'Celtic' fields in the eastern part of Salisbury Plain (Bradley *et al.* 1994), although it is rarely possible to suggest whether they pre- or postdate the fields.

Similarly, the settlement at Thorny Down may in fact have been quite open, as the 'enclosure' appears as a single length of bank and ditch that reflects the orientation of the local 'Celtic' field system. Whether the settlement is earlier or later than the surrounding fields is unclear. A little to the east, on Easton Down, lies a newly discovered, apparently square enclosure (RCHME archive, unpublished fieldwork) that, like others, is situated in close proximity to the system of linear ditches, lying in a quite isolated position on bleak, unsheltered higher downland at some distance from the valley floor.

East Chisenbury midden

Central to discussion of *place* is the massive Late Bronze Age midden at East Chisenbury, Wiltshire. Despite measuring some 200m in diameter and *c.* 3m deep at the centre, the mound has only recently been recognised, and appears to overlie an earlier ovoid enclosure and settlement (Brown *et al.* 1994). Here, in a small evaluation trench towards the perimeter, tips of ashed sheep dung were found to interleave with layers of bone-rich coprolitic material. Initial assessment by Dale Serjeantson of the great quantities of butchered bone from the site suggests that the largest proportion is from sheep with a significant quantity of neonatal lamb. Such large numbers of losses are by no means unknown at lambing time. However, it is worth considering other aspects of sheep husbandry. In parts of north Africa and Afghanistan, for example, shepherds still drive pregnant ewes into swamps, where they struggle and abort, in order to obtain the soft coat of the unborn lamb which is particularly sought after. Analysis of mandibles by Caroline Jenkins has concluded that sheep dairying may have been taking place, while the large number of spindle whorls from a small evaluation trench provides supporting evidence of an extremely high dependence on sheep.

With furrowed bowls occurring throughout the profile, with no Plain Ware or Scratch Cordon Ware present, and with a Sompting style socketed axe at the base of the deposit, the mound is likely to have accumulated in less than 100 years. The amount of sheep dung and bodies that it represents is enormous, and scaling up the bone count from the small excavated trench reveals figures of enough meat to feed some 10,000 people per year over a hundred year period. The implications are of an intensity of sheep farming on the Downs perhaps even rivalling that of the post-Medieval period.

The position of the mound on a prominent spur above the River Avon, with views across Salisbury Plain and to the Marlborough Downs, is a significant focal point. Chris Gingell pointed out that fields on the Marlborough Downs were manured up to the time that they were abandoned (Gingell 1992, 155). Almost certainly this practice was carried out on Salisbury Plain too. However, it would appear that during the seventh century BC, rubbish here was not put out on the fields as manure, but was being curated. The high percentage of butchered bone and personal ornaments from a small sample of the mound suggests that this is more than farmyard rubbish. Whether equipment such as the broken socketed axe was an everyday or prestige item is not clear, but in any case might be considered an unlikely everyday tool for local shepherds. Flat based fine tableware made for resting on flat surfaces is unlikely to represent the broken sherds from a shepherd's lunch. Equally, the high number of personal items in a small evaluation trench together with the presence of part of a deliberately placed human skull, an item that also preoccupied inhabitants at Swallowcliffe (Clay 1925, 90) and All Cannings Cross (Cunnington 1923), and the discovery of an alignment of a series of linear ditches and a post avenue focussing on the mound all add support to that view. Allowing for compaction and the effects of cultivation, the mound may have once been considerably higher and indeed must have been monumental. It is surely not the manure heap of a simple farmstead. It is not unknown for midden material to be used in a symbolic manner (Brück 1995; Luby and Gruber 1999). On one hand, it may represent the result of competitive or ritual feasting, or of communal festivals (it might be worth pointing out that the sacrifice of sheep in large numbers is still practised at some festivals by some societies and religions), but equally it may be that the mound itself was an expression of status.

Finale

It is important to consider that use was made of the whole of the landscape in Wessex, not just the upland chalk. Enclosures, large and small, as well as open sites all tend to cluster around the edge of the chalk (McOmish *et al.* forthcoming) and along the margins of the river valleys, and much of the extant archaeology that we see on the higher ground must have been at the limit of land units that also incorporated other soil types. Indeed, when looked at like this it becomes clear why so much apparently marginal chalkland was used for cultivation. At face value, the alternatives, the sand of the New Forest, or the nearby clays of the London Basin were inherently worse.

All this might sound a little too neat. What is missing are events that come about as a result of social friction, between family members or groups, where families split and move away, or of those pioneering, entrepreneurial instincts that drive some along a different path.

In contrast to the ephemeral field boundaries of the Middle Bronze Age, many of the more dramatic field lynchets and settlement earthworks visible on much of Salisbury Plain are Roman, but they too often fossilise an earlier, Bronze Age landscape, and in doing so demonstrate that prehistoric landscapes were being altered, adapted, developed and obscured at a very early date. This development invariably utilised 'green Celtic field' sites as domestic settlement units, while the former 'Celtic' fields themselves were reutilised, enhanced and emphasised by intensive agricultural use. In modern times, the ebb and flow of landscape utilisation has now almost come full circle, at least in the military areas, where use for combat training has ensured that much has returned to grassland. Among the apparent *space* of the military ranges, one is acutely aware of the same *places* that we started with – those provided by the natural landscape.

Acknowledgements

Many of the views outlined in this essay derive from a period of extensive fieldwork carried out by the former Royal Commission on the Historical Monuments of England and have benefited from discussion during that time with colleagues David McOmish and Graham Brown. Graham Brown and Mark Bowden both commented on an earlier draft although any errors remain my own responsibility.

Notes

1 There is no reason to assume that the scatters of pottery and stakeholes found underneath a number of the barrows at Snail Down should indicate settlement, given the many different activites that were probably carried out in this landscape.

References

Barrett, J., Bradley, R. and Green, M. 1991. *Landscape, Monuments and Society: the Prehistory of Cranborne Chase.* Cambridge: Cambridge University Press.

Bowen, H. C. 1975. Pattern and interpretation: a view of the Wessex landscape. In Fowler, P. J. (ed.) *Recent Work in Rural Archaeology*, 44–55. Bradford-on-Avon: Moonraker Press.

Bowen, H. C. 1978. 'Celtic' fields and 'ranch' boundaries in Wessex. In Limbrey, S. and Evans, J. G. (eds) *The Effect of Man on the Landscape: the Lowland Zone*, 115–122. London: Council for British Archaeology Research Report 21.

Bradley, R., Entwistle, R. and Raymond, F. 1994. *Prehistoric Land Divisions on Salisbury Plain: the Work of the Wessex Linear Ditch Project*. London: English Heritage Monograph 2.

Brown, G., Field, D. and McOmish, D. 1994. East Chisenbury midden complex, Wiltshire. In Fitzpatrick, A. P. and Morris, E. L. (eds) *The Iron Age in Wessex: Recent Work*. Salisbury: Association Francais d'Étude de l'Âge du Fer/Wessex Archaeology.

Brown, G., Field, D. and McOmish, D. Forthcoming. *The Midden at East Chisenbury, Wiltshire.*

Brück, J. 1995. A place for the dead: the role of human remains in Late Bronze Age Britain. *Proceedings of the Prehistoric Society* 61, 245–277.

Clay, R. C. C. 1928. An inhabited site of La Tène I date on Swallowcliffe Down. *Wiltshire Archaeologial and Natural History Magazine* 43, 59–94.

Cleal, R. and Allen, M. J. 1994. Investigation of tree-damaged barrows on King Barrow Ridge, Amesbury. *Wiltshire Archaeologial Magazine* 87, 54–84.

Cleal, R., Walker, K. E. and Montague, R. 1995. *Stonehenge in its Landscape*. London: English Heritage Archaeological Report 10.

Colt Hoare, R. 1812. *The Ancient History of Wiltshire*. London: Miller.

Cunnington, B. H. and Cunnington, M. E. 1913. Casterley Camp excavations. *Wiltshire Archaeologial and Natural History Magazine* 38, 53–105.

Cunnington, M. E. 1923. *The Early Iron Age Inhabited Site at All Cannings Cross*. Devizes: Wiltshire Archaeologial and Natural History Society.

Fowler, P. 1975. Continuity in the landscape? Some local archaeology in Wiltshire, Somerset and Gloucestershire. In Fowler, P. J. (ed.) *Recent Work in Rural Archaeology*, 121–136. Bradford-on- Avon: Moonraker Press.

Gingell, C. 1992. *The Marlborough Downs: a Later Bronze Age Landscape and its Environs*. Devizes: Wiltshire Archaeologial and Natural History Society Monograph 1.

Hawkes, C. 1939. The excavations at Quarley Hill, 1938. *Proceedings of the Hampshire Field Club* 14, 136–194.

Humphreys, C. 1997. Chiefly and shamanistic landscapes in Mongolia. In Hirsch, E. and O'Hanlon, M. (eds) *The Anthropology of Landscape*, 135–162. Oxford: Clarendon Press.

Legge, A. J. 1991. The animal remains from six sites at Down Farm, Woodcutts. In Barrett, J., Bradley, R. and Hall, M. (eds) *Papers on the Prehistoric Archaeology of Cranborne Chase*, 54–100. Oxford: Oxbow Monograph 11.

Luby, E. M. and Gruber, M. F. 1999. The dead must be fed: symbolic meanings of the shell mounds of the San Francisco Bay area. *Cambridge Archaeological Journal* 9(1), 95–108.

McOmish, D., Field, D. and Brown, G. Forthcoming. *The Field Archaeology of Salisbury Plain Training Area*. London: English Heritage.

Palmer, R. 1984. *Danebury: an Iron Age Hillfort in Hampshire*. London: Royal Commission on Historical Monuments of England Supplementary Series 6.

Piggott, S. 1973. The final phase of bronze technology, 1500bc–500bc. In Crittal, E. (ed.) *A History of Wiltshire* 1(2), 376–407. Oxford: Oxford University Press.

Shortt, H. de 1949. A hoard of bangles from Ebbesbourne Wake, Wiltshire. *Wiltshire Archaeologial and Natural History Magazine* 53, 104–112.

Smith, R. W. 1985. *Prehistoric Human Ecology in the Wessex Chalklands, with Special Reference to the Evidence from Valleys*. Unpublished Ph.D. thesis, University of Southampton.

Snead, J. E. and Preucel, R. W. 1999. The ideology of settlement: ancestral Keres landscapes in the northern Rio Grande. In Ashmore, W. and Knapp, A. B. (eds) *Archaeology of Landscape: Contemporary Perspectives*. Oxford: Blackwell.

Thomas, N. 1960. *A Guide to Prehistoric England*. London: Batsford.

Wainwright, G. W. 1971. The excavation of a Late Neolithic enclosure at Marden, Wiltshire. *Antiqaries' Journal* 51, 177–239.

7   Bronze Age agricultural intensification in the Thames Valley and Estuary

Dave Yates

Introduction

We are faced by a dichotomy in later prehistoric studies. We expect that a profound agricultural revolution occurred during the Neolithic period, transforming the lives of people and the nature of the landscape, and yet the archaeological record in southern England disproves this notion. In the uplands, the expected image of rapid colonisation is at odds with the environmental evidence where the overall picture is one of hills carrying an uneven patchwork of pasture, forest and scrub, and some limited traces of cultivation (Barrett 1994, 139). In the lowlands, the same picture emerges. There is little evidence for an economy based on stable mixed farming, no dramatic landscape transformation, few signs of a more settled mode of life and no proof that a food producing regime had replaced a food gathering lifestyle. Neolithic life did not experience large scale agricultural reform nor did it suddenly change the landscape. Instead, Neolithic society was driven by a need to honour its ancestors and create monuments within a largely untamed environment. This tradition of monument building was its distinguishing feature and remained a social priority for communities into the Early Bronze Age.

The agricultural revolution that we associate with the Early Neolithic emerges instead during the second millennium BC, during which a new landscape with distinct boundaries was created. This is the point at which agriculture and the domestication of life takes off. Now there is evidence of fixed settlements and archaeologically visible land divisions, and for the first time pottery and metals play a significant part in everyday activities. Unfortunately our knowledge of farming intensification is really defined around the evidence from upland areas.

The shock of a new managed and controlled landscape represents a momentous period of change in the lives of individuals and the priorities of communities. It is this lifestyle change and the intensification of agriculture that characterises the Later Bronze Age.[1] However, the pace of change was not confined solely to an agricultural revolution, for at the same time there was a fundamental shift in regional power and wealth toward the lowlands of eastern England (Barrett and Bradley 1980). But here we confront a second dichotomy, for although Later Bronze Age studies have established the emergence of a powerful lowland Britain (especially along the reaches of the River Thames), we have little knowledge of the lowland farming practices associated with these dramatic social changes. It was once even suggested that we would never know about these, and that in areas such as the Thames Valley the archaeological record would be entirely lost by the end of the twentieth century (Taylor 1972, 112).

Developer-funded archaeology has altered this gloomy prospect for lowland England and has reversed the problem confronting the researcher. It is no longer a question of too little information. Instead, as predicted by Thomas (1991), researchers are more likely to drown under a torrent of data flowing from contract excavation and evaluation.

Figure 7.1 shows the number of sites that now provide evidence of Later Bronze Age agricultural intensification. In this article, the appearance of field systems is held to indicate agricultural intensification. The fixing of such boundaries for long term use characterises a fully agricultural society. Throughout the study area, the integration of droveways and waterholes within the field systems suggests the predominance of livestock management. For parts of the Thames, pastoralism may have become the

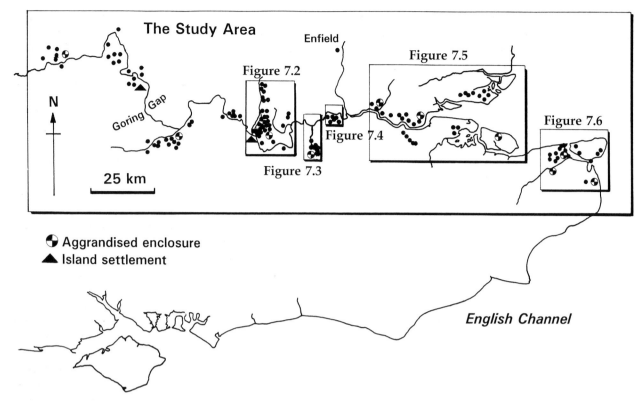

Fig. 7.1 *The River Thames and estuary approaches: evidence of Later Bronze Age land division*

paramount aim (Yates 1999, 167). Permanent field construction in this respect represented one response to the pressures of intensification since animals only have to be kept in fields when their population reaches a point where existing grazing land is under strain (Pryor 1998, 82). The increased scale of animal husbandry is also reflected in the construction of elaborate trackways, including metalled surfaces, as at Cranford Lane (Elsden 1996) and Hays, Dagenham (Meddens 1996, 326). At the latter site, environmental evidence of poaching (severe trampling by animals) supports the interpretation that such routeways were designed to handle the passage of large herds (*ibid.*, 326). The use of what are interpreted as community stockyards (Pryor 1996) and evidence of drafting gates (Elsden 1997, 6) also reflect the sophisticated and intensive style of livestock rearing.

The above outline indicates why field system construction can be equated with intensive livestock rearing. In respect of arable farming, a similar link between intensification and boundary construction can be argued (rather than being assumed). The construction of land allotments creates in effect a series of diverse micro-environments (Halstead and O'Shea 1989, 4; Pryor 1998, 79) in which a wide variety of crops can be grown. The fields therefore offer a strategy of diversification that is one of the buffering mechanisms used by farmers in intensive

farming to guard against total crop failure (Halstead 1981, 191). Field system construction is not confined solely to pastoral and arable intensification. For example, the communities at Reading Business Park constructed small fields for growing flax (Moore 1992, 120) and there was some evidence for leguminous crops, both of which represent highly intensive forms of cultivation.

This research paper, making use of commercially-generated information, offers an overview of intensive agricultural evidence along the entire River Thames corridor and its estuary approaches. It examines the chronology of the construction of field systems, paddocks, droveways and stock enclosures[2] in this powerful lowland zone and the relationship between the creation of land divisions and the emergence of new forms of settlement. Both archived contract excavation reports and evaluations are cited in this paper. Few of these records have been subject to the kinds of peer review of conventionally published works, but the volume and consistency of their findings have helped to identify distinct enclaves of Later Bronze Age activity. These zones of intensive agriculture are associated with concentrations of metal deposition, livestock herding and new forms of settlement. The discoveries by field units working along the River Thames reveal the complexity of land management practices associated with the emergence of a complex inter-regional exchange system based on social storage. The widespread demise of that system has also been recorded. Their discoveries of distinct patterns of occurrence of field systems will contribute to landscape characterisation, which can in turn improve protection and prediction.

The Upper and Middle Thames Valley

An earlier review of the evidence for Bronze Age field systems and the nature of agricultural intensification in the Upper and Middle Thames Valley[3] revealed that archaeologically visible field systems first appear during the Middle Bronze Age (Yates 1999). Field systems were not introduced simultaneously, but were established at different times during the Later Bronze Age sequence. The earliest ditched land divisions are associated with Deverel-Rimbury pottery and their general focus lies downriver. All the bounded landscapes were constructed with direct access to the main river course or tributaries of the River Thames.

By the Late Bronze Age, the bounded landscapes formed distinct enclaves along the river valleys; each was associated with stock raising, concentrations of river metal, new forms of settlement and often distinctive regional pottery styles (*ibid.*, 160). The regional groups form four distinct and separate clusters, two to the north and two to the south of the Goring Gap. The two groups downstream are named after well known sites at Runnymede-Petters and Marshall's Hill; north and west of the Goring Gap are the groups at Wallingford, associated with a rich riverside settlement, and Lechlade, which may have been controlled by the Burroway enclosure (*ibid.*, 161). This earlier analysis was wrong in one main respect. By selecting the traditional geographic divide of the Upper and Middle Thames Valley, the extent of the Runnymede-Petters managed land block was under-represented; subsequent research has revealed that if the arbitrary divide between the Middle and Lower Thames Valley is ignored, this regional group spills over onto the gravel terraces surrounding Heathrow airport. Consequently, it comprises the largest block of co-axial Bronze Age field systems along the course of the Thames Valley.

The West of London gravel terraces

The West of London gravels lie on the western edge of the Lower Thames Valley close to the Runnymede-Petters riverside regional power centre which dominates the confluence of the Thames and the Colne. In an area of approximately 150sq km bounded by the rivers Thames, Colne and Crane, an extensive zone of managed farming developed in the Middle and Late Bronze Ages (Fig. 7.2). The intensity of agrarian activity was matched by a spectacular level of river metal deposition. Communities here were exploiting the largest zone of lower terrace gravel that existed anywhere along the course of the River Thames. The pressure on available land was intense. The preferred prime land is represented by the main gravel terrace, but in addition, land divisions spill over into the flood plain gravels, brickearths and significantly the gravel islands within the alluvial floodplain of the river Colne. This area has the largest intensive cluster of Middle Bronze Age co-axial field divisions for the entire Thames Valley and the lands fringing the estuary in Kent and Essex. That degree of early farming pressure is also reflected during the Late Bronze Age .

None of the Late Bronze Age sites along the Thames Valley (on current evidence) support the notion that this was a major cereal producing zone. The West of London gravels area is no exception and there is evidence for the growing importance of animal husbandry. For example, at Perry Oaks Sewage Works, a major field system was laid out on the gravel terrace during the Middle Bronze Age and was later modified by the insertion of droveways and waterholes possibly in response to an intensification of stock keeping (Maloney 1999, 14). Work at Nobel Drive produced Middle/Late Bronze Age boundaries and significantly a stock management gateway similar to that first suggested by Pryor at Fengate (Elsden 1997). Thirty-nine sites are listed in Table 7.1 and mapped in Fig. 7.2; the wealth of evidence suggests a fully utilised environment with co-axial land divisions, water holes, droveways and ditched and banked enclosures with associated settlement.

The intensity of land use on the Taplow terraces is impressive, and this is heightened by the dramatic decline in activity that occurs during the Early Iron Age. Excavation teams consulted during this research pointed out the relative lack of Early Iron Age activity throughout this managed land block. For example, at Cranford Lane, Harlington, the transition from the Late Bronze Age to Early Iron Age was marked by the abandonment of the settlement within the area of excavation. Agricultural intensification is not witnessed again on this site until the Roman extensive field systems were constructed (Elsden 1996, 28). At Stanwell, the field systems were abandoned by the end of the Late Bronze Age with more open grazing and associated watering holes being used. No Iron Age material was discovered (O'Connell 1990). Similarly, at Heathrow Terminal 4, the silted fill of a waterhole indicated use over hundreds of years from the

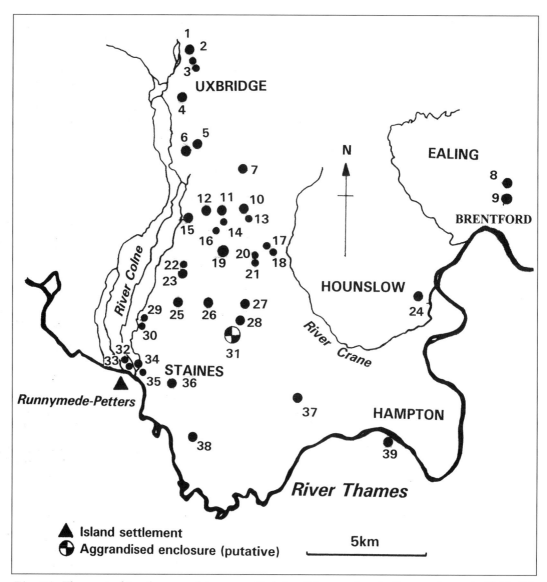

Fig. 7.2 *The west of London gravel terraces. Details of the numbered sites are shown in Table 7.1*

Middle Bronze Age, but it had finally silted up during the Later Bronze Age (MoLAS 1996, 13). The wider changes at the end of the Bronze Age may have had a profound impact on this once highly regimented zone of land tenure.

The River Wandle floodplain

In stark contrast to the pattern of agricultural intensification on the West of London Gravel Terraces, there is limited evidence for Middle Bronze Age farming activity along the River Wandle, which flows into the Thames at Wandsworth. One site at the former Kings College Sports Ground, Merton, has produced evidence of a field system that is associated with Middle Bronze Age metal deposition at nearby Merton and Mitcham (Bazely 1989). No

subsequent Late Bronze Age metal deposition or field systems occur in the vicinity.

A dramatic development occurs along this river valley during the Late Bronze Age (Fig. 7.3). The Merton fields are abandoned and the social focus shifts down towards Carshalton at the head of the valley. There is an explosion of activity with metal deposition, settlements, field systems, burnt mounds and metalled droveways being concentrated near to the source of the Wandle at Carshalton.

On the dipslope of the North Downs lies Queen Mary's Hospital, Carshalton, a Late Bronze Age ringwork site overlooking most of the surrounding area (Adkins and Needham 1985). More precisely, it overlooks the newly created busy landscape on the Wandle flood plain to the north of Carshalton. The enclosure's siting ensures that all the land divisions can be seen from the ringwork. Three definable

Table 7.1 *The West of London gravels sites. Site numbers refer to Fig. 7.2*

	Site name	Map ref.	Description	References
1	The former Jewsons Yard, Uxbridge	TQ 055 845	A major LBA/EIA boundary	Barclay et al. 1997
2	2-3 Windsor Rd, Uxbridge	TQ 056 840	BA boundary ditch	GLSMR 056024301
3	5-6 High Street, Uxbridge	TQ 056 840	BA gullies and parallel ditch to Windsor Rd site	GLSMR 050243
4	Try Builders' Yard, Uxbridge	TQ 051 828	Two parallel ditches possibly LBA	GLSMR 051032
5	Northolt Rd, Longford, Hillingdon	TQ 059 813	MBA settlement and possible field boundaries	MoLAS 1995
6	Former George Hopton site, Packet Boat Lane, Cowley	TQ 053 812	LBA/EIA linear ditch	Thompson et al. 1998, 83
7	Stockley Park	TQ 083 803	M/LBA pit, LBA pit	Mason and Lewis 1993, 25
8	36 Avenue Gardens, Acton	TQ 198 797	Possible MBA linear ditch	Thompson et al. 1998, 53
9	Former LRT bus works, Chiswick High Road, Hounslow	TQ 198 787	MBA/LBA ditches	Thompson et al. 1998, 96
10	Wall Garden Farm	TQ 078 784	MBA field boundary and possible enclosure	GLSMR 05046302
11	Holloway Lane	TQ 068 784	Ditches, stock enclosure and trackway with a range of LBA finds	GLSMR 05046105
12	M4 widening/gas main relocation	TQ 062 784	LBA pits and ditch	Mason and Lewis 1993, 30
13	Imperial College Sports Ground, Harlington	TQ 082 780	M/LBA subrectangular enclosures	Crockett 1996
14	Home Farm, Harmondsworth	TQ 071 777	MBA/LBA ditches	GLSMR 051109.3
15	Prospect Park, Harmondsworth, Hillingdon	TQ 050 775	LBA field system, possibly linked to the middle phases of the land divisions at Cranford Lane	Andrews 1996a,108; 1996b; Farwell et al. 1999
16	Home Farm, BFI quarries, off Harmondsworth Lane	TQ 067 774	BA field system, possible droveway and fencing	Maloney 1999, 14
17	Nobel Drive, north of Heathrow Airport	TQ 091 770	M/LBA field boundaries and drafting gate	Elsden 1997
18	Cranford Lane, Harlington	TQ 093 770	LBA coaxial field system and trackways	Elsden 1996
19	Airport Gate, Bath Road, Harmondsworth	TQ 070 770	MBA coaxial field system	Maloney 1999, 13
20	Neptune Road, Heathrow	TQ 085 768	LBA/EIA ditch	Elsden 1997
21	Heathrow northern runway	TQ 085 766	Pits and ditches	MoLAS 1998, 17
22	Heathrow Airport	TQ 052 766	2 undated ditches	Elsden 1997, 10
23	Perry Oaks sludge works and Heathrow Airport runway	TQ 055 765	MBA coaxial field system, LBA stock keeping, BA settlement	MoLAS 1997a, 12; Thompson et al. 1998, 80; Maloney 1999, 14
24	Bankside Close, Isleworth	TQ 158 749	MBA field boundaries	Hull 1998
25	Stanwell, Heathrow.	TQ 053 745	LBA field system	O'Connell 1990
26	Cargo Point development, Bedfont Road, Stanwell	TQ 065 745	Three phases of ditched boundaries	MoLAS 1998, 18
27	Heathrow Terminal 4, remote stands	TQ 080 745	Probable BA features	MoLAS 1998, 17
28	Stanwell Road, East Bedfont	TQ 077 740	Probable prehistoric ditch	Mason and Lewis 1993, 31
29	Lower Mill Farm, Stanwell	TQ 035 739	Possible Neolithic - EBA farmstead	Bird et al. 1994, 208
30	Poyle, Stanwell	TQ 032 738	BA settlement	Longley 1976, 8
31	Mayfield Farm	TQ 077 736	LBA ringwork	Cotton 1991
32	Church Lammas, NW Staines	TQ 028 722	MBA rectangular enclosure	Bird et al. 1994, 207
33	Church Lammas, NW Staines	TQ 027 721	2 successive field systems (undated)	Jackson et al. 1997, 211
34	Staines Central Trading Estate, Mustard Mill Lane	TQ 034 716	MBA/LBA field system	Fitzpatrick, pers. comm.
35	2-8 High Street, Staines	TQ 034 715	LBA occupation	Jackson et al. 1997, 212
36	Matthew Arnold School, Staines	TQ 053 706	BA ditches and settlement	Bird et al. 1991-2, 155
37	Vicarage Road, Sunbury	TQ 101 706	E?/MBA waterholes, grassland habitat	Bird et al. 1996, 201
38	Home Farm, Laleham	TQ 059 692	MBA/LBA settlement, possible BA boundary	Bird et al. 1994, 208; Jackson et al. 1997, 211
39	Hurst Park, East Molesey	TQ 145 689	E/M/LBA activity, probable LBA farmstead with associated field system	Andrews 1996a, 107; Farwell et al. 1999, 69

zones characterise this area of structured landscape: a) the small plateau on the North Downs dipslope on which the ringwork itself is sited; b) a belt of Late Bronze Age extramural settlement immediately to the north of the ringwork where the dipslope starts to level out onto the plain (the boundary of this zone may be marked by a series of metal deposits); and c)

the flood plain itself, where the majority of the land divisions and associated burnt mounds on the valley floor have been revealed.

Much further south, work in Sussex may add considerably to understanding the role of the enclosure at Queen Mary's Hospital and its relationship to the formal stockyards on the valley floor.

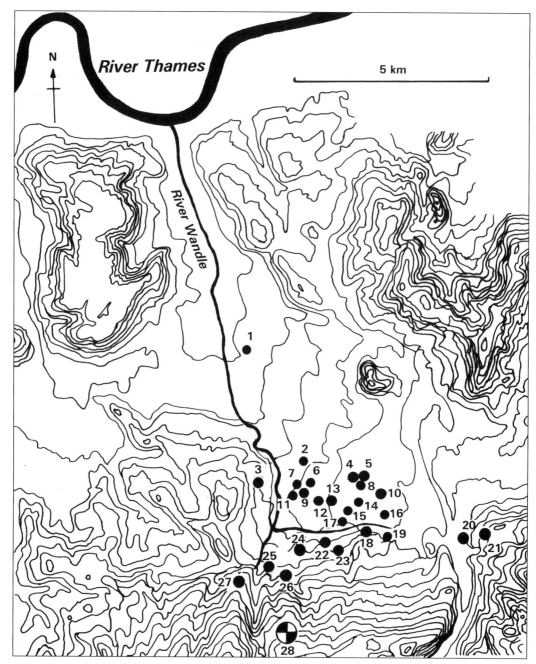

Fig. 7.3 *Queen Mary's Hospital, Carshalton: a Late Bronze Age ringwork overlooking a regimented landscape. Details of the numbered sites are shown in Table 7.2*

Hamilton and Manley note that first millennium BC enclosure sites (in Sussex) 'as a whole . . . seem to function best in terms of "looking out", perhaps to enable the co-ordination and planning of activities in the landscape that is being exploited around these sites (e.g. stock and people watching)' (Hamilton and Manley 1997, 101). This vantage point construction is similar to the ringwork site at Marshall's Hill which overlooks a considerable area of enclosed ground that may have been used for stockraising (Yates 1997). The link between stockraising and the

origin of early first millennium BC enclosures made by Hamilton and Manley follows the conclusion reached by Bradley back in 1971. Hamilton and Manley suggest that such enclosures are in effect 'points of view'. This is nowhere better seen than at Carshalton where every Late Bronze Age field system recorded to date was directly observable from the camp (Fig. 7.3). In this respect, the ringwork is of secondary importance to the parcelled landscape that it overlooks; the location of these field systems on the floodplain would have favoured

Table 7.2 *Wandle Valley sites. Site numbers refer to Fig. 7.3*

	Site name	Map ref.	Description	References
1	Kings College Sports Ground, Merton	TQ 272 698	A multi-phase MBA rectilinear field-system	Bazely 1989
2	Hundred Acre Bridge, Mitcham	TQ 285 670	LBA linear ditch and associated droveway, burnt mound, tree clearance	Tucker 1992
3	Wandle Valley Hospital, Carshalton	TQ 277 666	First millennium BC enviro-sedimentary sequence	Birley 1993
4	London Carriers Ltd, Beddington Road	TQ 299 666	Two truncated ditches, LBA pottery	Bird et al. 1991-92, 166
5	138 Beddington Lane, Croydon	TQ 300 666	BA rectilinear field-system, fence lines	Maloney 1999, 25
6	Interim Storage Pond, Beddington Sewage Works	TQ 287 665	LBA ditches, pits and flint scatters	Bird et al. 1990, 226
7	Wandle Meadows, London Road, Hackbridge	TQ 285 665	Ditches revealing LBA pottery	Bird et al. 1991-2, 166; GLSMR 021203
8	Royal Mail site, Beddington Farm	TQ 301 664	Prehistoric farming activity	Greenwood and Thompson 1992
9	Furlong Close, Sutton	TQ 286 664	Prehistoric finds, undated ploughsoils	GLSMR FLC96
10	Valley Park site, Purley	TQ 305 662	LBA field-systems, parallel linear ditches on 104 acre site	Heathcote 1989; Thompson et al. 1998, 50
11	London Road	TQ 285 662	Possible LBA linear features	GLSMR 021211
12	Beddington sewage farm	TQ 290 660	Ditches and shallow gullies	Greenwood and Maloney 1993, 106
13	Wandle Overflow	TQ 293 660	Prehistoric? field-systems	Bird et al. 1990, 226
14	Pegasus Way, Croydon	TQ 300 660	BA hearth and land surface	GLSMR IMW97
15	Beddington Lane, Beddington Roman Villa	TQ 297 658	Linear features, possibly LBA	Adkins and Adkins 1986; Adkins et al. 1986; GLSMR 02057502
16	Philips factory site, Beddington Farm Road	TQ 307 656	LBA pottery, possible burnt mound, undated linear ditch	Tucker 1963
17	NRA flood relief scheme, Beddington Park	TQ 296 655	Possible metalled prehistoric or Roman trackway, BA rectilinear field-system	Thompson, Westman and Dyson 1998, 231
18	34 Beddington Lane	TQ 302 654	Fire-fractured flint concentration	Saxby 1990
19	Aldwyk Road, Waddon	TQ 307 650	LBA assemblage	Gallant 1966, 169; GLSMR 030232; see also Lowther 1939, 180
20	Park Lane, Croydon	TQ 325 650	BA pits and gullies	Bird et al. 1996, 208
21	Stanhope Lane	TQ 330 650	LBA settlement	GLSMR 020299
22	Beddington Infants School	TQ 292 649	Ditch containing LBA pottery and flint	Heathcote 1989, 194
23	St Mary the Virgin Church Hall, Wallington	TQ 294 649	LBA pottery in primary colluvium	Bird et al. 1996, 225
24	Westcroft House, Westcroft Road, Carshalton	TQ 283 647	2 LBA/EIA ditches, LBA ritual pit containing sheep bones	Proctor 1999
25	St Philomena's Catholic Girls' School, Pound Street, Carshalton	TQ 274 646	LBA midden filling a gully	Maloney 1999, 26
26	Carshalton House	TQ 277 644	LBA/EIA ditch, PDR plain ware	Greenwood and Maloney 1993, 107
27	Kings Road and Harrow Road, Carshalton Camp	TQ 268 640	Agricultural terrace, LBA finds	GLSMR 030338; Turner 1963
28	Queen Mary's Hospital, Carshalton	TQ 279 622	LBA ringwork	Adkins and Needham 1985; Bird et al. 1996, 224

Table 7.3 Lambeth, Southwark and Bermondsey sites. Site numbers refer to Fig. 7.4

	Site name	Map ref.	Description	References
1	99-101 Waterloo Road, Lambeth	TQ 312 799	Linear ditch sealed by peat probably laid down in Tilbury IV regression	Thompson et al. 1998, 125
2	Bermondsey Abbey	TQ 334 793	Several small possibly Bronze Age gullies cut into natural sand and gravel	Thompson et al. 1998, 197
3	Phoenix Wharf, Bermondsey	TQ 337 799	EBA burnt mound and E/MBA plough, spade and hoe marks	Densem 1994
4	10-16 Lafone Street	TQ 337 798	Prehistoric ard marks and possible Neo/BA field boundary ditch	Bates 1996; 1997
5	Wolseley Street	TQ 339 797	MBA rip ard marks sealed by silty clay deposits and peats	Drummond-Murray 1994
6	Bramcote Grove, Bermondsey	TQ 349 780	MBA wooden trackways: access for hunting and fishing	Thomas and Rackham 1996.

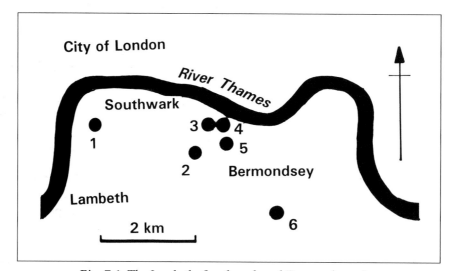

Fig. 7.4 The Lambeth, Southwark and Bermondsey sites

livestock management. In contrast to the intensity of Late Bronze Age activity, the Early Iron Age does not appear in the record (MoLAS 1995, 14). The Carshalton regional group of managed land therefore appears to follow the same decline as noted on the West of London gravels.

Farming in Southwark, Lambeth and Bermondsey

Further east from Wandsworth, excavations in Southwark and Lambeth provide the only direct evidence of Middle Bronze Age (and possibly earlier) cultivation in London (Fig. 7.4). However, river transgression occurred after a relatively short period of ground clearance (Drummond-Murray 1994) and therefore this early area of land pressure was never fully developed. Later prehistory in this area continued to be characterised by a pattern of shifting tidal inlets and interconnecting creeks but

this part of the Lower Thames Valley still remained a fully used (if waterlogged) landscape with occupation on higher ground with trackways joining those settlements (Thomas and Rackham 1996, 250).

The River Lea to Mucking

Crossing the river again and heading east further downstream, we meet the confluence of the rivers Lea and Thames. Needham and Burgess see the Lea river valley as the dry corridor linking the Thames and the prosperous East Anglian zone (1980, 453). The significance of this link is reinforced by recent finds from the former sewage treatment works at Rammey Marsh, Enfield, where a riverside Late Bronze Age field system has been recorded, sealed by alluvium containing Roman material (Maloney 1999, 11). My previous paper (1999) has shown the link between aggrandised enclosures and field systems. It is therefore of interest that this apparently isolated field system lies approximately 2km west of the old enclosure (*Eldeworth*) at Waltham Abbey which may have Late Bronze Age origins (Clarke *et al.* 1993, 111). Nearby at Aylands Allotments, a possible Late Bronze Age settlement suggests further activity in this area (Thompson *et al.* 1998, 56). This outlying block of managed land at Rammey Marsh is located on a major routeway linking the London basin with East Anglia.

The northern bank of the River Thames between the River Lea and Mucking comprises two distinct geological zones: alluvium and river terraces. A series of sites on the Thames alluvial margins suggests intensive and extensive exploitation roughly dating between 1600–1000 BC (Meddens 1996, 332). The area was divided by trackways and causeways and this floodplain was extensively used for animal grazing. At the Hays site, Dagenham, a substantial metalled causeway is interpreted as a principal access route to the marsh for a large number of relatively heavy animals (*ibid.*, 326). Further east at Bridge Road, Rainham, a rectangular enclosure likely to have been associated with animal husbandry was set at right angles to a brushwood trackway (*ibid.*, 325). This structure on the Ingrebourne river seems significant because from this point on the river terraces, field system evidence and components of a structured landscape increases (Fig. 7.5). At South Hornchurch, a ringwork with associated field systems and integrated droveways has recently been recorded. The enclosure and droveway design suggest a controlling interest in livestock movements (Guttmann and Last 2000).

Bronze Age field systems have been recorded at Whitehall Wood, Upminster (Greenwood 1986), Linford (Barton 1962, 61), Mucking (Jones 1993, fig. 4) and possibly Baker Street, Orsett (Wilkinson 1988, 13). Linear archaeology associated with the Horndon to Barking gas pipeline also confirmed land divisions in this area with possible Late Bronze Age ditched land divisions recorded at sites 4 , 5 and 9 (Wessex Archaeology 1994). Stock enclosures associated with field systems were recorded at Gun Hill, Tilbury (Drury and Rodwell 1973), and William Edwards School (Lavender 1998, 23), which appears to have a drafting gate similar to those suggested by Pryor (1998, 104). In a reappraisal of loomweight evidence in Essex, Barford and Major (1992) note that the greatest concentration in the county occurs in the zone around Thurrock surrounding Mucking. Significantly most of these are Late Bronze Age pyramidal loomweights (*ibid.*). Bond also concludes that the pastoral evidence at the North Ring, Mucking appears predominant (1988, 52). There are therefore two concentrations of managed land; one focused on the River Ingrebourne and the South Hornchurch ringwork, and the other as we move closer to the Mucking ringworks complex (Fig. 7.5). Both suggest an increasing pastoralist emphasis.

Southend-on-Sea Peninsula

20km east of Mucking lies the Southend-on-Sea peninsula which represents another distinct zone of Bronze Age activity (Fig. 7.5). This area has produced the largest concentration of Late Bronze Age metalwork deposits in Essex (Couchman 1980) and a remarkable concentration of Later Bronze Age settlement and intensive agricultural activity (Wymer and Brown 1995, fig. 95). The River Crouch defines the northern limit of the peninsula and its southern shoreline dominates the Thames estuary. As with all the enclaves of intensively used landscape up-river, the first ditched land divisions appear here in the Middle Bronze Age and there are further developments in the Late Bronze Age. Three sites to date are of Middle Bronze Age farming origin, none of which suggest continuity into the Late Bronze Age. Excavation at North Shoebury shows that the abandoned Middle Bronze Age enclosures are respected in part by later agricultural boundaries to the south and east.

Work associated with the Hullbridge project has provided valuable environmental data that may offer clues to the nature of the farming regime on the northern fringes of the peninsula. Excavation of the salt working hearth at Crouch Site 2 produced briquetage and a Deverel-Rimbury pot. Plant remains found in the briquetage included processed spelt wheat, emmer wheat and barley, and this implies that coastal economies at this time were based both on salt production and agriculture (Wilkinson and Murphy 1995, 164).

There are four Late Bronze Age field sites, including two developer-funded projects at London Southend Airport, that recorded components of a coaxial field system with no evidence of continuity into the Early Iron Age. In contrast, at the North Shoebury site, the major Late Bronze Age boundary remained in use for a considerable time and formed the axis of the subsequent Early Iron Age settlement (Wymer and Brown 1995, 21). Again, the exceptional environmental work associated with the Hullbridge project provides some insights into activity during the Late Bronze Age. The Hullbridge Crouch 22 site produced a wooden structure or hurdle likely to have been associated with seasonal sheep handling; this was dated to 1036–896 cal BC (HAR–5736: Wilkinson and Murphy 1995, 136). The discovery of an increasing number of loomweights on the peninsula might also suggest textile manufacture and inter-regional exchange of which woollen cloth formed a part. An emphasis on sheep in the regional

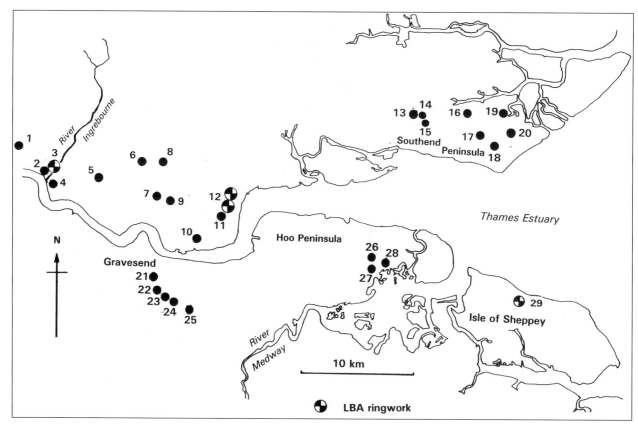

Fig. 7.5 *The lower reaches of the Thames and the estuary approaches*

Table 7.4 *River Lea to Mucking sites. Site numbers refer to Fig. 7.5*

	Site name	Map ref.	Description	References
1	Church Lane, Church St, Dagenham	TQ 499 848	Prehistoric ditches, LBA pottery	Maloney 1999, 1
2	Bridge Road, Rainham	TQ 521 825	MBA rectangular enclosure and droveway	Meddens 1996, 325
3	South Hornchurch	TQ 523 830	LBA ringwork, droveway, field system	Guttmann and Last 2000
4	Site 9, Horndon to Barking gas pipeline	TQ 526 815	Possible prehistoric parallel boundary ditches	Wessex Archaeology 1994
5	Whitehall Wood, Upminster	TQ 570 825	LBA/EIA field system	Greenwood 1986
6	Site 5, Horndon to Barking gas pipeline	TQ 606 840	LBA field boundary ditch	Wessex Archaeology 1994
7	William Edwards School	TQ 619 809	LBA stock enclosure	Lavender 1998, 23
8	Site 4, Horndon to Barking gas pipeline	TQ 624 840	LBA /EIA field boundary ditches	Wessex Archaeology 1994
9	Baker Street, Orsett	TQ 632 810	LBA open settlement, possible boundary gully (feature 21)	Wilkinson 1988, 15 -17
10	Gun Hill, Tilbury	TQ 655 778	LBA field system with spur ditch cutting off a promontory of grazing land	Drury and Rodwell 1973, 95
11	Linford	TQ 667 798	BA ditches	Barton 1962, 61
12	Mucking	TQ 674 806	LBA ringworks and MBA field system	Bond 1988; Clark 1993

economy suggests that farmers were managing the animals as a form of indirect social storage[4] to provide a buffer against disastrous farming years. As a form of live storage, the domestic animals could be used either directly (for food) or for inter-group exchanges which set up reciprocal obligations and maximised sharing during lean years (Flannery 1969, 87). The abundance of metalworking in this area and evidence of livestock rearing suggest a link between the two activities; both may have con-

Table 7.5 Southend-on-Sea Peninsula sites. Site numbers refer to Fig. 7.5

	Site name	Map ref.	Description	References
13	Eastwood, Southend	TQ 853 890	MBA/LBA enclosure	Wymer and Brown 1995, 177
14	London Southend Airport	TQ 875 891	LBA field system	Essex County Council 1998
15	South-eastern corner of Southend Airport	TQ 875 889	LBA field system	Germany and Foreman 1997
16	Butler's Farm Gravel Pit	TQ 905 892	Possible BA enclosure	Wymer and Brown 1995, 178
17	Wick Farm, Southchurch	TQ 906 872	Possible LBA enclosure	Bennett 1998, 202
18	North Shoebury	TQ 931 862	MBA sub-rectangular compounds and field system, LBA trackway and land division	Wymer and Brown 1995
19	Baldwin Farm Gravel Pits, Barling Magna	TQ 937 896	Possible MBA field gullies	Couchman 1977, 63
20	Alexandra Road, Great Wakering	TQ 940 870	MBA field system	Reidy 1997

Table 7.6 Gravesend-Hoo-Sheppey sites. Site numbers refer to Fig. 7.5

	Site name	Map ref.	Description	References
21	Springhead, Gravesend	TQ 617 728	Burnt mound under 1.7 m of colluvium, LBA/EIA pottery	Wessex Archaeology 1997b
22	Temple East of Springhead, Gravesend	TQ 623 719	Primary colluvium containing LBA pottery and burnt flint	Wessex Archaeology 1997a
23	Coldharbour Road, Gravesend	TQ 638 717	Co-axial system of land division and MBA/LBA linear ditches interpreted as a droveway with attached stock enclosure	Mudd 1994, 407
24	West of Northumberland Bottom, Gravesend	TQ 639 714	Possible BA enclosure ditches or field system	MoLAS 1997b
25	West of Church Road, Singlewell	TQ 652 705	Probable LBA field system	Oxford Archaeological Unit 1997
26	Malmaynes Hall Farm, Stoke	TQ 817 757	LBA/EIA linear boundary division	James 1999
27	Damhead Creek Power Station, gas feeder pipeline	TQ 817 745	BA linear ditch features and possible droveway	James, pers. comm.
28	Middle Stoke	TQ 828 755	MBA boundary ditch	James forthcoming
29	Kingsborough Farm	TQ 976 723	LBA ringwork	Stevens, pers. comm.

tributed to a process of added gift exchange that secured a longer term set of social obligations that could be called on in time of need.

This land block was also affected by the cessation of exchange networks at the end of the Bronze Age. Some of the field systems were abandoned and generally there are far fewer Early Iron Age sites in the Southend peninsula than Late Bronze Age ones (Wymer and Brown 1995, 157). Wymer and Brown suggest that perhaps the appearance of very large storage pits and the presence of at least one four-post structure reflect the greater self sufficiency of Early Iron Age sites on the peninsula (*ibid.*, 157).

Gravesend and the Hoo Peninsula

Opposite Thurrock on the southern shore of the Thames at Gravesend there appears to be another distinct zone of regimented landscape (Fig. 7.5). The first discovery was made at Coldharbour Road,

Gravesend, which revealed a droveway with a structure interpreted as an associated stockyard (Mudd 1994). Recent commercial archaeology in advance of major civil engineering work has revealed the extent of the formalised landscape in the area. Seven further sites have been discovered in the vicinity of Gravesend and on the Hoo Peninsula indicating field system construction and use during the Later Bronze Age. The new sites cannot be fully reported on because of commercial confidentiality, but they may suggest a land block that is bordered to the east by the River Medway which again has produced a considerable quantity of river metalwork.

North Shore-Highstead-Wantsum Channel

The last identifiable zone of agricultural intensification lies on the easternmost tip of the Thames estuary, where field systems, stock and settlement enclosures cluster on the Reculver Peninsula and land bordering either side of the Wantsum Channel (Fig. 7.6).

On the Isle of Thanet, there are enclosed Middle Bronze Age settlements, many of which have boundaries with defensive attributes suggesting that this area had a unique prehistory of its own. Perkins interprets these as specialist maritime havens on what was in effect a 'gateway island' (1994, 310; forthcoming). The only direct evidence for Middle Bronze Age field development relates to Netherhale Farm which lies on a spur of land originally overlooking the north eastern mouth of the Wantsum Channel (Macpherson-Grant 1993b). To the west of the Channel, there are no indications to date of field divisions; however, environmental evidence from the rivercourse along the Lower Sarre Penn river valley confirms that agricultural intensification (hazel woodland clearance) was underway during the Middle Bronze Age. The onset of colluviation appears to have occurred here between 1400–1000 BC (Cross 1992, 10). Again, there is a strong relationship between new forms of land exploitation and metal deposition as Middle Bronze Age metal artefacts have also been identified on the Isle of Thanet and along the northern shoreline off Whitstable and Herne Bay (Cross 1995, 23; Perkins forthcoming).

A far greater range of evidence exists on the nature of settlements and land use in the Late Bronze Age for this area. There are significant changes both on the Isle of Thanet and the 'mainland' to the west of the Wantsum Channel. On the Isle, there is a noticeable shift away from the northern and eastern coasts towards the southwestern shoreline, with a new focus on the Wantsum Channel. This settlement movement is accompanied by a noticeable shift in the distribution of metal deposits (Perkins 1994, 310). These new settlements directly overlooking the Wantsum navigable waters have regimented field systems. It is possible to conjecture that the settlement decline on the northern and eastern shoreline indicates the increasing importance of the Wantsum Channel.

On the 'mainland' western fringe of the Wantsum Channel, there is a particular intensity of land use, especially on the Reculver Peninsula. As Cross (1994b, 8) observes, a dense pattern of prehistoric settlement extends across the Reculver Peninsula, keeping to the high ground west of the Wantsum Channel. The most intensively studied area is the ancient landscape around the modern village of Highstead. Here, there is excavated material from the Neolithic through to the end of the Roman occupation. Highstead, an aggrandised Late Bronze Age enclosure sitting on the rise at Chislet, overlooks the channel and could oversee movement along this stretch of navigable water linking the English Channel and the Thames Estuary. It occupies a similar position to the siting of Marshall's Hill, Queen Mary's Hospital and Mucking North and South Rings. Highstead comprises a sub-square enclosure associated with a series of field ditches and what is perhaps a stockyard (Bennett 1997, 10). Linear archaeology to the immediate east of the enclosure has identified a wide area of regimented landscape partly buried beneath alluvial deposits (*ibid.*, 8).

The concentration of managed agricultural land close to the Highstead enclosure is not the only proof suggesting that this is a distinct territory, for the pottery evidence supports the notion as well. Macpherson-Grant notes a close pottery assemblage link between Highstead, Eddington Farm, Northdown at Margate, and Monkton Court Farm. He even suggests that the affinities between Highstead and Monkton Court Farm are such as to suggest one workshop (1992, 39). This marked degree of regionality is evident not just in the Late Bronze Age but also in the Middle Bronze Age (Macpherson-Grant 1993b, 63; Parfitt 1995). Stylistic differences in ceramic assemblages also separate this region from a region possibly based on the ringwork at Mill Hill (Macpherson-Grant 1992, 39).

Bronze Age activity is not confined solely to the North Shore and Reculver Peninsula in east Kent. There was settlement and land exploitation at Ashford and a possible Late Bronze Age enclosure in Canterbury (Boyle and Jenkins 1951; Macpherson-Grant 1991); both sites had access to the Wantsum Channel via the Great Stour river link. Champion noted in 1980 that pollen and snail sequences exist only from a very restricted area of east Kent, namely Devil's Kneadingtrough, Brook; Seabrook Stream near Folkestone; and Wingham in a small valley leading down to the River Stour. The general picture suggests considerable agricultural activity from at least the middle of the second millennium BC, with a phase of increased clearance from late in the Bronze Age (Champion 1980, 227). More recently, Scaife has re-examined Godwin's pollen sequence for Wingham. He has compared the Wingham sequences to his own unpublished data from Each End, Ash, and pollen analysis from the eastern fens including the Wantsum Channel. He concludes that there was increasing human pressure from the Middle to Late Bronze Age, and 'possible agricultural reorganisation during the Late Bronze Age' (Scaife 1995, 311). No conclusions have been reached on the nature of farming in the area immediately bordering the Late Bronze Age ringwork at Mill Hill, Deal.

As elsewhere, areas of Kent experienced a degree of social dislocation at the end of the Bronze Age.

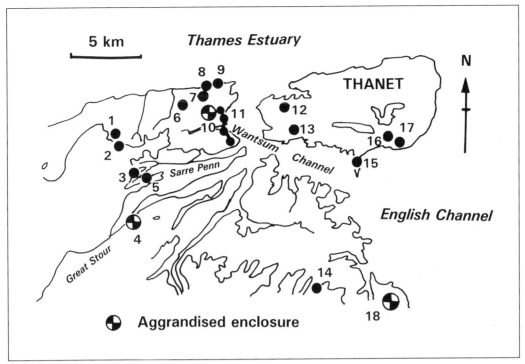

Fig. 7.6 *Northeast Kent. Site details are set out in Table 7.7*

Table 7.7 *Northeast Kent sites. Site numbers refer to Fig. 7.6*

	Site name	Map ref.	Description	References
1	South Street, west of Radfall Road	TR 130 645	LBA/EIA probable farmstead, iron slag associated with LBA/EIA pottery	Cross 1994a, Parfitt 1995
2	Radfall Corner, Thanet Way	TR 133 647	Metalled LBA/EIA droveway, extant wheel ruts, axle width 1.75 m	Cross 1994a, Parfitt1995
3	Lower Sarre Penn Valley, east of Tyler Hill	TR 144 605	MBA colluviation	Cross 1992, 2
4	10-11 Castle Street, Canterbury	TR 145 574	Possible LBA aggrandised enclosure	Boyle and Jenkins 1951; Macpherson-Grant 1991
5	Shelford Farm	TR 158 612	Ring ditch and associated field boundary	NAR TR16SE55
6	Eddington Farm	TR 172 672	LBA field ditches and enclosure	Houliston 1998; Macpherson-Grant 1993a
7	Dence Park, Herne Bay	TR 187 681	Possible LBA midden	SMR TR16NE7
8	Hillborough Road, Herne Bay	TR 188 684	LBA ceramics	Cross 1994b, 8
9	Beltinge Cliff	TR 195 683	Eight LBA/EIA ditch alignments and gullies	Cross1994b, 8; Hutchinson 1994; Parfitt 1996
10	Highstead, nr Chislet	TR 215 660	LBA aggrandised enclosure, series of field ditches and one possible stockyard	Bennett 1997, 3
11	Herne Bay wastewater treatment pipeline	TR 231 643	Four LBA/EIA field boundary ditches at Sarre Penn, 15 LBA/EIA ditches or gullies at Church Lane, Chislet (TR224648)	Parfitt 1996
12	Netherhale Farm	TR 275 675	MBA field system	Macpherson-Grant 1993b
13	Monkton Court Farm	TR 277 655	LBA enclosure boundary ditches and settlement	Perkins et al. 1994, 306
14	North of Venson Road, Whitfield Eastry improvement road	TR 308 533	Possible LBA/EIA field ditches	Rady 1995, 4
15	Ebbsfleet Farm, Minster	TR 333 630	Prehistoric linear features	Hearne et al. 1995, 244
16	Manston Road, Ramsgate	TR 361 656	Possible LBA enclosures or field boundaries	Wessex Archaeology forthcoming
17	Ramsgate Harbour approach road.	TR 362 645	LBA field-system	Shand 1998a; 1998b
18	Mill Hill, Deal.	TR 362 512	LBA ringwork	Champion 1980

Macpherson-Grant observes that Highstead is the only site producing reasonably clear evidence of continuity at the end of the Bronze Age (1992, 41). Monkton Court Farm and 10–11 Castle Street, Canterbury, suggest social discontinuity (Macpherson-Grant 1992, 48; Perkins *et al.* 1994, 281).

Conclusions

This study aimed to provide a comprehensive review and synthesis of all available data on Bronze Age agricultural intensification in the Thames Valley and Estuary. The attempt was only possible because of the recent proliferation of client reports. Many were site-specific relatively small-scale contracts, whereas others resulted from civil engineering work providing forms of linear archaeology (rail track routes, major roadways, flood relief schemes and gas pipelines) that involved wide transects through the urban and rural zones. Excavation and evaluation work along the course of such linear routes, together with the widespread imposition of PPG 16 stipulations on building work throughout the study area continues to reveal dense clusters of Bronze Age occupation and land divisions in relatively limited areas. The clustered distribution of field systems is therefore not a result of the lack of excavation in certain areas. The review did not confine itself to archaeological finds immediately bordering the river and estuary. All available developer-funded work was examined for entire county-wide areas along the estuary north and south of the Thames, and for each of the London Boroughs. The results consistently revealed a riverine and estuarine focus, with a series of socio-economic zones or hot spots along the valley and estuary foreshores in contrast to relatively empty areas elsewhere. Only two outlying inland zones of managed land were discovered, one at Carshalton on the River Wandle, and the other at Enfield on the River Lea, but both again lay on major connecting routes to the Thames linking through to the North Downs and East Anglia respectively.

Middle Bronze Age land division is absent from the extreme western limits of the study area and proliferates in particular between Abingdon and Isleworth. By the Late Bronze Age, the bounded landscapes formed distinct enclaves along the river course; each was associated with concentrations of metal deposition, specialist craft activity, new forms of settlement and often distinctive regional pottery styles. In Kent, metalworking deposition, pottery assemblages and settlement patterns may be so closely related that they define a distinct social shift focused on the Wantsum Channel (Macpherson-Grant 1992, 39; Perkins 1994, 310). This paper has

also cited work on Southend-on-Sea peninsula where a high volume of metal deposition is matched by intense settlement activity and field construction (Couchman 1980; Wymer and Brown 1995). The positioning of metalwork on this peninsula in an arc bordering dense farming and occupation sites (*ibid.*, 155) suggests that both fields and metals reinforce boundaries, in effect dividing up a working landscape (Bradley 1996, 42). The established relationship between metal deposits, new forms of settlement and managed agricultural land continues to be reaffirmed by new discoveries. For example, the long known concentration of river metals from the Thames at Taplow (Ehrenberg 1980) is now matched by the very recent discovery by Tim Allen of a Late Bronze Age palisaded enclosure overlooking the surrounding river terraces and known field systems.

The environmental evidence is very limited[5] but at present livestock management appears to be a major priority. All bounded landscapes are focused on the main river, its tributaries or direct access to the estuary. There is a degree of stylistic emulation between each of the regional groups in terms of 'estate' design, social beliefs and locational choice.

Social dislocation appears to have affected many of the farming communities at the end of the Bronze Age. The extent of collapse is so widespread that it suggests a general crisis and therefore long range exchange seems to have an international dimension. It is now a priority in the next stage of research to examine how the re-organisation of food production and land-holding are related to changes in the culture of exchange.

Acknowledgements

This research would not have been possible without the co-operation and generous access to new material provided by field personnel working along the Thames Valley and estuary. I would especially like to thank Richard Cross (Canterbury Archaeological Trust), Robin Densem (MoLAS), Alistair Barclay (Oxford Archaeological Trust), Nigel Brown (Essex County Council), Jonathan Cotton (Museum of London), Jonathan Last (Hertfordshire Archaeological Trust), Andrew Fitzpatrick (Wessex Archaeology), Dave Perkins (Thanet Archaeological Trust), Simon Mason (Kent County Council), Nick Elsden (MoLAS), Dave Dunkin (Archaeology South East), Simon Stevens (Archaeology South East), Richard James (Archaeology South East) and Pamela Greenwood. Special thanks are due to Bridget Neeve. I am most grateful to Richard Bradley for guidance and encouragement in this research. Any errors or omissions are entirely my own.

Notes

1 The term Later Bronze Age encompasses the traditional Middle and Late Bronze Age phases.

2 Stock enclosures are rectilinear in shape. Closely paired ditches create a bank that may have been hedged. Corner entranceways, connecting droveways and elaborate funnels characterise the more elaborate enclosures to create what have been interpreted as 'community stockyards' (Pryor 1996; 1998). Composite boundaries using both ditches and fence-lines may have provided an alternative reinforcement for the boundaries. Fencing and wattle hurdles may have subdivided the interiors. Waterholes are another commonly associated component.

3 The Upper Thames Valley is defined here as the section of the Thames between its source near Shorncote and the Goring Gap. The Middle Thames Valley is defined as the area between the Goring Gap and Staines, on the western fringe of London. The Lower Thames is defined as the stretch of river between Staines and the start of the Thames Estuary.

4 The use of livestock as a vehicle for the banking or 'indirect storage' of temporary agricultural surpluses (Halstead 1993, 63).

5 The recovery of biological remains on the river gravel terraces in particular is hampered by the adverse soil conditions (Sidell, Giorgi and Pipe 1999, 70).

References

Adkins, L. and Adkins, R. 1986. *Under the Sludge. Beddington Roman Villa: Excavations at Beddington Sewage Works, 1981–1983*. London: Beddington, Carshalton and Wallington Archaeological Society.

Adkins, L. and Needham, S. 1985. New research on a Late Bronze Age Enclosure at Queen Mary's Hospital, Carshalton. *Surrey Archaeological Collections* 76, 11–50.

Adkins, L., Adkins, R. and Perry J. G. 1986. Excavation at Prehistoric and Roman Beddington, 1984–85. *London Archaeologist* 5(6), 152–156.

Andrews, P. 1996a. Prospect Park and Hurst Park: the Settlements and the Landscape. In Andrews, P. and Crockett, A. *Three Excavations along the Thames and its Tributaries, 1994*, 105–111. Salisbury: Wessex Archaeology.

Andrews, P. 1996b. Prospect Park, Harmondsworth, London Borough of Hillingdon: settlement and burial from the Neolithic to the Early Saxon periods. In Andrews, P. and Crockett, A. *Three Excavations along the Thames and its Tributaries, 1994*, 1–50. Salisbury: Wessex Archaeology.

Barclay, A., Boyle, A., Bradley, P. and Roberts, M. R. 1997. Excavations at the former Jewson's Yard, Harefield Road, Uxbridge, Middlesex. *Transactions of the London and Middlesex Archaeological Society* 46, 1–25.

Barford, P. M. and Major, H. J. 1992. Later Bronze Age loomweights from Essex. *Essex Archaeology and History* 23, 117–120.

Barrett, J. C. 1994. *Fragments from Antiquity: an Archaeology of Social Life in Britain, 2900–1200 BC*. Oxford: Blackwell.

Barrett, J. C. and Bradley, R. J. (eds) 1980. *Settlement and Society in the British Later Bronze Age*. Oxford: British Archaeological Reports, British Series 83.

Barton, K. J. 1962. Settlements of the Iron Age and Pagan Saxon periods at Linford, Essex. *Transactions of the Essex Archaeological Society* (third series) 1(2), 57–104.

Bates, J. 1996. *10–16 Lafone Street, London SE1, London Borough of Southwark: an Archaeological Evaluation*. London: unpublished MoLAS Report.

Bates, J. 1997. *10–16 Lafone Street, London SE1, London Borough of Southwark: an Archaeological Report*. London: unpublished MoLAS Report.

Bazely, B. 1989. *Housing Development at Former Kings' College Sports Ground, Western Road, London Borough of Merton: Preliminary Report of Archaeological Investigation*. London: unpublished Museum of London Report.

Bennett, A. (ed.) 1998. Archaeology in Essex, 1997. *Essex Archaeology and History* 29, 194–215.

Bennett, P. 1997. *Highstead: Response to Proof of Evidence on Archaeological Matters*. Canterbury: unpublished Canterbury Archaeological Trust Report 1997/3.

Bird, D. G., Crocker, G. and McCracken, J. S. 1990. Archaeology in Surrey, 1988–89. *Surrey Archaeological Collections* 80, 201–227.

Bird, D. G., Crocker, G. and McCracken, J. S. 1991–2. Archaeology in Surrey, 1990. *Surrey Archaeological Collections* 81, 147–167.

Bird, D. G., Crocker, G., McCracken, J. S. and Saich, D. 1994. Archaeology in Surrey, 1991. *Surrey Archaeological Collections* 82, 203–219.

Bird, D. G., Crocker, G., Maloney, C. and Saich, D. 1996. Archaeology in Surrey, 1992–3. *Surrey Archaeological Collections* 83, 195–243.

Birley, M. 1993. *Wandle Hospital, Carshalton, London Borough of Sutton: an Archaeological Evaluation*. London: unpublished MoLAS Report.

Bond, D. 1988. *Excavation at the North Ring, Mucking, Essex: a Late Bronze Age Enclosure*. Chelmsford: East Anglian Archaeology 43.

Boyle, J. and Jenkins, F. 1951. Canterbury excavations at 10 and 11 Castle Street, 1950. *Archaeological News Letter* 3(9), 143–147.

Bradley, R. 1971. Stock raising and the origins of the hillfort on the South Downs. *Antiquaries' Journal* 51, 8–29.

Bradley, R. 1996. Rethinking the Later Bronze Age. In Bedwin, O. (ed.) *The Archaeology of Essex: Proceedings of the Writtle Conference*, 38–45. Chelmsford: Planning Dept., Essex County Council.

Champion, T. 1980. Settlement and environment in Later Bronze Age Kent. In Barrett, J. and Bradley, R. (eds) *Settlement and Society in the British Later Bronze Age*, 223–246. Oxford: British Archaeological Reports, British Series 83.

Clark, A. 1993. *Excavations at Mucking. Vol. 1: the site atlas*. London: British Museum Press.

Clarke, C. P., Gardiner, M. F. and Higgins, P. J. 1993. Excavations at Church Street, Waltham Abbey, 1976–87: urban development and prehistoric evidence. *Essex Archaeology and History* 24, 69–113.

Cotton, J. 1991. Prehistory in Greater London. *Current Archaeology* 11(4), 151–154.

Couchman, C. R. 1977. Work of Essex County Council Archaeology Section, 1977. *Essex Archaeology and History* 9, 60–94.

Couchman, C. R. 1980. The Bronze Age in Essex. In Buckley, D. G. (ed.) *Archaeology in Essex to AD 1500*, 40–46. Oxford: British Archaeological Reports, British Series 34.

Crockett, A. 1996. *Imperial Sports Ground, Harlington, 1996 Excavation*. Salisbury: unpublished Wessex Archaeology Report.

Cross, R. P. 1992. *Broad Oak Water Joint Steering Committee: Archaeological Evaluation Survey*. Canterbury: unpublished Canterbury Archaeological Trust Report 1992/14.

Cross, R. P. 1994a. *A299 Thanet Way Road Extension: Report on the Archaeological Evaluation*. Canterbury: unpublished Canterbury Archaeological Trust report 1994/35.

Cross, R. P. 1994b. *Reculver Road Caravan Park, Beltinge and Blacksoles Farm, Reculver Road, Herne Bay. Preliminary Historic Environment Assessment*. Canterbury: unpublished Canterbury Archaeological Trust Report 1994/26.

Cross, R. P. 1995. *Church Lane, Seasalter: Preliminary Historic Environment Assessment*. Canterbury: unpublished Canterbury Archaeological Trust Report 1995/42.

Densem, R. 1994. *Pheonix Wharf, Bermondsey, SE1, London Borough of Southwark: an Archaeological Preservation In-Situ Watching Brief*. London: unpublished MoLAS Report.

Drummond-Murray, J. 1994. *Wolseley Street, land adjacent to the Fire Station, SE1, London Borough of Southwark: an Archaeological Evaluation*. London: unpublished MoLAS Report.

Drury, P. J. and Rodwell, W. J. 1973. Excavations at Gun Hill, West Tilbury. *Transactions of the Essex Archaeological Society* 5, 48–101.

Ehrenberg, M. 1980. The occurrence of Bronze Age metalwork in the Thames: An Investigation. *Transactions of the London and Middlesex Archaeological Society* 31, 1–15.

Elsden, N. 1996. *Cranford Lane, Harlington, London Borough of Hillingdon: Post-Excavation Assessment Report*. London: unpublished MoLAS Report.

Elsden, N. 1997. Excavations at Nobel Drive, Harlington, and six sites to the north of Heathrow Airport, Hillingdon. *London and Middlesex Archaeological Collections* 48, 1–13.

Essex County Council 1998. *London Southend Airport, Essex*. Chelmsford: Essex County Council Report.

Farwell, D. E., Andrews, P. and Brook, R. 1999. *Prehistoric, Roman, and Early Saxon Settlement at Prospect Park, London Borough of Hillingdon*. Salisbury: Wessex Archaeology.

Flannery, K. V. 1969. Origins and ecological effects of early Near Eastern domestication. In Ucko, P. J and Dimbleby, G. W. (eds) *The Domestication and Exploitation of Plants and Animals*, 73–100. London: Duckworth.

Gallant, L. 1966. Three Early Iron Age sherds from Beddington, Surrey. *Surrey Archaeological Collections* 63, 169–171.

Germany, M. and Foreman, S. 1997. *The South-Eastern Corner of Southend Airport, Adjacent Warner's Bridge,*

Southend-on-Sea. Chelmsford: unpublished Essex County Council Report.

Greenwood, P. 1986. A Late Bronze Age-Early Iron Age field system and settlement at Whitehall Wood, Upminster. *London Archaeologist* 5(7), 171–5.

Greenwood, P. and Maloney, C. 1993. Excavation round-up, 1992, part 3. *London Archaeologist* 7(4), 104–110.

Greenwood, P. and Thompson, A. 1992. Excavation round-up, 1991, part 2. *London Archaeologist* 6(15), 415–423.

Guttmann, E. B. and Last, J. 2000. A Late Bronze Age landscape at South Hornchurch, Greater London. *Proceedings of the Prehistoric Society* 66, 319–359.

Halstead, P. 1981. From determinism to uncertainty: social storage and the rise of the Minoan palace. In Sheridan, A. and Bailey, G. N. (eds) *Economic Archaeology: Towards an Integration of Ecological and Social Approaches*, 187–213. Oxford: British Archaeological Reports, International Series 96.

Halstead, P. 1993. Banking on livestock: indirect storage in Greek agriculture. *Bulletin of Sumerian Agriculture* 7, 63–75.

Halstead, P. and O'Shea, J. (eds) 1989. *Bad Year Economics: Cultural Responses to Risk and Uncertainty*. Cambridge: Cambridge University Press.

Hamilton, S. and Manley, J. 1997. Prominent enclosures in 1st millennium BC Sussex. *Sussex Archaeological Collections* 135, 93–112.

Hearne, C. M., Perkins, D. R. J. and Andrews, P. 1995. The Sandwich Bay wastewater treatment scheme archaeological project, 1992–1994. *Archaeologia Cantiana* 115, 239–354.

Heathcote, J. 1989. Excavation round-up, 1989, part 2. *London Archaeologist* 6(7), 188–195.

Houliston, M. 1998. *An Archaeological Evaluation: Land South of the Thanet Way, Eddington, Herne Bay*. Canterbury: unpublished Canterbury Archaeological Trust Report 1998/51.

Hull, G. 1998. A Middle Bronze Age field ditch? at Bankside Close, Isleworth. *Transactions of the London and Middlesex Archaeological Society* 49, 1–14.

Hutchinson, A. 1994. *An interim report on the Archaeology of the Herne Bay Water Treatment pipeline*. Canterbury: unpublished Canterbury Archaeological Trust Report 1994/15.

Jackson, G., Maloney, C. and Saich, D. 1997. Archaeology in Surrey. *Surrey Archaeological Collections* 84, 195–243.

James, R. 1999. *An Archaeological Evaluation at Malmaynes Hall Farm (Kingsnorth Pipeline), Stoke, Kent*. Ditchling: unpublished Archaeology South-East Report.

James, R. Forthcoming. Archaeological investigations at Middle Stoke, 1995 and 1998. *Archaeologia Cantiana*.

Jones, M. U. 1993. Background. In Clark, A. *Excavations at Mucking. Vol. 1: the Site Atlas*. London: British Museum Press.

Lavender, N. J. 1998. Prehistoric and Romano-British activity at the William Edwards School, Stifford Clay Road, Grays: excavations 1997. *Essex Archaeology and History* 29, 19–32.

Longley, D. 1976. The archaeological implications of gravel extraction in north-west Surrey. *Research Volume of the Surrey Archaeological Society* 3, 1–35. Old Woking: Surrey Archaeological Society.

Lowther, A. W. G. 1939. Bronze and Iron Age. In Oakley K. P., Rankine, W. F. and Lowther, A. W. G. *A Survey of the Prehistory of the Farnham District*, 153–217. Guildford: Surrey Archaeological Society.

Macpherson-Grant, N. 1991. *A Re-Appraisal of the Prehistoric Pottery from 10–11 Castle Street, Canterbury*. Canterbury: unpublished Canterbury Archaeological Trust Report 1991/15.

Macpherson-Grant, N. 1992. A re-appraisal of Prehistoric pottery from Canterbury. *Canterbury's Archaeology*, 15th Annual Report (1990–91), 38–48.

Macpherson-Grant, N. 1993a. Eddington Farm, Herne Bay. *Canterbury's Archaeology*, 16th Annual Report (1991–1992), 40–41.

Macpherson-Grant , N. 1993b. A review of Late Bronze Age pottery from east Kent. *Canterbury's Archaeology*, 16th Annual Report (1991–1992), 55–63.

Maloney, C. 1999. Fieldwork round-up, 1998. In Maloney, C. and Holroyd, I. London fieldwork and publication round-up, 1998. *London Archaeologist* 9, supplement 1, 1–30.

Mason, S and Lewis, J. 1993. *The Developing Landscape of West London: Settlement, Economy and Environment on the Thames Gravels in the Prehistoric and Roman Periods, Post-Excavation Assessment Report and Updated Project Design*. London: unpublished draft MoLAS Report.

Meddens, F. M. 1996. Sites from the Thames estuary wetlands, England, and their Bronze Age use. *Antiquity* 70, 325–334.

MoLAS 1995. *Annual Review for 1994*. London: Museum of London.

MoLAS 1996. *Annual Review for 1995*. London: Museum of London.

MoLAS 1997a. *Annual Review for 1996*. London: Museum of London.

MoLAS 1997b. *West of Northumberland Bottom*. London: unpublished MoLAS Report.

MoLAS 1998. *Annual Review for 1997*. London: Museum of London.

Moore, J. 1992. Bronze Age activity: the site in its landscape. In Moore, J. and Jennnings, D. *Reading Business Park: a Bronze Age Landscape*, 118–123. Oxford: Oxford University Committee for Archaeology.

Mudd, A. 1994. The excavation of a Later Bronze Age site at Coldharbour Road, Gravesend. *Archaeologia Cantiana* 114, 363–410.

Needham, S. and Burgess, C. 1980. The Later Bronze Age in the Lower Thames Valley : the metalwork evidence. In Barrett, J. and Bradley, R. (eds) *Settlement and Society in the British Later Bronze Age*, 437–470. Oxford: British Archaeological Reports, British Series 83.

O'Connell, M. 1990. Excavations during 1979–1985 of a multi-period site at Stanwell. *Surrey Archaeological Collections* 80, 1–62.

Oxford Archaeological Unit 1997. *West of Church Road, Singlewell, Kent*. Oxford: unpublished Oxford Archaeological Unit Report.

Parfitt, K. 1995. *Archaeological Works on the Thanet Way, Sections 2–4, 1995 Assessment*. Canterbury: unpublished Canterbury Archaeological Trust Report 1995/47.

Parfitt, K. 1996. Herne Bay waste water pipeline. *Canterbury's Archaeology*, 19th Annual Report (1994–95), 16–19.

Perkins, D. R. J. 1994. Discussion. In Perkins, D. R. J., Macpherson-Grant, N. and Healey, E. Monkton Court Farm evaluation, 1992. *Archaeologia Cantiana* 114, 305–312.

Perkins, D. Forthcoming. *A Gateway Island: the Later Prehistory of the Isle of Thanet*. Ph.D. thesis, Institute of Archaeology, University College London.

Perkins, D. R. J., Macpherson-Grant, N. and Healey, E. 1994. Monkton Court Farm evaluation, 1992. *Archaeologia Cantiana* 114, 237–316.

Proctor, J. 1999. Late Bronze Age/Early Iron Age placed deposits from Carshalton. *London Archaeologist* 9(2), 54–60.

Pryor, F. 1996. Sheep, stocklands and farm systems: Bronze Age livestock populations in the Fenlands of eastern England. *Antiquity* 70, 313–324.

Pryor, P. 1998. *Farmers in Prehistoric Britain*. Stroud: Tempus.

Rady, J. 1995. *Whitfield-Eastry Improvement Road: Report on Trial Trenching Project North of Venson Road*. Canterbury: unpublished Canterbury Archaeological Trust Report 1995/24.

Reidy, K. 1997. Middle Bronze Age occupation at Great Wakering. *Essex Archaeology and History* 28, 1–11.

Saxby, D. 1990. *Preliminary Report of the Archaeological Evaluation on the Land Adjacent to 34 Beddington Lane, Beddington, London Borough of Sutton*. London: unpublished MoLAS Report.

Scaife, R. G. 1995. Pollen analysis from the Wantsum Channel. In Hearne, C. M., Perkins, D. R. J. and Andrews, P. The Sandwich Bay wastewater treatment scheme archaeological project, 1992–1994. *Archaeologia Cantiana* 115, 303–313.

Shand, G. 1998a. A Neolithic causewayed enclosure in Kent. *Past* 29, 1.

Shand, G. 1998b. *Ramsgate Harbour Approach Road 1998: Interim Report, Areas A, B (North) and C*. Canterbury: unpublished Canterbury Archaeological Trust Report.

Sidell, J., Giorgi, J. and Pipe, A. 1999. Environmental archaeology in London, 1995–1998, part 1. *London Archaeologist* 9(3), 67–71.

Taylor, C. C. 1972. The study of settlement patterns in pre-Saxon Britain. In Ucko, P. Tringham, R. and Dimbleby, G. (eds) *Man, Settlement and Urbanism*, 109–113. London: Duckworth.

Thomas, C. and Rackham, J. (eds) 1996. Bramcote Green, Bermondsey: a Bronze Age trackway and palaeo-environmental sequence. *Proceedings of the Prehistoric Society* 62, 221–253.

Thomas, R. 1991. Drowning in data? Publication and rescue archaeology in the 1990s. *Antiquity* 65, 822–828.

Thompson, A., Westman, A. and Dyson, T. (eds) 1998. *Archaeology in Greater London, 1965–1990: a Guide to Records of Excavations by the Museum of London*. London: Museum of London.

Tucker, S. L. 1991. *The Philips Factory Site, Beddington Farm Road, Croydon*. London: unpublished MoLAS Report.

Tucker, S. L. 1992. *Hundred Acre Bridge, Mitcham: Report of an Archaeological Evaluation*. London: unpublished MoLAS Report.

Turner, D. J. 1963. Excavations at Carshalton, 1961. *Surrey Archaeological Collections*, 70, 50–53.

Wessex Archaeology 1994. *Horndon to Barking Natural Gas Transmission Pipeline Archaeological Investigations, 1993.* Salisbury: unpublished Wessex Archaeology Report.

Wessex Archaeology 1997a. *Archaeological Evaluation at Temple East of Springhead, Gravesend, Kent.* Salisbury: unpublished Wessex Archaeology Report.

Wessex Archaeology 1997b. *Archaeological Evaluation at Springhead, Gravesend, Kent: Contract 194/870.* Salisbury: unpublished Wessex Archaeology Report.

Wessex Archaeology Forthcoming. Excavations on a Late Bronze Age, Anglo-Saxon and Medieval settlement at Manston Road, Ramsgate 1995-7. *Archaeologia Cantiana.*

Wilkinson, T. J. 1988. *Archaeology and Environment in South Essex: Rescue Archaeology Along the Grays By-Pass, 1979–80.* Chelmsford: East Anglian Archaeology 42.

Wilkinson, T. J. and Murphy, P. L. 1995. *The Archaeology of the Essex Coast, Vol. 1: the Hullbridge Survey.* Chelmsford: East Anglian Archaeology 71.

Wymer, J. J. and Brown, N. R. 1995. *Excavations at North Shoebury: Settlement and Economy in South-East Essex, 1500 BC–AD 1500.* Chelmsford: East Anglian Archaeology 75.

Yates, D. T. 1997. *Bronze Age Field systems in Lowland Britain: the Thames Valley.* Unpublished MA dissertation, Dept. of Archaeology, University of Reading.

Yates, D. T. 1999. Bronze Age field systems in the Thames Valley. *Oxford Journal of Archaeology* 18(2), 157–170.

8   The 'community of builders': the Barleycroft post alignments

Christopher Evans and Mark Knight

This paper concerns things that are essentially non-analogous, or at least without a sense of ready reference – an extraordinary series of 'screen-like' post alignments involving upwards of one thousand substantial timbers that extended across the flood-plain terraces of the River Great Ouse east of Needingworth (Cambridgeshire; TL 35707150; Figs 8.1 and 8.2). They were discovered in the course of the Barleycroft Farm/Over investigations carried out by the Cambridge Archaeological Unit and relate to Bronze Age fieldsystems that have been traced there across more than 350ha on both sides of the river. Sealed by up to 0.75–1.5m of alluvium, and generally lying below the maximum depth of aerial photographic detection, the recovery of these systems belies Fox's declaration (1923, 62) regarding the paucity of Bronze Age occupation within the Ouse Valley. Not only does the fieldwork provide a

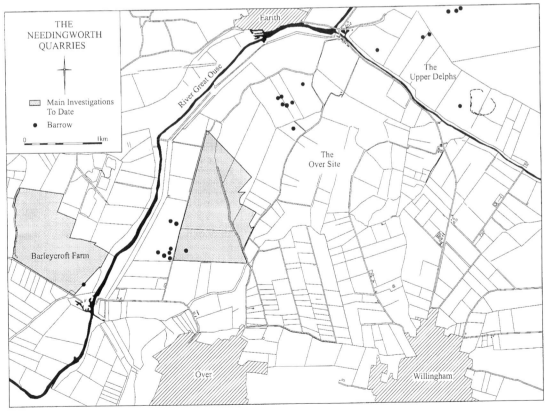

Fig. 8.1 *Location map (note Haddenham causewayed enclosure on Upper Delphs terrace, upper right of picture)*

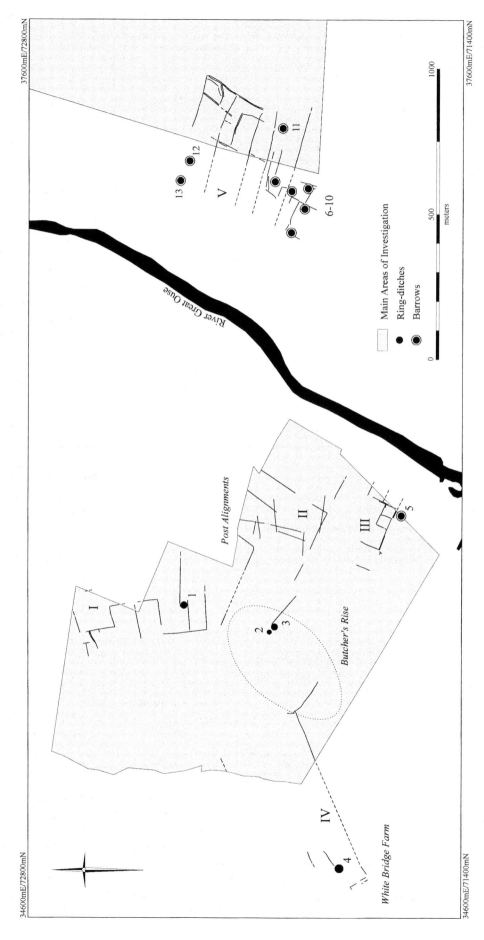

Fig. 8.2 The Barleycroft/Over Bronze Age Landscape showing Field Blocks I–V. While the Block IV system largely lies beyond the area of investigations, the White Bridge Farm cropmarks clearly correlate with a substantial ditch boundary found running southwest from the flank of Butcher's Rise 'hill'-top. It is anticipated that the investigations will shortly extend into the eastern riverside swathe proper, where barrows 6–10 are 'framed' by the fieldsystem's axes. (Under excavation at the time of writing, Field Block VI – located north of 'V' on the east bank – is not shown)

context for the barrow cemeteries along the river's lower reaches (Hall and Coles 1994, fig. 52; Hall 1996; Hodder and Evans forthcoming), but also it details the situation of the ring-ditches in this area (Field 1974).

These are *landscape-scale* investigations in the fullest sense of the word, of which Bronze Age land-use is only one component. Formal sampling procedures have been employed throughout, and much emphasis has been given to the teasing out of buried soil artefact densities to address earlier modes of residential mobility. The project's methodologies and the results of the first years of fieldwork have already been outlined in interim publications (Appendix 1; Evans, Pollard and Knight 1999; Evans and Knight 2000). Eventually continuing across more than 700 ha (with approximately one third investigated to date), the study/quarry area falls on the river's floodplain terraces just above its junction with the fens at Haddenham and Earith. Accordingly, one of the fieldwork's prime research directives is the status of a major river in prehistory, variously its potential as both a landscape corridor – facilitating interaction among the communities of its middle and lower reaches – and/or a territorial divide.

It is argued here that the post alignments, in relation to other features within the immediate Bronze Age landscape, formed part of a vast ceremonial space. They are certainly reflective of group construction and possibly related to large-scale gatherings. Owing to the character of the archaeological record of the British Bronze Age – apparently without a distinct class of major 'extra-domestic' enclosures aside from those associated with its funerary rituals (e.g. Barrett 1988) – little emphasis has been given to the theme of mass assembly in studies of the period. This is in contrast to the Neolithic with its causewayed enclosures and henges, and the hillforts, cult sites/shrines and other 'centres' of the Iron Age.[1] Perhaps due to the need to root the period's readily evident metalwork and barrows in an appropriate domestic base, in recent years attention has largely focused on individual settlements. This has certainly contributed a new perspective to the period's archaeology, yet it is one often lacking any sense of large group dynamic. Increasingly, there is an ethos of the 'site as universe' with an emphasis on its attendant domestic rituals, as if the intentional closure of pits or houses constituted the totality of social life. Important though these approaches are to off-set the sweep of metalwork typologies, there is surely now a need to redress the balance and acknowledge something other than just the interaction of communities on a daily, face-to-face level. It is only by admitting a larger scale dynamic to the period's studies that the social 'works'; in such networks, the possibility for group reproduction through cross-lineage intercourse, the exchange of goods and the transmission of material culture styles lies.

Lowland divides – beyond settlement

Working at such a scale as at Barleycroft/Over challenges precepts concerning bounded landscapes and any easy distinction between ritual and domestic/agricultural domains (cf. e.g. Malim 2000). Within the investigations to date, four main field-system 'blocks' on three distinct alignments have been identified on the Barleycroft side alone (Fig. 8.2, I–IV). No northern or southern end has yet been identified to the overall fieldsystem complex. Moreover, each block is associated with ring-ditches and, in the case of the southernmost, a barrow. Begging the question of where does one system begin and another end, are these field blocks to be seen as representative of distinct communal sub-sets or as simply determined by immediate topographic factors? Given its extent and sub-division, the evidence suggests that this was a *seamed landscape* involving major axial shifts, with ring-ditch monuments and topographic features serving as nodal points.

There is not the scope here to outline the organisation of the Ouse-side fieldsystems in any detail. Firmly radiocarbon dated to the mid to later second millennium BC (see *Postscript* to Evans and Knight 2000), with Deverel-Rimbury ceramics recovered in association (although somewhat earlier, Collared Urn-attributed origins remain a possibility), these are 'big' systems with wide axial divisions 80–120m apart. Equally, they are quite open with substantial gaps between, and interruptions along, their ditched boundaries. Only in the southeasternmost Barleycroft block were droveway-like double-ditched lines recovered. Demonstrably a 'late' elaboration, the gap between these was consistently narrow (1.5–2m) and, in each instance, one of the pairs was very minor being little more than a discontinuous trough. Accordingly, these are thought to attest to hedged embankments and elsewhere this manner of demarcation may have extended between interrupted ditch lengths (see Pollard 1996 and Evans 1998 concerning 'hedge' recovery). Otherwise, and perhaps telling in the light of how much emphasis is given to their logistical determination at Fengate (Pryor 1996), droveways are completely absent within the Barleycroft/Over system. This need not be indicative of a paucity of animals, but rather may show that their movement did not require such rigid or permanent delineation.[2]

Although for the sake of convenience, the term 'fieldsystem' is retained here, the Barleycroft/Over boundaries appear reave-like and seem to relate to a

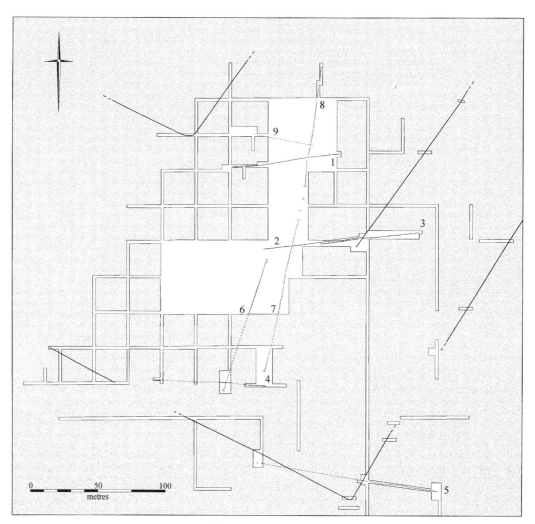

Fig. 8.3 The Barleycroft alignments: 1–9 post alignments (unnumbered black linears are ditched Bronze Age boundaries; Romano-British boundaries omitted)

more general parcelling of land. Yet, in contrast to the great Dartmoor systems (Fleming 1988), the layout at Barleycroft/Over, although primarily oriented in reference to immediate stretches of the river, was clearly more responsive to variations in local topography. Nevertheless, the manner of its large-scale axial blocking does not seem directly analogous to 'familiar' agricultural usage. In keeping with the dispersed character and low density of its accompanying settlement, its operations do not appear to have been governed by principles of economic maximisation (cf. Pryor 1996; 1998).

Among the major highlights of the excavations to date has been the recovery of an indisputable longhouse set in a separate ditched compound alongside a terrace-edge settlement including round-houses, wells and four posters that skirted the fieldsystem within the Paddocks sub-site (Block I; Evans and Knight 2000, 97, 101, fig. 9.8). Excavation of a pair of ring-ditches on the Butcher's Rise knoll in 1996 demonstrated that one of these – double-

ditched with a central 'primary' *in situ* cremation pyre post-dating an inhumation phase – became the focus of a major cremation cemetery with 35 sub-sequent interments (*ibid.*, figs 9.6 and 9.7). During the course of the southern field investigations at Barleycroft, a flat cemetery of 11 cremations was recovered within the axes of the southernmost field block (Block III). Potentially an instance of denying a 'past' linkage, the situation of the latter is partic-ularly telling as the hedged perimeter of those paddocks would probably have screened the barrow located immediately south of it; the question that arises here is why, given local precedent, these cremations were not interred within the monument.

Aside perhaps from the longhouse, all of the above are now well-established components within the fabric of the Later Bronze Age landscapes of southern England (e.g. Barrett, Bradley and Green 1991; Needham 1992; Brück 1999). In contrast, the post alignments discovered in the course of the final phase of the Barleycroft fieldwork are without direct

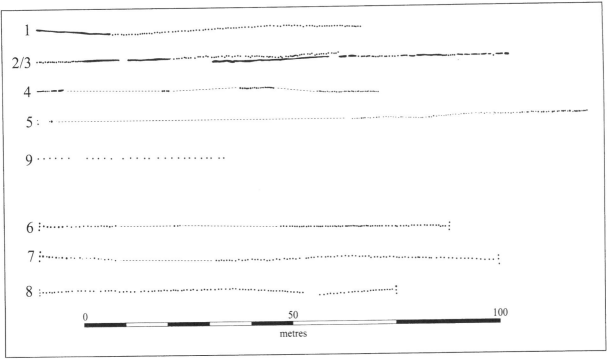

Fig. 8.4 *The Barleycroft alignments: Lines 1–5 and Line 9, east-west orientation; Lines 6–8, north-south (note the 'T'-set terminals of the latter and the wider intervals between the posts of Line 9)*

parallel. The eight main 'lines' extended across *c.* 6 ha of the western floodplain and lay at a height of 3–3.5m OD (Lines 1–8, plus one minor, Line 9; Fig. 8.3). Although their limits were ostensibly determined, it is conceivable that they continue into the uninvestigated field immediately to the north. Apart from Lines 2/3 and 5, they occurred within the bounds of the largest single field exposed within the Barleycroft system, terminating well inside its surrounding ditches. Their secondary status, and that the ditches were then still 'active' or at least apparent when the first alignments were erected, is indicated by the fact that the eastern end of Line 2 appears to terminate just before it reaches one of the northeast-southwest oriented ditches, although its eastern extension (Line 3) cut through the same ditch. Although reflecting some degree of respect, it is nevertheless difficult to see how the ditch system could continue to operate when cross-cut by the post lines. Less ambiguous is the evidence of the southernmost line (Line 5) whose posts clearly cut the fills of one of the ditch system's main axes.

The post alignments proper were not recognised for what they were in the course of the evaluation fieldwork. However, test pit sampling indicated relatively high densities of struck and burnt flint throughout the area (Evans and Knight 2000, fig. 9.4). Consequently, as part of the main excavation phase, the sampling programme was intensified to a 25m interval and this immediate swathe was target-ed for open-area investigation, although admittedly not at the scale to which it eventually extended. In the course of excavation, pit clusters of both Later Neolithic and Early Bronze Age date were recovered (as well as tree throw assemblages attesting to Early Neolithic activity; see Evans, Pollard and Knight 1999). These pit clusters predate the fieldsystem. Although very slight traces of two roundhouses were discovered, which are likely to have been broadly contemporary with the post lines, aside from a few small pits of Late Bronze Age/post-Deverel Rimbury attribution, there is little direct evidence of occupation/'use' associated with the timber alignments. (While the alignments have not as yet been absolutely dated, no Iron Age material whatsoever was recovered from the terrace on which they were located. The area as a whole has a paucity of occupation of Iron Age date and the post lines are therefore unlikely to be of post-Bronze Age attribution).

Varying in length from 77.5 to 129m, there is a basic distinction between the east-west and north-south lines (Fig. 8.4). Whereas the former were somewhat irregular and locally involved minor bedding trenches, the latter were much more formally executed with regular post intervals and had 'T'-set ends with posts off-set at right angles to their terminal uprights. Yet, even these were not perfect in their layout, and kinks along their lengths suggest segmented or successive bedding. Line 9, a return to Line

Post alignment 2

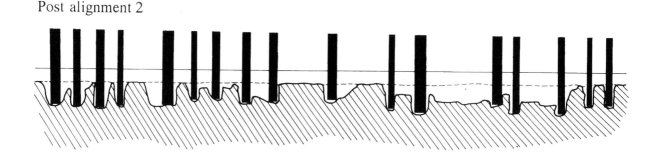

Post alignment 7

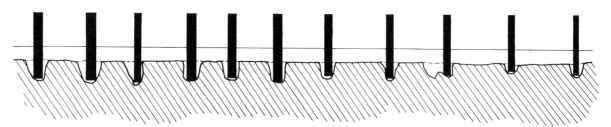

Fig. 8.5 *The Barleycroft alignments: comparative longitudinal sections with post settings reconstructed*

8, was only *c.* 50m long and had extremely irregular settings whose average spacing was twice that of any other; this would seem to be still another 'type'.

This is a matter of 'small post architecture' (i.e. 'non-totem pole' scale). With their uprights on average only *c.* 0.2m in diameter, the alignments were not, for example, comparable to the mass timber constructions of the Neolithic. Instead, any 'monumentality' would have lain in their collective impact, particularly the closeness and regularity of their interval (0.5–1.1m). Generally, the postholes were 0.2–0.45m deep, although the depth of the overlying buried soil should also be added (*c.* 0.25m; Fig. 8.5). From this, it can be estimated that the posts, at most, would have stood only *c.* 1–2m high. However, they could have been considerably higher and more substantial had their lower portions been supported by turf-stack banks. The existence of such upstanding features can perhaps be inferred by the 'T'-set terminals of the north-south lines (i.e. these may have formed an end revetment), and in the stand-off of those settings where lines overlapped (e.g. Lines 1 and 8; Lines 2 and 7) or ran parallel (Lines 2 and 3). From this, the existence of *c.* 1m high and 1m wide flanking banks could be postulated and, if so anchored, these could have supported posts standing 2–4m above ground level. Yet, the evidence is far from conclusive and traces of local-ised burning in their upper subsoil-level profiles could contradict this (see below). It is, of course,

equally possible that the interval between the posts was itself closed, perhaps by wattle panels. Yet, by the open 'singularity' of the alignments (i.e. without corners whatsoever), *enclosure* does not seem to be their purpose as this could have been achieved by more widely spaced post settings.

From their arrangement and intersections, it is clear that not all of the post alignments could have been contemporary, or at least raised at the same time. The most obvious relationship is that of Lines 7 and 8. Seemingly paired, together they extended over 217.5m and had an off-centre 'interruption' some 24m across (Fig. 8.6). Arguably, the latter was a major entrance as both lines terminated in 'T's at this point, and situated within the opening were, roughly equidistant, a four-square post setting and a two-post setting. Given this arrangement, Line 4 may mark a westward return along the southern side of this area (with a broad corner gap) and, in the north, Line 9 could also be associated (Fig. 8.7C). If collectively interrelated, although surely quite imposing, this would still have been a very open and an almost facade-like setting. Its entrance post settings contribute to the impression of its formality. Obviously not relating to any manner of 'closeable' gateway, they seem to have been free-standing structures. Within an immediate landscape context, the four-square setting evokes the arrangement of the core interments within the flat cremation cemet-ery in the southeastern field block. Yet, equally, it

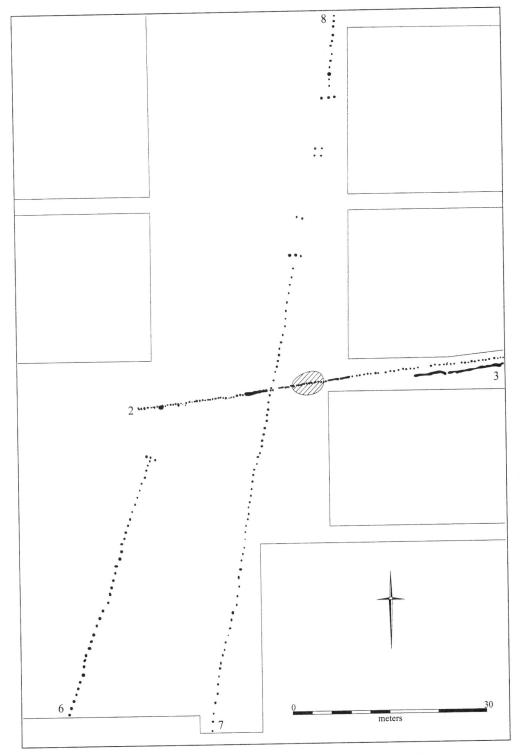

Fig. 8.6 *The Barleycroft alignments: the facade entranceway (note two- and four-post structures; hachuring indicates extent of burning along Line 2*

also evokes domestic structures – roundhouse porches and granary structures – and thereby raises the long-rehearsed ambiguities concerning four posters (e.g. Ellison and Drewett 1971).

The formality of this layout contrasts with its unelaborated origins, for two of the east-west lines evidently pre-date the north-south 'facade': Line 8 clearly cut through Line 1, and a post of Line 7 recut a setting in Line 2. The latter relationship was unequivocal; despite the fact that the bedding trench of Line 2 appeared to interrupt the north-south line, Line 7 must have been set through a gap within it. It

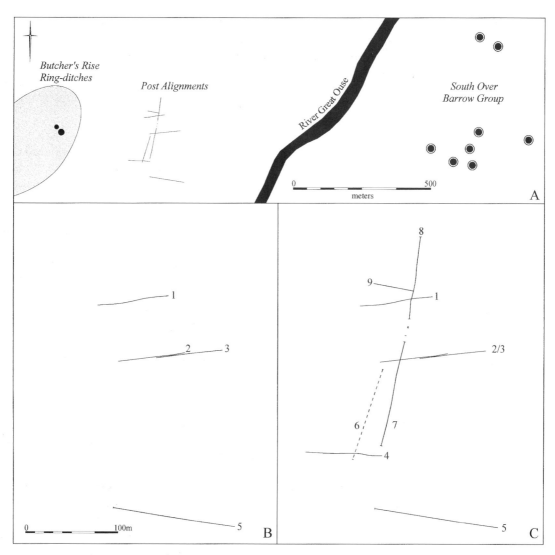

Fig. 8.7 *The Barleycroft alignments. A: The larger cross-river complex; B: Primary east-west 'screens' (with Lines 3 and 5 probably secondary additions); C: The developed facade (the dashing of Line 6 indicates its ambiguous status)*

is 'logical' – if normative phasing precepts can be applied to such constructions – that Line 3, the extension to Line 2, was contemporary with Line 5 in the south, as their east-west terminals roughly correspond (Fig. 8.7B). Given this developmental sequence, Line 6 may represent the first of the north-south lines set to block the western end of axes Lines 2/3 and 5 (a post on its projected alignment had been set into Line 2; the west end of Line 5 in the south had a distinct two-post terminal, going some way to match or at least anticipate the three-post ends of the north-south lines). However, the status of Line 6 is ambiguous; its relationship with Line 4 was undefined and it could even be secondary to the Line 7/8 facade.

A number of points arise from this schema. Whereas its final facaded format seems a distinctly 'timber-type' construction (i.e. quasi-structural), the original east-west lines appear more akin to the earlier ditched boundaries in that they emphasise directional orientation and not 'blockage', although their alignment was off-set to the ditches. Yet, does this sequence really express phasing with its implication of structural succession or should we see instead a cumulative layout with earlier lines left standing despite increasingly divergent alignments? The latter seems possible in that what were probably the original east-west lines – 1 and 2 – directly complemented the entrance of the final north-south facade. Not only did Line 8 interrupt Line 1, but the layout of Lines 1 and 2 were complementary to the facade's entrance and equidistantly flanked it (by *c.* 20m, roughly comparable to the entrance interval itself). Similarly, the western end of Line 5 seems to correspond to the facade's alignment, with the 65m gap between Lines 5 and 7 being comparable to the interval between Lines 1 and 2/3 (60m). Whatever term is applied to the post alignments' sequence, *transformation* is certainly apparent – from a series of relatively simple east-west oriented 'screens' to a more formal north-south facade structure with funnelled entrance access.

It is imperative that the sheer scale of the construction of the alignments is appreciated. In total, it is estimated that this would have involved more than 950 uprights. This is a massive quantity of timber and represents, for example, the amount needed to build 15–20 longhouses. Assuming in the light of the postholes' uniformity that the alignments were built of managed timber, they would have required the clearance of some 2–4 ha of woodlot (upper and lower estimates dependent on overall length of posts and whether two could be generated from each trunk). Of course, this cannot be taken as any manner of absolute gauge. However, there was no evidence for the digging out or re-use of posts and, even if the lines were cumulative, their lifespan may have been as little as 25–50 years duration. If so, and presuming that *c.* 25 year-old oak was largely employed for their construction (R. Darrah, pers. comm.), then this would still have the potential for two cuttings over its span. Yet, even if factored down, their construction represents a enormous draw of prime wood that could otherwise have been allocated to more pragmatic purposes.

Albeit at a much reduced scale, the extravagant use of timber in the alignments has affinities with its bulk employment at Flag Fen. This, the scale of the period's fieldsystems and the short-lived nature of its settlements (i.e. the lack of evidence for direct rebuilding) – just as, too, the mass stripping of soil cover for the period's turf-stack barrows – could suggest expansive attitudes towards landscape. Certainly, it seems difficult to see these communities as 'gentle custodians' of the land, practising a careful husbandry of its resources. Yet, belying such a judgement, when compared to Seahenge (Pryor 2001), the Barleycroft alignments are entirely a product of a *domesticated landscape* and not the 'wildwood'. Their sheer scale must imply a degree of successful land-use management (i.e. the production of a surplus), at least in the short-term.

A cross-ground complex

Fence lines are part of the grammar of second millennium BC settlement (e.g. Fig. 8.8C; Bond 1988, 13, fig. 12; Fleming 1988, 89–91; Moore and Jennings 1992, 27, fig. 9; Guttmann and Last 2000, 327, fig. 7), and have also been found sub-dividing contemporary fieldsystems (Yates 1999, 166). Extensive, palisade-type constructions are also known from the period that are generally attributed to either defence or stock management (e.g. Redgate Hill, Hunstanton: Healy, Cleal and Kinnes 1993, 72–75; Rams Hill: Bradley 1975; see also Knight 1984, 190, 196). By their scale and 'openness', it is not possible to ascribe the Barleycroft post lines to any manner of either defensive, strictly domestic or agrarian/pastoral enclosure, which the marked regularity of their settings could itself further support. Given this, how is any sense of their 'meaning' to be established – through broad morphological analogy or immediate landscape context?

The Flag Fen timber alignment provides an obvious parallel. The Barleycroft constructions lack the extraordinary ritual deposits that accompanied this, but then they did not cross the 'wet', only lowlying gravel terraces. The appropriateness of this comparison rests upon how the Peterborough settings are themselves interpreted, whether as a series of reset and highly irregular post lines or as a much rebuilt causeway (Pryor 1991; forthcoming; cf. Evans forthcoming a). Both imply linear progression and/or division, and these principles also seem integral to the Barleycroft settings. Yet, as is apparent in Fig. 8.8, the regularity and cross-axes of the Ouse-side post alignments markedly contrast with the Flag Fen 'avenue' and, except at the most basic level, it is difficult to see them as being of the same category of construction.

Although generally of a somewhat later date, as a regularly permeable boundary, pits alignments also offer a basis for comparison (e.g. Knight 1984, 259–262). Apart from the fact that they were 'earthen actions' (*vs.* standing structures), where they differ is that whereas pit alignments essentially define and partially encircle landscape/territorial zones, the Barleycroft alignments are more a matter of straight axial 'screens'.[3] In some respects, within the British sequence, it is the stone rows of the upland zone whose arrangement offers the closest parallel to these (e.g. Fig. 8.8E; Fleming 1988, 95–100). Postulating this, we have, of course, to set aside differences in material and dating (generally ascribed to the Later Neolithic, the attribution of most is far from secure). Nevertheless, the affinities between the Barleycroft alignments and stone rows may also extend to their linkages with funerary monuments, for a number of stone rows extend from burial-related cairns (it is argued below that the Barleycroft settings have an indirect relationship to the Over barrow group).[4] Although potentially reflective of the complex interaction of timber and megalithic constructions, and having general affinities with other forms of linear-type settings, that indirect parallels can be found for the Barleycroft alignments should not deflect us from, what at least thus far, is their unique character.

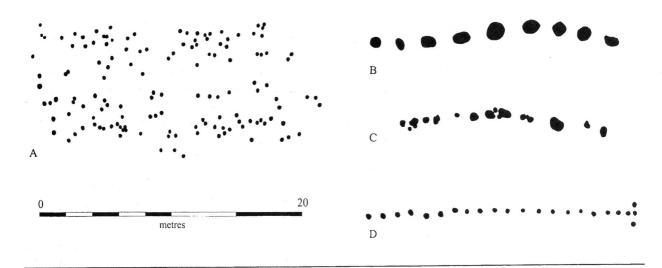

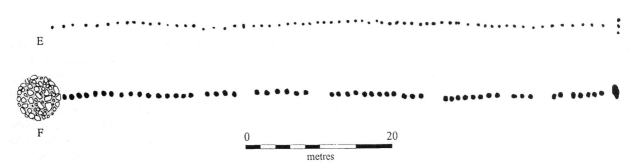

Fig. 8.8 *Comparative 'linears'. A: Flag Fen, Power Station alignment/causeway (after Taylor 1992, fig. 8); B: Post alignment, Site 5, Plantation Quarry, Willington, Bedfordshire (after Dawson 1996, fig. 17); C: Fence line/timber 'screen', North Ring, Mucking (after Bond 1988, fig. 3; see Parker Pearson 1993, fig. 114 for reconstruction); D: Barleycroft Line 6 (note that of these four examples, only the full length of the Mucking 'screen' is shown, with the remainder of the illustrations depicting representative segments only); E: Barleycroft Line 7 (northern portion); F: Stone row, Drizzlecombe, Dartmoor (after Fleming 1988, fig. 60)*

That a length of Line 2 at Barleycroft – immediately east of its junction with Line 7 – had evidently been torched provides further evidence of the 'nonfunctional' associations of the Barleycroft post settings (Fig. 8.6). Scorching of the surrounding natural indicates that the quantities of charcoal and reddened clay in the upper posthole fills at this point derived from *in situ* firing. That burnt human bone also occurred within them, mainly skull fragments, suggests ritual activity. However, this specific event is unlikely to explain the phenomenon of the alignments as a whole.

The post settings more closely conform to the alignment of Field Block I and, given that they generally seem to post-date the immediate Block II boundaries, this could imply the later dominance of the more northerly field system (Fig. 8.2). However, their broader situation within the floodplain may be more telling of their role as they fall between two major components of its cultural topography: the Butcher's Rise 'knoll' and the barrow cemetery on the east bank opposite. It is the shift in the orientation of the post lines in relation to the earlier field boundaries, and particularly the intentional fronting of the main north-south facade towards the barrows, that most clearly links these far flung components (Fig. 8.7A). However, it is also suggestive that, looking east, the 'fanning' of the northern and southernmost east-west lines would have roughly framed the barrow group. From the outset of the investigations, the Butcher's Rise hilltop suggested itself as an obvious area of occupation and a distinct locale within the subtle topography of the floodplain. This potential gradually became more apparent when it was realised that the main axes of the fieldsystem 'spun' upon its crown (Fig. 8.2) and that a contemporary ditch encircled its lower southwestern flanks. Yet, despite intensive trial trenching, no substantive settlement remains were located. From this, and from the existence of the pair of ring-ditches on its eastern side (the one, as noted above, attracting a major cremation cemetery), it is clear that this rise was a recognised place within the second millennium landscape. Yet, it seems without a readily defined function and is essentially an 'empty' centre.[5]

Having three immediate outliers, the cluster of five round barrows on the east bank of the Ouse is an impressive monument group, whose crowns still stand *c.* 1m high. Now scheduled, these are un-investigated aside from geophysical survey (see Evans and Knight 2000, fig. 9.9). However, the one barrow that falls within the east bank quarry (Fig. 8.2, 11) has been dug and found to have a primary *in situ* pit-pyre cremation. Analogous with those investigated in the course of the Haddenham Project (Evans and Hodder forthcoming), it has secondary Collared Urn-associated interments, and its primary construction probably dates between 1800 and 1500 BC (radiocarbon determinations forthcoming). The geophysical survey demonstrated that the east bank fieldsystem postdated the barrow group with its axes boxing the mounds. Despite this apparent infringement, seen at a distance, their mounds would still have made a striking impression and they were probably considered a place of ancestors, whether 'real' or by invention.

If we are correct in seeing the post lines as interrelating the western hill-top and the eastern riverside barrow group, then this would encompass a vast complex extending over some 1.5km (Fig. 8.7A). Visually linked, this would have been almost a theatrical arena. Yet, aside from the burnt segment of Line 2, and the presence of body parts (possibly displayed on posts), there is no direct evidence of the 'performances' that took place here. Although the character of the alignments' construction suggests a wide draw of labour and resources from multiple communal sub-sets, unfortunately there is not means by which to establish their precise function and the scale of the participatory 'audience'. Indeed, visual 'fixing' may have been their sole purpose.[6] However, even this implies viewers and, although there is no basis on which to demonstrate it, this leads us to suspect that they related to *en masse* meetings. Overlooking interpretative ambiguities, if this was to be the case, then – probably centred on ancestral cults – associated activities could equally have ranged from exchange (e.g. of stock, metals or marriage partners) to mass perambulation (the latter, possibly involving the direction of the participants' vision and movement, may have had vague affinities to the operation of earlier cursus monuments and, effectively, would have involved the construction of a socio-ceremonial 'field' or 'way'). The complex's associations could have referenced both the domestic and ritual domains;

consistent with the nature of 'public' space in general, it is unlikely to have had only a single attribution (i.e. multi-faceted usage). What the larger Barleycroft/Over complex points to is a 'componented' sense of inter-communal group space, with its 'totality' reflecting the assembly of distinct parts. Again, this has parallels with Flag Fen, variously its droveway approach, timber 'avenue' and great platform, which extend over some 1.1km in total. Both sites involve the linkage of diverse components, and their sheer scale might explain why comparable venues have not been recognised previously in the archaeology of the later second millennium BC.

That such a vast 'ceremonial' space could potentially be erected (and ceremonies enacted) within the bounds of what had been a fieldsystem at Barleycroft may be reflective of the place of ritual, specifically that it need not be removed from the domestic fabric. A point variously reinforced by the siting of the cemetery within the axes of the southeastern field block (Block III), and the incorporation of ring-ditches and barrows within the larger boundary system, the situation of the post alignments suggests that there was little intrinsic sense of 'sacred lands'. *Situation* seems crucial here, and this equally applies to the duration of the post lines, as their usage could not have extended over more than 50–100 years at most. Although perhaps having 'monumental' characteristics, they cannot themselves be counted as any manner of long-term monuments and might be better considered as some manner of *community project* (Evans 1988). Yet, if their role was essentially to facilitate a cross-river linkage between the east bank barrows and the ring-ditches opposite (and possibly frame group gatherings), then, once established, this association could well have continued beyond the span of the timber constructions themselves.

Familiar landscapes?

The extraordinary character of the Barleycroft post lines challenges arguments that the later second millennium saw the advent of familiar patterns of land-use (e.g. Pryor 1998, 125). Through contrast to previous modes of residential mobility (e.g. Edmonds, Evans and Gibson 1999; Pollard 1999), this ethos essentially hinges on the evidence of field-systems and maintains that 'settling down' initiated practices of agricultural land-use comparable to those of the ethno-historical present. Yet, in the case of the Barleycroft/Over investigations, is it just the 'Lines' that create a sense of disquiet or does this extend to the system of land boundaries itself? Can its great axes really be seen, for example, as analogous to the fabric of the Medieval/post-Medieval landscape – effectively 'our world'? By their vast scale and interval (and many gaps), they do not seem to fulfil normative expectations of fieldsystem enclosure. Ultimately governed by concepts of economic need, the 'normativism' of Bronze Age fieldsystems is equally undermined by the fact that they did not then occur on the Continent. Certainly with comparable and probably locally higher population densities, the Scandinavian, Dutch and German Bronze Ages, for example, evidently thrived without such formalised systems – how can they be 'necessary'?

The Barleycroft/Over systems, particularly the giving over of what had been a field to the post 'screens', would similarly question the accepted longevity of later prehistoric fieldsystems. Although now tied down to the latter half of the second millennium BC, further analysis and dating is expected to tighten their span. Although some blocks were locally elaborated by additional ditches and, arguably, hedge lines, generally there seems to have been little active maintenance of the boundaries. The regularity of their profiles and adherence to straight alignments cannot attest to long-term mucking out. Although they undoubtedly left lingering earthwork scars, most seem to have been cut and simply left to silt up.[7]

Through alluviation, drainage and the construction of the river's barrier banks, the 'phenomenology' of this landscape has been lost (cf. Tilley 1994). Nevertheless, the singular character of the post alignments encourages speculation concerning their symbolism. This could vary from the 'sacrifice' of wood to the direct equation of posts with people.[8] Although the possibilities are many, the excavated evidence offers few insights into any intended ritual content. However, given their 'in-field' location and materials (*managed* wood and land), in terms of structuralist precepts, their interrelationships do not primarily seem to pertain to oft-cited nature/culture distinctions but rather – framing the cross-river mortuary complexes and including human remains – to the living and dead (i.e. the ancestors). *De facto*, the activities carried out here must have involved references time/locale and, thereby, must have encompassed crucial parameters of community and place.

With a linkage established between monuments straddling the Ouse, and in reference to the larger project's prime research directive, the role of the river should, accordingly, be considered. Although surely it must have been many things simultaneously, generally it would have to be said that it seems 'neutral' with complementary sites and densities (and fieldsystems) occurring on both sides.[9] However, there is patterning that could suggest some degree of bankside difference, in particular the almost exclusive occurrence of the barrows cemeteries on the east side. Although isolated exemplars are known on the west bank, they do not occur in anything like the density that they do on the eastern side (a single ring-ditch has also been recovered on the east side and the geophysical surveys suggest that others may occur within the main Over barrow group).

What are we to make of this – are we to postulate separate barrow and ring-ditch 'folk'? This, of course, is implausible and in all likelihood these distributions were primarily determined by environmental and topographic factors. Foremost among these was the marine inundation that occurred across the southwestern fens during the Later Neolithic/Early Bronze Age. Correlating with the deposition of Fen Clay beds (Waller 1994), this had its limits along the northern side of the lower reaches of the Ouse. Not illogically, the riverside barrow cemeteries throughout the Haddenham Level (in the fen immediately northeast of Over) were constructed on its dry southern terraces. In other words, they were not built in the wet and their distribution may, in fact, have participated in the delineation of that divide. The east bank location of the Over barrows may therefore represent an up-river extension of this pattern. In terms of the immediate topography of the Barleycroft/Over floodplain, the gravel terraces on that side are considerably more limited (i.e. linear) and of less 'use-value' than the more extensive plain of the west bank. The Bronze Age fieldsystems were probably first laid out across the latter. Therefore, although there were possibly distinctions *viz.* prime/core and marginal lands, during the second millennium BC, it seems unlikely that the riverside marked a socio-territorial divide. If further proof of this is needed, the shared characteristics of the Bronze Age fieldsystems on both sides could be enlisted. Even more potentially telling are the post alignments and their postulated role in unifying the Butcher's Rise hill-top (and its ring-ditch cemetery) and the east bank barrow field.

When compared with the 'bounded', readily defined domestic units of the Iron Age,[10] among the central challenges of Bronze Age archaeology would be that of scale. Focusing, as the subject has been prone to, on specific sites – one settlement cluster or ring-ditch – it becomes difficult to mesh this immediacy with the scale of its fieldsystems. Despite their size, and no matter how many hundreds of hectares they may have extended over, their axes could be walked in a matter of hours if not minutes. Certainly, it is wrong to see them as self-contained 'worlds'. People would regularly have escaped the geometry of their boundaries, and equally crucial is what lay beyond: the woodlands, wetlands and, eventually, other fieldsystems and communities. A key issue, therefore, that the interpretation of the Barleycroft alignments poses, is where or at what level did 'community' reside? Was it in the face-to-face interaction of the fieldsystems' dispersed settlement clusters, the presumably lineage-based collective of ring-ditch, secondary barrow and flat cemetery populations, or something larger and more nebulous? It must, of course, have encompassed all three and certainly would have included the latter – in effect, the broader 'community of builders'. The period's daily groupings would have been far too small to function as reproductive units and social networks must (through incest taboos) have involved the dovetailing of at least three lineages. Still requiring resolution is the degree to which any larger group interactions were formalised and under whose auspices they occurred – collective 'neighbourhood groups', elected headman 'kings' (Fleming 1988, 120–122) or more removed, chieftain-like modes of authority (see Evans and Knight 2000, 101). Be this as it may, the period's fieldsystems can themselves be considered as integrating structures, knitting together communal sub-sets. The open 'parcelling' of such systems as at Barleycroft/Over could well reflect the provision of a framework to abet permanent residence, perhaps by groups previously practising modes of residential mobility revolving around the area's ring-ditches. If so, they may simultaneously have facilitated *both social proximity and distinction*. Cross-cutting this, just as in earlier 'rounds' dispersed social groups would have come together for diverse exchanges (probably in the context of festivals and ceremonies), so too would such rites have been integral to 'fieldsystem life'. By this, such systems may be considered as much a basis of social interaction as a means of agricultural delineation. Similarly, the negotiations required to variously erect and extend the Barleycroft post lines may have been central to the enactment of broader social relations.

Acknowledgements

The Barleycroft/Over fieldwork has been funded by Hanson Aggregates, where it has been promoted by B. Chapman and J. Bown. Equally, the successive support of B. Sydes, L. Austin and S. Kaner of Cambridgeshire County Council has been instrumental to it.

We are indebted to the many who have participated within the excavations themselves, and thank C. Begg and A. Hall whose graphics feature in this contribution. Long-term specialist collaboration with Josh Pollard (ceramics and flint) and Charly French (environmental) has been fruitful and a key component to the fieldwork. Discussion with and advice variously provided by K. Gdaniec, D. Gibson, J. D. Hill, T. Lane, G. Lucas, S. Needham, F. Pryor, N. Sharples, M. L. S. Sorensen and D. Yates has been greatly appreciated; we are particularly grateful in this instance for information supplied by Prof. R. Bradley, R. Darrah and A. Mawson.

Notes

1 Previously, the period's gatherings have only really been discussed in relation to modes of 'animal-driven' transhumant activity (e.g. Bradley 1975; cf. Needham and Ambers 1994; see Evans 1987 for overview); but see Needham and Spence 1996 and Yates 1999 concerning 'aggrandised enclosures' and also the role of meetings at/visits to higher status settlements.

2 Unlike Barleycroft/Over, Fengate has an extensive gravel terrace hinterland and its droves may not have been dictated by its immediate fen-edge population alone, but by the need to drive the herds of more distant communities down to seasonally available pastures through their fields (in other words, to get to Flag Fen).

3 Of Middle Iron Age attribution, a post alignment excavated at Plantation Quarry, Bedfordshire (Dawson 1996), seems, effectively, a timber rendering of a pit alignment-type boundary (Fig. 8.8B).

4 See Wilhelmi 1987 for German Bronze Age mortuary-associated timber alignments/'causeways'. M. Green's excavation of a Later Bronze Age timber avenue at Ogden Down also provides a parallel. There, two alignments extended down towards the Dorset Cursus from a post circle surrounding a Neolithic ring-ditch that was apparently reworked during the Late Bronze Age (R. Bradley pers comm.).

5 A sense of facaded orientation is also expressed in the early phases of the main Butcher's Rise ring-ditch, its respective antennae- and horseshoe-plan ditches (accompanied by an inhumation on their central axis dated to 2040–1770 BC: OxA–8113) being oriented just south-of-east (Evans and Knight 2000, fig. 9.7A and B).

6 What is proposed is certainly not any manner of absolute geometry, but rather rough orientation. More detailed analysis of the alignments could be attempted; for example, the Line 7/8 facade-entrance opens onto the core barrows of the group. Yet, unless the north-south and east-west lines were of different heights, this perspective would have been blocked by its funnelled access alignments (Lines 1 and 2/3).

7 A major part of the argument for the long-term maintenance of the Fengate system was the homogeneity of its ditch fills, thought to derive from extended reworking (Pryor 1980). However, subsequent excavation has established that extensively leached, near-uniform deposits are frequently characteristic of pre-Iron Age archaeology on lowland gravels as a whole, and do not require explanatory recourse to special circumstances. See Evans and

Pollard forthcoming concerning a shorter chronology (i.e. post-Late Neolithic origins) for the Fengate system based on a reappraisal of the Storey's Road sub-site.

8 Providing this paper's title, in 1983, Mawson witnessed the re-building of a circular byre/shrine among the Agar Dinka of the southern Sudan, an event that occurs, at least ideally, on an eight year cycle (Mawson 1989). After protracted negotiations by diverse tribal/territorial sub-sets concerning who is responsible for the renewal of what portion (and the supply of materials), the re-building itself happens quickly and is accompanied by much ceremony and ritual. As part of this, the interior ring of its double-post wall circle is entirely renewed, with the posts of the inner circle trimmed and shifted to the outer circuit. Lengths of its perimeter are the responsibility of specific communal sub-sets, with the participants encircling the shrine and undertaking this re-setting *en masse*. Specific groups are, thereby, identified with specific portions of the building and its wall posts. Similarly evoking the equation of people and timber, there are stories in Dinka religious mythology that relate the direct substitution of the gods' requirement of human sacrifice with that of wood (Mawson 1989 and in Evans and Hodder forthcoming; see Evans, Pollard and Knight 1999 concerning 'wood'/tree associations).

9 It must be presumed that the river was always a landscape corridor facilitating movement, with its light terrace sub-soils attracting a high density of prehistoric settlement (investigations on the clays of Needingworth Ridge immediately to the west – what Fox characterised as the valley's 'cold claylands' (1923, 62) – failed to identify any substantial prehistoric presence: Schlee 1995; cf. Evans forthcoming b). However, there is evidence to suggest that the Ouse Valley was a major divide during the Iron Age. This ranges from the recovery of a series of pit alignments along the bankside of a palaeo-channel at Meadow Lane, St Ives (Pollard 1996; see also Malim 2000, fig. 8.10), to the broader distribution of coinage, pottery types and mortuary rites (Hill, Evans and Alexander 1999; Evans and Hodder forthcoming).

10 However, an element of off-site seasonal activity has been recognised in the period's land-use, involving the utilisation of fen-fast barrows as marshland foraging stations (Evans and Hodder forthcoming).

Appendix 1: Cambridge Archaeological Unit – Barleycroft/Over Reports

Evans, C. 1992. *The Archaeology of Willingham/Over: a Desktop Study.* Cambridge: Cambridge Archaeological Unit.

Evans, C. 1995. *Archaeological Investigations at Barleycroft Farm, Bluntisham, Cambridgeshire, 1994.* Cambridge: Cambridge Archaeological Unit (Barleycroft Farm/ARC Paper 1).

Evans, C. and Gibson, D. 1996. *Floodplain Investigations: Barleycroft Farm, Cambridgeshire, 1995.* Cambridge:

Cambridge Archaeological Unit (Barleycroft Farm/ARC Paper 4).

Evans, C. and Knight, M. 1997a. *The Over Lowland Investigations, Cambridgeshire: the 1996 Evaluation.* Cambridge: Cambridge Archaeological Unit (Over/ARC Paper 3).

Evans, C. and Knight, M. 1997b. *The Barleycroft Paddocks Excavations, Cambridgeshire.* Cambridge: Cambridge Archaeological Unit (Barleycroft Farm/ARC Paper 5).

Evans, C. and Knight, M. 1998. *The Butcher's Rise Ring-ditches: Excavations at Barleycroft Farm, Cambridgeshire, 1996.* Cambridge: Cambridge Archaeological Unit (Barleycroft Farm/ARC Paper 6).

Evans, C. and Knight, M. 2001. *Excavations at Barleycroft Farm: the Southern Field Investigations.* Cambridge: Cambridge Archaeological Unit (Barleycroft Farm/Hanson Paper 7).

Evans, C. and Pollard, J. 1995. *The Excavation of a Ring-Ditch and Prehistoric Fieldsystem at Barleycroft Farm, Bluntisham, Cambridgeshire, 1994.* Cambridge: Cambridge Archaeological Unit (Barleycroft Farm/ARC Paper 2).

Gdaniec, K. 1992. *Archaeological Observations at Barleycroft Farm, Bluntisham.* Cambridge: Cambridge Archaeological Unit.

Gdaniec, K. 1995. *Archaeological Investigations at Barleycroft Farm: the Plant Extension Site.* Cambridge: Cambridge Archaeological Unit (Barleycroft Farm/ARC Paper 3).

Knight, M. 1999. *Willingham/Over Pipeline Re-routing: Archaeological Investigations.* Cambridge: Cambridge Archaeological Unit (Over/Hanson Paper 5).

Pollard, J. 1998. *Excavations at Over: Late Neolithic Occupation (Sites 3 & 4).* Cambridge: Cambridge Archaeological Unit (Over/ARC Paper 4).

References

Barrett, J. C. 1988. The living, the dead, and the ancestors: Neolithic and Early Bronze Age mortuary practices. In Barrett, J. C. and Kinnes, I. (eds) *The Archaeology of Context in the Neolithic and Bronze Age: Recent Trends,* 30–41. Sheffield: Department of Archaeology and Prehistory, University of Sheffield.

Barrett, J. C., Bradley, R. J. and Green, M. 1991. *Landscape, Monuments and Society: the Prehistory of Cranborne Chase.* Cambridge: Cambridge University Press.

Bond, D. 1988. *Excavation at the North Ring, Mucking, Essex.* Chelmsford: East Anglian Archaeology Monograph 43.

Bradley, R. 1975. The Bronze Age occupation in its wider context. In Bradley, R. and Ellison, A. *Rams Hill: a Bronze Age Defended Enclosure and its Landscape,* 150–170. Oxford: British Archaeological Reports, British Series 19.

Brück, J. 1999. Houses, lifecycles and deposition on Middle Bronze Age settlements in southern England. *Proceedings of the Prehistoric Society* 65, 145–166.

Dawson, M. 1996. Plantation Quarry, Willington: Excavations 1988–91. *Bedfordshire Archaeological Journal* 22, 2–49.

Edmonds, M., Evans, C. and Gibson, D. 1999. Assembly and collection – lithic complexes in the Cambridgeshire Fenlands. *Proceedings of the Prehistoric Society* 65, 47–87.

Ellison, A. and Drewett, P. 1971. Pits and post-holes in the British early iron age: some alternative explanations. *Proceedings of the Prehistoric Society* 37, 183–194.

Evans, C. 1987. Nomads in 'waterland'?: prehistoric transhumance and fenland archaeology. *Proceedings of the Cambridge Antiquarian Society* 76, 27–39.

Evans, C. 1988. Acts of enclosure: a consideration of concentrically organised causewayed enclosures. In Barrett, J. C. and Kinnes, I. (eds) *The Archaeology of Context in the Neolithic and Bronze Age: Recent Trends*, 85–96. Sheffield: Department of Archaeology and Prehistory, University of Sheffield.

Evans, C. 1998. The Lingwood Wells: a waterlogged first millennium BC settlement at Cottenham, Cambridgeshire. *Proceedings of the Cambridge Antiquarian Society* 87, 11–30.

Evans, C. Forthcoming a. *Power and Island Communities: Excavation of the Wardy Hill Ringwork, Coveney, Ely.* Chelmsford: East Anglian Archaeology Monographs.

Evans, C. Forthcoming b. Metalwork and 'cold claylands': pre-Iron Age occupation on the Isle of Ely. In Lane, T. and Coles, J. (eds) *Through Wet and Dry: Proceedings of a Conference in Honour of David Hall.* Lincolnshire Archaeology and Heritage Report 5/WARP Occasional Paper 17.

Evans, C. and Knight, M. 2000. A fenland delta: later prehistoric land-use in the lower Ouse Reaches. In Dawson, M. (ed.) *Prehistoric, Roman and Saxon Landscape Studies in the Great Ouse Valley*, 89–106. London: Council for British Archaeology Research Report 119.

Evans, C., Pollard, J. and Knight, M. 1999. Life in woods: tree-throws, 'settlement' and forest cognition. *Oxford Journal of Archaeology* 18, 241–254.

Evans, C. and Hodder, I. Forthcoming. *Marshland Communities and Cultural Landscape: the Haddenham Project 1981–87, Vol. II.* Cambridge: McDonald Institute Research Series.

Evans, C. and Pollard, J. Forthcoming. Storey's Bar Road sub-site – a re-appraisal. In Pryor, F. *Archaeology and Environment of the Flag Fen Basin.* London: English Heritage Archaeological Report.

Field, K. 1974. Ring-ditches of the Upper and Middle Great Ouse Valley. *Archaeological Journal* 31, 58–74.

Fleming, A. 1988. *The Dartmoor Reaves: Investigating Prehistoric Land Divisions.* London: Batsford.

Fox, C. 1923. *The Archaeology of the Cambridge Region.* Cambridge: Cambridge University Press.

Guttmann, E. B. A. and Last, J. 2000. A Late Bronze Age landscape at South Hornchurch, Essex. *Proceedings of the Prehistoric Society* 66, 319–354.

Hall, D. N. 1996. *Cambridgeshire Survey: Isle of Ely and Wisbech.* Cambridge: Fenland Project Report 10/East Anglian Archaeology Monograph 79.

Hall, D. N. and Coles, J. 1995. *The Fenland Survey: an Essay in Landscape and Persistence.* London: English Heritage.

Hill, J. D., Evans, C. and Alexander, M. 1999. The Hinxton Rings – a Late Iron Age cemetery at Hinxton, Cambridgeshire, with a reconsideration of northern Ayles-ford-Swarling distributions. *Proceedings of Prehistoric Society* 65, 243–274.

Healy, F., Cleal, R. M. J. and Kinnes, I. 1993. Excavations on Redgate Hill, Hunstanton, 1970 and 1971. In Bradley, R., Chowne, P., Cleal, R. M. J., Healy, F. and Kinnes, I. 1993. *Excavations on Redgate Hill, Hunstanton, Norfolk, and at Tattershall Thorpe, Lincolnshire*, xii, xiv, 1–77. Chelmsford: East Anglian Archaeology Monograph 57.

Hodder, I. and Evans, C. Forthcoming. *The Emergence of a Fen-edge Landscape: the Haddenham Project 1981–87, Vol. I.* Cambridge: McDonald Institute Research Series.

Knight, D. 1984. *Late Bronze Age and Iron Age Settlement in the Nene and Great Ouse Basins.* Oxford: British Archaeological Reports, British Series 130.

Malim, T. 2000. The ritual landscape of the Neolithic and Bronze Age along the middle and lower Ouse Valley. In Dawson, M. (ed.) *Prehistoric, Roman and Saxon Landscape Studies in the Great Ouse Valley*, 57–88. London: Council for British Archaeology Research Report 119.

Mawson, A. 1989. *The Triumph of Life: Religion and Politics among the Agar Dinka of Southern Sudan.* Unpublished Ph.D. thesis, University of Cambridge.

Moore, J. and Jennings, D. 1992. *Reading Business Park: a Bronze Age Landscape.* Oxford: Oxford Archaeological Unit.

Needham, S. P. 1992. The structure of settlement and ritual in the Late Bronze Age of South-East Britain. In Mordant, C. and Richard, A. (eds) *L'Habitat et l'Occupation du Sol à l'Âge du Bronze en Europe*, 49–69. Paris: Editions du Comité des Travaux Historiques et Scientifiques. Documents Prehistoriques 4.

Needham, S. and Ambers, J. 1994. Redating Rams Hill and reconsidering Bronze Age enclosure. *Proceedings of the Prehistoric Society* 60, 225–243.

Needham, S. and Spence, T. 1996. *Refuse and Disposal at Area 16 East Runnymede, Runnymede Bridge Excavations*, vol. 2. London: British Museum Press.

Parker Pearson, M. 1993. *Bronze Age Britain.* London: Batsford.

Pollard, J. 1996. Iron Age riverside pit alignments at St. Ives, Cambridgeshire. *Proceedings of the Prehistoric Society* 62, 93–115.

Pollard, J. 1999. 'These places have their moments': thoughts on occupation practices in the British Neolithic. In Brück, J. and Goodman, M. (eds) *Making Places in the Prehistoric World: Themes in Settlement Archaeology*, 76–93. London: UCL. Press.

Pryor, F. M. M. 1980. *Excavation at Fengate, Peterborough, England: the Third Report.* Northamptonshire Archaeological Society Monograph 1/Royal Ontario Museum Archaeological Monograph 6.

Pryor, F. M. M. 1991. *Flag Fen.* London: Batsford.

Pryor, F. M. M. 1996. Sheep, stockyards and field systems: Bronze Age livestock populations in the Fenlands of Eastern England. *Antiquity* 70, 313–324.

Pryor, F. M. M. 1998. *Farmers in Prehistoric Britain.* Stroud: Tempus.

Pryor, F. M. M. 2001. *Seahenge: New Discoveries in Prehistoric Britain.* London: HarperCollins.

Pryor, F. M. M. Forthcoming. *Archaeology and Environment of the Flag Fen Basin*. London: English Heritage Archaeological Report.

Schlee, D. E. 1995. *Excavation of a Romano-British Settlement on the Needingworth Bypass*. Cambridge: Cambridgeshire County Council Field Archaeological Unit Report 99.

Taylor, M. 1992. Flag Fen: the wood. *Antiquity* 66, 476–498.

Tilley, C. 1994. *A Phenomenology of Landscape*. Oxford: Berg.

Waller, M. 1994. *Flandrian Environmental change in Fenland*. Norwich: East Anglian Archaeology Report 70/Fenland Project Report 9.

Yates, D. T. 1999. Bronze Age field systems in the Thames Valley. *Oxford Journal of Archaeology* 18, 157–170.

Wilhelmi, K. 1987. Zur Besiedlungsgenese Englands und des nordwestlichen Kontinents von 1500 vor bis Christi Geburt. *Acta Praehistorica et Archaelogica* 19, 71–84.

9 'Breaking new ground': land tenure and fieldstone clearance during the Bronze Age

Robert Johnston

In upland areas during the second millennium BC, people cleared stone from the soil in order to improve the land for cultivation and pasture. The stone was used to build cairns and field banks that survive today as a durable signature of extensive human occupation in what are now agriculturally marginal environments. This activity marked a variation in the way upland areas were inhabited, and it is often presented as evidence for the widespread changes in agriculture and settlement that distinguish the earlier from the later Bronze Age. The boundaries and clearance cairns are, in broad terms, accepted as evidence for a change in the way that rights to resources were articulated within and between communities. Although it is evident when considering archaeological remains such as the 'Celtic' fields on the Marlborough Downs that tenure over land was of critical concern to groups occupying the region, it is not so obvious how tenure was articulated among the plots and small cairns in the uplands. The subtlety with which tenure over resources was expressed in the uplands is evident at the later Bronze Age unenclosed settlements of Green Knowe, Peeblesshire, and Standrop Rigg, Northumberland.

The timber houses at Green Knowe, constructed on roughly circular terraces on the hillside, were each surrounded by a bank of stone originating from the surrounding fields (Jobey 1981). As the fields were farmed, the stone was cleared and piled up around each house with only a slight gap left for the entrance. On one of the platforms (platform 2), where there had been at least two structures built on the same terrace, the bank of stone was particularly large (Fig. 9.1). Among the stones, by the entrance, there was a substantial quantity of refuse, including broken pottery, fragments of two shale objects and numerous stone rubbers. The amount of stone around platform 2 increased during the life of the

house that it surrounded, as evidenced by the interleaving of midden layers and stone. The clearest contrast, and one that may not have been obvious to the inhabitants of the settlement, was between the impermanent decaying house and the durable ring of fieldstone with which it was surrounded. When the platform was no longer in use, the ring of stone would have been a reminder to those who returned to the locale of the size and shape of the house, fossilised in the ring of stone.

At Standrop Rigg, investigations were undertaken in the area of six huts associated with numerous low banks, lynchets and small cairns (Jobey 1983). Most of the cairns lay within the fields, although two were conjoined with the banks of the field system. As at Green Knowe, some of the platforms were surrounded by low banks of stone. These were formed during the life of the houses, but in at least one case they continued to be the focus for the deposition of stone even after the house had fallen out of use; the shape of the original house was respected and remembered in the ring of stone (Fig. 9.1). The field system that had built up around the houses at Standrop Rigg was in several places attached directly to the rings of stone. The field banks did not differ in composition from the rings of stone; they never stood as walls, nor was there any evidence for there having been a hedge or a row of posts. The low banks would seem to have marked out areas of land in the same way as the rings of stone delimited the house.

At both Green Knowe and Standrop Rigg, fieldstone was deliberately placed around the exterior of domestic structures. The house was incorporated within the field system, and therefore included within the material network that defined resources for the purpose of initiating or asserting usufruct. The evident symbolism of such an act – relating the domain of the family (the house), associated with

Green Knowe
Platform 2

Standrop Rigg
Hut 4

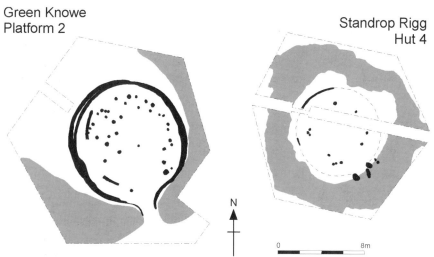

Fig. 9.1 *The 'rings' of fieldstone deposited around the later Bronze Age huts at Green Knowe, Peebleshire, and Standrop Rigg, Northumberland. The post-holes and ring grooves of the huts are depicted in black, and the bank of stone is shaded grey (after Jobey 1981 and 1983)*

structures of kinship and inheritance, to the field, associated with agricultural production, fertility and subsistence – can now only be crudely represented. The close connections between these social domains were elements of daily life, expressed during the activities undertaken in both house and field. The material traces of fieldstone clearance enforced the informality of this process. However, once the stone had accumulated, it would have contributed to any structuring or negotiation of land tenure since both house and field were demarcated in stone.

For such an interpretation to be acceptable, land tenure cannot be explained in terms of a static relationship between social organisation and land. Instead, tenure varies according to the agricultural practices that reproduce it and the social networks of which it is a part. In this paper, I intend to consider, firstly, how tenure might be defined as a structural rule and resource, and secondly, what difference such a definition makes to the interpretation of later prehistoric fieldstone clearance.

Perspectives on land tenure

Tenure has long been of interest to those studying the relations between humans and the land. Practitioners in the fields of ethnography, anthropology, history and jurisprudence have left a substantial record of the many different forms of land tenure found throughout the world. A central catalyst for this research has been the conflict between indigenous, otherwise known as customary or traditional, and colonial systems of land tenure. As a result, we have a large archive of sources through which we can study the great variety of land tenure systems.

Although there is an obvious bias in many cases towards communities that have undergone significant changes as a result of contact with Western societies, the emphasis on history and process is in contrast to the rather ahistoric representations of social life that can be found in other ethnographic accounts written in the first half of this century – a factor of the dynamic, eristic context in which the research was undertaken. A central concern of many studies has been to explore the dynamic nature of land tenure systems, often graduating from the parcels of nested rights over resources associated with communal forms of tenure to the direct ownership of land to be found among Westernised communities (e.g. Damas 1994; Migot-Adholla and Bruce 1994; Spear 1997). Such a historical perspective on ownership and tenure originates in the models inspired by nineteenth century evolutionists such as Lewis Henry Morgan who believed the move to the private ownership of property was a sudden and dramatic change that marked the commencement of civilisation (Netting 1993, 168; cf. the ecological rationale of Fredrich Engels 1972, 202).

The definitions of land tenure employed in most anthropological accounts equate tenure with the rights to land and the rights to farm or work the land as held by groups or individuals. The legal connotations that are associated with the term 'tenure' are somewhat distractive since in most respects the forms of tenure have little in common with modern Western attitudes to property and ownership (cf. Meek 1948; Elias 1951). It is better to think of tenure as polysemic, including in its definition not only property but also concepts such as obligation, attachment and usufruct. At the broadest level, tenure makes up the bundles of rights that people hold over the land: 'it is the relation of man to the soil in the widest sense' (Malinowski 1935, 319). This ecological dimension to tenure is often considered to be its most important feature. Land tenure is a mediator between the social and the natural world: '[it] is a system of patterns of behaviour that specifically serve to control a society's use of environmental resources' (Crocombe 1974, 2). Tim Ingold was referring to this relationship between social and natural worlds when he defined tenure as 'an aspect of that system of relations which *constitutes* persons as productive agents and directs their purposes' (Ingold 1986, 130, original emphasis; see Kitchen this volume for further discussion). Tenure is therefore not simply the relationship between people and the soil, it represents the appropriation and transcendence of the natural world by humans: '*tenure engages nature in a system of social relations*' (Ingold 1986, 136, original emphasis). A social perspective recognises that 'rights to land' presuppose relations between people as well as between people and the land (Digim'rina 1995, 3). Robert Netting, for example, uses tenure to represent the rights to private property (including resources) held by individuals and families (Netting 1993, 157). Defining tenure in terms of the social world does not limit at what scale tenure is structured; for some researchers, it is almost solely a local concern operating and changing at the level of the family or village, whereas for others, tenure is affected by broader socio-political, demographic and technological factors (e.g. Ward and Kingdom 1995).

Among communities practising cultivation, the range of forms of tenure is impressive. It is usual to find a diverse range of practices, with various types of tenure associated with different resources and the means of acquiring those resources. Tenure can operate in three dimensions. For example, trees are often an important resource, and each tree may provide a variety of products over which different members of a group have access. The tenure of a type of tree can be split between gender groups, with women having rights over deadwood and leaf litter, and men having access to trunks for foundation beams and beehives located in the trees (Rocheleau and Edmunds 1997). These nested rights of access and use are also temporal: cultivated land is held by a family for growing crops, but when the crop has been harvested the stubble is a resource that any member of the community may use for pasture. In the Pearl River delta of south China, these nested rights are taken a stage further, as different rights are conferred on topsoil and 'bottom soil' (Siu and Faure 1995). Communal ownership is often resolved into 'clusters of specific rights which groups and individuals hold over a piece of land, its uses, and its products' (Gluckman 1943, 27).

Time is another variable quality of systems of land rights. Tenure implies, after all, resource use through time, and the dictionary definition of tenure equates it with time. Historically, land is enmeshed in the biographies of subjects and within the trajectories of groups (Ingold 1986, 137). As the words of a Nigerian herder quoted by Lane illustrate, 'land belongs to a vast family of which many are dead, few are living and countless members are still unborn' (Lane 1998, 1). The herder mentions three temporally distinct groups, but they remain part of the same family and they hold equal rights to the land. Time is therefore a crucial aspect of tenure as social relations. Past and future usufruct have a potent relationship with the present. Time is also a feature of the everyday reworking of land tenure relations. In Mai Weini, Eritrea, time is the measure of space, and it cannot be disassociated from the practices undertaken in that space. The villagers measure the size of a plot in *tsimidi* – the amount of land a pair of oxen are capable of ploughing in one day (Tronvoll 1998, 241). This amount varies with the quality of the soil, the relative difficulty of the local climate for working (hot weather will require a longer mid-day break), and the distance of the plot of land from the village (the day lasts from when the farmer reaches the field in the morning until he stops work in order to get home before dark). Aside from time and temporality, tenure is also influenced by tempo: the rhythms of the seasons, the growth of crops and the regeneration of gardens. Swidden fields, for example, have life-cycles around which resource use and land tenure are organised.

The four dimensions of space and time make up the multi-dimensionality of land tenure (cf. Kelly 1992, 60). The rights to resources are governed by historical precedents of access and use, identity, social relations of power, daily patterns of use and management and the long term investment of labour (Rocheleau and Edmunds 1997, 1352). Considering this variety, it is clear why descriptions of land tenure often reveal 'complex parcels of divergent practices' (Ward and Kingdom 1995, 8). Nevertheless, it does not explain why studies of long term change tend to come to similar conclusions about topics such as the individuation of land holding and the impact of agricultural intensification (e.g. Boserup 1965). The categories that have been set up in order to facilitate the synthesis of land tenure systems is partly responsible for this, but these categories should not be seen as infallible:

> Tenure is not either private or communal; property does not parse neatly into open access, common, and private; groups are not either closed-corporate or open-atomistic. Rights in the same physical field may be partitioned among private owners, temporary cultivators, possessors of trees or buildings

on the land, those with rights of easement to travel across the land, and a whole community permitted to graze their animals on the crop stubble. Where private property rights have great importance, as they do among smallholders, they can become legally complex and richly diversified. The several types of property use, holding, inheritance, transfer, and administration that are actively present, known and enforced in a community of intensive cultivators (as opposed to the laws on the books and the official regulations of the state) represent a careful adjustment of social rules and practices to ecological facts (Netting 1993, 182).

Gardening and magic in Papua New Guinea

One of the earliest anthropological monographs on agricultural practice and land tenure is Bronislaw Malinowski's detailed study of a village community on the Trobriand Islands (Malinowski 1935). Gardens are important among the Trobriand Islanders because there is a close ontological connection between the soil and human beings: the origins of humanity are in the soil, and the ancestors of a sub-clan or local group emerged from the ground bringing their knowledge of 'garden magic' with them. The location where this first emergence took place becomes the hereditary territory of the group. As a consequence of the value attributed to gardens, the work that is undertaken is not confined to everyday behaviour, but is linked to a complex suite of rites and small-scale ritual performances that come under the general term of 'magic': 'The two ways, the way of magic and the way of garden work – *megwa la keda, bagula la keda* – are inseparable' (Malinowski 1935, 76). There is a strict sequence to the activities that are carried out in the main yam gardens or *leywota* – carefully tended plots that are representative of gardens in general. In the first instance, the individual plots are allocated to families by the chief or headman. These ceremonial and strictly formal components are then superseded by small-scale rituals that are performed by the garden magician. Clearance of the plots can only be undertaken once these rites have been performed. The preparation of gardens is a complex, meaningful activity that is concurrently a part of day-to-day life and a formalised expression of people's origins and place in the world.

Lawrence, during his research among the Garia in the Madang district, Papua New Guinea, also observed a close connection between gardening and magic (Lawrence 1955). The key figures involved in the preparation of the Garia gardens are the garden leaders. They hold a monopoly on ritual knowledge which they use to regulate the stages of garden production. Lawrence considered land tenure to be closely related to social structure, and taking a functionalist position, he identified a irrefutable relationship between kinship, economy and ritual:

> Ultimately, therefore, religion is the cornerstone of land tenure, for it validates the system. On the one hand, fear of retribution from the spirits of the dead induces respect for both personal and patrilineage land rights, and rationalises the complex of relationships which they promote. On the other, ritual beliefs and practices justify traditional agricultural techniques and set in motion the system of land use by co-ordinating the activities of heterogeneous clusters of fellow cultivators (Lawrence 1955, 45).

The stress that both Malinowski and Lawrence place on social relations rather than land use as a determinate of land tenure is supported in Digim'rina's study of the Basima, Milne Bay Province, Papua New Guinea (Digim'rina 1995). He accepts that the availability of land is relevant, but argues that the main determining factor is social relations, characterised by group and individual claims to land. The contradictions between group and individual rights come into being when the two become interwoven:

> The social complexities of "ownership" are sometimes such that paradoxes and contradictions in man-property relations are revealed whenever there is disputation over land and the rhetorical, ideological claims of the group are woven into the pragmatic claims of individuals (Digim'rina 1995, 194).

Land is part of a social geography that encompasses the relations within a group as well as external contacts between communities. The identity of the group is manifested in the various types of land that it holds: the area around the hamlet centred on the hole of emergence, cultivated land, foraging and hunting ground, and *susu* (community)-owned land. Together, these form a community's identity, primarily through the historical attachment to place articulated in ancestral myths and continued in existing social relationships: 'a group's special relationship to the land it calls its own is immutable, non-transferable, and inalienable, for it is principally from the group-land relationship that the *susu* derives its identity, belonging, power and prestige' (Digim'rina 1995, 199).

There is a strong relationship between people and the land in the examples from Papua New Guinea. Neither Malinowski, Lawrence nor Digim'rina relate this to the practicalities of food production; it is for deeply embedded reasons allied to a community's origin myth. The link between a group and its local area is centred on the hole of emergence where the founding ancestors left the soil in order to establish the village. The formality of the society-land relations that this expresses is maintained in the small-scale rites that accompany the allocation of gardens and the clearance of the plots for agriculture. This magic is a visible and no doubt at times discursive means of maintaining the ontological basis of the villagers' attachment to place. Although not discussed above, it is also closely related to the fertility of the soil and the growth of crops – another and more quotidian aspect of the relations between humans and the soil. Practical non-discursive actions such as the clearance of stone from the fields and formal activities such as garden magic are bound together in the generation and reproduction of the same structures. To what extent the latter can be said to be discursively motivated is not clear from the functional studies of Malinowski and Lawrence, but it would seem that routine everyday actions are combined in quite complex ways with so-called ritual practices, and together both are implicated in the long-term maintenance of the ontological link between a community and the soil.

Not one of the three studies, knowingly or otherwise, agrees with the link Ester Boserup (1965) made between land tenure and land use. In each case, the system of rights to land and inheritance is interpreted as a consequence of social relations, entirely independent of the type of agriculture practised. It is reasonable to argue that social relations are implicated during day-to-day conduct, as Lawrence rightly recognised; the relations of kinship and land tenure were 'further reinforced by daily contact' (Lawrence 1955, 44). Nonetheless, this entirely socialised world would seem to lack an explicit physicality that must certainly have existed. The evidence for this is implicit in both Malinowski's and Digim'rina's accounts. In the latter, the plots and gardens have different land tenure regimes associated with each of the various classes of land use. A distinction is made between rights over hunting grounds and rights to cultivated land close to the village. The Trobriand Islanders also have different categories of gardens, with the formal rites of garden magic used in the main yam gardens or *leywota*. The way in which we choose to interpret this evidence depends on whether or not precedence is given to land use or to social structure. In light of the rethinking of these frameworks, it is possible to interpret tenure as dependent on and influencing practice rather than isolating either land use or social identity.

Summary

Land tenure varies across time-space according to the practices with which the resource is associated. This relationship between land use and tenure is widely recognised but the multi-dimensional contextual character of tenure is far from accommodated within general models of land tenure. Instead of seeing tenure as being a direct consequence of agricultural practices, it should be both a medium and an outcome of land use. Agricultural practice structures land tenure and is itself structured by land tenure. The tenure over particular resources is therefore both multi-dimensional and contextual: multi-dimensional in that it varies according to practices situated in time-space, and contextual in its dualistic relationship to land use.

One of the principal themes illustrated by the examples from Papua New Guinea is the process by which tenure is established over an area of land. The initiation of rights over resources is situated within existing structures of significance and domination. Such structures may include the history of the locale and its connection with particular elements of a group's history, for instance the association of ancestral spirits with the resource. This 'myth of the original ancestors' is characteristic of many pastoral communities – the land comes to be held by the living community as a gift from the ancestors. The gift of land establishes an inalienable bond between the givers and receivers. The Orang Suku Laut, sea nomads from Indonesia, consider land in such a way (Chou 1997).

The material expression of resource tenure cannot be restricted to the physical enclosure of land, but must also be associated with the practice of working land or using a resource and the material residues consequential with resource use. In some cases, the only visible material signature of land tenure may be evidence for the practical negotiation by communities with existing structures, such as an ancestral past. The establishment of rights to a plot of land by clearance and by cultivation is often to be found among small-scale farmers. The Ibo of southeast Nigeria and some Maori groups establish tenure through cultivation (Green 1941; Kawharu 1977). The Wa-Bena in Tanzania acquire tenure over land following its clearance – 'my field' reverting to 'my old field' after cultivation of the plot has ceased (Meek 1949, 19). In Mai Weini in Eritrea, rights to habitation in the village – *tisha* – are based on the construction of a house (Tronvoll 1998, 232). In Basima, discussed above, there are two aboriginal groups, *tutupawa*, whose claim to land is ahistoric and incorporates large areas that their ancestors had 'walked upon', made tracks, laid stones, planted trees and cultivated (Digim'rina 1995, 200*ff*). However, there were many areas of garden land that were not 'claimed', and these were appropriated by immigrant groups, *wagawaga*, who acquired rights by clearing, cultivating or simply by trekking over the land and naming places during the process. These claims are historical and called simply *gabu* meaning 'burn'. The material manifestation of tenure, if it exists at all, may therefore be both varied and subtle.

Bronze Age fieldstone clearance in northern England

The construction of prominent boundary systems during the second millennium BC, such as those found on Dartmoor or the Wessex chalkland, are routinely presented as evidence for an increased emphasis on control or tenure over areas of land. The extension of this argument to include the irregular systems of plots, linear clearance features and small cairns found in upland areas is much more difficult (see also Kitchen this volume). In many cases, the straggling banks of stone do not completely enclose an area of land, and the cairns do not define prominent places that might be associated with larger territorial boundaries, as has been suggested for earlier Bronze Age ritual monuments, particularly barrows. Despite this, there is evidence in the structure of some of the small cairns, for instance the incorporation of token burials, to suggest that they are implicated in establishing, asserting or maintaining rights to land by acting as temporal markers to critical moments in the history of the field (Johnston 2000). This interpretation of the cairnfields is weakened by the use of a definition of tenure that relies almost entirely on its association with time and temporality. What is clear from the discussion in the previous section is that rights to land, and more importantly the initiation of rights to land, should be discussed in terms of the practices associated with resource use and the structures that generate and are reproduced by such practices. The following interpretative analysis of fieldstone clearance in Cumbria attempts to link the clearance of fieldstone, as the material signature of resource use, with structures of legitimation that facilitated the initiation of resource use.

Cairnstone: cairnfields on the Cumbrian fells

The mixture of informal activity creating divisions and emphasis within the immediate environs of daily life, and the formal expression of resource usufruct preserved as fieldstone clearance is apparent in the structure of the small cairns found among the fields at sites such as Standrop Rigg. Such cairnfields consist of groups of small cairns of varying sizes and shapes numbering from only a few to many hundreds (e.g. Cherry 1961; Jobey 1968; Fleming 1971). They are generally located on flat or gently sloping southerly facing sites, and are often found in association with large, more elaborate cairns, ring cairns or cists. In some regions, they are located within small systems of plots and close to settlements.

A central concern in the study and excavation of cairnfields has been the distinction between cairns with a sepulchral function and those built as a consequence of agricultural activity (e.g. Ashbee 1957; Graham 1959; Yates 1984; Young and Welfare 1992; Barnatt 1994; Barber 1997). The use of this dualism has several implications: 'clearance' cairns are interpreted as being informal and unstructured; they are consequently discussed in collective terms – the cairnfield – and rarely, if ever, considered singly. The cairnfields are used as evidence for economic activity, as demonstrated by the unsophisticated structure of the cairns. As a result, cairnfields, and the 'intensive' agricultural regimes with which they are associated, are isolated from socio-ritual explanations of other upland monuments such as burial mounds. The evidence from sites such as Chatton Sandyford, High Knowes and Millstone Hill in Northumberland does not support this division between cairns for clearance and cairns for burial (Johnston 2000). So-called clearance cairns have evidence for deliberate deposits of charred material and artefacts, their structure includes elements of careful construction similar to burial monuments, and they incorporate pre-existing features such as earthfast boulders. Taken together, these elements are evidence for formalised clearance practices. In the following examples from Cumbria, these patterns will once more be emphasised, and a clearer interpretation of the role of fieldstone clearance in structuring resource tenure will be discussed.

The large cairnfield of Barnscar, located on Birkby Fell, near Ravenglass in western Cumbria, consists of approximately four hundred small cairns of varying sizes and shapes spread over 25.5 hectares of the southerly slopes of the fellside. They were first recorded in the nineteenth century by C. W. Dymond who, uncharacteristically for the time, recognised and surveyed even the more irregular and ephemeral stone heaps and traces of stone banks: 'In ancient areas of cultivation, similar banks are frequently found: and, in many such cases, it is natural to suppose that they may have been cast up to define the limits of holdings' (Dymond 1893, 180*ff*). He went on to excavate 14 of the cairns: 'In these [cairns] were found, in an inverted position, several small cinerary urns, of the type commonly called "British", a few fragments of pottery, and some burnt bone' (Dymond 1893, 186). Two of the pottery vessels have survived; both are collared urns. A further ten cairns at Barnscar were investigated by Walker in the 1950s (Walker 1965). Two were structureless heaps of stones resting on the subsoil, while the other eight sealed anthropogenic deposits and features. Although individual descriptions were not published for the cairns, a general sequence of deposits was provided. Above the boulder clay and weathered brash, there was a darker 'loamy' clay that was interpreted as a buried

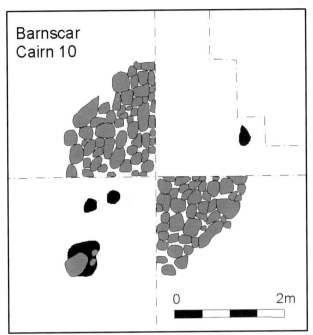

Barnscar
Cairn 10

0   2m

Fig. 9.2 A simplified plan of cairn 10, Barnscar,
showing the four pits filled with charred material and
burnt stone - depicted in black - and the covering
mound of stones - shaded grey (after Walker 1965)

mounds disturbed in the nineteenth century. Yet, the cairns that Dymond excavated were undistinguished: they were neither particularly large, nor were they in prominent locations within the cairnfield. Of the other ten cairns that he examined, we can only presume that they were either structureless or covered insubstantial pits or hollows, as with those dug sixty years later. The cairns without burials are nevertheless interesting. The hollows and pits may be the result of clearing tree stumps as Walker tentatively suggests (Walker 1965, 62). They may also relate to the deliberate 'quarrying' of stones from the boulder clay in order to build the cairn. At cairn 10, for example, there were four pits (Fig. 9.2). Three of these were small, no more than 0.3m in diameter and 0.1m deep, and preserved beneath the stone. Another more substantial pit, 0.3m deep, had been cut into the disturbed boulder clay/brash 2m beyond the limit of the covering mound. If it were not for the charcoal and burnt stones in the fill of these cut features, they might have been disregarded as stone holes. Although that may be the means by which they were formed, the presence of a deliberate fill and the effort to seal them with a layer of clay suggests that this activity was formalised. A sequence that began with the clearance of vegetation and the breaking of new ground was completed by the deliberate 'filling in' of burnt material, including stone, and the sealing of the 'wounds' with fresh clay and a mound of stones.

The presence of formalised structural elements and unusual or special deposits at Barnscar can be paralleled at other excavated cairnfields in the region. On Carrock Fell, on the northeastern edge of the Cumbrian Fells, three cairnfields with over two hundred cairns were investigated on several occasions. At one, an area of rammed clay with charcoal was used as the base for a ring of boulders that was in turn heaped over with stones; there were two flint flakes recovered from the mound (Spence 1935, 174). Three other cairns produced similar results: an elliptical mound overlay a deposit of reddish earth and charcoal; a second cairn had been heaped over a 0.1m thick deposit of 'yellow earth' and charcoal; the third also overlay a deposit of yellow earth and charcoal, on this occasion with a continuous thin layer of charcoal (Barker 1951, 201–202). Another of the cairns overlay a central pit containing charcoal and burnt bone (Barker 1934, 108). On Corney Fell in west Cumberland, two cairns were examined in a cairnfield of roughly seventy cairns. One of the cairns (4.25m in diameter) did not contain unusual deposits although the stone had been placed in a structured manner with the larger stones at the centre and smaller stones forming the top and periphery of the mound. Another cairn, approximately 8m in diameter, was structured with the

soil by the excavator. It survived in patches most frequently located towards the centre of the cairn; elsewhere it had been stripped before the stones were piled on top, or it had since eroded. In the areas where the buried soil had been stripped, there were frequent shallow pits filled with partially burnt stones and a dark brown loam with charcoal fragments. These pits were roughly circular to irregular in plan, and less than 0.5m across. The profiles varied from very shallow dished features to steep sided, flat bottomed pits, 0.2–0.4m deep. What was to become the interior of the cairn was then sealed with a sterile layer of boulder clay that may have been the spoil excavated from the pits. The cairn material, made up of stones excavated from the pits and collected from the surrounding area, was piled on top of this spoil, although no effort was made to seal all the pits or stripped ground surface.

Pollen recovered from the mineral soil underlying the cairn was dominated by tree taxa, particularly birch, oak, alder and hazel. This led Walker to suggest that the cairns were associated with the primary clearance of the woodland, probably during the Bronze Age. However, he did not feel that the cairns resulted from field clearance: 'The use of excavated clay in their construction, as well as the great likelihood that many of the stones were themselves obtained by excavation, suggests that the cairns were made for some particular purpose' (Walker 1965, 61). The 'purpose' is not at all obvious. There were cremations buried in several of the larger stones around the outside and smaller stones towards the centre. The mound overlay a central deposit of 'pink and white ash flecked with charcoal' (Ward 1977, 1). At Bolton Wood, a small cairn had been constructed on top of a large boulder. Beneath the boulder was a 0.3m thick deposit of black earth along with charcoal, some small fragments of burnt bone and a charred hazelnut (Spence 1937, 47). At Threlkeld, on the northern Cumbrian Fells, three excavated cairns in a cairnfield were shown to be structured with large stones in the centre making up the core of the feature and small stones on top and around the periphery (Dymond and Hodgson 1902, 48*ff*). One of three cairns at Threepow Rise, Moor Divock, contained 'pockets of charcoal' and a single deposit of dark earth and charcoal at the base (Spence 1935). Five further cairns were excavated at the small cairnfield at Milkingstead, in Eskdale (Hodgson 1928). All of the cairns here contained at least two stone lined pits, some of which had intact covering stones. There were no finds from the structures excepting a burnt area beneath one of the mounds.

Small cairns, that are to all intents monuments for the deposition of fieldstone, are in many cases deliberately structured. They are not ubiquitously amorphous, structureless heaps of stone. The most obvious feature of the cairns is the presence of burnt or charred deposits beneath the stone mound. These may be ephemeral features such as those under the cairns at Carrock Fell and Corney Fell, or they may be relatively substantial features such as those investigated at Barnscar. Cairns are built on 'found-ation' deposits that in many cases are marked by slight traces of burning, and exceptionally consist of human burials, for instance the cremated bone recovered at Bolton Wood. The mound of fieldstone that makes up the body of the cairn can include structural features reminiscent of burial monuments, such as the outer kerbs of stone that defined the limits of one of the cairns in Carrock Fell. However, elsewhere, the structure of the monument may be no more complex than the grading of stone with large stones in the centre and smaller stones outside. Together, these features represent a temporal and spatial commemoration of fieldstone clearance. The significance of this in terms of identifying resource tenure in the archaeological record is discussed in the following section.

'Breaking new ground' and the transformation of fieldstone into cairnstone

For archaeology, the clearance of fieldstone has defined the agricultural landscapes of the second millennium BC in the uplands of Britain. The stones may have been cleared for a variety of reasons, just one of which might have been in order to improve cultivated land. At a regional scale of analysis, the distribution of cairnfields is discontinuous, with clear evidence for patterning. In Dumfriesshire and the North York Moors, for example, the cairnfields are situated on predominately southerly facing slopes at altitudes below 300m OD (Fleming 1971, 21; Yates 1984, 220–223; RCAHMS 1997, 46, fig. 41). This patterning is undoubtedly the result of many different factors. Nonetheless, the commonsensical observation that the cairnfields are situated in places more suitable for cultivation cannot be avoided. Whatever the exact context of fieldstone clearance, which in any case cannot be established from the examples from Cumbria discussed above, it is evident that the process of clearing stone involved labour with the soil. The construction of the cairn, field bank or ring of stone around a house involved a practical engagement between the individuals involved and the land.

The chronological context of this activity is important. There is clear and unambiguous bias in both the radiocarbon dates and the structural evidence towards the second millennium BC. In northern England, the radiocarbon dates from six excavated cairnfields all calibrate to the end of the third millennium BC or the first half of the second millennium BC (Johnston 2000, 58 with additions). In support of this, the tradition of building burial monuments was at its most prolific and structured during the second millennium BC. The small cairns that otherwise have no evidence for a burial may contain rough kerbs, central pits, spreads of charcoal and deposited artefacts. These features are in no sense ubiquitous but they are sufficiently frequent, with at least one or two examples from every prehistoric cairnfield excavated under modern conditions. The presence of these material components in the construction of the cairns is not only relevant to how the cairns were conceived and constructed in a meaningful way, it links the mounds more or less directly into a wider cairn-building tradition. Whatever the long-term history of the cairnfield locales, and it is probable that such places were occupied intermittently over many centuries in the second millennium BC (Kitchen 2000), there is a discrete, radiocarbon-dated phase of cairn con-struction during the Bronze Age. The fact that samples suitable for radiocarbon dating are only likely to be found in cairns with special deposits does offer some indication as to why this coherency exists, and warns us against extrapolating these dates to include all cairnfields, or indeed to include all the cairns in the same locale.

The relationship between temporality and tenure is important. Yet, as I have attempted to demonstrate through a review of anthropological accounts of land tenure, there needs to be an 'opening out' of the definition of resource tenure encapsulating not only land use but the structuring properties of agricultural practices. A development of this idea is that resource tenure embodies the 'duality of structure', whereby it is both medium and outcome of the practices it recursively organises (Giddens 1984, 25). This can be illustrated using the archaeological examples presented in the previous section. Clearing stone from a field results in the building of physical markers, the cairns, that define and lay testimony to the labour of clearance. These markers record the clearance of a plot of land. Of course, there are other perhaps more formal markers that might have been used, such as lines of wooden sticks or more simply the limits of disturbed soil or vegetation. The difference between the cairns and other less durable markers is that once constructed, the stone monuments remained as physical reminders of the location of a once-cleared plot and the intensity or duration of occupation. Their meaning within an agent's memory – consisting of a knowledge of when, how and why they were constructed – structured future resource tenure at the locale.

If cairns are structuring features of both the physical and the social world, it is important to understand their temporal relationship with the locale in which they are situated. Fields have histories of occupation of which the cairnstone is a part. There is some dispute as to what period in a field's history the clearance of stone should be assigned. It could represent a gradual and cumulative effort over many years – the clearing of fieldstone being a recurring event closely associated with the short-term tempo of agricultural practice. Clearance could also be a special event linked to critical conditions in the history of the field, for instance the first working of the ground or a final attempt to restore fertility to a depleted and eroded soil. The archaeological and environmental evidence is rarely able to provide even a suggestion as to what practices were undertaken, and a broader study of ethnographic sources can only extend the range of possibilities. Yet, in considering the social conditions through which clearance was practised and the principles that were followed in the construction of the cairns, it is possible to suggest the relationship between fieldstone clearance and the history of the field.

At Barnscar, the cairns overlay stoneholes that had been filled with charred material and carefully covered with clay. The quarrying of stone and the deposition of what could be 'ritual offerings' to ensure the subsequent fertility of the land are best interpreted as an act of 'breaking new ground'. This first clearance of fieldstone was important because

of the social conditions that it reproduced: specifically, tenure over the land and/or its resources, and the relations between agents and the structures that tenure, in turn, relied on. For example, kinship, inheritance and the historical associations of the locale all contributed to legitimating the initiation of a field. Token deposits of human bone, as found at Bolton Wood, and the complete cinerary urns from Barnscar are a more conspicuous example of formal practices that legitimated tenure. Such practices are comparable to the accounts of gardening and magic in Papua New Guinea in terms of the intensity of the relationship expressed between people and the land. The relationship between people and the land they worked was a bonding of blood and soil. Even when new groups sought to colonise land, they did so in respect of an ancestral presence that could be legitimated only by naming and mythologising the surrounding landscape.

The informality apparent in the way fieldstone was cleared around the exterior of the houses at Green Knowe and Standrop Rigg may not appear conspicuous; nonetheless, it too legitimates tenure. The fieldstone joined the fields and the houses. The domestic and agricultural domains were critically linked through the lives and wider network of relationships of the inhabitants, and, as with the Nigerian herder quoted earlier, with the past and future members of the community. The enclosure of houses and fields within the same banks of stone was not accidental, although the resulting durable signature of both houses and fields had an unintended role in structuring future inhabitation of the locales. The houses and fields differ from the cairnfields in that they did not legitimate resource use in terms of long-term social networks such as the ancestral past. In contrast, the deposition of burnt material and human remains in the cairns deliberately linked occupation of the plot into formally expressed and pre-existing networks of tenure and belonging. This contrast is important as it demonstrates that cairnfields and field systems were inhabited in different ways. Although the agricultural practices undertaken may have appeared superficially similar, the structural conditions in which they were undertaken were significantly different.

Taken together, the anthropological and archaeological examples emphasise the importance of social relations in the reproduction of tenure and encourage us to look more closely at links between agricultural practices and structures of kinship, tenure and inheritance. Cairnstone, as a resource connected to the domains of both life and death, and as a medium through which all three of the previously mentioned networks were structured, is a vital archaeological resource with which to explore the social context of fieldstone clearance during the second millennium BC.

Acknowledgements

The research for this paper was undertaken while the author was in receipt of an AHRB studentship. The work was presented at the first meeting of the Bronze Age Forum in Cambridge, 1999, and I am grateful to Jo Brück for her support and efforts in organising the conference, and her subsequent patience in waiting for a written draft of the paper. The ideas that form the basis for the research have been developed over several years, and I am indebted to colleagues at seminars and conferences in Newcastle, Birmingham, Gothenburg and Sheffield for their stimulating questions and discussion.

References

Ashbee, P. 1957. Excavations on Kildale Moor, North Riding of Yorkshire, 1953. *Yorkshire Archaeological Journal* 39, 179–192.

Barber, J. (ed.) 1997. *The Archaeological Investigation of a Prehistoric Landscape: Excavations on Arran 1978–1981*. Edinburgh: Scottish Trust for Archaeological Research.

Barker, M. M. 1934. Tumuli near Carrock Fell. *Transactions of the Cumberland and Westmoreland Antiquarian and Archaeological Society* 34 (New Series), 107–112.

Barker, M. M. 1951. Some excavations in the Carrock Area. *Transactions of the Cumberland and Westmoreland Antiquarian and Archaeological Society* 50 (New Series), 201–202.

Barnatt, J. 1994. Excavation of a Bronze Age unenclosed cemetery, cairns, and field boundaries at Eaglestone Flat, Curbar, Derbyshire, 1984, 1989–1990. *Proceedings of the Prehistoric Society* 60, 287–370.

Boserup, E. 1965. *The Conditions of Agricultural Growth: The Economics of Agrarian Change under Population Pressure*. London: George Allen and Unwin.

Cherry, J. 1961. Cairns in the Birker Fell and Ulpha Fell area. *Transactions of the Cumberland and Westmoreland Antiquarian and Archaeological Society* 61 (New Ser), 7–15.

Chou, C. 1997. Contesting the tenure of territoriality: the Orang Suku Laut. *Bijdragen tot de Taal-, Land- en Volkenkunde* 153(4), 605–629.

Crocombe, R. 1974. An approach to the analysis of land tenure systems. In Lundesgaarde, H. P. (ed.) *Land Tenure in Oceania*, 1–17. Honolulu: University Press of Hawaii.

Damas, D. 1994. *Bountiful Island: A Study of Land Tenure on a Micronesian Atoll*. Waterloo, Ontario: Wilfred Laurier University Press.

Digim'rina, L. S. 1995. *Gardens of Basima: Land Tenure and Mortuary Feasting in a Matrilineal Society*. Unpublished Ph.D. Thesis, Australian National University,.

Dymond, C. W. 1893. Barnscar: an ancient settlement in Cumberland. *Transactions of the Cumberland and West-moreland Antiquarian and Archaeological Society* 12 (First Series), 179–187.

Dymond, C. W. and Hodgson, T. H. 1902. An ancient village near Threlkeld. *Transactions of the Cumberland and Westmoreland Antiquarian and Archaeological Society* 2 (New Series), 38–52.

Elias, T. O. 1951. *Nigerian Land Law and Custom*. London: Routledge and Kegan Paul.

Engels, F. 1972. *The Origin of the Family, Private Property and the State*. London: Lawrence and Wishart.

Fleming, A. 1971. Bronze age agriculture on the marginal lands of north-east Yorkshire. *Agricultural History Review* 19, 1–24.

Giddens, A. 1984. *The Constitution of Society: Outline of a Theory of Structuration*. Cambridge: Polity Press.

Gluckman, M. 1943. *Essays on Lozi Land and Royal Property*. Livingstone: The Rhodes-Livingstone Institute.

Graham, A. 1959. Cairnfields in Scotland. *Proceedings of the Society of Antiquaries of Scotland* 90, 7–23.

Green, M. M. 1941. *Land Tenure in an Ibo Village in South-Eastern Nigeria*. London: Percy Lund.

Hodgson, E. 1928. Excavations above Milkingstead, Eskdale. *Transactions of the Cumberland and West-moreland Antiquarian and Archaeological Society* 28 (New Series), 149–151.

Ingold, T. 1986. *The Appropriation of Nature: Essays on Human Ecology and Social Relations*. Manchester: Manchester University Press.

Jobey, G. 1968. Excavations of cairns at Chatton Sandyford, Northumberland. *Archaeologia Aeliana* 46 (Fourth Series), 5–50.

Jobey, G. 1981. Green Knowe unenclosed platform settlement and Harehope cairn, Peebleshire. *Proceedings of the Society of Antiquaries of Scotland* 110, 72–113.

Jobey, G. 1983. Excavation of an unenclosed settlement on Standrop Rigg, Northumberland, and some problems related to similar settlements between Tyne and Forth. *Archaeologia Aeliana* 11 (Fifth Series), 1–21.

Johnston, R. 2000. Dying, becoming and being the field: prehistoric cairnfields in Northumberland. In Harding, J. and Johnston, R. (eds) *Northern Pasts: Interpretations of the Later Prehistory of Northern England and Southern Scotland*, 57–70. Oxford: British Archaeological Reports, British Series 302.

Kawharu, I. H. 1977. *Maori Land Tenure: Studies of a Changing Institution*. Oxford: Clarendon Press.

Kelly, R. L. 1992. Mobility/sedentism: concepts, archaeological measures and effects. *Annual Review of Anthropology* 21, 43–66.

Kitchen, W. H. 2000. *Later Neolithic and Bronze Age Land Use and Settlement in the Derbyshire Peak District: Cairnfields in Context*. Unpublished Ph.D. thesis, University of Sheffield.

Lane, C. R. 1998. Introduction: overview of the pastoral problematic. In Lane, C. R. (ed.), *Custodians of the Commons: Pastoral Land Tenure in East and West Africa*, 1–25. London: Earthscan.

Lawrence, P. 1955. *Land Tenure among the Garia: The Traditional System of a New Guinea People*. Canberra: Australian National University.

Malinowski, B. 1935. *Coral Gardens and their Magic Vo.l 1: A Study of the Methods of Tilling the Soil and of Agricultural*

Rights in the Trobriand Islands. Bloomington: Indiana University Press.

Meek, C. K. 1948. *Colonial Law: A Bibliography with Special Reference to Native African Systems of Law and Land Tenure*. London: Oxford University Press.

Meek, C. K. 1949. *Land Law and Custom in the Colonies* (second edition). London: Oxford University Press.

Migot-Adholla, S. E. and Bruce, J. W. 1994. Introduction: are indigenous African land tenure systems insecure? In Bruce, J. W. and Migot-Adholla, S. E. (eds), *Searching for Land Tenure Security in Africa*, 1–13. Iowa: Kendall Hunt.

Netting, R. M. 1993. *Smallholders, Householders: Farm Families and the Ecology of Intensive, Sustainable Agriculture*. Stanford: Stanford University Press.

RCAHMS 1997. *Eastern Dumfriesshire: An Archaeological Landscape*. Edinburgh: The Stationery Office.

Rocheleau, D. and Edmunds, D. 1997. Women, men and trees: gender, power and property in forest and agrarian landscapes. *World Development* 25(8), 1351–1371.

Siu, H. F. and Faure, D. 1995. Introduction. In Faure, D. and Siu, H. F. (eds) *Down to Earth: The Territorial Bond in South China*, 1–19. Stanford: Stanford University Press.

Spear, T. 1997. *Mountain Farmers: Moral Economies of Land and Agricultural Development in Arusha and Meru*. Oxford: James Currey.

Spence, J. E. 1935. Report of the Committee for Prehistoric Studies. *Transactions of the Cumberland and Westmoreland Antiquarian and Archaeological Society* 35 (New Series), 170–181.

Spence, J. E. 1937. Bolton Wood enclosure. *Transactions of the Cumberland and Westmoreland Antiquarian and Archaeological Society* 37 (New Series), 43–48.

Tronvoll, K. 1998. *Mai Weini, a Highland Village in Eritrea: A Study of the People, their Livelihood and Land Tenure during Times of Turbulence*. Laurenceville NJ: Red Sea Press.

Walker, D. 1965. Excavations at Barnscar, 1957–58. *Transactions of the Cumberland and Westmoreland Antiquarian and Archaeological Society* 65 (New Ser), 53–65.

Ward, J. E. 1977. Cairns on Corney Fell, West Cumberland. *Transactions of the Cumberland and Westmoreland Antiquarian and Archaeological Society* 77 (New Series), 1–5.

Ward, R. G. and Kingdom, E. 1995. Land use and tenure: some comparisons. In Ward, R. G. and Kingdom, I. (eds) *Land, Custom and Practice in the South Pacific*, 6–35. Cambridge: Cambridge University Press.

Yates, M. J. 1984. Groups of small cairns in northern Britain – a view from SW Scotland. *Proceedings of the Society of Antiquaries of Scotland* 114, 217–234.

Young, R. and Welfare, A. T. 1992. Fieldwork and excavation at the Crawley Edge cairnfield, Stanhope, Co. Durham. *Durham Archaeological Journal* 8, 27–49.

10 Tenure and territoriality in the British Bronze Age: a question of varying social and geographic scales?

Willy Kitchen

In the introduction to his 'Age of Stonehenge' (1980), Colin Burgess lays out the underlying premise on which his argument rests:

> . . . by the third millennium, Britain and Ireland . . . had already been divided fairly rigidly into territories by stratified societies, which, confined within their borders, were much more static than has usually been conceived . . . The[se] territories . . . can be likened to a cellular structure in which each cell (or territory) develops in sympathy with its neighbours. Thus the inhabitants of any territory will be aware of developments not only in adjoining territories but indirectly in others much further removed . . . Those cells or territories it touches will together form a "tradition block" . . . Cells, or territories, which consistently share a wide range of traditions will together form a "community of tradition" . . . Applying the "constant culture contact" model, we can see that it is not the people within their territories who change, but their ideas, which adapt to each innovation (Burgess 1980, 20–22).

This puts me in mind of some insane system of apian prehistoric peer polity interaction, each bee policing its own cell within the honeycomb, and occasionally sending the whole colony into a frenzy of activity by the performance of a bee dance. Burgess's conception of the landscapes of the British Bronze Age is all structure and no agency. Further, as Burgess himself readily admits, such a model requires that we accept 'a much more settled and highly developed landscape and much larger population figures than those usually entertained' (*ibid.*, 20).

Little, if any, progress has been made in our understanding of Bronze Age population demographics in the two decades that now separate us from the publication of Burgess's book. However, for a number of more recent authors, the extent to which the landscapes of the second millennium BC

and earlier might be regarded as 'settled and highly developed' – implying systematic and long-lasting compartmentalisation of the landscape into discrete territories – has diminished markedly. In its place, we find the beginnings of an alternative model, according to which group mobility, fluidity of landuse, and tenure over paths and places, but not fixed land surfaces, is said to have prevailed well into the second half of the second millennium BC (Barrett 1994; Tilley 1994; Whittle 1997, 19). However, if life in the Bronze Age was characterised more by movement, it is not at all easy to conceive of the geographical scales over which those lives were lived. Barrett, for example, concentrates more on the temporal dimensions of such lifeways, whereas Whittle has defined a 'spectrum of relative mobility' without ever explicitly discussing the distances over which such mobile communities might have ranged. Furthermore, identifying the point of transition from these third or second millennium 'landscapes of becoming' to the 'landscapes of being' that are said by Barrett to characterise the later second and first millennia BC is not a straightforward task in many regions of Britain (Barrett 1994, 136–153).

Somewhere between these two poles, it can be suggested, lies Andrew Fleming's most recent call for a distinction to be drawn between different conceptions of prehistoric political geography, encompassing 'large' and 'small terrains' respectively (Fleming 1998). As Fleming rightly observes, '[i]f spatial scale and a sense of landscape are to be bound into coherent models of social structure and agency, "territory" is an essential bridging concept' (*ibid.*, 45). However, 'territory', as a concept, should not necessarily be collapsed into some restless search for the location in space of discrete boundaries, frozen in particular historical epochs, and etched across the landscape in material form. As Fleming also notes, 'ultimately a landscape-centred prehistory which privileged place over people would fail as an historical enterprise' (*ibid.*).

In particular, it is essential that we maintain a clear distinction between the quite separate concepts of tenure and of territoriality (Ingold 1986, 130–164). Thus, following Ingold, the former can be defined as 'an aspect of that system of relations which *constitutes* persons as productive agents and directs their purposes' (*ibid.*, 130); original emphasis and the latter can be defined as 'an aspect of the means through which those purposes are put into effect under given environmental circumstances' (*ibid.*, 130–131). In purely analytical terms, tenure is a mode of appropriation related to social relations of production that 'engages nature in a system of social relations' (*ibid.*, 136), whereas territoriality is a mode of communication related to the material forces of production that 'engages society in a system of natural relations' (*ibid.*, original emphasis removed). Whereas the former can be understood as an ongoing process, the latter more closely approximates 'a succession of synchronic states' (*ibid.*).

It is this distinction that Fleming fails to maintain in his own discussion of political geography. Thus, he suggests in passing that territory might be understood 'in the sense of occupancy of land' (Fleming 1998, 45), before going on to query how comparatively more fluid human social networks, or communities, routinely reproduced through the performance of subsistence tasks or ceremonial rites, might have intersected across the more rigid territorial boundaries he seeks to identify as emergent in prehistory on Dartmoor and elsewhere in the later second millennium BC (*ibid.* 51–56; 1979; 1983; 1984). The point is that his largely static understanding of territory in terms of the 'occupancy' of land conflates Ingold's definitions of tenure and of territoriality, and therefore fails to grasp the point that it is these particular social networks, relevant to tenure, not territoriality, that must form the focus of our enquiry.

Fleming maintains that it may have been common in prehistory 'for claims to occupancy of land to be vested in a large terrain with an area upwards of, say 100 square kilometres – a kind of "folk territory", with the emphasis as much on the people as on defined areas of the earth's surface' (*ibid.* 52), yet he goes on to suggest that:

> Large terrains might be occupied with varying degrees of social inclusiveness; their boundaries might be more or less permeable; they might vary and change in the manner and degree of their ethnic identity. Within these large terrains there would have been scope for different modes and strengths of socio-political organisation, which might have influenced the form of subsequent sub-divisions. Large terrains would have varied in size, and the

interstices between them would doubtless have been occupied by small (affiliated?) terrains (Fleming 1998, 52–53).

A certain tension clearly exists between these related statements, since Fleming appears to assert a particular durability for the geographic integrity of his large terrains that is incompatible with his additional definition of their boundaries as delimiters of 'folk territories'. Furthermore, he appears to imply a rather static conception of later prehistoric patterns of inhabitation that remains to be demonstrated in many regions of the country.

By way of illustration, let us consider a couple of brief examples that might serve to focus our discussion on the importance of varying scales of geographic mobility tied to prehistoric patterns of landuse that necessarily cross-cut the kinds of territorial 'frameworks' that Fleming seeks to construct.

An example from the North York Moors

Consider, for example, the different scales of mobility and landuse implied in three different interpretations of round barrow and cairnfield distributions recorded on the North York Moors (Fleming 1971a; Spratt 1981; Harding with Ostoja-Zagórski 1994).

A decade before the publication of the 'Age of Stonehenge', and relying on environmental evidence (Dimbleby 1962) that has been only partially confirmed in subsequent studies (for example, Atherden 1976; Jones *et al.* 1979), Fleming described a landscape initially populated by shifting cultivators who intensively exploited cereal plots over very short periods of time before moving on to clear and cultivate neighbouring areas in a ceaselessly changing pattern of clearance, cultivation and soil degradation. The degree of population mobility evoked is wholly incommensurate with that envisaged by Burgess. The ridge top barrows that these people built on the Blackamore uplands are taken to represent a proxy record of their relentless progress across the region, but are not said to have acted recursively to tie people more permanently to the land where their ancestors were buried, or to delineate particular territorial or tenurial boundaries. The cairnfields, which are typically located at rather lower altitudes between 200m and 300m OD on drier, gently sloping land, represent for Fleming the 'aftermath' of this earlier colonisation. Their construction, he argues (1971a, 23), followed 'the inevitable decline and fragmentation of the original population, and the development of a slightly different type of agriculture', under which pastoralism gradually supplanted cereal cultivation as the principal means of subsistence in the region.

Spratt, by contrast, argues that such cairnfields represent the remains of 'subsidiary' or 'satellite camps' utilised predominantly by Bronze Age herders attached to small farming communities who were more permanently settled in valley-side settlements, in each case located less than an hour's walk away. He develops a settlement model that comprises a series of spatially-constrained, small-scale, mixed-farming communities settled within discrete 'estates' of approximately 8km² each. Such a model, *prima facie*, corresponds quite closely with Burgess's conception of 'territorial cells'. Individual tenurial boundaries were physically delineated by lines of intervisible round barrows located on the immediate watersheds surrounding the headwaters of the River Rye, and by a series of smaller streams feeding this same river (Spratt 1981; Fig. 10.1). However, Spratt fails to distinguish chronologically between round barrows and cairnfields, with the apparent implication that both were constructed as part of the same contemporary system of landuse and tenurial control (*contra* Fleming 1971a, 20–23). Significantly, for our purposes, he notes that barrows sited along watersheds might also have marked the line of upland routes through the region, 'an idea which can obviously be integrated with the boundary thesis' (Spratt 1981, 100). This point will be taken up again below.

Harding, like Spratt, sees the cairnfields as indicative of a mixed farming regime that incorporated more or less regular exploitation of upland pastures. However, he is prepared to countenance a rather more extensive pattern of Bronze Age 'transhumance' than Spratt, suggesting that exploitation of the cairnfields might have taken place within a system of landuse that would have regularly taken the occupants of some North Yorkshire cairnfields at least as far as the more fertile lowlands around Stokesley, some 15km to the west (Harding with Ostoja-Zagórski 1994, 64–65). Accordingly, the nature of landuse at Danby Rigg, the particular cairnfield examined by Harding, might have been 'restricted in extent either spatially or temporally or both' (*ibid.*, 66), while in the Bronze Age at least, the larger open expanses of Blackamore itself 'are most unlikely to have been cleared on a large scale at a single moment' (*ibid.*). In such circumstances, we might envisage a relatively low intensity system of Bronze Age landuse more in keeping with certain forms of woodland forest-farming (Evans 1999, 83–87), scrub- or bush-fallow (Pryor 1998, 145), than with those more intensive agricultural systems that, through the development of field lynchets perhaps as much as the purposive construction of field walls, are likely to account for the development of Celtic field systems in Wessex and elsewhere in the Later Bronze Age (Barrett 1994, 144, 148–149).

Both Spratt and Harding seem to be in broad agreement as to the nature of the landuse practices pursued at the various cairnfield locales. However, the different scales of movement into which they might choose to integrate these places imply very different connections between the people who worked the cairnfields and the land itself. In the former case, those who worked the land remained more or less constantly within an hour's walk of the cairnfield in question, and would have dwelt largely within their own closely defined community's area of land-holding. The geographic area known today as the North York Moors was entirely covered by a system of fixed tenurial boundaries, such that it was always possible to say which land fell within the jurisdiction of which groups, and hence to exclude outsiders. In the latter case, by contrast, those who worked the land would presumably have spent longer periods of time at a much greater distance, and in moving with their animals to upland pastures or 'common or garden' cairnfields (Harding with Ostoja-Zagórski 1994, 68), would have passed through tracts of landscape that formed part of the traditional ranges of a series of different groups. The implications for how the wider landscape was understood, experienced and inhabited are profound, and it becomes necessary in such circumstances to consider which members of individual groups habitually moved to the uplands, and which remained elsewhere (Barrett 1989, 122–123). Superficially subtle differences in scales of movement, aligned to rather different conceptions of tenurial control over land, may have fundamental implications for the ways in which different communities organised and understood themselves.

A further example from the Peak District of Derbyshire

Over the past two decades, successive studies of archaeological evidence from the Peak District of Derbyshire have made a series of claims superficially similar to those of Spratt with respect to the tenurial compartmentalisation of land in the region in the third and second millennia BC (Hawke-Smith 1979; 1981; Bradley and Hart 1983; Barnatt 1987; 1996a; 1996b; 1999). These analyses have drawn primarily on recorded distribution plots of extant cairnfields, round barrows and a number of ceremonial monuments of more uncertain nature, including in particular the 'classic' henge monuments at Arbor Low and the Bull Ring (Harding with Lee 1987, 110–115; Barnatt 1990, 31–41). A series of much smaller ringworks, including embanked stone circles and ringcairns, are also found in the immediate vicinity of many cairnfields, primarily situated on the

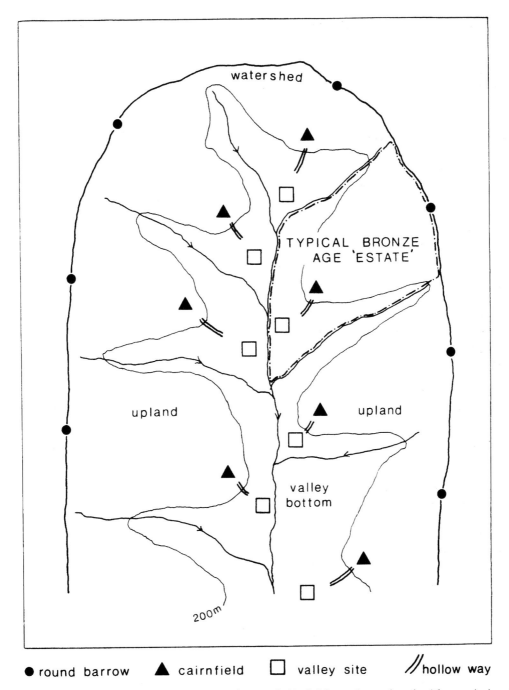

● **round barrow**   ▲ **cairnfield**   □ **valley site**   ∥**hollow way**

Fig. 10.1 *Spratt's model of Bronze Age 'estates' on the North York Moors (reproduced with permission from Spratt 1981, fig. 7.6)*

dipslopes behind a succession of dramatic gritstone edges that overlook the Derwent Valley in the northeast of the region (Fig. 10.2; Radley 1966a; Barnatt 1986; 1987; 1999).

The Peak District as a whole has traditionally been seen as the preserve of largely pastoralist populations in prehistory (Armstrong 1956; Radley 1966b; Hicks 1972; Bramwell 1973; Green 1980, 153, 190; Vine 1982). However, following the publication of Hawke-Smith's study of 'man-land relations' in the region, an agricultural function has been more readily inferred for the cairnfields in particular, although the extent to which these represent the remains of arable fields, 'common or garden' plots, or more extensive hay meadows and pasturage varies from author to author (Hawke-Smith 1979; Bradley and Hart 1983; Barnatt 1987; 1994; 1999). Be that as it may, each of these later authors has been happy to see cairnfield exploitation as having taken place within a largely static pattern of tenurial

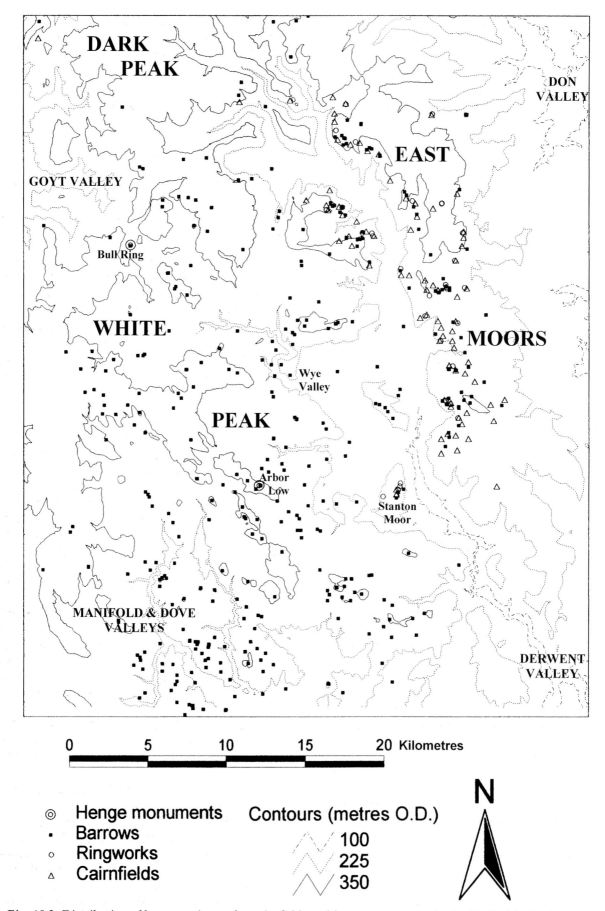

Fig. 10.2 *Distribution of barrows, ringworks, cairnfields and henge monuments in the Derbyshire Peak District*

control that might in each case be said to mirror Spratt's model of Bronze Age 'estates'. Thus, Hawke-Smith (1981, 66) suggests that,

> [t]he land-tenurial system that best suits the data would have been a lattice of interlocking territories, maintained fairly strictly over several centuries by different groups . . . [in a landscape] governed by a closely structured system of compound territories in which certain grazings [*sic*] were held in common.

However, nowhere does he spell out the individual extent of these compound territories.

Bradley and Hart were rather more cautious and broad-brush in their treatment, noting in particular the inadequacies of the environmental evidence from Derbyshire when seeking to test Hawke-Smith's models. However, at the scale of Fleming's 'large terrain landscapes', they were happy to suggest an '*expansion* of the settled landscape' (Bradley and Hart 1983, 192, original emphasis) from the third into the second millennium BC. This period saw the colonisation of the East Moors by small family groups responsible for the construction of the cairnfields, which were said by these authors at least to be representative of 'lower ranking settlements' than those already established on the limestone 'core area' of the White Peak (*ibid.*).

Finally, Barnatt has most recently written of the Peak District in prehistory in the following terms:

> The picture which now emerges . . . for much of the Bronze Age is one where sedentary farming of similar character was the norm throughout. This is a time for which the archaeological evidence stresses the local. Each farming "family" had its own fields and small monuments nearby (Barnatt 1999, 48).

According to Barnatt, this process of tenurial compartmentalisation became possible through the emergence of an 'hierarchy of monuments' in the Later Neolithic, including the two large communal henges, six or more 'great barrows' comparable with those of the Great Wolds Valley in East Yorkshire (Manby 1988), and several hundred small 'family barrows', each indicative of different scales of social organisation and tenurial control (Barnatt 1996b, 52). Successive monumental scales might relate to different levels of social organisation, with monumental complexes developing at a number of different landscape foci that may have been related to specific 'traditional agricultural zones' (Barnatt 1996a, 65–66; Fig. 10.3). Within this nested landscape of discrete social territories, Barnatt sees his small 'family barrows' as defining the boundaries of individual family land-holdings in a manner very similar to that envisaged by Spratt. On the East Moors in particular, topographic boundaries defined by local watersheds, or more obviously perhaps by gritstone edges, may also have been significant,

while most such areas of individually held land-holdings also incorporated at least one ringwork associated with its primary cairnfield (Barnatt 2000).

Barrows as social markers or spatial boundaries?

When considering the territorial functions fulfilled by Bronze Age round barrows, it is essential that one distinguishes carefully between systems of 'social boundary defence', most relevant to our understanding of territoriality, and 'spatial' or 'perimeter boundary defence', which is more relevant to our understanding of tenurial relations in prehistory (Cashdan 1983; Ingold 1986, 142; Smith 1988, 247–248; Barnard 1992). Whereas Spratt and Barnatt's conception of Bronze Age monuments as being predominantly located either at the centre or on the periphery of specific family land-holdings implies some degree of spatial or perimeter defence of specific areas of land, social boundary defence by contrast represents a mode of reciprocal communication most often observed among gatherer-hunters and pastoralists. It is, Ingold (1986, 143) argues, 'a means of effecting co-operation over an extensive but common range in an ecological situation (the exploitation of dispersed fauna or flora) which precludes regular face-to-face contact between co-operating units in the course of extractive activities'.

Thus, the initial construction of monuments, and in particular the multi-phased construction of many in the Peak District (Barnatt 1999, 38), might as easily relate to the ways in which practical exploitation of such places were organised (where, when and by whom) as to the social appropriation of the land itself. As Ingold (1986, 143) argues, 'territorial compartmentalisation may be perfectly compatible with the collective appropriation of nature', without this necessarily requiring that the landscape itself was physically or conceptually carved up into discrete tracts of land, whereby particular social groups exercised an exclusive right to exploit and enjoy specific resource areas.

Visible traces of the recent exploitation of land, as at cairnfields perhaps, or of the recent observance of a number of possible rituals, only one of which might have been burial within round barrows or ringworks, would serve as sufficient indication that others passing through should do just that, rather than pausing to exploit further resources that had already been grazed that season. If the larger monuments, henges for example, may have seen the coming together of quite large groups of people from time to time, the very considerable numbers of smaller round barrows or ringworks might relate more to the seasonal or less periodic comings and

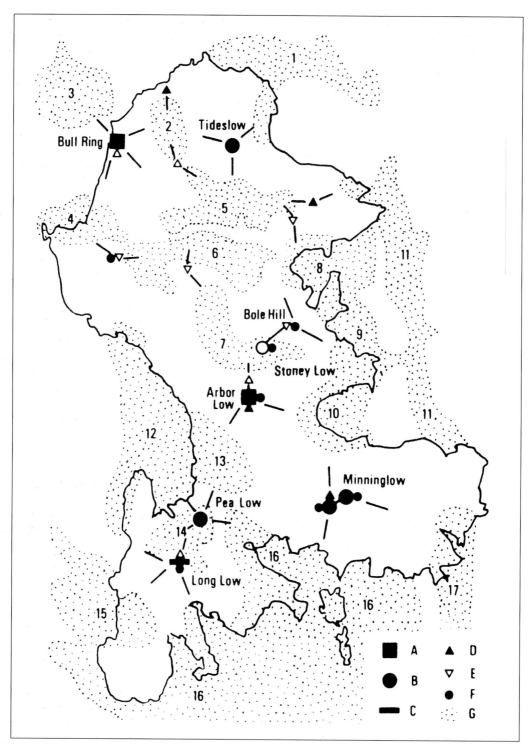

Fig. 10.3 *Monument complexes and 'traditional agricultural zones' in the White Peak (reproduced with permission from Barnatt 1996a, fig. 1.17.4). A: henges; B: 'great barrows'; C: bank barrows; D: long barrows with superimposed round barrows; E: other chambered and long barrows; F: round barrows; G: 'traditional agricultural zones'*

goings of pastoralists or agro-pastoralists, as Fleming argued long ago for many of the Wessex barrow cemeteries (Fleming 1971b). Unless we can confidently ascribe more sedentary systems of agricultural landuse to these particular populations, there is nothing to prevent us from seeing such smaller monuments as representative of a continuing system of essentially mobile landuse based predominantly on the husbanding of animals. The sheer quantity and superficial homogeneity of these monuments, rather than evidencing the settling down of equals across a now divided landscape, might instead indicate the enduring success of existing systems of landuse and mobility in preserving a large degree of political autonomy between different groups, each of which may have practised different burial rites at the *same* barrow sites.

As Burnham (1979, 350–351) has argued,

> in nomadic pastoral societies, the actual pattern of local grouping resulting from reallocation of political allegiances by individuals and groups via residential mobility is probably more determinative of genealogical structure over the long term than vice versa . . . Once established as a principle of political organisation, fluidity of local grouping proves to be a remarkably resistant feature of any society. In particular, spatial mobility greatly inhibits the development of political centralisation and, although perhaps to a lesser extent, class stratification . . . it is a source of structural conservatism that must be analysed and dealt with in any attempt to understand the transformation of nomadic pastoral societies from relatively egalitarian, acephalous forms toward greater stratification and centralisation.

The ways in which barrows and other monuments came to be embodied within wider discourses of landscape might then have operated at a series of different social scales. Humphrey, for example, has shown how the annual addition of stone to *oboo* cairns on the mountain tops of Mongolia, and the cairns themselves, might serve as 'occupation-marks' for their builders, as 'orientation marks' for travellers, and as sites of ritual observance at which latent tensions between competing views of the world, chiefly and shamanic, might be played out (Humphrey 1995, 138, 146, 148). In this respect, it is less easy to maintain Spratt's position that pathways and boundaries might be straightforwardly integrated within the same hypothesis. It is possible, rather, to suggest that barrows in the Peak District or on the North York Moors remained embedded within a series of different routines tied to the exploitation of different pastures, and that individual barrows continued to hold meanings, perhaps different meanings, for a series of different groups or peoples. Indeed, it is even possible to accept that certain of these barrows were built by increasingly sedentary groups of cultivators or agro-pastoralists, while still maintaining that the majority were more often utilised by more mobile groups of agro-pastoralists who continued to exploit seasonal pastures and move over much wider tracts of land. Further, it is implicit in Burnham's analysis that the composition of individual family groups, task groups, or wider social groupings, may have been inherently unstable for much of the period.

In the Peak District, such a model can be seen to account satisfactorily for a number of aspects of the burial record that distinguish it from some more exhaustively studied areas within the British Isles. Thus, for example, barrows in the region occur either singly or in groups of two or three, and cemeteries of the type identified in Wessex are entirely absent. Further, there is little evidence for status differentiation between individuals, at least as this might be inferred by differential treatment of corpses or the provision of gravegoods (Barnatt 1996a; 1999, 40–42). Indeed, the evidence rather suggests that a profusion of very different burial rites may have been practised at the time, both within and between individual barrows. Barnatt seeks to explain this apparent heterogeneity of practice in terms of the 'inherent variability' of barrow funerals over time, such that the infrequent performance of funerary rites, witnessed by only a few mourners at a time, led to idiosyncratic developments at individual burial locales (Barnatt 1996a, 40). However, it is equally possible to suggest that such heterogeneity rather reflects cultural differences between individual social or task groups who were entitled to make use of a series of different barrows across the landscape at different times, perhaps according to the particular pastures over which their herds or flocks were running at the time of a death or of a burial.

Indeed, Hawke-Smith himself has suggested that individual barrows evidencing both inhumation and cremation rites might have fallen within areas of commonly held upland grazing land on the White Peak where the interlocking 'compound territories' of individual groups overlapped (Hawke-Smith 1979, 181, 183; 1981, 66). We can easily accept such an analysis without also insisting on the economic primacy of the cultivation of cereal crops, as Hawke-Smith chose to do (space does not allow a sufficient consideration of landuse here; for a detailed discussion see Kitchen 2000). Thus, we might begin to conceive of a system of landuse and of socio-spatial mobility in the third and second millennia BC in the Peak District that only commences at the scale of Fleming's 'large terrains'. The territorial dimensions of resource extraction and production at the time may have corresponded to a series of overlapping 'large terrains' marked on the ground today by a pattern of regularly-spaced monumental complexes. Nevertheless, these large terrains may have been essentially open-ended entities, tied into much broader axes of movement into and out of the Peak District, which focussed on the valleys of the Goyt, Don, Derwent, Dove and Manifold Rivers respectively. Thus, different groups may have moved more or less frequently from the Peak District to the Yorkshire and Lincolnshire Wolds in the east and northeast along the Don and Rother Valleys, to the Cheshire Plain or Morecambe Bay in the northwest

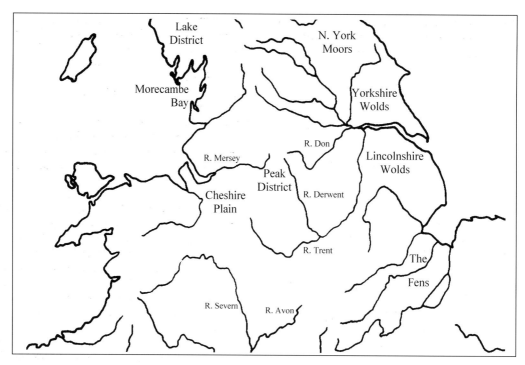

Fig. 10.4 *Map of central and northern England showing major rivers and areas named in the text*

along the Goyt Valley, to the Fens in the southeast initially by way of the Derwent and Trent, or to the Severn and Avon valleys in the southwest again initially by way of the Manifold or Dove (Fig. 10.4). Such movements might then have provided the context through which significant quantities of flint, commonly used in preference to locally occurring cherts, were imported into the region (Garton 1991, 18–19; Kitchen 2000).

In at least two of these more distant areas (the Wolds and the Fens), we find evidence for large-scale division of land in the Later Bronze Age of a type quite unknown in the Peak District. As such, we might note that intensification of production among predominantly pastoralist communities need not necessarily require any reduction in group mobility, or investment in the laying out of permanent systems of intensive livestock management. Humphrey and Sneath have demonstrated clearly that in present day Mongolia at least, similar intensification can be achieved by increasing seasonal group mobility (Humphrey and Sneath 1996). Indeed, contrary to commonly held perceptions that seasonal migration is a 'primitive survival technique' (*ibid.*, 18), Gilles and Gefu have suggested that forced sedentarisation in certain countries in Africa and Asia in recent times has actually undermined livestock production in circumstances where animal movements became too severely restricted (Gilles and Gefu 1990, 106).

It is therefore quite possible that rather different responses to social and/or environmental stresses in the Later Bronze Age led to the physical demarcation of pasture land in only certain regions of the country, and it is in a context in which these different responses may have registered a profound impact in areas geographically very distant from one another that we might begin to understand the phenomenon of the emergence, for example, of isolated fortified hilltop enclosures at the turn of the first millennium BC in northern England. An understanding of Bronze Age lifeways conceived on this scale might help to account both for the wide distribution of similar suites of material culture in the Earlier Bronze Age, and for the apparent increase in regionalisation in the Later Bronze Age and Iron Age, since these emerging regional blocks may represent the crystallisation of more specific axes of long-distance movement that had been used for millennia in different parts of the country. Clearly, such an understanding also requires that we adopt a position in many ways diametrically opposed to that proposed by Burgess and implicitly followed by a number of subsequent authors (Hawke-Smith 1979; Spratt 1981; Barker 1985, 207).

Acknowledgements

My thanks to Mark Edmonds and John Barrett, who supervised my thesis, but have not had sight of this paper. They are therefore more than usually absolved of any responsibility for this particular piece of work. Thanks also are due to John Barnatt and John Collis for permission to reproduce Figs 10.1 and 10.3.

References

Armstrong, A. L. 1956. Palaeolithic, Neolithic and Bronze Ages. In Linton, D. L. (ed.) *Sheffield and its Region: a Scientific and Historical Survey*, 90–110. Sheffield: British Association for the Advancement of Science.

Atherden, M. A. 1976. The impact of late prehistoric cultures on the vegetation of the North York Moors. *Transactions of the Institute of British Geographers* 1, 284–300.

Barker, G. 1985. *Prehistoric Farming in Europe*. Cambridge: Cambridge University Press.

Barnard, A. 1992. Social and spatial boundary maintenance among southern African hunter-gatherers. In Casimir, M. J. and Rao, A. (eds) *Mobility and Territoriality: Social and Spatial Boundaries among Foragers, Fishers, Pastoralists and Peripatetics*, 137–151. Oxford: Berg.

Barnatt, J. 1986. Bronze Age remains on the East Moors of the Peak District. *Derbyshire Archaeological Journal* 106, 18–100.

Barnatt, J. 1987. Bronze Age settlement on the East Moors of the Peak District of Derbyshire and South Yorkshire. *Proceedings of the Prehistoric Society* 53, 393–418.

Barnatt, J. 1990. *The Henges, Stone Circles and Ringcairns of the Peak District*. Sheffield: University of Sheffield, Sheffield Archaeological Monographs 1.

Barnatt, J. 1994. Excavation of a Bronze Age unenclosed cemetery, cairns and field boundaries at Eaglestone Flat, Curbar, Derbyshire, 1984, 1989–1990. *Proceedings of the Prehistoric Society* 60, 287–370.

Barnatt, J. 1996a. Barrows in the Peak District: a review and interpretation of extant sites and past excavations. In Barnatt, J. and Collis, J. (eds) *Barrows in the Peak District: Recent Research*, 3–94. Sheffield: Sheffield Academic Press.

Barnatt, J. 1996b. Moving beyond the monuments: paths and people in the Neolithic landscapes of the Peak District. *Northern Archaeology* 13/14, 43–59.

Barnatt, J. 1999. Taming the land: Peak District farming and ritual in the Bronze Age. *Derbyshire Archaeological Journal* 119, 19–78.

Barnatt, J. 2000. To each their own: later prehistoric farming communities and their monuments in the Peak. *Derbyshire Archaeological Journal* 120, 1–86.

Barrett, J. C. 1989. Time and tradition: the rituals of everyday life. In H.-Å. Nordström and A. Knape (eds), *Bronze Age Studies: Transactions of the British-Scandinavian Colloquium in Stockholm, May 10–11, 1985*, 113–126. Stockholm: Museum of National Antiquities.

Barrett, J.C. 1994. *Fragments from Antiquity: an Archaeology of Social Life in Britain, 2900–1200 BC*. Oxford: Blackwell.

Bradley, R. and Hart, C. 1983. Prehistoric settlement in the Peak District during the third and second millennia bc:
a preliminary analysis in the light of recent fieldwork. *Proceedings of the Prehistoric Society* 49, 177–193.

Bramwell, D. 1973. *Archaeology in the Peak District: a Guide to the Region's Prehistory*. Stafford: Moorland Publishing Company.

Burgess, C. 1980. *The Age of Stonehenge*. London: J. M. Dent and Sons.

Burnham, P. 1979. Spatial mobility and political centralization in pastoral societies. In L'Equipe écologie et anthropologie des sociétés pastorales (ed.) *Pastoral Production and Society*, 349–360. Cambridge: Cambridge University Press.

Cashdan, E. 1983. Territoriality among human foragers: ecological models and an application to four Bushman groups. *Current Anthropology* 24, 47–66.

Dimbleby, G. W. 1962. *The Development of British Heathlands and their Soils*. Oxford: Clarendon Press.

Evans, J. G. 1999. *Land and Archaeology: Histories of Human Environment in the British Isles*. Stroud: Tempus.

Fleming, A. 1971a. Bronze Age agriculture on the marginal lands of north-east Yorkshire. *Agricultural History Review* 19, 1–24.

Fleming, A. 1971b. Territorial patterns in Bronze Age Wessex. *Proceedings of the Prehistoric Society* 37, 138–166.

Fleming, A. 1979. The Dartmoor Reaves: boundary patterns and behaviour patterns in the second millennium BC. *Proceedings of the Devon Archaeological Society* 37, 115–131.

Fleming, A. 1983. The prehistoric landscape of Dartmoor. Part 2: north and east Dartmoor. *Proceedings of the Prehistoric Society* 49, 195–241.

Fleming, A. 1984. The prehistoric landscape of Dartmoor: wider implications. *Landscape History* 6, 5–19.

Fleming, A. 1998. Prehistoric landscapes and the quest for territorial pattern. In Everson, P. and Williamson, T. (eds) *The Archaeology of Landscape: Studies Presented to Christopher Taylor*, 42–66. Manchester: Manchester University Press.

Garton, D. 1991. Neolithic settlement in the Peak District: perspective and prospects. In Hodges, R. and Smith, K. (eds) *Recent Developments in the Archaeology of the Peak District*, 3–21. Sheffield: J. R. Collis Publications, Sheffield Archaeological Monographs 2.

Gilles, J. L. and Gefu, J. 1990. Nomads, ranchers and the state: the sociocultural aspects of pastoralism. In Galaty, J. G. and Johnson, D. L. (eds) *The World of Pastoralism: Herding Systems in Comparative Perspective*, 99–118. London: Guildford Press.

Green, H. S. 1980. *The Flint Arrowheads of the British Isles: Part 1*. Oxford: British Archaeological Reports, British Series 75(i).

Harding, A. F. with Lee, G. E. 1987. *Henge Monuments and Related Sites of Great Britain: Air Photographic Evidence and Catalogue*. Oxford: British Archaeological Reports, British Series 175.

Harding, A. F. with Ostoja-Zagórski, J. 1994. Prehistoric and Early Medieval activity on Danby Rigg, North Yorkshire. *Archaeological Journal* 151, 16–97.

Hawke-Smith, C. F. 1979. *Man-Land Relations in Prehistoric Britain. The Dove-Derwent Interfluve, Derbyshire: a Study in Human Ecology*. Oxford: British Archaeological Reports, British Series 64.

Hawke-Smith, C. F. 1981. Land use, burial practice and territories in the Peak District *c*. 2000–1000 bc. In Barker, G. (ed.) *Prehistoric Communities in Northern England: Essays in Social and Economic Reconstruction*, 57–72. Sheffield: Dept. of Prehistory and Archaeology, University of Sheffield.

Hicks, S. P. 1972. The impact of man on the East Moor of Derbyshire from Mesolithic times. *Archaeological Journal* 129, 1–21.

Humphrey, C. 1995. Chiefly and shamanist landscapes in Mongolia. In Hirsch, E. and O'Hanlon, M. (eds) *The Anthropology of Landscape: Perspectives on Place and Space*, 135–162. Oxford: Clarendon Press.

Humphrey, C. and Sneath, D. 1996. *Pastoralism and Institutional Change in Inner Asia: Comparative Perspectives from the Meccia Research Project*. London: Overseas Development Institute, Pastoral Development Network Paper 39b.

Ingold, T. 1986. *The Appropriation of Nature: Essays on Human Ecology and Social Relations*. Manchester: Manchester University Press.

Jones, R. L., Cundill, P. R. and Simmons, I. G. 1979. Archaeology and palaeobotany on the North York Moors and their environs. *Yorkshire Archaeological Journal* 51, 15–22.

Kitchen, W. 2000. *Later Neolithic and Bronze Age Land Use and Settlement in the Derbyshire Peak District: Cairnfields in Context*. Unpublished Ph.D. thesis, University of Sheffield.

Manby, T. G. 1988. The Neolithic in Eastern Yorkshire. In Manby, T. G. (ed.) *Archaeology in Eastern Yorkshire:* *Essays in Honour of T. C. M. Brewster*, 35–88. Sheffield: Dept. of Archaeology and Prehistory, University of Sheffield.

Pryor, F. 1998. *Farmers in Prehistoric Britain*. Stroud: Tempus.

Radley, J. 1966a. A Bronze Age ringwork on Totley Moor and other Bronze Age ringworks in the Pennines. *Archaeological Journal* 123, 1–26.

Radley, J. 1966b. Fifty arrow-heads from the gritstone moors of the southern Pennines, with a consideration of other arrow-heads from the Peak District. *Transactions of the Hunter Archaeological Society* 9(2), 110–114.

Smith, E. A. 1988. Risk and uncertainty in the 'original affluent society': evolutionary ecology of resource-sharing and land tenure. In Ingold, T., Riches, D. and Woodburn, J. (eds) *Hunters and Gatherers. Vol. 1: History, Evolution and Social Change*, 222–251. Oxford: Berg.

Spratt, D. A. 1981. Prehistoric boundaries on the North Yorkshire Moors. In Barker, G. (ed.) *Prehistoric Communities in Northern England: Essays in Social and Economic Reconstruction*, 87–104. Sheffield: Dept. of Prehistory and Archaeology, University of Sheffield.

Tilley, C. 1994. *A Phenomenology of Landscape: Places, Paths and Monuments*. Oxford: Berg.

Vine, P. M. 1982. *The Neolithic and Bronze Age Cultures of the Middle and Upper Trent Basin*. Oxford: British Archaeological Reports, British Series 105.

Whittle, A. 1997. Moving on and moving around: Neolithic settlement mobility. In Topping, P. (ed.) *Neolithic Landscapes*, 15–22. Oxford: Oxbow Monograph 86.

11   A Later Bronze Age landscape on the Avon Levels: settlement, shelters and saltmarsh at Cabot Park

Martin Locock

Summary

Excavation on a proposed development site at Cabot Park, Avonmouth, in 1997 identified an extensive horizon within the alluvial silts representing a stabilised upper saltmarsh surface of Later Bronze Age date (at about 1200 cal. BC). Associated with the horizon were a group of features comprising burnt stone, pottery, animal bone and charcoal. Structural evidence is limited to shallow post-settings and stakeholes.

Similar sites have been identified on the Severn foreshore at Chapeltump, Rumney Great Wharf and Cold Harbour, and can be firmly contrasted with conventional roundhouse occupation sites in drier locations. Temporary or seasonal occupation, perhaps involving 'industrial' activities (e.g. salt-making), coastal grazing and hunting, seems likely. The pottery has strong parallels with Brean Down Unit 4, Combe Hay and Chapeltump II.

In interpreting such sites, simple models of 'permanent' and 'temporary' settlement foci and marginality are unhelpful; the range of activities has a spatial and temporal dimension, and thus the prehistoric landscape needs to be considered as a whole. The Cabot Park sites presumably represent one part of a complex pattern whose other components included occupation of the bedrock margin, agriculture, and ritual and burial on Lawrence Weston Hill. The Later Bronze Age trackways and timber structures in channels found elsewhere in the Estuary were probably linked to a similar diversity of environment and practice.

Introduction

Although archaeologists have long recognised that much of past behaviour needs explanation at a landscape rather than a site scale, the lack of detailed data to provide a context often limits what can be said. This problem is generally a matter of the low definition of information about other sites in the area (lack of close dating in particular), and perhaps limited evidence for vegetation. In a dynamic environment such as the Severn Levels, even the basic topography that prevailed at any specific point in the past can be hard to establish. It is only now that a critical mass has been reached when it becomes possible to do more than note sites within an uncertain context. This paper is an attempt to reconstruct the Later Bronze Age landscape for part of the North Avon Level, based mainly on the data from recent excavations on the alluvium, but also drawing on previous discoveries on the inland margin whose significance can now be better appreciated. The model for the exploitation and use of the landscape is complex, with numerous interlinked elements; the applicability of 'core and periphery' and central place models for spatial organisation is discussed in the light of the model.

The Levels landscape

The landscape of the Severn Levels has four well-defined topographic areas, from conventional bedrock 'dry land', reclaimed and drained alluvial plain, the exposed foreshore and saltmarsh, and the river itself. Between the River Avon at Avonmouth and Oldbury-on-Severn is the area known as the Avonmouth Level, varying in width from 2–5km. The inland edge comprises a narrow scarp foot bench (0.5km wide) rising to steep ridges up to 100m OD.

The alluvial deposits have formed since the end of the last glaciation, and have been characterised by Allen and Rae (1987) as the Wentlooge Formation. The large tidal reach experienced in the Bristol Channel led to the creation of very extensive salt-

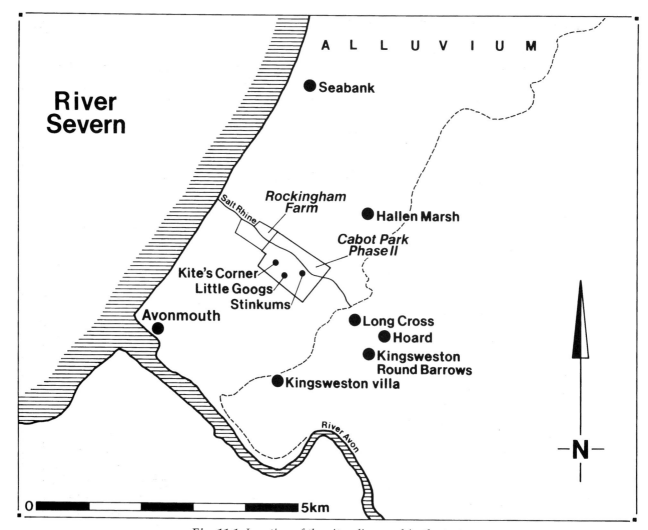

Fig. 11.1 *Location of the sites discussed in the text*

marsh areas, the inland margins of which became stabilised periodically. The Formation includes estuarine silts and peat deposits, representing saline/brackish and freshwater conditions respectively. Although for some parts of the estuary it has been possible to establish a general sequence of peat and silt formation (for example the Caldicot Level), it seems that the Avonmouth Level was a more fragmented landscape and peat growth was localised (Lawler *et al.* 1992).

In the historic period there have been successive attempts to protect the area from estuarine flooding, leading to the creation of a system of rhines (drainage ditches), sea walls and gouts (sluice gates). The main rhines probably originated as natural channels. Although the chronology of reclamations (or more properly land-claim) is uncertain, there are indications of initial occupation on the present ground level from the eleventh century AD and documentary evidence suggesting that some drainage had occurred in the Saxon period (Rippon 1996; 1997). The fully-protected and drained landscape as

currently seen probably dates to the seventeenth century.

Outside the sea wall lies the active saltmarsh (limited in extent on the North Avon coast, which seems to be in an erosive phase) and the silt-covered intertidal zone, covering some exposures of glacial gravels and bedrock (Riley 1998).

Recent work in Avonmouth

The agricultural landscape of the Levels has seen a shift to industrial use over the past 100 years, following the construction of the Avonmouth Docks in the 1890s and the subsequent construction of chemical works on the coast. The pace of development has been increased recently by the construction of the Second Severn Crossing and its linking motorways, and the good transport links have led to a series of proposals for distribution and warehousing units. These have prompted intensive archaeological investigations (Fig. 11.1), whose results have provided a firm sequence for the changes in the environment, as well as identifying sites including an Iron Age hut group at Hallen Marsh (Barnes 1993).

The Cabot Park development (Fig. 11.1) covers an area of 200 hectares on the north edge of Avonmouth, Bristol (in the 1974–1996 county of Avon, and pre-1974 Gloucestershire; in the historic parish of Henbury tithing of Lawrence Weston), between the A403 Aust-Avonmouth road and the M49 motorway. It includes a railfreight terminal and distribution units. The first phase of the development lay at the northwest, closest to the coast, around the eighteenth century buildings of Rockingham Farm. Evaluation and excavation of the area was concentrated on a medieval moated site, but also located a late prehistoric stabilised soil horizon within the alluvial silts (Locock 1997a; Locock and Lawler 2000). Palaeoenvironmental analyses on the horizon showed that it probably formed in an upper saltmarsh environment, presumably during a temporary break in estuarine silting.

The current phase of development lies immediately southeast of Rockingham Farm, covering an area of 60 hectares along the banks of the Salt Rhine. A nested programme of investigation has been undertaken, with a borehole survey and trial pits to map the deep stratigraphy, investigation of surface features and known sites, and evaluation trenching within building footprints (Locock *et al.* 1998; Locock in press). The principal features of the alluvial stratigraphy are two horizons: an organic clay of Neolithic date, and an extensive gleyed layer representing a Late Bronze Age stabilised soil, as seen at Rockingham Farm. In between these horizons, and above and below, there are unbroken estuarine silts. No peat deposits occur in the area.

The stabilised soil has been examined for a range of palaeoenvironmental evidence, which has revealed a consistent picture of an upper saltmarsh location, with soil ripening, salt/brackish diatoms, and pollen devoid of trees. In some places, the gleyed horizon dips into palaeochannels, presumably contemporary creeks; in general it seem to form a flat, undifferentiated surface. The gleying is concluded to be the result of a rapid rise in water table during the renewed onset of estuarine flooding (the interpretation of these soils is discussed at greater length elsewhere: see Locock 1999).

The Cabot Park sites

In three locations within the study area, the gleyed horizon produced evidence of human activity. These sites have been named after field names on a 1772 estate map as Little Googs, Kites Corner and Stin-

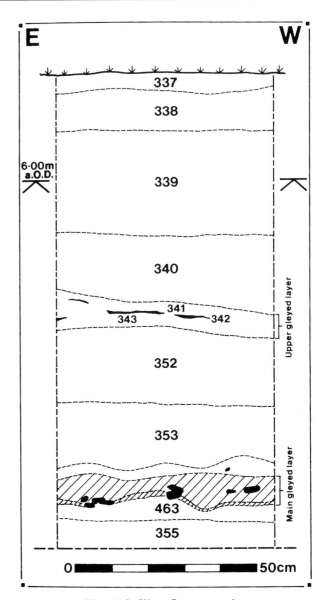

Fig. 11.2 *Kites Corner, section*

kums. They are similar in form: a dense scatter of charcoal and burnt stone extending over an area of 5–8m diameter, associated with numerous pottery fragments and animal bone (see for example Figs 11.2 and 11.3). There is very limited evidence for structures.

Radiocarbon dates are available for the Kites Corner site but these are unfortunately inconsistent (see Table 11.1); that from the upper gleyed layer, with a very low carbon content might be considered unreliable, but there are also wide variations from the charcoal samples. Although the surface may have been exposed for decades, the full date range seems improbable.

The Little Googs site was revealed in two evaluation trenches; it occupies the southwest bank of a broad palaeochannel that runs across much of the Cabot Park area. The site lies outside the proposed

Table 11.1 *Radiocarbon dates from Kites Corner*

Lab. ref. no.	Source	Measured radiocarbon age	Calibrated two sigma
Beta 129554	Surface of dense charcoal patch (462)	2610 ± 70 BP	890–530 cal BC
Beta 134900	Dense charcoal patch (462)	2970 ± 60 BP	1390–1000 cal BC
Beta 134901	Charcoal spread (351)	3350 ± 60 BP	1760–1505 cal BC
Beta 134902	Upper gleyed layer (341)	2850 ± 40 BP	1120–910 cal BC

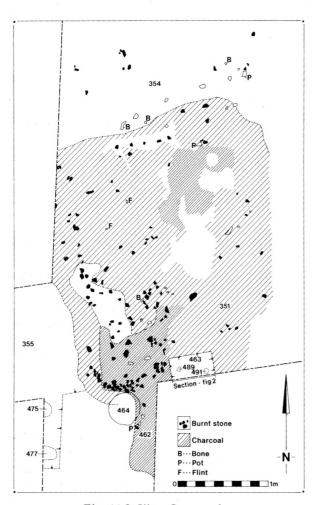

Fig. 11.3 *Kites Corner, plan*

Table 11.2 *Pollen and charcoal in order of decreasing frequency*

CHARCOAL	POLLEN
Oak	High % herbs
Ash	High % spores
Elm	High % aquatic
cf Hawthorn	Small no. arboreal: pine, alder, limes, hazel
cf Blackthorn	
Hazel	
Alder	
Birch	
Holly	
Willow	

tures, the lack of spatial differentiation of occupation, activity and refuse areas, and the very small numbers of flints suggest that they are not conventional permanent settlements. The materials present point to a range of activities.

The presence of stone is in itself surprising; at this point, bedrock lies 15m below present ground level, with the intervening material comprising sands and clays. Its occurrence on the site is not accidental; it must have involved deliberate collection and transport to the site. Its source has not been established, but it is very mixed and small in size. It has been suggested for a similar site at Rumney Great Wharf, Cardiff (Allen 1996), that the stone was from exposures of glacial gravels in the river bed, and this seems likely at Cabot Park too.

The charcoal and burnt stone is evidence for extensive or repeated pyrotechnic activities. Since the upper saltmarsh was devoid of trees, the fuel (which comprised shrub-type sticks rather than timber) must also have been transported from further inland (the pollen from the site contains few tree species typical of alder carr, suggesting that the woodland lay some distance away) (see Table 11.2). The pottery is simple and relatively undecorated in contrast to the assemblages from bedrock settlement sites such as Thornwell, Chepstow, Monmouthshire (Hughes 1996). It has strong parallels with the pottery from Unit 4 at Brean Down, Somerset, and Combe Hay, Somerset, but is considered likely to have been made in the locality (Price and Watts 1980; Bell 1990). Certainly, clay, stone for temper and evidence of burning are all present on the Cabot Park sites.

Among the animal bones present, cattle predominates, although deer is also found; there were

building footprint and will be preserved within the development. The site at Kites Corner was fully exposed during the evaluation in 1998 in order to examine the site in plan, and was excavated in 1999. Two shallow central postholes and a few stakeholes were the only evidence for structures. The Stinkums site was again seen in evaluation trenching, and in fact comprises three scatters over a distance of 70m, separated by blank areas (possibly channels). These will be investigated when that part of the development is commenced.

When these were first exposed, interpretation concentrated on two questions: do they represent permanent settlements, and if not, where is the settlement? The absence of roundhouse-type struc-

very few sheep/goat. Fish bones were found in the sieved samples. In contrast, contemporary bedrock sites yield little or no wild fauna (Tinsley and Grigson 1981, 223), suggesting either that hunting was not a significant food source, or (more likely) that the pattern of butchery, consumption and discard associated with hunting is not reflected in assemblages from settlements. Thus the Cabot Park assemblage reflects a distinctly different pattern of meat consumption than was usual.

Despite the minimal structural evidence, the quantity and variety of materials present suggest something more than a temporary structure; rather, a seasonal camp might be proposed, used as a base for foraging, cattle pasturing and craft activities. The recognition of these sites as a distinctive site type rather than the eroded remains of roundhouses has led to the identification of several previously re-ported sites on the Welsh foreshore as examples, including Rumney Great Wharf 2, Cardiff (Allen 1996), Cold Harbour, Newport (Whittle *et al.* 1989), and Chapeltump II, Monmouthshire (Whittle *et al.* 1989; Locock *et al.* 2000). At Chapeltump II, bone points and the presence of balls of fired clay sug-gested on-site pot making.

Perhaps the most critical question remains the reason for the presence of the burnt stones. In some ways, the Cabot Park sites are similar to burnt mounds (situated close to water; stone and charcoal present in profusion; limited evidence for struc-tures), but there are also significant differences, particularly the presence of the large assemblage of pottery. Although the stone may have been used in cooking or to provide temper for pottery, the effort involved in transporting the stone seems dispro-portionate. It is possible that the stone and fuel were being used as part of a salt making process, as Barfield (1991) suggests, albeit using a technique that does not involve briquetage vessels as found at Brean Down, Somerset (Bell 1990) and Droitwich, Worcestershire (Barfield 1991). Extensive sampling was undertaken during the excavations at Kites Corner to check for enhanced salt levels in the soil, but returned negative results. However, the need for access to saltwater would explain the location of the sites at the boundary between the dry areas and the saltmarsh, which otherwise seems unnecessarily close to the tidal waters.

Exploitation of the Levels landscape

By using the evidence from the materials found at Cabot Park and other sites in the area sharing the Levels environment, it is possible to draw up a detailed model of Late Bronze Age use of the various topographic zones (Fig. 11.4).

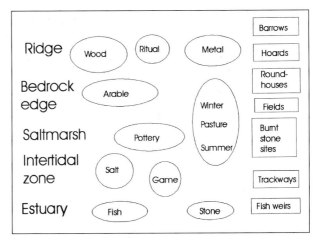

Fig. 11.4 *Activities in the Later Bronze Age landscape*

Intertidal zone

Although direct evidence from the Bronze Age intertidal zone is limited, the excavation of a river channel at Caldicot, Monmouthshire, revealed evi-dence for both a well built boat and a series of wooden fish weirs in the bed (Nayling and Caseldine 1997). There is little doubt that the food resources of the estuary were well used, as is implied by the construction of trackways in order to reach them. The collection of stone from exposures in the estuary would probably have been easier than quarrying from bedrock.

Saltmarsh-edge

The Cabot Park-type sites provide evidence for the use of this zone for craft activities and hunting, and probably seasonal cattle pasture and possibly salt-making. In addition, Later Bronze Age trackways have been noted on the Welsh foreshore at Cold Harbour Pill (Whittle *et al.* 1989; Locock 1997b).

Bedrock margin

The discovery of Bronze Age pottery along the bedrock margin (Boore 1996; Burchill 1996) suggests that a settlement lies somewhere in the area, pre-sumably associated with arable fields. The limited space available may have restricted the extent of the fields. The recovery from Kites Corner of four carbonised cereal grains (two wheat, two barley) is the only direct evidence of agriculture in the area. The settlement might be expected to conform to the roundhouse-type model, as found at Thornwell, Monmouthshire (Hughes 1996) and Atlantic Trading Estate, Barry, Vale of Glamorgan (Sell 1998). There are also antiquarian reports of unlocated flints from Kingsweston (Tratman 1947).

Fig. 11.5 *The Kingsweston Hill hoard (photo: Bristol City Museums and Galleries; BCMG 31/1982)*

Bedrock ridge

A small group of barrows is spread along the crest of the ridge. The remains are four low mounds, excavated in the 1920s (Tratman 1923; 1924). The main barrow, T2, was described as 40 feet (12m) in diameter. It covered a cremation as well as a hearth associated with a spread of burnt stone that extended over an area of 10 feet (3m). The pottery was of a soapy fabric with fingertip decoration and was described as being 'of Hallstatt type'; animal bone included horse, pig, ox and sheep. An Early Iron Age date was proposed, mainly on the basis of the presence of an iron cheek piece with Hallstatt affinities and the transitional Bronze Age/Iron Age pottery (Tratman 1924, 239; 1947, 171, 176). The dating has since been questioned; the radiocarbon dates for the burials in the barrow at Court Hill, Tickenham (primary burial 1375 ± 100 bc; secondary burial 715 ± 130 bc), led Green (1973) to suggest a firmly Bronze Age date for Kingsweston Hill T2 and its pottery. Tratman (1975) defended the original dating; the pottery cannot be re-examined because it

was destroyed during the Second World War. Although certainty is not possible, it would appear likely that the pottery implies a use of the barrow in the final stages of the Bronze Age. Given that this 'monument' produced charcoal, burnt stone, pottery and animal bone, it would have borne a marked resemblance to the Cabot Park sites.

A more precisely dateable find from the ridge was the Kingsweston hoard of the Ewart Park phase, discovered by metal detectorists just east of the barrows in 1982 (Fig. 11.5). The hoard has not been published; a photograph and brief mention were included in a paper by Grinsell (1986), and a fuller account was prepared by Plowright in 1983 (unpublished). The hoard comprised 28 objects recovered over a period of weeks from an area of 10m diameter. 20 of these are socketed axes, of which one was complete and five largely so. Three casting jets and part of a possible socketed sickle were also present. The axes had casting faults, and many of the objects had ragged breaks and had been torn and bent, making the identification as a metalworking hoard probable. The axes include two Sompting types, one with pelleted rib decoration and a small spur at the base of the loop, and one with two pairs of diverging ribs. The Sompting material has parallels with the Llyn Fawr hoard at the very end of the Bronze Age (Savory 1980), and a date of *c.* 920–700 cal. BC can be suggested (Needham *et al.* 1997).

It is assumed that the bedrock ridge may also have been the source of the wood used on the saltmarsh.

Later Bronze Age landscapes

Although there is still debate about the date at which sedentism became general, a typical model of dryland settlement in the later prehistoric period would include a permanent domestic site surrounded by its fields, with more distant areas used for pasture, wood and other resources. The evidence for extensive field systems around settlement sites in the Thames Valley, in turn surrounded by areas with limited use (apart from metal hoards), might be seen to fit this model (Yates 1999). David Clarke's model (1972) of a wetland landscape at Glastonbury is similar in intent, with the settlement surrounded by infield, outfield and uncultivated 'scrub' zones. These models share an approach based on core and periphery oppositions, in which key functions and activities occur at the centre.

This is perhaps an inevitable component of the analysis of peasant-type arable subsistence, where daily travelling time constrains the extent of different landuses. It is unfortunate, nonetheless, because it is easy to conflate peripheral location, social marginality, and low economic productivity as a logical package (Young and Simmonds 1995). Peripheral and marginal locations need not be of limited significance. Anthropologists have little use for the term 'marginality', but are very interested in the related topics of liminality and boundaries. It is boundaries that define group identity, group membership and territory in reference to other groups. On this basis, we should expect activities that define group identity to occur not at the centre, but rather along the boundaries, a pattern that is indeed suggested by the distribution of human remains in the Later Bronze Age (Brück 1995). It is tempting to see the use of the Kingsweston barrows as a statement of ownership. It may also be possible to see the association of metalworking hoards with the areas between settlements as being part of this 'claiming' of the land, while also perhaps reflecting the opportunities for trade and exchange responsible for the wide distribution of metals and finished tools. Lobb's study of Later Bronze Age activity in a river valley context in Berkshire noted the use of upland, 'marginal' land for barrow groups away from the main settlements on the river gravels; in contrast, timber structures were found on the river bank itself (1992, 174).

In economic terms, too, it may be easy to underestimate the relative importance of summer pasture, wood and other resources, as opposed to arable cultivation. At Cabot Park, with the constrained area for fields, it seems reasonable to assume that the economy concentrated on the resources that were available, and relied on trade in craft goods in return for grain. It may be that this emphasis in the economy was accompanied by a different settlement pattern, in which much of the population spent much of the time based at temporary shelters.

It may be, then, that to look for the settlement associated with Cabot Park is fruitless; as has been shown, there was a complex pattern of exploitation across the topographic zones, whose use was interdependent. Evidence from upland Later Bronze Age landscapes in the Marlborough Downs (Gingell 1991) and on Dartmoor (Fleming 1978; 1983; 1988), as well as from lowland landscapes such as the Hampshire coast (Gardiner and Allen 2001), shows that by the Later Bronze Age, land was precious, and the question was not whether to use it, but rather what to use it for. It should therefore comes as little surprise to see the intensive exploitation of the opportunities presented by the Levels landscape.

Acknowledgements

The fieldwork at Cabot Park was undertaken by GGAT; individual elements were directed by Martin Lawler, Martin Locock, Sarah Robinson, Richard Roberts, Steve Sell, and Adam Yates. Specialist reports were prepared by Nigel Cameron, Astrid Caseldine, John Crowther, Jenny J. Hall, Su Johnson, Richard Macphail, Lorraine Mepham, Mark Noël and Mike Walker.

The work was funded by the developers, Western Properties Ltd, AMEC Construction Ltd and Burford Group PLC. We are grateful to Bob Jones and Jon Brett of Bristol City Council, Vanessa Straker, Julie Jones and Denise Druce of University of Bristol, and Andrew Davison and Neil Linford of English Heritage for their help during the project, and to Gail Boyle of Bristol Museum for her assistance with the Kingsweston hoard.

The author is grateful to his colleague Paul Jones for preparing the figures, and to Paul Graves Brown for his comments on the text.

References

Allen, J. R. L. 1996. Three Final Bronze Age occupations at Rumney Great Wharf on the Wentlooge Level, Gwent. *Studia Celtica* 30, 1–16.

Allen, J. R. L. and Rae, J. E. 1987. Late Flandrian shoreline oscillations in the Severn Estuary: a geomorphological and stratigraphical reconnaissance. *Philosophical Transactions of the Royal Society of London* 315 (series B), 185–230.

Barfield, L. H. 1991. Hot stones: hot food or hot baths? In Hodder, M. A. and Barfield, L. H. (eds) *Burnt Mounds and Hot Stone Technology*, 59–68. West Bromwich: Sandwell Metropolitan Borough Council.

Barnes, I. 1993. Second Severn Crossing, English approaches: an interim report on the 1992/93 fieldwork. *Archaeology in the Severn Estuary* 4, 5–30.

Bell, M. 1990. *Brean Down Excavations, 1983–1987*. London: English Heritage Archaeological Report 15.

Boore, E. 1996. Kings Weston Road/Long Cross, Lawrence Weston. *Bristol and Avon Archaeology* 13, 83.

Brück, J. 1995. A place for the dead: the role of human remains in Late Bronze Age Britain. *Proceedings of the Prehistoric Society* 61, 245–278.

Burchill, R. 1996. Survey and re-excavation at Kingsweston Roman villa. *Bristol and Avon Archaeology* 13, 47–52.

Clarke, D. L. 1972. A provisional model of an Iron Age society and its settlement system. In Clarke, D. L. (ed.) *Models in Archaeology*, 801–869. London: Methuen.

Fleming, A. 1978. The prehistoric landscape of Dartmoor, part 1: south Dartmoor. *Proceedings of the Prehistoric Society* 44, 97–123.

Fleming, A. 1983. The prehistoric landscape of Dartmoor, part 2: north and east Dartmoor. *Proceedings of the Prehistoric Society* 49, 195–241.

Fleming, A. 1988. *The Dartmoor Reaves: Investigating Prehistoric Land Divisions*. London: Batsford.

Gardiner, J. and Allen, M. J. 2001. The occupation of the developing harbour landscape. In Allen, M. J. and Gardiner, J. *Our Changing Coast: a Survey of the Intertidal*

Archaeology of Langstone Harbour, 203–219. York: CBA Research Report 124.

Gingell, C. 1992. *The Marlborough Downs: a Later Bronze Age Landscape and its Origins.* Devizes: Wiltshire Archaeological and Natural History Society Monograph 1.

Green, H. S. 1973. The excavation of a round cairn at Court Hill, Tickenham, north Somerset. *Proceedings of the Somerset Archaeology and Natural History Society* 117, 33–46.

Grinsell, L. V. 1986. Bronze Age settlement and burial ritual. In Aston, M. and Iles, R. (eds) *The Archaeology of Avon: a Review from the Neolithic to the Middle Ages,* 29–40. Bristol: Avon County Council.

Hughes, G. 1996. *The Excavation of a Late Prehistoric and Romano-British Settlement at Thornwell Farm, Chepstow, Gwent, 1992.* Oxford: British Archaeological Reports, British Series 244.

Lawler, M., Parkhouse, J. and Straker, V. 1992. *Archaeology of the Second Severn Crossing: Assessment and Recommendations for the English Approaches.* Swansea: Glamorgan-Gwent Archaeological Trust Report to the Second Severn Crossing Group.

Lobb, S. J. 1992. Development of the landscape. In Butterworth, C. A. and Lobb, S. J. *Excavations in the Burghfield Area, Berkshire,* 172–177. Salisbury: Wessex Archaeology Report 1.

Locock, M. 1997a. Rockingham Farm, Avonmouth, 1993–1997: moated enclosures on the North Avon Level. *Archaeology in the Severn Estuary* 8, 83–88.

Locock, M. 1997b. A prehistoric trackway at Cold Harbour Pill, Redwick, Gwent. *Archaeology in the Severn Estuary* 8, 9–12.

Locock, M. 1999. Buried soils of the Wentlooge Formation. *Archaeology in the Severn Estuary* 10.

Locock, M. In press. A bonfire in the saltmarsh, spring, 1200 BC: the archaeology and environment of a temporary shelter. In Hinman, M. (ed.) *Interpreting Stratigraphy* 11.

Locock, M. and Lawler, M. 2000. Moated enclosures on the North Avon Level: survey and excavation at Rockingham Farm, Avonmouth, 1993–1997. *Transactions of the Bristol and Gloucestershire Archaeological Society* 118, 93–122.

Locock, M., Robinson, S. and Yates, A. 1998. Late Bronze Age sites at Cabot Park, Avonmouth. *Archaeology in the Severn Estuary* 9, 31–36.

Locock, M., Trett, B. and Lawler, M. 2000. Further late prehistoric features on the foreshore at Chapeltump, Magor, Monmouthshire: Chapeltump II and the Upton trackway. *Studia Celtica* 34, 17–48.

Nayling, N. and Caseldine, A. (eds) 1997. *Excavations at Caldicot, Gwent: Bronze Age Palaeochannels in the Lower Nedern Valley.* York: Council for British Archaeology Research Report 108.

Needham, S., Bronk Ramsay, C., Coombs, D., Cartwright, C. and Pettit, P. 1997. An independent chronology for British Bronze Age metalwork: the results of the Oxford Radiocarbon Accelerator Programme. *Archaeological Journal* 154, 55–107.

Plowright, G. Unpublished. *An Analysis of the Late Bronze Age Hoard from King's Weston Down, Bristol, and Some Problems Associated with its Display.* Museums' Association Diploma Project, 1983 (Bristol Museum 31/1982).

Price, R. and Watts, L. 1980. Rescue excavations at Combe Hay, Somerset, 1968–1973. *Proceedings of the Somerset Archaeology and Natural History Society* 124, 1–49.

Riley, H. 1998. Intertidal survey at Avonmouth and Oldbury-on-Severn. *Archaeology in the Severn Estuary* 9, 79–82.

Rippon, S. 1996. *Gwent Levels: the Evolution of a Wetland Landscape.* York: Council for British Archaeology Research Report 105.

Rippon, S. 1997. *The Severn Estuary: Landscape Evolution and Wetland Reclamation.* London: Leicester University Press.

Savory, H. N. 1980. *Guide Catalogue of the Bronze Age Collections.* Cardiff: National Museum of Wales.

Sell, S. H. 1998. Excavations of a Bronze Age settlement at the Atlantic Trading Estate, Barry, South Glamorgan (ST 134 673). *Studia Celtica* 32, 1–26.

Tinsley, H. M. and Grigson, C. 1981. The Bronze Age. In Simmons, I. and Tooley, M. (eds) *The Environment in British Prehistory,* 210–249. London: Duckworth.

Tratman, E. K. 1923. First report on King's Weston Hill, Bristol. *Proceedings of the University of Bristol Spelaeological Society* 2(1), 76–82.

Tratman, E. K. 1924. Second report on King's Weston Hill, Bristol. *Proceedings of the University of Bristol Spelaeological Society* 2(2), 238–243.

Tratman, E. K. 1947. Prehistoric Bristol. *Proceedings of the University of Bristol Spelaeological Society* 5(3), 162–182.

Tratman, E. K. 1975. The excavation of a round cairn at Court Hill, Tickenham, north Somerset, 1969, and the King's Weston Hill Barrows, Bristol. *Proceedings of the Somerset Archaeology and Natural History Society* 119, 56–57.

Whittle, A., Antoine, S., Gardiner, N., Milles, A. and Webster, P. 1989. Two Later Bronze Age occupations and an Iron Age channel on the Gwent foreshore. *Bulletin of the Board of Celtic Studies* 36, 200–223.

Yates, D. T. 1999. Bronze Age field systems in the Thames valley. *Oxford Journal of Archaeology* 18, 157–170.

Young, R. and Simmonds, T. 1995. Marginality and the nature of later prehistoric settlement in the north of England. *Landscape History* 17, 5–17.

12 Reading Business Park: the results of phases 1 and 2

Adam Brossler

Summary

This paper examines the evidence recovered from two phases of excavation undertaken at the site of Reading Business Park, Berkshire (Moore and Jennings 1992; Brossler and Early forthcoming). The aim of the paper is to provide a brief synopsis of the activity found, highlighting points of interest, such as the relationship between the Middle Bronze Age fieldsystem and the placement of two cremation deposits. The final section is concerned with the management of space on the Late Bronze Age settlement. An attempt has been made to divide the area into activity zones, based on the spatial pattern of structures, features and artefacts.

Background

The site of Reading Business Park is located in the lower Kennet Valley, 1km to the south of the River Kennet and 3.5km from the centre of Reading; it encompasses an area of *c.* 80ha (Fig. 12.1). Two phases of excavation were undertaken at the Business Park (Fig. 12.2). The first phase, undertaken in 1987–1988, comprised seven excavation areas, and was published in 1992 by John Moore and David Jennings. The second phase of excavation was carried out in 1995; publication of this is forthcoming (Brossler and Early forthcoming).

Pre-Bronze Age activity

An excavation, located to the north of the Late Bronze Age settlement, identified the presence of Neolithic activity, which comprised a rare example of a segmented ring ditch, 20 pits, 15 postholes and a substantial quantity of flint work, along with a sherd of Grooved Ware and a sherd of Peterborough Ware pottery.

Early Bronze Age activity

The earliest Bronze Age activity is represented by a ring-ditch, tentatively dated to the Early Bronze Age. It was located to the west of the Middle Bronze Age fieldsystem, and measured 3m in internal diameter. No dateable material was recovered from the fills of the ring-ditch. However, similar examples of Early Bronze Age ring-ditches have been identified at Shorncote Quarry, Gloucestershire. One of these measured 4m in internal diameter and had an internal pit (Barclay *et al.* 1995, 31), while a further two examples measured 5.4m and 5.7m in internal diameter respectively (Hearne and Adam 1999, 42).

Middle Bronze Age activity

The fieldsystem

During the Middle Bronze Age, activity in the Business Park area and its environs appears to have become more intensive. In Areas 3100 and 3000B, a coaxial fieldsystem was identified (Fig. 12.3). A further four excavation areas all contained ditches that were also thought to be parts of coaxial fieldsystems (Moore and Jennings 1992).

The fieldsystem in Areas 3100 and 3000B appears to have undergone a certain amount of change, with at least three identifiable phases of activity (Fig. 12.3). The phases were based on the stratigraphic relationship between the ditch-cuts and appear to have utilised different areas of land, which may suggest that some form of field-rotation system was being practised during this period. This system of

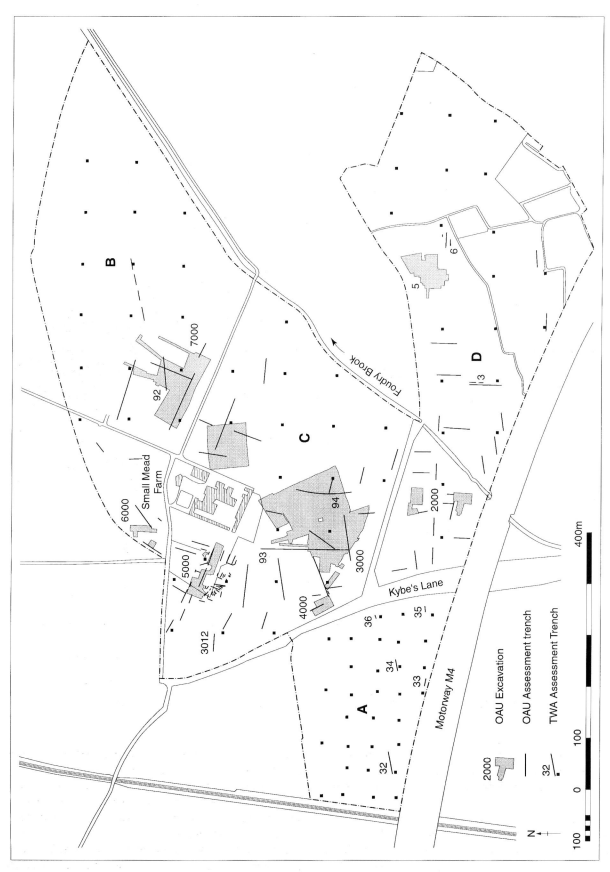

Fig. 12.1 Location map (drawn by Mike Middleton)

Fig. 12.2 *Plan of 1988 and 1995 excavation areas (drawn by Mike Middleton)*

rotation may indicate a degree of specialisation in agricultural activities. There is evidence to suggest that both pastoral and arable agriculture were being practised at the site from the Late Neolithic period. The environmental evidence indicates that cereal crops were being cultivated during the Late Neolithic and Late Bronze Age (Campbell forthcoming), while the animal bone assemblage indicates that the cows were the main domesticate (Wilson forth-

coming). Further evidence that suggests that pastoralism was the dominant form of agricultural practice lies in the presence of a waterhole. This was located close to the fieldsystem and probably acted as a water source for animals, rather than providing water for a settlement. An example of another Middle Bronze Age waterhole located adjacent to fieldsystems can be seen at Eight Acre Field, Radley (Mudd 1995). The placement of waterholes adjacent

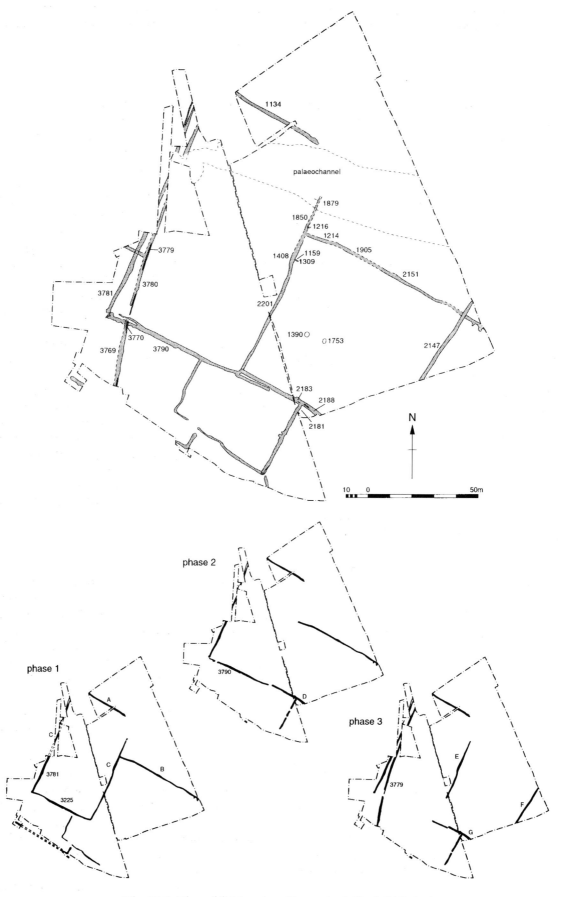

Fig. 12.3 Plan of field system (drawn by Mike Middleton)

to fieldsystems is of significance, and is practised through into the Iron Age (Brossler *et al.* forthcoming).

The fieldsystem and cremations

The fact that the fieldsystem appears to be aligned on the earlier ring-ditch is of some significance. The ring-ditch is located at the junction of two field boundaries, which respect it rather than cutting through it. Recent arguments suggest that Middle and Late Bronze Age fieldsystems often respect earlier funerary monuments (Yates 1999; Field this volume). At Reading Business Park, continuing interest in pre-existing monuments can also be seen in the re-use of the Late Neolithic segmented ring-ditch. A cremation deposit was identified in one of the fills of the feature, and produced a calibrated radiocarbon date-range of 1732–1723 BC, 1688–1431 BC at 95% confidence (NZA 9508: Brossler and Early forthcoming).

Another interesting note is the placement of two cremation deposits next to one of the ditches. This may indicate that funerary remains were used as markers to strengthen ancestral ties to land. Brück argues that in the Late Bronze Age human remains may have been used to symbolise identity and liminality (1995, 263). The placement of the cremations may represent an attempt to establish control over an area of land that was located beyond the immediate reach of a settlement. Cohen argues that ritual forms part of a symbolic device, 'through which community boundaries are affirmed and reinforced' (1985, 50). This observation supports the possibility that the cremation deposits were deliberately placed to affirm both physical and spiritual rights to land. An interesting point is that the fieldsystem changes location, possibly indicating that the claim to the land was either short lived, or that the attitude towards such types of funerary remains changed, much as the attitude towards inhumation appears to have changed in the preceding period.

Late Bronze Age activity

The focal point of the Late Bronze Age activity is represented by the settlements in Areas 3100 (Moore and Jennings 1992) and 3000B (Brossler and Early forthcoming) (Fig. 12.2). Another settlement was identified in Area 5 (Moore and Jennings 1992), but will not be discussed in this paper. The settlement in Areas 3100 and 3000B was concentrated in the central area of the two excavations and comprised twelve roundhouses, and eleven four-post and two-post structures, along with 154 pits, numerous postholes, eight waterholes and a burnt mound. The burnt mound and the waterholes are of particular interest.

Burnt mound

The burnt mound measured *c.* 85m in length, *c.* 25m in width and 0.2m in depth. The mound, orientated northeast-southwest, was located to the northeast of the settlement (Fig. 12.2). A number of other examples of burnt mounds have been identified throughout the British Isles. The largest comparable mound was identified at Chalfont St Giles; this measured *c.* 40m in length (Smithson 1984).

The function of burnt mounds remains unclear, although various theories have been suggested. In Ireland, they are thought to be open air cooking areas (Ó Drisceoil 1988). Other suggestions include their use as prehistoric saunas (Barfield and Hodder 1987) or facilities for textile production (Jeffery 1991).

As very few finds were recovered from the burnt mound at Reading Business Park, it is difficult to suggest the function it served. A total of 259 sherds of Late Bronze Age pottery was recovered from the burnt mound, some of which seem to have been exposed to intense heat, to the extent that the material appears vitrified (Morris forthcoming). The charcoal assemblage indicates that the deposit was built up over a period of time (Gale forthcoming). However, it is unclear whether this was as a result of an industrial process or deliberate dumping of domestic refuse.

Waterholes

Eight Late Bronze Age waterholes were identified during the 1995 excavations. The difference between a waterhole and well is that the latter is assumed to be structural, whereas the former is a simple cutting to access water. The basic criterion for the identification of a waterhole is that the feature cuts below the projected Bronze Age watertable. The level of the watertable is based on Lambrick's hydrology model of the Upper Thames Valley (1992). He argues that the watertable had dropped significantly by the Bronze Age period, and it was only during the Late Bronze Age/Early Iron Age that the watertable began to rise again (*ibid.*, 217). Although a palaeochannel was identified at the site, environmental evidence suggests that it had silted up prior to the Late Bronze Age (Robinson forthcoming). As a result, the waterholes would have provided the only access to water during the period in which the settlement was in use.

The features contained evidence that indicated three phases of activity (Fig. 12.4). The primary

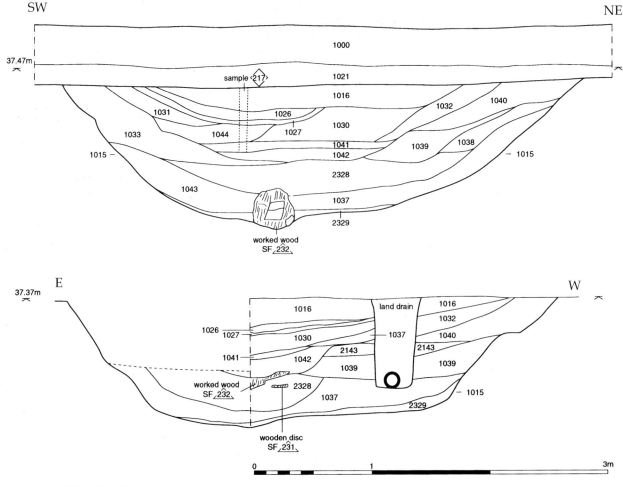

Fig. 12.4 Section through one of the Late Bronze Age waterholes (drawn by Mike Middleton)

phase fills are represented by silts and/or clays that contained varying frequencies of gravel and sand, which suggest natural slumping and silting. The second phase seems to represent a period of disuse. The fills associated with this phase are similar to phase 1; however, they appear to seal the features. In the third phase, the fills contain varying frequencies of charcoal, animal bone, pottery, loomweights and other evidence of domestic settlement. By this phase, it becomes clear that the waterholes were being used as rubbish pits.

The pattern of filling can be paralleled on a number of other sites including Stanwick, Hampshire (Fox 1928; 1930), Berinsfield, Mount Farm (Barclay and Lambrick 1995), Eight Acre Field, Radley (Mudd 1995), and Shorncote Quarry, Gloucestershire (Hearne and Heaton 1994; Brossler *et al.* forthcoming). At Stanwick, a large pit was excavated in the 1920s, the bottom fill of which was identified as being estuarine clay which surrounded a wooden post (Fox 1930). This layer was sealed by more clay fills, which were in turn sealed by a charcoal layer measuring *c.* 0.05m in depth. A total of 20 cylindrical

loomweights and a fragment of saddle quern were recovered from a deposit above the charcoal layer (Fox 1928; 1930).

During the phase 1 excavations at Reading Business Park, a linear arrangement of pits was excavated and interpreted as flax retting pits (Moore and Jennings 1992, 41). Given the evidence, it is probable that these features were in fact waterholes. The pattern of the fills followed the same phasing as noted above, with evidence of waterlogged material identified in the primary fills; the final fills, as noted by Moore, again comprised domestic rubbish, including oven plates or fragments of pit linings (1992, 40).

The placement of waterholes offers some idea of how space was organised within the settlement. In Area 3000B, two waterholes were located at the southern edge of the settlement, mirroring the porch orientation (Fig. 12.5). A further waterhole was identified to the north of the settlement area. The placement of waterholes around the edge of settlements has been recognised by Richard Bradley, who noted the similarity in the placement of the pond at

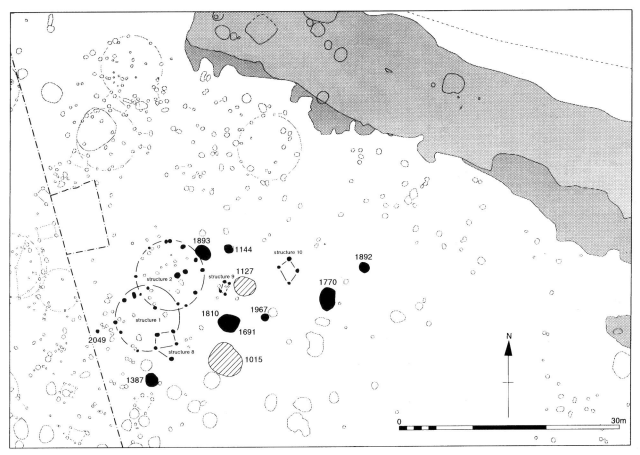

Fig. 12.5 *Detail of spatial relationship of structures and waterholes (drawn by Mike Middleton)*

Aldermaston Wharf to sites on the chalklands of Wessex and Sussex (Bradley *et al.* 1980, 290). A number of other sites in the Upper Thames Valley appear to display the same placement of waterholes; these include Shorncote Quarry, Gloucestershire (Hearne and Heaton 1994; Brossler *et al.* forthcoming), and Eight Acre Field, Radley (Mudd 1995). The waterholes at Shorncote Quarry were located to the southeast of a ring-gully, at the furthest southeastern extent of the settlement. The waterholes at Eight Acre Field were located to the northwest of a ring-gully. An interesting parallel can be drawn between the position of the waterholes at the Middle Bronze Age site at Black Patch, Sussex (Drewett 1982), and a number of those excavated in Area 3000B. In both cases, these features are positioned towards the front of the roundhouses, which suggests that their function was to provide water for human consumption; their location may also explain why, in some cases, they later become used as rubbish pits.

Activity areas

The placement of waterholes is not the only spatial pattern that can be identified on Late Bronze Age

settlements. At Reading Business Park, the main settlement area can be divided into three activity zones (Fig. 12.6). These zones represent areas where consumption, processing and production of materials took place. The zones are not rigid, and it is accepted that a degree of overlapping took place in the definition of the zones.

The primary zone (Zone 1), represented by the main domestic settlement (including roundhouses and four-post structures), was the consumption zone. The secondary zone (Zone 2) was the processing zone, and is represented by the presence of four-post structures, pits and waterholes. The tertiary zone (Zone 3) was the production zone where crops were grown and harvested, animals grazed and woodland managed.

The idea of zones allows for a tentative interpretation of the function of the pits, post-built structures and feature alignments. The main feature-type identified in the primary zone was postholes; only a small number of pits were identified in this zone. The lack of deep pits suggests that four-post structures were used for storage in the primary zone. These appear to be clustered in the western part of this area, which may indicate sub-divisions or deliberate spacing within the zones. This spacing

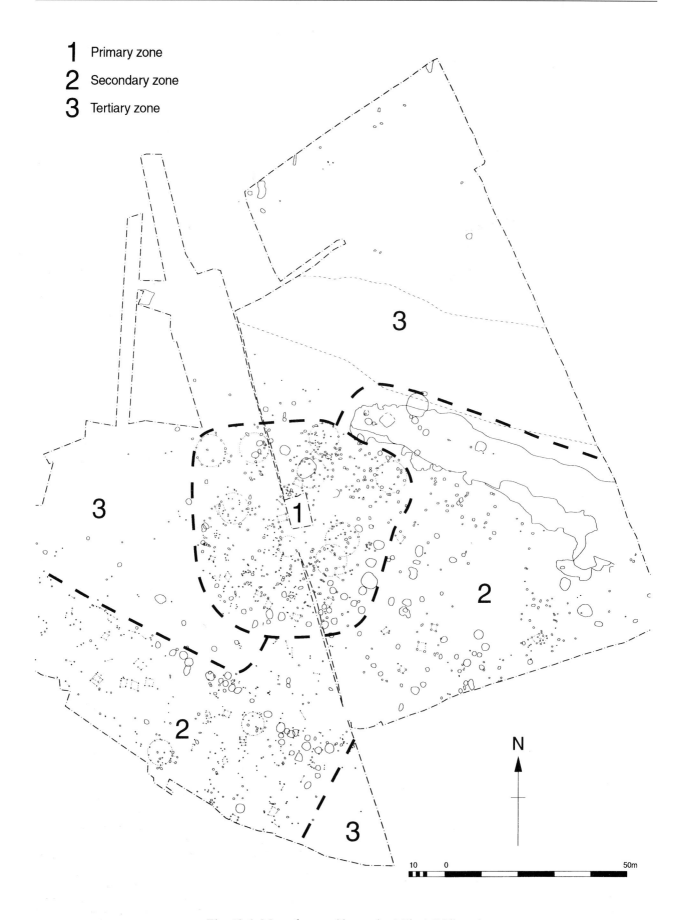

1 Primary zone
2 Secondary zone
3 Tertiary zone

Fig. 12.6 Map of zones (drawn by Mike Middleton)

may have been to divide domestic areas from storage or activity areas. The presence of loomweights indicates that textile production was taking place within the settlement, possibly within the roundhouse structures.

The secondary zone, or processing zone, was characterised by an increase in the frequency of pits. The number of two-post and four-post structures in this area was similar to that of the primary zone. However, it is probable that the function of these structures may have differed. The pit types in this area were predominantly scoop-profiled, although a number of basin-profiled pits were also recorded. It is possible that these two different pit types may have fulfilled task-specific functions. The scoop-profiled pits may have functioned as working areas, possibly for the processing of cereal products, whereas the basin-profiled pits types may have been used for short-term storage, or as containers to place the end product. The four-post structures in this zone may have acted as convenient storage areas for the products that were to be processed, such as barley, wheat and flax. This would indicate that the four-post structures were temporary constructions built for specific tasks, rather than static structures that people revolved around.

The tertiary zone (Zone 3) would have comprised both woodland and areas of agriculture. The evidence for the location of this zone is based on the low frequency of identified features. Very little structural activity can be identified in the area to the east and north of the primary zone, and to the area to the extreme south of Area 3100. The low frequency of four-post structures in this zone most probably relates to the agricultural demands placed on the area. The four-post structures were perhaps for the temporary storage of crops during periods such as harvest.

Discussion

The development of the Business Park area and surrounding landscape through the Bronze Age provides an interesting insight into the life of Bronze Age communities. The presence of certain types of features, such as waterholes and burnt mounds, allows some understanding of the physical day-to-day tasks that were being undertaken, and offers a glimpse into how the landscape was being used. The evidence indicates that woodland management and agriculture were being undertaken, which would suggest that communities had a developed understanding of the landscape that they inhabited. The presence of loomweights and a possible cheese-press indicates specialist knowledge of the material they were harvesting. Only further study of this landscape will allow a greater understanding of the motivating factors that affected the socio-economic practices of the communities that lived there during this period.

Acknowledgements

I am grateful to Angela Boyle for her comments on the original text.

References

Barclay, A., Glass, H. and Parry, C. 1995. Excavations of Late Neolithic and Early Bronze Age ring-ditches, Shorncote Quarry, Sommerfield Keynes, Gloucestershire. *Transactions of the Bristol and Gloucestershire Archaeological Society* 113, 21–60.

Barclay, A. and Lambrick, G. 1995. *Berinsfield, Mount Farm*. Oxford: Oxford Archaeological Unit Post-Excavation Assessment and Research Design.

Barfield, L. H. and Hodder, M. 1987. Burnt mounds as saunas, and the prehistory of bathing. *Antiquity* 61, 370–379.

Bradley, R., Lobb, S., Richards, J. and Robinson, M. 1980. Two Late Bronze Age settlements on the Kennet gravels: excavations at Aldermaston Wharf and Knights Farm, Burghfield, Berkshire. *Proceedings of the Prehistoric Society* 46, 217–295.

Brossler, A. and Early, R. Forthcoming. *Excavations of an Early Prehistoric Landscape at Reading Business Park: Phase 2*. Oxford: Oxford Archaeological Unit, Thames Valley Landscape Series.

Brossler, A., Gocher, M., Laws, G. and Roberts, M. Forthcoming. Excavations of a late prehistoric landscape in the Upper Thames Valley at Shornecote Quarry. *Transactions of the Bristol and Gloucestershire Archaeological Society*.

Brück, J. 1995. A place for the dead: the role of human remains in Late Bronze Age Britain. *Proceedings of the Prehistoric Society* 61, 245–277.

Campbell, G. Forthcoming. The charred remains. In Brossler, A. and Early, R. *Excavations of an Early Prehistoric Landscape at Reading Business Park: Phase 2*. Oxford: Oxford Archaeological Unit, Thames Valley Landscape Series.

Cohen, A. P. 1985. *The Symbolic Construction of Community*. Chichester: Ellis Horwood and Tavistock.

Drewett, P. 1982. Later Bronze Age downland economy and excavations at Black Patch, East Sussex. *Proceedings of the Prehistoric Society* 48, 321–400.

Fox, C. F. 1928. A Bronze Age refuse pit at Sanwic, Hants. *Antiquaries' Journal* 8, 331–336.

Fox, C. F. 1930. The Bronze Age pit at Sanwic, Hants. *Antiquaries' Journal* 10, 30–33.

Gale, R. Forthcoming. The wood charcoal. In Brossler, A. and Early, R. *Excavations of an Early Prehistoric Landscape at Reading Business Park: Phase 2*. Oxford: Oxford Archaeological Unit, Thames Valley Landscape Series.

Hearne, C. M. and Heaton, M. 1994. Excavations at a Late Bronze Age settlement in the Upper Thames Valley at Shornecote Quarry, near Cirencester. *Transactions of the Bristol and Gloucestershire Archaeological Society* 112, 17–57.

Hearne, C. M. and Adam, N. 1999. Excavation of an extensive Late Bronze Age settlement at Shornecote Quarry, near Cirencester, 1995–6. *Transactions of the Bristol and Gloucestershire Archaeological Society* 117, 35–73.

Jeffery, P. 1991. Burnt mounds, fulling and early textiles. In Hodder, M. A. and Barfield, L. H. (eds) *Burnt Mounds and Hot Stone Technology*, 97–107. West Bromwich: Sandwell Metropolitan Borough Council.

Lambrick, G. 1992. Alluvial archaeology in the Holocene in the Upper Thames Basin, 1971–1991: a review. In Needham, S. and Macklin, M. G. (eds) *Alluvial Archaeology in Britain*, 209–226. Oxford: Oxbow Monograph 27.

Moore, J. and Jennings, D. 1992. *Reading Business Park: a Bronze Age Landscape*. Oxford: Oxford Archaeological Unit/Oxford University Committee for Archaeology, Thames Valley Landscape Series Vol. 1.

Morris, E. Forthcoming. Later prehistoric pottery. In Brossler, A. and Early, R. *Excavations of an Early Prehistoric Landscape at Reading Business Park: Phase 2.* Oxford: Oxford Archaeological Unit, Thames Valley Landscape Series.

Mudd, A. 1995. A Late Bronze Age/Early Iron Age site at Eight Acre Field, Radley. *Oxoniensia* 60, 21–66.

Ó Drisceoil, D. A. 1988. Burnt mounds: cooking or bathing? *Antiquity* 62, 671–680.

Robinson, M. Forthcoming. Soils, sediments and hydrology. In Brossler, A. and Early, R. *Excavations of an Early Prehistoric Landscape at Reading Business Park: Phase 2.* Oxford: Oxford Archaeological Unit, Thames Valley Landscape Series.

Smithson, S. 1984. The burnt mound of Chalfont St. Giles. *Records of Buckinghamshire* 26, 113–116.

Wilson, R. Forthcoming. The animal bone. In Brossler, A. and Early, R. *Excavations of an Early Prehistoric Landscape at Reading Business Park: Phase 2.* Oxford: Oxford Archaeological Unit, Thames Valley Landscape Series.

Yates, D. T. 1999. Bronze Age field-systems in the Thames Valley. *Oxford Journal of Archaeology* 18(2), 157–170.

13 Leaving home in the Cornish Bronze Age: insights into planned abandonment processes

Jacqueline A. Nowakowski

'Places where the temperature changed as you stepped in from the street. Places with an undeclared history and a disturbing sense of potential: that something should be enacted in present time to mollify an unresolved past. These theatres of memory took the breath away'.
Rodinsky's Room by Rachel Lichtenstein and Iain Sinclair 1999, 192.

My paper sets out to examine the evidence for abandonment of settlement and for this purpose examines a set of data from a number of settlements dating to the second millennium BC which have been excavated in Cornwall. The archaeological study of the processes of abandonment is still in its infancy (see Tomka and Stevenson 1993) and in a volume entitled *Abandonment of Settlements and Regions: Ethnoarchaeogical and Archaeological Approaches* edited by Cameron and Tomka in 1993, it is evident that methodological and theoretical frameworks are only just beginning to emerge. I would suggest that the study of abandonment has much to reveal about psychological responses to place and as such its examination becomes a vital and legitimate area for archaeological research. I would also like to suggest that these types of studies may aid understanding of the nature of cultural practice and by doing so may reveal something about the concept of place. A room that becomes abandoned may, by that process, make it visible in a way in which it was not when it was occupied (cf. Rodinsky's Room 1999). For the archaeologist, abandonment processes condition the entry of material culture from past lives into the primary archaeological inventory of a site or 'place' (Cameron 1993, 3), thereby creating a sense of place. This I would suggest has considerable implications for our interpretations of the histories of places. For the purposes of this paper my study is limited to one particular type of abandonment and that is the evidence for planned abandonment of

settlement in the Cornish Bronze Age. It is argued that if planned abandonment can be demonstrated as an integral part of the life history of a settlement, then this will affect our conceptual approaches towards the studies of those places that we classify as settlements and villages. As a consequence, there are obvious effects for how we go about investigating the material remains of such places as well how we interpret the behavioural meanings of the spatial patterns and distributions we observe in our excavated data (cf. Moore 1982).

There may be many reasons why places, and in particular settlements become abandoned. Catastrophic environmental events may enforce desertion, as in the case of the Roman city of Pompeii or the Neolithic settlement of Skara Brae in Orkney. Mass evictions of towns, villages and indeed whole regions which result in the abrupt cessation of a culturally distinct way of life through manipulative political processes as we have witnessed through widespread ethnic cleansing in regions such as Bosnia, Kosovo or Rwanda leave behind bereft landscapes. Modernisation and the progression towards a modern age where traditional lifestyles are no longer capable of being sustained may result in the depopulation of village and countryside so that no more than echoing ruins are left behind, as was the case following the 1930s evacuation of St. Kilda (Steel 1975). There will be the inevitable unpredictable variety in the survival of material things following events such as evacuation, eviction or desertion. The recent razing and torching of evacuated buildings in the Balkans, although systematic, may result in random survival. In contrast, the gradual abandonment of a place represents a process of control, and what survives into the future may well be dependant on a number of factors, not least the feelings of those who follow. However, just as the desertion of distinctive landscapes and lifestyles may be represented by particular material consequences, responses to such changes will be varied as newer communities differ in their responses to what has been left behind and what may survive into the future. This was very evident during a study of abandoned nineteenth century farm buildings on Bodmin Moor in Cornwall, where differing attitudes towards old buildings were expressed in a variety of ways by a moorland community (Nowakowski 1987).

There are also other less tangible factors that might be responsible for abandonment; the processes may be the result of economic intensification resulting in overcrowding and the inability to sustain a certain way of life. Ghosts of the past, redolent with disease, death and destruction, may haunt places prohibiting reoccupation and/or resettlement. The direct inclusion of death into the archaeologically defined 'domestic' sphere, such as the disposal of human remains in a former place of residence, may mark a significant end event for a community or a place within that community (cf. Brück 1995; this volume). Ethnographic accounts demonstrate how abandonment is often powerfully influenced by ritual practice. For example, Gow has shown that when an adult person dies on the Bajo Urunmamba in western Amazonia, the house in which she or he once lived is abandoned. As the dead soul is potently attached to place within this society, it may threaten the living. The dead soul is an image of memory, incapable of any kinship action except invoking the pity of its kin and, as such, it exerts a powerful hold over the future of a place. As a consequence, any surviving kin avoid the places where the dead soul may be encountered (Gow 1997, 53–54). These powerful reactions may not only be limited to the beliefs of other cultures outside the western European cultural sphere; in our own backyards the impact of any destructive eradication of something which is 'local' may provoke very emotional and hostile reactions. The demolition of a farmhouse on Bodmin Moor caused great consternation among the locals during the 1980s (cf. Nowakowski 1987). The act of destruction in this instance was locally viewed as a powerful transformation and transgression of the traditional notion of how a moorland community may and should behave.

It is not my intention here to provide any clearcut explanations for the reasons underlying the abandonment of some settlements in the Cornish Bronze Age, but merely to present the evidence, reveal some of its variability and to offer some interpretations of the evidence currently available to us. For this purpose, I will concentrate on data from three sites of Middle Bronze Age date which have been recently excavated. I will then illustrate this discussion further by presenting other broadly contemporary sites where similar processes may be evident. As will become apparent in this study, good site preservation is the main factor that permits a relative degree of confidence in our interpretations of the past narratives of each individual place.

Identifying planned abandonment processes in the Cornish Bronze Age: the Middle Bronze Age settlement at Trethellan Farm

In 1987, the Cornwall Archaeological Unit excavated the Bronze Age settlement at Trethellan Farm in Newquay in Cornwall (Nowakowski 1991). Prior to this time, the site was unknown and it was found entirely by accident. The excavation provided the most extensive and arguably comprehensive view of a Bronze Age lowland village in the county to date. The results of the excavation were analysed and published within five years of the fieldwork, and a full account appears in *Cornish Archaeology* (Nowakowski 1991). For the purposes of the present paper, I have revisited the site and present below a synthetic account of what I believe to be one of the most significant results of this work, that is a further consideration of the processes of abandonment.

The settlement comprised at least seven roundhouses built of wood and stone sited on a natural terrace on the south-facing slopes of the Gannel estuary (Fig. 13.1). Each structure (with one exception) had been built within a purpose-dug hollow. These varied in depth. The radiocarbon dates indicated a history of settlement of about 300 years during the fifteenth to thirteenth centuries cal. BC (*c.* 1200–975 bc). The village seemed to exhibit signs of formal arrangement, with the larger residential houses standing to the east and smaller ancillary buildings positioned on the west. Most of the buildings had undergone several phases of rebuilding or modification, suggesting individual as well as collective changing life histories. However, despite this, the formal division of residential and ancillary buildings appeared to be maintained during the history of occupation. Despite minor structural changes, the original uses of each individual building therefore appear to have been perpetuated. This is an important consideration to highlight as it may not only reveal the significance of each building over generations, but may also have affected the ways in which the buildings eventually became abandoned. As Rothschild *et al.* have observed, 'implicit in the discussions of abandonment is the idea that the full-time use of structure as a residence or workplace is the only use that counts' (1993, 124).

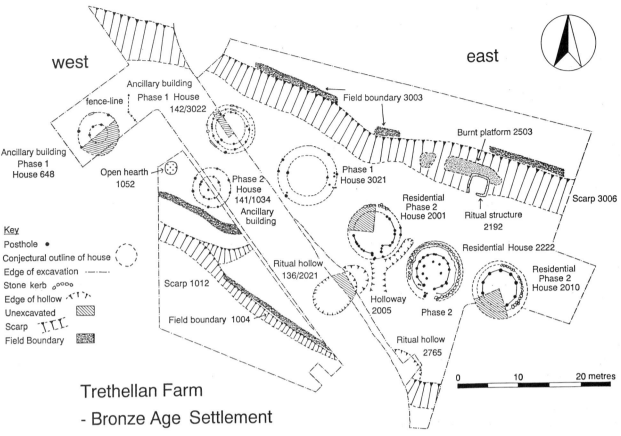

Key

Posthole •
Conjectural outline of house (͑ ͗)
Edge of excavation ·—·—·
Stone kerb ₒºººₒ
Edge of hollow ᐟᐪᐟᐟ
Unexcavated ▨
Scarp ꓔꓔꓔ
Field Boundary ▦

Trethellan Farm
- Bronze Age Settlement

Fig. 13.1 *Plan of Trethellan Farm showing organisation of space and activities*

At Trethellan Farm, the evidence for the final condition of the site, as revealed after the mechanical removal of a massive (up to 2m deep) overburden, signalled a systematic and rather 'tidy' demolition of the village, presumably by the hands of its former occupants. Even without precise dates, it appears that the abandonment of the settlement was planned – the processes of departure being most thorough and akin to burial – as if the settlement had died and the community had moved on lock, stock and barrel. The archaeological evidence for this was graphic. Some of the activities during this process were very destructive but were carried out methodically rather than by random vandalism. For example, in house 2001, two postholes (2317 and 2324) that had once held structural timbers had been backfilled and blocked up. Small stones had been crammed into the mouths of these backfilled holes. Similar activities were noted within house 141/1034, and in houses 648 and 2010 where the tops of some postholes (such as 2498) were cut away, prohibiting re-use. In houses 141/1034 and 2010, following the removal of structural wooden posts either in their entirety (with the resulting sockets backfilled) or by having been cut off at their bases, many postholes were finally sealed by large flat slates. The shadows of former wooden posts in the form of postpipes

were found in at least three of the residential buildings, houses 2001, 2010, 2222.

Slate-lined hearths and raised hearths found within the buildings were buried intact beneath levelling layers and on abandonment these features – especially in houses 2001, 2010 – were undisturbed. No attempt had been made to salvage or reuse clearly useful building materials. This behaviour calls to mind the Welsh ethnographer Iorwethe Peate's observation that in the traditional Welsh farmhouse, once the 'pentanfaen' or hearth stone was in place, 'it was an offence to remove it. The house itself might be destroyed, the owner may desert the site . . . but the pentanfaen was never removed' (1944, 123).

Pits within house interiors were backfilled and in one house (2001) seven intact rubbing stones were found in pit 2027 beneath an intact saddle quern. In house 648, the burnt fragments of a smashed granite saddle quern were found scattered throughout the upper 'abandonment' and demolition layers. 85% of the entire stonework assemblage – typically dominated by food processing tools – was made up of many quern fragments found scattered throughout occupation layers. A high proportion of all classes of material culture – dominated by an enormous ceramic assemblage (a total of 5795 sherds weighing

Table 13.1 *Trethellan Farm houses: quantities of all classes of finds from residential structures, all phases*

Phases of occupation	House 2001	House 2222	House 2010
Phase 1	18	161	25+
Phase 2	83	111	123
Phase 3	55+	44	559
			Abandonment
Phase 4	201	243	
	Abandonment	Abandonment	
Overall totals	357+	559	707+

Table 13.2 *Trethellan Farm houses: quantities of all classes of finds from non-residential structures, all phases*

Phases of Occupation	House 648	House 141/3022	House 141/1034	House 3021
Phase 1	10	33	37	2
				Abandonment
Phase 2	136	734	71	0
Phase 3	196	250	161	0
	Abandonment		Abandonment	
Phase 4	0	319	0	0
		Abandonment		
Overall totals	342	1336	269	2

Table 13.3 *Trethellan Farm: quantities of all classes of finds from all structures from occupation to abandonment. Table 13.3 shows that the processes of abandonment at Trethellan Farm created a variable and complex site inventory of material culture remains. Whereas relatively low quantities of finds were recovered from earlier phases of habitation and activities in all of the buildings, it is clear that the processes of abandonment resulted in increased quantities of all classes of finds towards the end of each structure's life. The significant variation in the composition and density of each individual building's inventory is likely to have been a reflection of the differential treatment of each structure as well as its original and/or changing function. In addition, the absence of data is also a reflection of this. As has been discussed in the text, house 3021 was treated in a different fashion to its neighbours*

Occupation phases	1	2	3	4	Abandonment	Overall totals
House 2001	18	83	55+	201	=55 + 201 = 256	357+
House 2222	161	111	44	243	= 44 + 243 = 287	559
House 2010	25+	123	–	–	559	707+
House 648	10	136	196	–	196	342
House 142/3022	33	734	250	–	319	1336
House 141/1034	37	71	–	–	161	269
House 3021	2	–	–	–	2	2

78.8kg and representing the largest collection of domestic pottery recovered from a site of this period in Britain as a whole (see Woodward in Nowakowski 1991, 103)) – was recovered from the levelling or demolition layers in the hollows where the buildings had once stood (see Tables 13.1 and 13.3). There was a striking absence of any domestic debris in any of the spaces outside the buildings; this was just as true for the macroplant fossils remains (of which there were 0.43 litres) (see Straker in Nowakowski 1991, 170) as for other classes of data.

In some instances, there is clear evidence for staged abandonment (see below) where following final occupation, a series of levelling episodes signalled a precursor to final demise. For example, in house 2010, following the blocking or infilling of features such as interior pits, hearths and postholes, the partial demolition of the surrounding stone kerb took place and in the northwestern section of the house, slates were laid flat on top of earlier evidence for occupation, concealing this. At the same level in the southern section of the building, an extensive stony rubble spread (2547) over 0.50m in thickness was laid down lapping up against the inner faces of surviving kerb stones. A similar scenario was documented in house 648. In an act probably leading up to final abandonment, an open fire was lit on the demolition layers of house 2010, and this produced extensive spreads of charred cereal and wild plant seeds as well as old (oak) wood. These spreads were found beneath a characteristically sooty but extensive soil layer that was also notably rooty, perhaps some indication that the area lay exposed for a while prior to its final abandonment. As a matter of interest, a number of macroplant remains of species characteristic of abandoned or waste places were recorded from the Bronze Age deposits at Trethellan Farm, for example the small nettle and the stinging nettle, cleavers, mallow and brome (see Straker in Nowakowski 1991). The very small artefact assemblage associated with the main phase of activity within house 648 (ten items in total: see Table 13.2) contrasts dramatically with the material recovered from its abandonment layers – over 196 items. This may reflect that prior to abandonment the building was 'cleaned out', although this contrasts quite graphically with the scenario within house 142/3022 (see Table 13.2) where, following a domestic use in phase 2, the hollow appears to have been infilled with a great deal of domestic debris, including over 1000 sherds of pottery (Table 13.3). As Woodward and Cane have noted, these comprised fragments of a whole range of vessel types, 'as if the whole spectrum of pottery from the settlement itself is represented here' (see Woodward and Cane in Nowakowski 1991, 127). Yet despite this, the area where the building had once stood continued to be used, albeit in a piecemeal way, as it became the location of a clay oven (see Nowakowski 1991).

All the evidence has the hallmarks of systematic and deliberate behaviour, that of burying all traces of the village. This was so wholesale, so complete, that even a rather odd stone building that had been built into the foot of a slope at the back of the settlement lay undetected by the excavation team for some time, and its eventual discovery was therefore a complete surprise. This was an unusual stone building (called ritual structure 2192: see Nowakowski 1991, 96–100). It had been neatly built into the foot of a scarp and was square in plan but small, measuring 3.2m x 3.2m, and it therefore provided no more than 10.24 sq. m of interior space. Much of its drystone walls remained; three had been built as revetted faces into the slope and the fourth was free-standing and formed the front wall of the building where an entrance was discovered. The actual function of the structure was enigmatic and eluded us, which is why it was interpreted as a 'ritual' building (see Nowakowski 1991, 99–100), but in common with the other Bronze Age buildings on the settlement, the evidence showed that it had been partly dismantled and then buried under its own structural material. The upper walling was taken down and then used to infill the interior. This was done in such a fashion that the tops of the remaining undemolished walls were shaved to fit in with the angle of the slope.

At Trethellan Farm the wholesale character of this behaviour was striking. However, underlying this story is another that highlights a degree of variability that is worth discussion. The excellent preservation of the buildings at Trethellan owed much to the final events that befell this village. However, the histories of some of the buildings did differ and point up several important processes that may have underlain their final demise. A consideration of these paints the settlement as a living entity that changed throughout its 300 or so year history: some buildings became redundant, fell out of use, or maybe were reused in a different way – all processes that reflect an evolving lifecycle. House 3021 is one such example of this process at Trethellan. Unlike its neighbours, it had not been built within a hollow, contained virtually no finds and therefore appears to have become redundant; it was not reused while the other buildings around were still occupied (see Table 13.2). Of interest was the absence of any attempt to rebuild another structure in its place, considering that each of the three principal residential houses were clearly refurbished over several generations.

A similar scenario can be drawn up for house 2222, which stood on the eastern side of the settlement. When this large residential building fell out of use, it was buried under its own rubbish. The largest collection of pottery from the building (over 500 sherds) was recovered from the extensive infill and levelling layers spread across its entire ground plan. These ceramics tended to be sherds of more than average weight when compared to the entire site assemblage as a whole (see Woodward and Cane in Nowakowski 1991). This could suggest that material dumped here was possibly wholly connected with the building itself and the sherds were not brought in as rubbish from elsewhere. The distribution of the material was less intensive, more sporadic and notably laterally extensive. Of further interest, house 2222, although similar in size and architecture to its immediate neighbours, exhibited the signs of a less complex history of use with minimal evidence for rebuilding, but it also contained human remains. The very fragmentary remains of an articulated adult male found under the central hearth had been buried there while the house was still occupied. This was the only location on the entire site where human remains contemporary with the settlement were found. As the discussion above illustrates, these two houses, so integral to the village as a whole, provide different and contrasting abandonment stories, but the behaviour for deliberate burial and concealment is strongly evidenced in both cases.

I would now like to turn to two other features discovered at this settlement as they shed further light on the variety of burial and concealment behaviour I have so far discussed. On the eastern side of the settlement, in 'front' of houses 2001 and 2222, two oval-shaped hollows were found. These had been deeply dug into the terrace; one (136/2021) was complete and only a small part of the second hollow (2765) survived (see Fig. 13.1). Excavation revealed that these had not been roofed structures, and the possibility that these represented the remains of further 'houses' was therefore discounted. The features and finds recovered from these two areas appeared to be substantially and qualitatively different from the finds excavated from the houses and it was for this reason that they became described as 'ritual' features (see Nowakowski 1991, 86–96).

In hollow 136/2021, caches of pot sherds, animal bone and shellfish were found filling pits that had been capped by flat pieces of slate. The earliest pit found in the base of the hollow was substantial and contained some of the best preserved animal bone found on the entire site. It has to be said here that the condition of animal bone on the site as a whole was very poor (see Payne in Nowakowski 1991, 180–182), but animal bone from deposits associated with these hollows were noticeably better preserved. Localised spreads of wood charcoal signifying the positions of small open fires together with spreads of macroplant fossil remains – in particular wild plant foods – covered the floor of the hollow (see table 70A in Straker in Nowakowski 1991, 170–171). The lowest layers were then covered with dumps of shillet (degraded bedrock) and charcoal, and during a later episode, a slate pavement was laid across the southern half of this hollow. Towards the centre of this pavement, cup-marks were found pecked on the underside of two flat slates. A scatter of over 250 pottery sherds were found distributed on the periphery of this feature but confined to the hollow. To the east, further sealed pits were found, and one notably deep pit contained a piece of red deer antler. Alongside this pit was a dense concentration of crushed mussel shell that lay under a flat slate slab but that was not itself contained in a pit. Hollow 2765 only partially survived (it had been cut through by the site developers prior to the discovery of Trethellan), but this too exhibited signs of activities similar to those recorded in its neighbour hollow 136/2021.

Unlike the interiors of the houses with their distinctive floor surfaces and associated structural features, these two hollows had been the foci for the deposition of caches of artefacts and dumps of rich organic material. Dense pockets of charcoal indicated the positions of small open fires that appeared to have been lit time and time again. There was a pattern of repetition in the arrangements of pits and fires suggesting a sustained and continuous, if perhaps infrequent pattern of behaviour over time. These events were then marked by levelling episodes that betray a desire to conceal evidence for what had taken place within these hollows. The radiocarbon dates obtained from these hollows would suggest that the events that took place within them occurred during the life of the village, that is while the neighbouring roofed buildings were in use.

What took place in the hollows appeared to result in a materially different outcome from the deposits found in the 'houses'. However, the activities that resulted in concealment were similar to those processes that ultimately befell the houses, their deliberate burial and abandonment. Why were the houses at Trethellan abandoned in this way? Why were they not just left to ruin? It is clear that choices were made about how distinctive places were to be left, and it can be argued that any interpretation of these events derive their meaning as much from the ways this was executed as from what did not take place, for there is little clear evidence for gradual decay and neglect. Is what we have documented at Trethellan unique to this particular site, or have any other broadly contemporary sites produced such tantalising evidence for planned abandonment processes?

Evidence for planned abandonment at other Cornish sites

I would now like to turn to the data excavated at two other sites of this period in Cornwall; in both cases, detailed post-excavation analysis is anticipated in the near future and the results discussed here represent preliminary findings.

In 1993, a single oval house of Bronze Age date was found on the edge of an Iron Age round at Penhale Farm, Fraddon, in Indian Queens in mid-Cornwall (Nowakowski 1998). Despite much later activity (associated with the round) within the vicinity of this house, the preservation of the Bronze Age structure was excellent, just as at Trethellan. The building lay within a scooped hollow and was relatively small, measuring 6m x 5m, and providing just over 23.76 sq. m of interior floor space. Post-excavation analysis to date reveals two main occupation horizons within the structure. In its earliest phase it was a wooden building. This was burnt down and later replaced by a building in wood and stone. On its abandonment, the later building appears to have been levelled and deliberately back-filled. It contained a large amount of Middle Bronze Age pottery (780 sherds). No central hearth pit was found in either phase and there was a general dearth of plant remains (Straker in Nowakowski 1998).

Given the absence of a hearth, pits and other internal fittings and features, its interpretation as a domestic ancillary shack or farm building seems likely. Despite being refurbished, it did not appear to have changed in function over the time it was in use. In common with the buildings excavated at Trethellan Farm, domestic debris infilled the entire surface area of the hollow on abandonment. In the main, this was pottery, although some flint and stonework, including a broken mould and quern stone, were found. Two main events of debris deposition were recorded. The stratigraphically lower group of pottery had the appearance of being dumped after the original wooden building had burnt down. However, the collection of pottery from the upper levels, which had been dumped as part of the demolition process, had the appearance of being burnt and then redeposited into the presumably now abandoned ruin (Quinnell in Nowakowski 1998). Thus in both major episodes of use, the interior had been employed for the disposal of domestic debris that we assume to have been associated with the active history of this structure during the Bronze Age. Despite the close proximity of this solitary Bronze Age building to the site of a later prehistoric and Romano-Cornish round, the entire structure survived intact; perhaps strong local taboos or a folk memory of its place ensured its survival as an archaeological ruin some 2000 years later. Radiocarbon dates for this building are yet awaited but the ceramics are characteristic Trevisker wares placing it chronologically into the same cultural lifestyle as that of the villagers at Trethellan Farm.

During the following year, 1994, another Bronze Age site was found during the construction of the Indian Queens bypass less than 1/4 mile from the solitary building found at Penhale Round. Here, at Penhale Moor, a geophysical survey had detected two circular anomalies within the road corridor. Upon detailed excavation, these proved to be circular hollows in which two Bronze Age buildings had once stood (Nowakowski 1998). In common with the other sites so far discussed in this paper, the domestic debris that infilled both hollows comprised pottery of Bronze Age date, flint and stonework. One hollow (1013) was larger than the other (1018). The larger has been interpreted as a specialised residential building with a large central hearth, the smaller was simpler in plan and may have been a contemporary ancillary building. Both structures were surrounded by extramural features such as pits, cobbled surfaces and fencelines represented by lines of posts. As with all the other sites discussed so far, no formal midden deposits were identified at Penhale Moor, and indeed in this instance, the general absence of macroplant remains as evidence for crop cultivation and food processing

could suggest that occupation here was of a specialised kind different to the dwelling (residential) buildings found at Trethellan Farm (Straker in Nowakowski 1998). A modest collection of pottery was found within the larger of the buildings (1013 produced 148 sherds), whereas 87 sherds were found in its smaller neighbour (1018). The ceramic assemblage is diagnostic of Trevisker ware, so occupation on this site was broadly contemporary with Trethellan Farm and the building at Penhale Round. As in the case of Penhale Round, radiocarbon dates are awaited.

Preliminary post-excavation assessment has revealed that many sherds in hollow 1013 were burnt and small. This is especially true of those found in the upper levels (Quinnell in Nowakowski 1998). The general impression from preliminary analysis is that the ceramic distribution is of a kind to be expected from a structure where pottery was in regular use and where broken pieces had subsequently become incorporated into floors or had been used as post-packing material. Pieces of one large storage vessel were found in both hollows, linking usage and emphasising their contemporaneity. The pattern of ceramic distribution in the smaller hollow (1018) was markedly different. It was observed that here cord-impressed sherds (diagnostic of Trevisker ware), although often of better quality than the rest of the assemblage, had been worn or abraded to some degree (Quinnell in Nowakowski 1998). Some had clearly been selected for re-use as post-packing material.

Of great interest, in terms of the general rarity of contemporary metalwork found in archaeologically defined 'domestic' contexts in the southwest, was the discovery of a very poorly preserved copper-alloy side-looped spearhead (S. Needham, pers. comm.). This was found piercing the upper earthen floor of structure 1013 at an 70° angle, and had the appearance of having been speared into the floor as though it was used to 'kill the house' (Nowakowski 1998). It is likely that it was in a broken condition when it was discarded in this fashion (S. Needham, pers. comm.). Brück (1999) has argued that the discard or burial of 'odd' deposits within houses may have taken place at critical junctures of the lifecycle of a house which may have mirrored important events or changes in the lives of its inhabitants. The clearly unusual method of disposal of a broken object as seen here at Penhale Moor suggests intent rather than accidental or casual loss (cf. Bradley 1990), and as Pollard has pointed, out it is 'unwise to separate the practical functions of (objects) from the potential for their manipulation in symbolic expression through deposition' (Pollard 1995, 143).

On abandonment, both hollows were levelled and infilled, and in the case of 1013, the discard of the spearhead could have precipitated the final demise of the structure and hence life of the settlement. The behaviour documented at Penhale Moor is again striking in its resonance of deliberate and systematic burial and concealment providing yet further compelling evidence of planned abandonment.

Throughout the examples I have summarily discussed above, the common thread I would suggest is clear archaeological evidence for deliberate, planned abandonment of places within the landscape of Middle Bronze Age Cornwall. By reviewing records of past excavations of other broadly contemporary settlements, I would argue that evidence for equivalent behaviour can be identified (see also Brück this volume). For example, the excavators of the well known Cornish Bronze Age settlement found at Trevisker in the parish of St. Eval (which was excavated in the late 1950s) found the remains of two timber roundhouses and no formal domestic midden. However, a variety of finds filled the hollows where the two houses had once stood. In common with the three sites discussed above, no complete pots were found, and the condition of the ceramic assemblage varied from those sherds that were freshly broken to those that were very worn and sometimes even burnt (ApSimon and Greenfield 1972, 334). There were other signs of deliberate abandonment processes as the ditches of the houses appeared to have been kept scrupulously clean during occupation but had been filled with domestic debris once they were no longer in use (*ibid.*, 337). In common with the buildings at Penhale Moor, some artefacts (in this instance, stone) were used as packing materials and some were buried in pits. On abandonment, some of the outer postholes in House A had their posts withdrawn and their vacant holes were filled with tightly packed quartzite and shillet. Three of the inner ring had been 'deliberately blocked with stones' (*ibid.*, 307).

Arthur ApSimon suggested that house A ceased to be occupied following a fire 'which heavily scorched the floor', but whether this caused abandonment or took place during demolition remains uncertain (*ibid.*, 309). However, he also suggested that the blocking of the postholes might be considered 'a symbolic act against a possible reinstatement' (*ibid.*, 337). The Bronze Age site at Trevisker was reoccupied during the Iron Age when new houses were built over their Bronze Age predecessors. However, despite this, sufficient material and detail survived for us to reconstruct the Bronze Age story of the site, this to a large degree being a direct consequence of the earlier settlement having been so well concealed during abandonment.

Although the full story of life at Bronze Age Gwithian in west Cornwall remains yet to be told in detail (Thomas 1958), the wealth of material evidence for settlement abandonment, successive reuse of place and re-occupation is one well recounted in the archaeological texts for this period (see for example Burgess 1980). It is hoped that one day the full details of this story may be available, allowing a similar level of scrutiny (Nowakowski 1989).

On present evidence, it would be unwise to extrapolate the general trends that have been recorded at sites such as Trethellan Farm, Penhale Round and Penhale Moor and present them as typical behaviours for lowland settlement of this period as a whole. However, further evidence of the systematic demolition (and hence abandonment) of a Bronze Age building has been observed at the recently excavated lowland site of Callestick (Jones forthcoming). All these examples, including Trevisker, and perhaps Tredarvah near Penzance (Pearce and Padley 1977), Kynance Gate on the Lizard (Thomas 1960) and indeed Gwithian in the sand dunes near Hayle (Thomas 1969), have produced exceptional data in terms of our understanding of the varied character of life in the lowlands of Cornwall during the second millennium BC. It could be argued that this was the result of the ways in which each site was abandoned by its original inhabitants. Of interest is the contrasting way in which contemporary moorland (and therefore upland) sites were left. At excavations of Stannon Down on Bodmin Moor, for example, Roger Mercer demonstrated that the Bronze Age roundhouses were simply left and were notably devoid of material finds (Mercer 1970). In this instance, no systematic attempt had been made by the inhabitants to erase all traces of their settlement. The same can be said for the Later Bronze Age site at Trewey Downs in Zennor in west Cornwall (Dudley 1941).

Towards the idea that abandonment can create a sense of place

Throughout prehistory, the creation of place has manifested itself in a variety of fashions. For earlier prehistory, the ceremonial monuments erected for burial and ritual were clearly created by particular communities living and working in specific locales, particular landscapes. Excavations have shown that these monuments were reused time and time again and eventually became potent symbolic landmarks, creating a sense of place, and giving to the landscapes within which they continued to stand visible time-depth for later generations. The final episodes at many Earlier Bronze Age barrows and cairns, for example, appeared to be representative of 'the closing down' of a place (cf. Barrett 1994). Many were marked by the construction of a mound of stone and earth and these sites (and places) were effectively deliberately buried. In doing so, they became fossilised in time and space.

Can similar types of processes be happening over a thousand years later in settlements? Is this what is happening at sites such as Trethellan Farm and Penhale Round? Did the communities who built these places and lived and raised their children within them, purposely close these settlements down once the life cycle of their community had come to an end? And does the process of planned abandonment both eradicate that sense of place for that community as well as, rather ironically perhaps, perpetuating and making it visible by investing it with a grave-like significance? Richard Bradley has recently argued that the significance of monuments is their ability to create place (Bradley 1998). Was planned settlement abandonment symptomatic of the process of the creation of a kind of tangible landmarking – immortality brought into the 'domestic sphere', that is the domain of the settlement? Was abandonment a ritual process that was neither confined to specific types or classes of places nor to particular phases within the cultural period we call the Bronze Age? And finally, can such processes as abandonment reveal the prevalence of a moral geography that reflects an integral world view or mindset? I would argue that this evidence is compelling and requires us to consider such fundamental issues as what is, and what was, the meaning of place in the prehistoric past.

The past can be maintained, manipulated, changed and re-invented in a variety of ways. However, it can also be denied. Planned abandonment is one form of behaviour where continuities can be concealed as well as created and by doing so, such practices offer us a dynamic tool that reveals much about the processes underlying the creation, maintenance and destruction of place.

Acknowledgements

An earlier shortened version of this paper was presented at the forum 'Place and Space in the British Bronze Age' held at Cambridge University in April 1999. The author would like to thank Joanna Brück for her invitation to submit this version to the current volume and for allowing her to look at her forthcoming discussion on the lifecycles of Middle Bronze Age houses in southern England. Thanks also go to my colleagues Peter Herring, Nicholas Johnson, Henrietta Quinnell and Adam Sharpe for their encouragement and comments on this paper and to Andy Jones for permission to use material from his forthcoming paper on the Callestick structure. Especial thanks go to John Gould and Peter Gathercole for their support and interest.

References

ApSimon, A. and Greenfield, E. 1972. The excavation of the Bronze Age and Iron Age settlement at Trevisker Round, St. Eval, Cornwall. *Proceedings of the Prehistoric Society* 38, 302–381.

Barrett, J. C. 1994. *Fragments from Antiquity: an Archaeology of Social Life in Britain, 2900 – 1200 BC*. Oxford: Blackwells.

Bradley, R. 1990. *The Passage of Arms: an Archaeological Analysis of Prehistoric Hoards and Votive Deposits*. Cambridge: Cambridge University Press.

Bradley, R. 1998. *The Significance of Monuments*. London: Routledge.

Brück, J. 1995. A place for the dead: the role of human remains in Late Bronze Age Britain. *Proceedings of the Prehistoric Society* 61, 245–277.

Brück, J. 1999. Houses, lifecycles and deposition on Middle Bronze Age settlements in southern England. *Proceedings of the Prehistoric Society* 65, 145–166.

Burgess, C. 1980. *The Age of Stonehenge*. London: Dent.

Cameron, C. M. 1993. Abandonment and archaeological interpretation. In Cameron, C. M. and Tomka, S. A. (eds) *Abandonment of Settlements and Regions: Ethnoarchaeological and Archaeological Approaches*, 3–7. Cambridge: Cambridge University Press.

Cameron, C. M. and Tomka, S.A. (eds) 1993. *Abandonment of Settlements and Regions: Ethnoarchaeological and Archaeological Approaches*. Cambridge: Cambridge University Press.

Dudley, D. 1941. A Late Bronze Age settlement on Trewey Downs, Zennor, Cornwall. *Archaeological Journal* 98, 103–130.

Gow, P. 1997. Land, people, and paper in western Amazonia. In Hirsch, E. and O'Hanlon, M. (eds) *The Anthropology of Landscape: Perspectives on Place and Space*, 43– 62. Oxford: Clarendon Press.

Jones, A. Forthcoming. The excavation of a Later Bronze Age structure at Callestick. *Cornish Archaeology*.

Lichtenstein, R. and Sinclair, I. 1999. *Rodinsky's Room*. London: Granta Books.

Mercer, R. 1970. The excavation of a Bronze Age hut circle settlement, Stannon Down, St. Breward, Cornwall. *Cornish Archaeology* 9, 17–46.

Moore, H. L. 1982. The interpretation of spatial patterning in settlement residues. In Hodder, I. (ed.) *Symbolic and Structural Archaeology*, 74–79. Cambridge: Cambridge University Press.

Nowakowski, J. A. 1987. Staddle-stones and silage pits: successional use in an agricultural community. In Hodder, I. (ed.) *Archaeology as Long-term History*, 43–53. Cambridge: Cambridge University Press.

Nowakowski, J. A. 1989. *Gwithian: an Assessment of the Bronze Age Excavations 1954–1961*. Truro: Cornwall Archaeological Unit.

Nowakowski, J. A. 1991. Trethellan Farm, Newquay: excavation of a lowland Bronze Age settlement and Iron Age cemetery. *Cornish Archaeology* 30, 5–242.

Nowakowski, J. A. 1998. *A30 Project, Cornwall: Archaeological Investigations Along the Route of the Indian Queens Bypass 1992–1994, Assessment and Updated Project Design*. Truro: Cornwall Archaeological Unit.

Peate, I. C. 1944. *The Welsh House: a Study in Folk Culture.* Liverpool: Brython.

Pearce, S. and Padley, T. 1977. The Bronze Age find from Tredarvah, Penzance. *Cornish Archaeology* 16, 25–41.

Pollard, J. 1995. Inscribing space: formal deposition at the Later Neolithic monument of Woodhenge, Wiltshire. *Proceedings of the Prehistoric Society* 61, 137–156.

Rothschild, N. A., Mills, B. J., Ferguson, T. J. and Dublin S. 1993. Abandonment at Zuni farming villages. In Cameron, C. M. and Tomka, S. A. (eds) *Abandonment of Settlements and Regions: Ethnoarchaeological and Archaeological Approaches*, 123–137. Cambridge: Cambridge University Press.

Steel, T. 1975. *The Life and Death of St. Kilda.* London: Fontana.

Thomas, A. C. 1958. *Gwithian: Ten Years' Work (1949–1958).* Privately published.

Thomas, A. C. 1969. The Bronze Age in the South West. *Archaeological Review* 4, 3–13.

Thomas, I. 1960. Excavations at Kynance 1953–60. *The Lizard* 1(4), 5–16.

Tomka, S. A. and Stevenson, M.G. 1993. Understanding abandonment processes: summary and remaining concerns. In Cameron, C. M. and Tomka, S. A. (eds) *Abandonment of Settlements and Regions: Ethnoarchaeological and Archaeological Approaches*, 191–195. Cambridge: Cambridge University Press.

14 Body metaphors and technologies of transformation in the English Middle and Late Bronze Age

Joanna Brück

Introduction

This paper begins by exploring the metaphorical connections between people, houses, pots and quernstones during the English Middle and Late Bronze Age (*c.* 1500–700 BC). It is argued that during this period, analogies were drawn between the lifecycles of houses, their inhabitants, and certain categories of objects, notably pottery and quernstones. Houses, pottery and quernstones were treated in similar ways to the human body at critical points in their use-lives, of which 'death' is the most archaeologically visible. This suggests that quernstones, pots and houses stood in a metaphorical relationship with human bodies; it may even have been the case that these were considered at some level to be 'living' entities themselves. As such, the activities surrounding the use of objects such as quernstones and pottery provided ways of thinking about social relationships, just as the characteristics of such artefacts formed potent metaphors for understanding what it meant to be human. Social practices that engaged with the lifecycles of houses, pots and quernstones thus furnished ways of conceptualising and coping with such processes as biological and social ageing (cf. Fitzpatrick 1997).

The second main theme in this paper concerns physical fragmentation. The breaking of objects and the destruction of houses at the end of their lives provided metaphors for understanding the passage of time. Furthermore, the treatment and deposition of human remains and of certain classes of material culture suggests that the process of physical fragmentation was considered an essential element of the ongoing cycle of death and the regeneration of life. In many societies, life is considered a limited good (Bloch and Parry 1982); only when the world of the ancestors receives a new member can another human life be released into the society of the living.

As such, death is the source of life and fertility. There is much to suggest that English Middle and Late Bronze Age societies shared a concern to harness and control the regenerative power of death. The possibility that the process of physical fragmentation and breakage may have been viewed in a positive light has important implications for the interpretation of founders' hoards that will be considered at the end of this paper. Drawing on this, we may suggest that the imagery of cyclical creation, transformation and regeneration that underlay Bronze Age understanding of the human lifecycle informed and facilitated the development of technological processes such as metalworking and pottery production.

Settlement lifecycles

The relationship between houses and people provides a useful starting point (for a full discussion, see Brück 1999). Middle and Late Bronze Age settlements generally consisted of a single household group occupying several post-built roundhouses (e.g. Ellison 1981; 1987; Drewett 1982; but see Barrett 1989a). These were often accompanied by other features, for example ponds, pits and four-post structures (usually interpreted as raised granaries) (Fig. 14.1). Many sites were set within an enclosure and associated field system. On the basis of the finds inventories from Middle Bronze Age settlements, Ellison (1981) and Drewett (1982) have identified two main types of building: major residential structures (food consumption, tool production and maintenance, weaving, etc.) and ancillary structures (food preparation, animal housing, etc.). According to this model, settlements generally comprised one major residential structure plus one or more ancillary structures.

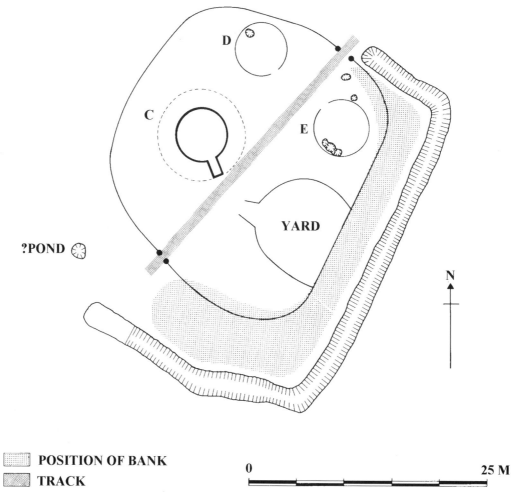

D

C

E

YARD

?POND

N

POSITION OF BANK

TRACK

0   25 M

Fig. 14.1 Schematic plan of the settlement at Down Farm, Dorset (after Barrett, Bradley and Green 1991: fig. 5.41)

In many cases, Middle and Late Bronze Age settlements can be shown to have several phases of construction (e.g. Ellison 1978; Barrett, Bradley and Green 1991, section 5.3). New buildings were erected and old ones remodelled or demolished, fences built and dismantled, ponds dug and refilled with refuse, and so on. Moreover, the distribution of finds suggests that the function of both external and internal activity areas could change over time (Nowakowski 1991). I have argued elsewhere (Brück 1999) that the changing structure and use of space at these sites can be understood as reflecting the developmental cycle of the household group. Over time, the demographic, social and economic circumstances of the household changed (cf. Goody 1958; Moore 1986, 91–102). Children were born, married and moved away, while dependant elderly relatives may have joined the co-residential group. Similarly, as the household reached the peak of its socio-economic status, the resources may have become available to erect new buildings or other structures; these might have fallen out of use and into poor

repair as the economic circumstances of the household declined. These observations suggest that lifecycle of the settlement was intimately connected with that of its inhabitants.

However, the lifecycles of Middle and Late Bronze Age settlements were not simply connected in practical terms with those of their occupants. More interestingly, there was also a close symbolic relationship between the two. This is demonstrated by particular depositional practices. It is a noticeable feature of these sites that critical points in space were marked out through the deposition of objects in pits, ditches and postholes or under ramparts (e.g. Brück 1995; 1999). Boundaries, entrances, corners and similar significant points in space had attention drawn to them by the dumping of concentrations of artefacts (broken and whole) or by the deposition of single finds that otherwise defy modern rationalist explanation, for instance animal burials, human skulls, whole pots or quernstones, bronze objects (that could have been recycled) and so on. Examples include the concentrations of mould debris (for the

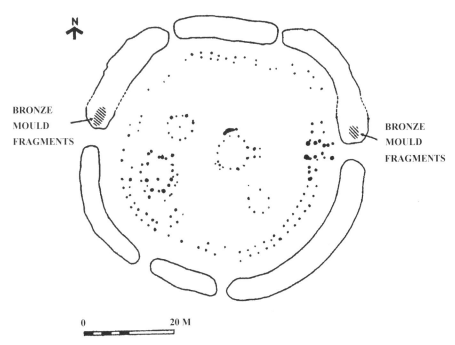

Fig. 14.2 *Location of the dumps of mould fragments at Springfield Lyons, Essex (after Buckley and Hedges 1987: fig. 5)*

production of swords, artefacts of considerable social significance) at the eastern and western entrances to the settlement at Springfield Lyons, Essex (Fig. 14.2; Buckley and Hedges 1987), the skull fragments from the palisade enclosure at Staple Howe, Yorkshire (Brewster 1963), the chalk phallus from a posthole in the porch of roundhouse D, Itford Hill, East Sussex (Burstow and Holleyman 1957), and the bronze objects buried in three of the four corners of the enclosure ditch at South Lodge Camp, Dorset (Barrett, Bradley and Green 1991; see also Barber this volume).

Now, just as some objects were placed as a means of emphasising important points in space, we may suggest that other similar finds from settlement contexts acted as event-marking deposits, accentuating certain moments in time. I would argue that critical points in the life of the settlement and its occupants were marked out through acts of deposition (Brück 1999). We are familiar with the idea of a foundation deposit associated with the construction of a building, but the remodelling and abandonment of a roundhouse or other structure may have required similar acts. The 'death' of certain roundhouses provides interesting data. However, in order to understand the symbolic significance of the practices surrounding the abandonment of such buildings, we first need to consider what happened to human bodies on death. Throughout the Middle Bronze Age and in parts of Eastern England during the Late Bronze Age, the normative funerary rite for the human dead was cremation (Ellison 1980). In

many cases, the cremated bone appears to have been deliberately crushed prior to burial (e.g. Dacre and Ellison 1981). Recent studies cast some doubt on this assertion (McKinley 1993; pers. comm.), although the nature of the cremation process itself can be seen to have a similar effect – the fragmentation of the human body. Although the vast majority of burials were unaccompanied or accompanied only by pottery, grave goods such as bronze knives, bracelets or spearheads occasionally occur (Ellison 1980; Petersen 1981, 117; see also McKinley's discussion (1997: 130, 132) of evidence for pyre goods).

Returning to the settlement evidence, analogies can be drawn at several levels. At some sites, special closing deposits appear to have been made on the abandonment of the house, just as gifts were occasionally given to members of the human dead (cf. Barrett and Needham 1988; Barrett 1989b). In the case of Chalton, Hampshire, for example, a bronze knife, awl and palstave were placed on the floor of hut 1 on abandonment (Cunliffe 1970). At Trethellan Farm, Cornwall, the houses were 'buried' at the end of their life, deliberately sealed and levelled with spreads of rubble, earth and occupation debris, perhaps evoking metaphorical connections with the burial of the dead (Nowakowski 1991). At another site in Cornwall, Penhale Moor, a roundhouse appears to have been symbolically 'killed' by driving a spearhead into the floor (Nowakowski this volume). In some cases, houses appear to have burnt down, as for example at Mile Oak, East Sussex (M. Russell, pers. comm.). Although difficult to demonstrate archaeologically, this may have been a deliberate act designed to formally signify the end of the building's life (cf. Stevanovic 1997; Chapman 1999). On other sites, houses were dismantled, as at Winterbourne Stoke Crossroads, Wiltshire (Richards 1990). It is not difficult to see that analogies may have been drawn between the treatment and disposal of the dead by burning the body and crushing the bones and the deliberate firing or dismantling of 'dead' roundhouses. More telling still, at Broom in Bedfordshire (Mortimer and McFadyen 1999; McFadyen, pers. comm.), 9g of cremated human bone was recovered from one of the porch postholes of the roundhouse (structure 5). On abandonment, approximately half of the posts in the central post-ring were removed and the postholes silted up. The remainder of the post-ring (an arc of posts to the south and southeast) was left *in situ* (the presence of post-pipes attests to this). The human bone was recovered from the only post in the porch structure to remain standing. The location of these fragments within the upper fill of the posthole suggested to the excavators that the bone had entered this feature very late on in the occupation history of the building. Furthermore, the nature of this fill was similar to that of a pit which had demonstrably been cut at the end of the construction sequence. The amount of bone is small, and one could argue for accidental inclusion. However, the location of the deposit in the entrance-way to the roundhouse is significant and fits the general pattern for finds of human remains on settlement sites of this period (Brück 1995); we shall come back to this point below. Here, then, we can suggest that a token deposit of cremated human bone was made on abandonment of the roundhouse, infusing this moment with the imagery of death (Mortimer and McFadyen 1999).

These examples suggest that during the English Middle and Late Bronze Age, houses were conceptualised as living entities with lifecycles intimately related at both a practical and symbolic level to those of their inhabitants (see also Nowakowski this volume; cf. Bailey 1990; Chapman 1997). Votive deposits were made both at critical points in the existence of the house (construction, rebuilding and abandonment), and at important junctures in the lives of its human occupants, such as birth, marriage, death and other *rites de passage*, not least because these may have coincided temporally with equivalent points in the life of a building. For instance, the death of a person may have required the symbolic death through burning or dismantling of the house with which they were associated during life. I would suggest that finds such as the dump of burnt grain recovered from a pit in hut E at Itford Hill, East Sussex (Burstow and Holleyman 1957), the animal burial under the floor of hut 1 at South Lodge Camp,

Dorset (Barrett, Bradley and Green 1991), and the awl in one of the porch postholes of hut 3, Black Patch, East Sussex (Drewett 1982), may be interpreted as examples of these kinds of life cycle rites. Of course, such ideas do not simply apply to roundhouses but may be equally relevant at both a larger and smaller scale: the lifecourses of individual pits and of entire settlements seem to have been commemorated through similar sets of depositional practices (cf. Hill 1995).

Bodies, pots and quernstones

I want to move away now from the evidence provided by roundhouses to consider the analogies drawn between human lifecycles and those of other artefact categories, notably pottery and quernstones. Human bodies, pots and querns seem to have been treated similarly on 'death'. As such, quernstones and pottery may have been conceptualised, at some level, as having lifecycles similar to their owners. Finds from funerary contexts provide some of the most telling evidence. Although most cremations of this period were placed in complete pottery vessels, many were accompanied by collections of sherds. This can be interpreted as the deliberate breaking of vessels to signify the closure of the social relations that these sustained (cf. Tilley 1996, 317–318). At the end of the human life for which it provided nourishment, the pot was also symbolically killed. Like the human body, which was broken down through the process of cremation and subsequent crushing of the bones, pots were also smashed into many small pieces. The cemetery at Bromfield, Shropshire (Stanford 1982), provides some interesting evidence for this practice. Here, the differential burning of potsherds recovered from the area of the funeral pyre indicates that pots were deliberately broken at the pyre-side. In other words, the sherds recovered were not simply collected up from a nearby refuse source for deposition with the burial, but were broken as part of the funerary ritual in a way that metaphorically linked pots and human bodies through the process of fragmentation.

Outside of the funerary context, similar practices appear to have taken place. At Trethellan Farm, Cornwall, the smashed and burnt fragments of a quern were discovered in the levelling layers of house 648 (Nowakowski 1991; see Seager Thomas 1999: 41 for other examples). Here, the death of a house was accompanied by the death of one of the objects central to the household's material and social reproduction. Like its owner, this quern (essential for the preparation of food and thus a potent symbol of life, fertility and productivity) was burnt, broken and buried upon death. Pottery was often treated in a similar way. At Broom in Bedfordshire (Mortimer and McFadyen 1999), two pits were cut on the abandonment of the roundhouse (structure 5) and infilled with large amounts of broken pottery, signifying the end of the physical and social life of the house (the building itself was largely dismantled). The pottery assemblage from the two pits comprised parts of at least fourteen or fifteen vessels, including both fine and coarseware pots as well as a wide range of vessel shapes and sizes (*ibid.*). The excavators note that a high proportion of the sherds show fresh breaks, and one can perhaps suggest that here the pottery inventory belonging to the house during life was deliberately smashed and buried on abandonment.

Like humans, the broken sherds of a pot were often deposited with evident care. At Patteson's Cross, Devon, several large sherds of bucket urn had been placed on the base of a pit under a single fill that itself produced no artefacts (Fitzpatrick, Butterworth and Grove 1999, 73). At North Shoebury in Essex, large sherds from a bucket urn and a small bossed vessel had been laid flat on the base of a shallow depression (Wymer and Brown 1995, 80, 153). Whole pots were also buried in pits and ditches at many Middle and Late Bronze Age settlements; examples include an almost complete pot standing upright in a pit at Westbury, Hampshire (Lewis and Walker 1976), as well as a number of whole vessels from features at Reading Business Park, Berkshire (Moore and Jennings 1992). The latter included a fine burnished bowl as well as a pot that had been deposited inverted, making it difficult to accept the traditional interpretation of such vessels as storage facilities. Moving from pots to other materials, we may recall here the deposits of burnt (cremated?) barley from pits inside roundhouses at Black Patch and Itford Hill, both in East Sussex (Burstow and Holleyman 1957; Drewett 1982); the symbolism surrounding grain and grinding will be explored further below, but the fact that barley was burnt and buried as part of the rites enacted over the course of a household's lifecycle is surely interesting.

Fragmentation and regeneration

Now, we have traced the metaphorical connections between the lifecycles of humans, the houses they lived in, and certain classes of material culture, notably pottery and quernstones. But what did it mean that people, houses and objects were broken down upon death? I'd like to argue that the breaking and burning of objects was not simply destructive but facilitated new cycles of regeneration. There are several sources of evidence suggesting a concern with the symbolic regeneration of life and fertility

through the harnessing of death in the British Middle and Late Bronze Age.

One of the most intriguing lines of information is the treatment and deposition of human remains during the Late Bronze Age. In this period, the practice of cremation no longer appears to have been the normative funerary rite for most of the population and, with a few exceptions, burials are no longer archaeologically visible. Several archaeologists have suggested that human remains may have been routinely exposed to the elements (e.g. Cunliffe 1992, 76). Whatever the case, fragments of human bone were frequently collected and reused in non-funerary contexts (Brück 1995). Examples include possible amulets from settlement contexts, for instance the pierced roundel of skull from All Cannings Cross, Wiltshire (Cunnington 1923), and the fragment of a similar disc again with a drilled perforation from a waterhole at Reading Business Park, Berkshire (A. Boyle, pers. comm.). Human bone, particularly whole skulls or fragments of skull, was also used and deposited during various non-mortuary rituals (Brück 1995). It is found in contexts such as rivers, lakes and bogs, as well as in caves and occasionally with bronze hoards. More frequently, fragments of human bones are recovered from boundary locations on settlement sites, for example enclosure ditches and pits or postholes in and around the entrance to the settlement. I have argued elsewhere (*ibid.*) that such material played an important role in activities such as rites of passage or other rituals concerned to mark out space and/or time because of its potential to symbolise states of transition (death being the ultimate transformation between categories of being).

Moreover, fragments of human bone are often found as components of refuse deposits during this period. However, before we can consider the conceptual links between human bone and refuse, we need to explore the nature of 'rubbish' in Bronze Age societies. Several lines of evidence suggest that the value-judgements attached to refuse in the Bronze Age were not the same as in the modern western world (Brück 1995; cf. Hill 1995; Chapman 2000). Broken objects were often used and deposited in ways that suggest they held particular symbolic significance. As we have seen above, for example, at Springfield Lyons in Essex (Buckley and Hedges 1987), large dumps of clay mould fragments were recovered from the butt ends of the enclosure ditches at the major entrances, marking out the points of transition from inside to outside (Fig. 14.2). At other sites, broken potsherds form part of votive deposits. For example, at Runnymede, Surrey (Needham 1991, 110), a pit in Area 6 contained large parts of a single horse skeleton, the forelimbs of which had been crossed. Over this lay a neatly inverted hearth, beside and below which were large potsherds including pieces from a fineware bowl. At Monkton Court Farm, Kent, a quern fragment had been placed on the base of a pit and at its centre (Perkins, Macpherson-Grant and Healey 1994, 248). The quern was surrounded by a ring of eight hammerstones. Above this was a deposit of large sherds representing the *in situ* breakage of a large coarseware jar (*ibid.*). Anthropological studies of ritual have pointed out that ritual practices often surround states of transformation; rites of passage such as initiation, marriage and death are obvious examples. In the Bronze Age, the breaking of objects and the use of fragmentary artefacts in ritual acts such as those described above no doubt made symbolic reference to the social transitions effected by such rites, signifying not only a change in state but the ending and replacement of old sets of social relations with new ones. In a similar way, broken objects were deposited as a means of drawing attention to the crossing of boundaries in space, as in the example of Springfield Lyons above.

Thus, like human bone, rubbish appears to have been conceived of as a powerful medium for symbolising states of transition. The ambiguous nature of decaying refuse – containing artefacts no longer fit for the use they were intended – may have been one reason why it was seen as a source of such symbolism. It seems likely too that metaphors were drawn between refuse and death during this period. For example, at Broom in Bedfordshire (Mortimer and McFadyen 1999), parts of the roundhouse were deliberately covered with domestic rubbish on abandonment. Furthermore, in many societies, refuse (or certain categories of refuse) is perceived as 'dirty', 'dangerous' or 'ambivalent' (Douglas 1966; Hodder 1982, 155–163; Okely 1983, 77–89). As such, it may come to symbolise the 'other' and may therefore be dumped at the edges of the safe, familiar world contained within the settlement. The deposition of such powerful material in boundary ditches in the Middle and Late Bronze Age drew attention to the significance and possible danger of crossing the line between inside and outside.

Although refuse may have been considered a dangerous and ambivalent substance at one level, it appears to have been viewed more positively at another. It has been suggested that midden material was used to fertilise the fields during the Middle and Late Bronze Age (e.g. Gingell 1990); scatters of artefacts recovered from old land surfaces or trapped within lynchets may be interpreted in this way. As such, refuse may have been considered a source of fertility (Brück 1995; Parker Pearson 1996). If so, then conceptual linkages may have been made between death and decay on the one hand and life, fertility and rebirth on the other (see Fitzpatrick

1997; Hingley 1997 for related ideas applied to the British Iron Age). Materials that were dead in one sense provided a life-giving source of fertility to the fields. Another interesting conceptual link between refuse and ideas of growth and life is provided by Middle and Late Bronze Age settlements in Shetland. In some cases, buildings were actually set into earlier middens whereas at other sites middens grew up around houses over the course of their lives (Downes and Lamb 2000). At Sumburgh, for example, midden material was continuously deposited just outside the walls of the house, so that the walls essentially grew in thickness over time (*ibid.*). In southern England, monumental middens up to several metres deep are known from a number of Late Bronze Age sites, for example at Runnymede, Surrey (Needham 1991; Needham and Spence 1996), and Potterne, Wiltshire (Lawson 1994). These sites have also produced more 'high status' objects, for example bronze or amber artefacts, than other sites of similar date. It may be that the accumulation of refuse was another way of signifying status, by providing visible evidence of animal ownership, high levels of craft production and of substantial consumption of food, pottery and other artefacts (McOmish 1996; Needham and Spence 1996, 242–248). Parker Pearson (1996) refers to these sites as 'hoards of fertility'. Midden material, although redolent of death and decay at one level, was a source of life at another; no doubt the presence of such monumental middens in the landscape sent significant messages about those who were in a position to accumulate such 'hoards'.

Interestingly, human bone is a frequent component of these midden deposits. In many cases, fragments of human bone probably went through a cycle of use as amulets or in particular ritual activities before being incorporated into a midden with other refuse. In other instances, bone appears to have been deposited in a formalised manner within the midden matrix. At East Chisenbury, Wiltshire, for example, a piece of human skull had been placed on a prepared surface within the midden and a fragment of sarsen stone and several potsherds arranged around this (Brown, Field and McOmish 1994). In either case, whether human remains were deposited intentionally or not, the fact that they are subsumed within a mass of refuse may be significant. Like rubbish, human bone can be viewed as a dangerous, ambivalent substance, redolent of liminal states of being (Metcalf and Huntingdon 1991). On the other hand, in a society that sees life as a limited good, it may also have been considered a source of fertility. In many cultures, mortuary rituals are associated with imagery of fertility and rebirth (Bloch and Parry 1982). The death of one person facilitates the birth of another.

By conceptualising life as a cyclical process, the finality of death is negated and the rent to the social fabric repaired. We have already seen above that during the Late Bronze Age human remains were used to symbolise states of transition, for example by marking out spatial and temporal boundaries on settlements and in other contexts. It may be that this association between death and transformation hints that the renewal of life was thought of as a cyclical process.

Furthermore, the funerary rites of the period challenged the sudden and arbitrary nature of death. We have seen that cremation and exposure were probably the normative treatments afforded to the dead during the Middle and Late Bronze Age respectively. Cremation is a multi-stage process, with the potential for both temporal and spatial distance between the cremation itself and final deposition of the burnt bone in the ground (Barrett 1991, 121–122). Similarly, where exposure of human bodies is the norm, secondary phases of the mortuary rite may take place once the bones are defleshed (Metcalf and Huntingdon 1991). In either case, although bodily death may occur unexpectedly, the point of social death (i.e. the final incorporation of the deceased into the realm of the ancestors) is carefully controlled through the timing of the later stages of the mortuary rite. Thus, the arbitrary and destructive nature of death can be challenged and it can be harnessed for the good of society. In such a context, an understanding of death as a source of life might not be surprising. Indeed, during the Middle Bronze Age, cremation burials were often concentrated in the southeastern side quadrant of barrows (I am grateful to M. Wysocki for drawing my attention to this); by orienting the dead towards the rising sun, death was permanently linked with life and with the cyclical rebirth of the day (cf. Parker Pearson and Richards 1994; Fitzpatrick 1997; Oswald 1997; Owoc 1999).

A concern with fertility and the regeneration of life through the control of death is suggested by several other lines of evidence. During both the Middle and Late Bronze Age, cooking appears to have resulted in the production of prodigious quantities of burnt flint as evidenced by the widespread presence of burnt mounds. It is widely accepted that hot flint was used as a means of heating water or other liquids in large ceramic vessels that could not themselves have stood direct heat from a hearth. It is possible that analogies may have been drawn between the process of cremation and cooking. Like human bone, the flint shattered and fractured on burning. It become brittle and often acquired a marked bluish-white tinge, similar to that of burnt bone. Both cooked food and burnt bone were placed in ceramic containers. In a similar way,

grain (stored in pits) and the remains of the dead were buried in the ground; presumably, storage in the belly of the earth protected and nurtured the life-giving qualities of both these substances. At least some of the burnt flint produced during cooking and other thermal activities was crushed (like cremated human bone) and used as a tempering agent for pottery.[1] Broken vessels were also used as a source of filler (grog) for the production of new pots. In this way, materials that were no longer usable in the manner originally intended entered the cycle of production at a new point. The death of a pot, like the burning and breaking of flint, facilitated the creation of new vessels (Morris 1994: 38; Brown 1995, 127; cf. Cleal 1995, 192). Again, we can envisage death as the source of fertility and new life. Indeed, the very structure of the open bonfires in which pots were fired may have called to mind cremation pyres, although there is no way of demonstrating constructional similarities.

Drawing the analogy further, the activity of grinding (burnt flint, human bone and grain) seems to have been so closely associated with the process of transformation from one state to another that quernstones must have been redolent with the symbolism of death and rebirth. It is surely this that explains the presence of so many quernstones in event-marking deposits on Middle and Late Bronze Age settlements (Brück 1999; Seager Thomas 1999: 43; examples include complete quernstones placed on the bases of pits in huts A and E at Itford Hill, East Sussex, and in a posthole of a roundhouse at New Barn Down, West Sussex: Burstow and Holleyman 1957; Curwen 1934). Indeed, the very fact that burnt human bone was treated like grain (itself an essential and symbolically potent element of life in agricultural societies) is surely also significant, reminding us again that the remains of the dead could be understood as a source of fertility (cf. Hingley 1997). Middle Bronze Age burials are rarely accompanied by grave goods (but see McKinley's discussion (1997: 130, 132) of evidence for pyre goods). However, grinding equipment is not unknown from such contexts; the rubbing stone or grinder found "jammed under the rim" of an inverted urn in the Knighton Heath cemetery, Dorset, is one such example (Petersen 1981: 56). The upper portion of this urn had been destroyed prior to excavation and it is not known if it originally contained a burial. Whether this item belonged to one of the individuals buried in the cemetery, was emplyed to prepare a funerary meal for the mourners, or was used for the crushing of human bone is far from clear, although it is tempting to suggest the latter (however, note McKinley's reservations (1993) concerning evidence for the deliberate crushing of bone prior to deposition).

The interpretation of broken objects in bronze hoards

The process of fragmentation may therefore have had positive connotations during this period. This has important implications for archaeological interpretation of finds such as bronze hoards. Broken bronzes are usually interpreted in one of two ways. Many of the rapiers and swords from the River Thames, for example, appear to have been deliberately cut or snapped. Bradley (1990) has argued that these may have been deposited in the river as surrogate funerary offerings during a period in which the dead were not accompanied by lavish grave goods. He suggests that these swords and rapiers may have been deliberately broken to signify the death of their owner.

Broken objects are also found in dryland contexts, notably 'founders' hoards'. However, in this case, they are widely interpreted as 'refuse', material come to the end of its use life and awaiting recycling. Several Continental scholars have challenged this interpretation for European scrap hoards (Worsaae 1866–1871, 64–68; Hundt 1955, 99–100; Müller-Karpe 1958, 34; Verlaeckt 1998) but in Britain functionalist explanations remain common (but see Coles 1968–1969, 33; Barrett and Needham 1988, 136; Needham 2001; Barber this volume). However, interpretations of such hoards as simple collections of scrap metal are not always fully satisfactory. For example, Needham (Barrett and Needham 1988, 136) points out that there is a discrepancy in many parts of Britain between the full range of bronze types produced (including those known from moulds and settlement contexts) and those that were actually deposited as part of founders' hoards. This suggests that certain bronze types were excluded from deposition in scrap hoards, a fact that does not sit easily with their supposed utilitarian significance. There is also interesting patterning in terms of the treatment afforded to artefacts in Late Bronze Age founders' hoards (Turner 1998; R. Maraszek, pers. comm.); these studies are beginning to suggest that different bronze types were fragmented in specific ways and that certain parts of the broken artefacts were excluded from deposition, suggesting that non-functionalist rationales governed certain choices for inclusion in such hoards. Verlaeckt (1998) has identified similar patterning in Danish hoards. He points out that hoards of both broken and unbroken artefacts can be seen to comprise normative combinations of object types (for example hanging vessels and spiral armrings, or socketed axes and sickles) and he notes that bronze types recovered from contemporary burials were usually excluded from hoards of broken artefacts. His analysis also demonstrates that there is a negative correlation

between the degree of fragmentation and the presence of casting jets, and that certain categories of object, for example swords, are much more likely to be found broken than others.

Returning to the English evidence, it is also possible to challenge purely functionalist explanations for dryland hoards on the basis of evidence for the careful arrangement of objects. At South Dumpton Down, Kent, for example, a bronze hoard was deposited in a small pit cut into the side of the enclosure ditch surrounding a Middle Bronze Age settlement (D. Perkins, pers. comm.; Barber this volume). Four bronze palstaves had been placed in a fan shape on the bottom of the pit. Over these, in the middle fill of the pit, a piece of tabular flint had been laid on top of which were piled another palstave and fragments of two bangles. In this case, it is not only the evidence for careful arrangement that is significant, but also the presence of broken bronze objects. If we accept a 'votive' explanation for the deposition of these bronzes, then the presence of broken bronzes need not be antithetical to a ritual explanation for at least a proportion of dryland hoards. Indeed, a number of writers (e.g. Worsaae 1866–1871, 64–68; Nebelsick 1997; Verlaeckt 1998) have suggested that broken bronzes in certain Continental hoards were deliberately destroyed as part of a ritual act, practices similar to the destruction of pots in the British Middle Bronze Age funerary rites discussed above.

Given these considerations, the presence of broken objects in founders' hoards cannot necessarily be used as evidence to support functional explanations for these collections (indeed, the contradictory interpretations posed for broken objects from wet and dry contexts tell us more about the nature of archaeological interpretation than about Bronze Age social or economic practices). As we have seen above, broken objects and 'refuse' can be symbolically redolent of particular processes or conditions and, as such, may have been purposefully included in hoards buried with votive intent. What, then, is the significance of broken objects in founders' hoards? Can their presence help us to understand why these hoards were deposited? In many societies, metalworking is seen as a magical activity, associated with the transformation of rock into metal and of one object into another (e.g. Welbourn 1981; Budd and Taylor 1995; Hingley 1997). Like any activity that involves processes of transformation, the liminal period during which the transition takes place may be viewed as a source of danger, and smelting and casting are therefore often surrounded by secrecy and taboo. As such, the whole process of metalworking may be drawn on as a potent metaphor for transformation (Herbert 1993; Hingley 1997). Materials such as casting debris and broken items awaiting recycling symbolise this process. No doubt such items could have acted as a means of metaphorically marking out liminal states, or points of transition in space and time, and their deposition may therefore have occurred in the context of a range of ritual practices unconnected with metalworking (Barber this volume). As Needham (2001) notes, although founders' hoards may have been accumulated as part of the process of bronze production, there is no reason to suppose that their deposition was always an integral element of metalworking activities (contrary to interpretations in which such hoards are interpreted as temporary stores of metal indicative of seasonal smithing). In other words, it is possible that there was a ritual intention behind the deposition of collections of broken metalwork even if the bronzes had originally been gathered together as part of the metalworking process.

Of course, a ritual interpretation does not mean that the deposition of scrap hoards was never associated with metalworking activities. Ethnographic studies of metalworking indicate that ritual is often an integral part of metal production precisely because of the potential danger of this transformative process (e.g. Welbourn 1981; Herbert 1993; Budd and Taylor 1995). Votive deposition of scrap material may have been seen as an essential step in the successful production of bronze, as Worsaae (1866–1871) so long ago suggested. Let us explore this possibility further.

Bronze Age technology and the production of the self

The preceding discussion reminds us that the recycling of objects through breaking and remelting was an essential stage in bronze production. Bronze, like people, was transformed from one state to another and reborn into a new life through the process of fragmentation and the medium of fire. One might note here that there is occasional evidence that bronze objects from ritual contexts were subjected to heat; much of the metalwork recovered from Duddingston Loch, Edinburgh (mostly swords and spearheads), was not only broken or bent, but was also partly melted (Coles 1959–1960, 29, 117). Like the practice of breakage, fire was considered to be a medium of transformation (and probably also of creation) and no doubt played an essential role in many ritual practices. Relating these ideas again to the process of bronze production, copper ores would initially have been given up by the earth and then crushed, smelted and cast to convert them into a very different material, metal (Jones 1999; cf. Hingley 1997). The preparation of pottery clay and tempering agents (involving grinding and mixing), and the transformation of these materials into ceramics through firing were analogous processes (Jones 1999). As Jones (*ibid.*) has observed, the series of transformative cycles into which copper was drawn finally ended when the copper or bronze objects (themselves often broken) were consigned to the ground as hoards. Here, the mutualistic relationship between people and the environment is clear (cf. Brück 1999); what was taken from the earth had to be restored to it, if it was to continue to provide for its human inhabitants. Doubtless, similar ideas lay behind the deposition of objects or materials such as pottery, grain and animal carcasses. It was the earth that produced and nourished; hence gifts had to be given to the earth to sustain the productivity of land and livestock (cf. Cunliffe 1992). However, as a *caveat*, it should be underlined that the transformative processes in question here do not necessarily imply the kind of culture-nature dualism envisaged in classic structuralist works (e.g. Levi-Strauss 1970). A strict culture-nature dichotomy in which humans are envisaged as taming, controlling and transforming nature into a cultural product cannot be envisaged for this period (see Brück 1999).

This discussion suggests that the technological processes in which humans engaged (including bronze and pottery making, and the preparation and cooking of food) were conceptualised as cycles of birth, death and regeneration through the metaphor of transformation by fire, crushing and grinding. The process of biological and social growth among humans appears to have been understood and conceptualised in a similar way. Technologies such as metallurgy acted as metaphors for the production of the self. Humans, like other materials, underwent rites of passage at critical stages in their lives which required the destruction of the old social persona and the relationships this sustained, and the creation of a new self identity. At death, this was achieved through the fragmentation and burning of the body itself, although at other points in the lifecycle, the breaking and deposition of artefacts that stood in a metaphorical relationship with the human body (for example pots) would have achieved the same purpose.

This reminds us that technology is never divorced from social context and cannot be simply understood in functionalist terms (e.g. Lemmonier 1986; 1993; Pfaffenberger 1988; *World Archaeology* 27). Rather, its specific forms arise out of an historical context in which social relations, knowledge and ideas about the materials and substances that make up the world, and culturally-particular understandings of causal processes together combine to form the resources out of which people build their productive practices. The complex web of metaphorical relationships that binds humans and the inanimate universe together has a major impact on people's judgement of what is effective action. Technological processes cannot therefore be considered neutral or value-free; solutions to particular problems were chosen not simply for 'functional' reasons (of course, the concept of 'functionality' is itself culturally constructed), but because of the meanings that materials, substances or processes might have held. What I would like to suggest here is that by thinking about human life as a series of transformative cycles involving heating and crushing, Bronze Age people were provided with the conceptual tools essential for the smelting of metal out of rock. It was because they conceptualised biological and social development in this way, that the process of bronze production became 'thinkable'.

Conclusion

This paper has tried to discuss some of the focal metaphors that Bronze Age people used to describe and understand technological, social and natural processes. The idioms of transformation and regeneration were central cultural metaphors through which people conceptualised the passage of time, the production of food and other categories of material culture, and the creation of social agents. Conceptual linkages suggest that the human life-cycle was compared with and understood in relation to such technological processes as pottery and bronze production. Conversely, at death, the human body was broken and burnt just as grain was ground by the quernstone and cooked on the hearth to provide essential nourishment for the continuance of biological and social life. In other words, such creative/transformative activities as cooking, cremation, metalworking and potting were considered analogous processes because each was effected through heating and crushing. As discussed above, this has important implications for functionalist interpretations of Bronze Age technology. No doubt, further work may elucidate more fully the nature and origins of the cultural metaphors discussed in this paper.

Notes

1   Although this similarity does not extend to the use of bone as temper, for which there is no evidence during this period.

Acknowledgements

I would like to thank Angela Boyle, Andrew Fitz-patrick, Lesley McFadyen, David Perkins and Miles Russell for information on several of the sites discussed in this paper. I am grateful to Regine Maraszek for information from her Ph.D. research and to Mick Wysocki for discussion on Middle Bronze Age burial practices. Nigel Brown, Andrew Fitzpatrick, Richard Hingley, Andy Jones, Nigel Macpherson-Grant, Jacqueline McKinley and Jacky Nowakowski kindly commented on some of the ideas presented here. Thanks also to Stuart Needham for sight of his forthcoming paper on bronze hoards and for discussing the Continental literature with me. Of course, responsibility for the interpretations presented here rests solely with myself.

References

Bailey, D. 1990. The living house: signifying continuity. In R. Samson (ed.), *The social archaeology of houses*, 19–48. Edinburgh: Edinburgh University Press.

Barrett, J. C. 1989a. Food, gender and metal: questions of social reproduction. In Sørensen, M. L. S. and Thomas, R. (eds) *The Bronze Age-Iron Age Transition in Europe*, 304–320. Oxford: British Archaeological Reports, International Series 483(2).

Barrett, J. C. 1989b. Time and tradition: the rituals of everyday life. In H.-Å. Nordström and A. Knape (eds), *Bronze Age Studies: Transactions of the British-Scandinavian Colloquium in Stockholm, May 10–11, 1985*, 113–126. Stockholm: Museum of National Antiquities.

Barrett, J. C. 1991. Mortuary archaeology. In Barrett, J. C., Bradley, R. and Green, M. *Landscape, Monuments and Society: the Prehistory of Cranborne Chase*, 120–128. Cambridge: Cambridge University Press.

Barrett, J. C. and Needham, S. P. 1988. Production, circulation and exchange: problems in the interpretation of Bronze Age bronzework. In Barrett. J. and Kinnes, I. (eds), *The Archaeology of Context in the Neolithic and Bronze Age: Recent Trends*, 127–140. Sheffield: Dept. of Archaeology and Prehistory.

Barrett, J. C., Bradley, R. J. and Green, M. 1991. *Landscape, Monuments and Society: the Prehistory of Cranborne Chase*. Cambridge: Cambridge University Press.

Bloch, M. and Parry, J. (eds) 1982. *Death and the Regeneration of Life*. Cambridge: Cambridge University Press.

Bradley, R. 1990. *The Passage of Arms: an Archaeological Analysis of Prehistoric Hoards and Votive Deposits*. Cambridge: Cambridge University Press.

Brewster, T. C. M. 1963. *The Excavation of Staple Howe*. Wintringham: East Riding Archaeological Research Committee.

Brown, G., Field, D. and McOmish, D. East Chisenbury midden complex. In Fitzpatrick, A. P. and Morris, E. L. (eds) *The Iron Age in Wessex: Recent Work*, 46–49. Salisbury: Trust for Wessex Archaeology/Association Française d'Etude de l'Age du Fer.

Brown, N. 1995. Ardleigh reconsidered: Deverel-Rimbury

pottery in Essex. In Kinnes, I. and Varndell, G. (eds) *'Unbaked Urns of Rudely Shape': Essays on British and Irish Pottery for Ian Longworth*, 123–144. Oxford: Oxbow Monograph 55.

Brück, J. 1995. A place for the dead: the role of human remains in the Late Bronze Age. *Proceedings of the Prehistoric Society* 61, 245–277.

Brück, J. 1999. Houses, lifecycles and deposition on Middle Bronze Age settlements in southern England. *Proceedings of the Prehistoric Society* 65, 145–166.

Buckley, D. G. and Hedges, J. D. 1987. *The Bronze Age and Saxon Settlements at Springfield Lyons, Essex: an Interim Report*. Chelmsford: Essex County Council Occasional Paper 5.

Budd, P. and Taylor, T. 1995. The faerie smith meets the bronze industry: magic versus science in the interpretation of prehistoric metal-making. *World Archaeology* 27,133–143.

Burstow, G. P. and Holleyman, G. A. 1957. Late Bronze Age settlement on Itford Hill, Sussex. *Proceedings of the Prehistoric Society* 23, 167–212.

Chapman, J. 1997. Places as timemarks – the social construction of prehistoric landscapes in Eastern Hungary. In Nash, G. (ed.) Semiotics of landscape: archaeology of *mind*, 31–45. Oxford: British Archaeological Reports, international series 661.

Chapman, J. 1999. Deliberate house-burning in the prehistory of central and eastern Europe. In Gustafsson, A. and Karlsson, H. (eds) Glyfer och arkeologiska rum – en vänbok till Jarl Nordbladh. Göteborg: Univsity of Göteborg Press, Gotarc Series A, vol. 3.

Chapman, J. 2000. 'Rubbish dumps' or 'places of deposition': Neolithic and Copper Age settlements in central and eastern Europe. In Ritchie, A. (ed.) Neolithic Orkney in its European context, 347–362. Cambridge: McDonald Institute monograph.

Cleal, R. 1995. Pottery fabrics in Wessex from the fourth to second millennia BC. In Kinnes, I. and Varndell, G. (eds) *'Unbaked Urns of Rudely Shape': Essays on British and Irish Pottery for Ian Longworth*, 185–194. Oxford: Oxbow Monograph 55.

Coles, J. 1959–1960. Scottish Late Bronze Age metalwork: typology, distributions and chronology. *Proceedings of the Society of Antiquaries of Scotland* 93, 16–34.

Coles, J. 1968–1969. Scottish Early Bronze Age metalwork. *Proceedings of the Society of Antiquaries of Scotland* 101, 1–110.

Cunliffe, B. 1970. A Bronze Age settlement at Chalton, Hampshire (site 78). *Antiquaries' Journal* 50, 1–13.

Cunliffe, B. 1992. Pits, preconceptions and propitiation in the British Iron Age. *Oxford Journal of Archaeology* 11(1), 69–83.

Cunnington, M. E. 1923. *The Early Iron Age Inhabited Site at All Cannings Cross Farm, Wiltshire*. Devizes: George Simpson.

Curwen, E. C. 1934. A Late Bronze Age farm and Neolithic pit-dwelling on New Barn Down, Clapham, near Worthing. *Sussex Archaeological Collections* 75, 137–170.

Dacre, M. and Ellison, A. 1981. A Bronze Age cemetery at Kimpton, Hampshire. *Proceedings of the Prehistoric Society* 47, 147–203.

Douglas, M. 1966. *Purity and Danger: an Analysis of the Concepts of Pollution and Taboo*. London: Routledge and Kegan Paul.

Downes, J. and Lamb, R. 2000. *Prehiatoric Houses at Sumburgh in Shetland: Excavations at Sumburgh Airport, 1967–74*. Oxford: Oxbow Books.

Drewett, P. 1982. Later Bronze Age downland economy and excavations at Black Patch, East Sussex. *Proceedings of the Prehistoric Society* 48, 321–340.

Ellison, A. 1978. The Bronze Age in Sussex. In P. Drewett (ed.), *Archaeology in Sussex to AD 1500*, 30–37. London: Council of British Archaeology Research Report 29.

Ellison, A. 1980. Deverel-Rimbury urn cemeteries: the evidence for social organisation. In Barrett, J. C. and Bradley, R. J. (eds) *Settlement and Society in the British Later Bronze Age*, 115–126. Oxford: British Archaeological Reports, British series 83.

Ellison, A. 1981. Towards a socioeconomic model for the Middle Bronze Age in southern England. In Hodder, I., Isaac, G. and Hammond, N. (eds) *Pattern of the Past: Studies in Honour of David Clarke*, 413–438. Cambridge: Cambridge University Press.

Ellison, A. 1987. The Bronze Age settlement at Thorny Down: pots, post-holes and patterning. *Proceedings of the Prehistoric Society* 53, 385–392.

Fitzpatrick, A. 1997. Everyday life in Iron Age Wessex. In Gwilt, A. and Haselgrove, C. (eds) *Reconstructing Iron Age Societies: New Approaches to the British Iron Age*, 73–86. Oxford: Oxbow Monograph 71.

Fitzpatrick, A. P., Butterworth, C. A. and Grove, J. 1999. *Prehistoric and Roman Sites in East Devon: the A30 Honiton to Exeter Improvement DBFO, 1996–9. Vol. 1: Prehistoric Sites*. Salisbury: Trust for Wessex Archaeology.

Gingell, C. 1992. *The Marlborough Downs: a Later Bronze Age Landscape and its Origins*. Devizes: Wiltshire Archaeology and Natural History Society Monograph 1.

Goody, J. (ed.) 1958. *The Developmental Cycle in Domestic Groups*. Cambridge: Cambridge University Press.

Herbert, E. 1993. *Iron, Gender and Power: Rituals of Transformation in African Societies*. Bloomington: Indiana University Press.

Hill, J. D. 1995. *Ritual and rubbish in the Iron Age of Wessex: a study on the formation of a particular archaeological record*. Oxford: British Archaeological Reports, British Series 242.

Hingley, R. 1997. Iron, ironworking and regeneration: a study of the symbolic meaning of metalworking in Iron Age Britain. In Gwilt, A. and Haselgrove, C. (eds) *Reconstructing Iron Age Societies: New Approaches to the British Iron Age*, 9–18. Oxford: Oxbow Monograph 71.

Hodder, I. 1982. *Symbols in Action: Ethnoarchaeological Studies of Material Culture*. Cambridge: Cambridge University Press.

Hundt, H.-J. 1955. Versuch der Deutung der Depotfunde der nordischen jüngeren Bronzezeit, unter besonderer Berücksichtigung Mecklensburgs. *Jahrbuch des Römisch-Germanischen Zentralmuseums, Mainz*, 2, 95–140.

Jones, A. 1999. *A Biography of Colour: Colour, Technology and Transformation in the Early Bronze Age of Britain*. Paper presented at the fifth annual meeting of the European Association of Archaeologists, Bournemouth, Sept. 1999.

Lawson, A. 1994. Potterne. In A. P. Fitzpatrick and E. L. Morris (eds), *The Iron Age in Wessex: Recent Work*, 42–

46. Salisbury: Trust for Wessex Archaeology/Association Française d'Etude de l'Age du Fer.

Lemmonier, P. 1986. The study of material culture today: toward an anthropology of technical systems. *Journal of Anthropological Archaeology* 5, 147–186.

Lemmonier, P. 1993. (ed.) *Technological Choices: Transformation in Material Cultures since the Neolithic*. London: Routledge.

Levi-Strauss, C. 1970. *The Raw and the Cooked: Introduction to a Science of Mythology, Vol.1*. London: Jonathan Cape.

Lewis, E. R. and Walker, G. 1976. A Middle Bronze Age settlement site at Westbury, West Meon, Hampshire. *Proceedings of the Hampshire Field Club and Archaeological Society* 33, 33–34.

McKinley, J. 1993. Bone fragment size and weights of bone from modern British cremations and its implications for the interpretation of archaeological cremations. *International Journal of Osteoarchaeology* 3, 283–287.

McKinley, J. 1997. Bronze Age 'barrows' and funerary rites and rituals of cremation. *Proceedings of the Prehistoric Society* 63, 129–145.

Metcalf, P. and Huntingdon, R. 1991. *Celebrations of Death: the Anthropology of Mortuary Ritual*. Second edition. Cambridge: Cambridge University Press.

Moore, H. 1986. *Space, Text and Gender: an Anthropological Study of the Marakwet of Kenya*. Cambridge: Cambridge University Press.

Moore, J. and Jennings, D. 1992. *Reading Business Park: a Bronze Age Landscape*. Oxford: Oxford Archaeological Unit.

Morris, E. 1994. Pottery. In Hearne, C. M. and Heaton, M. J. Excavations at a Late Bronze Age settlement in the Upper Thames Valley at Shorncote Qaurry near Cirencester, 1992. *Transactions of the Bristol and Gloucestershire Archaeological Society* 112, 34–43.

Mortimer, R. and McFadyen, L. 1999. *Investigation of the Archaeological Landscape at Broom, Bedfordshire: phase 4*. Cambridge: Cambridge Archaeological Unit Report 320.

Müller-Karpe, H. 1958. Neues zur Urnenfelderkultur Bayerns. *Bayerische Vorgeschichtsblätter* 23, 4–34.

Nebelsick, L. 1997. Auf biegen und brechen: ekstatische Elemente bronzezeitlicher Materialopfer – ein Deutungsversuch. In Hänsel, A. and Hänsel, B. (eds) *Gaben an die Götter: Schätze der Bronzezeit Europas*, 35–41. Berlin: Freie Universität Berlin/Staatliche Museen zu Berlin, Preussischer Kulturbesitz.

Needham, S. P. 1991. *Excavation and Salvage at Runnymede Bridge, 1978: the Late Bronze Age Waterfront Site*. London: British Museum.

Needham, S. 2001. When expediency broaches ritual intention: the flow of metal between systemic and buried domains. *Journal of the Royal Anthropological Institute* 7.2, 275–298.

Needham, S. and Spence, T. 1996. *Refuse and Disposal at Area 16 East, Runnymede*. London: British Museum Press.

Nowakowski, J. 1991. Trethellan Farm, Newquay: the excavation of a lowland Bronze Age settlement and Iron Age cemetery. *Cornish Archaeology* 30, 5–242.

Okely, J. 1983. *The Traveller Gypsies*. Cambridge: Cambridge University Press.

Oswald, A. 1997. A doorway on the past: practical and mystic concerns in the orientation of roundhouse doorways. In Gwilt, A. and Haselgrove, C. (eds) *Reconstructing Iron Age Societies*, 87–95. Oxford: Oxbow Monograph 71.

Owoc, M. A. 1999. *Munselling the mound: the use of soil colour as metaphor in British Bronze Age funerary ritual*. Paper presented at the 5th annual meeting of the European Association of Archaeologists, Bournemouth, Sept. 1999.

Parker Pearson, M. and Richards, C. 1994. Architecture and order: spatial representation and archaeology. In Parker Pearson, M. and Richards, C. (eds) *Architecture and Order: Approaches to Social Space*, 38–72. London: Routledge.

Parker Pearson, M. 1996. Food, fertility and front doors in the first millennium BC. In Champion, T. and Collis, J. (eds) *The Iron Age in Britain and Ireland: Recent Trends*, 117–132. Sheffield: J. R. Collis Publications.

Perkins, D. R. J., Macpherson-Grant, N. and Healey, E. 1994. Monkton Court Farm evaluation, 1992. *Archaeologia Cantiana* 114, 237–316.

Petersen, P. F. 1981. *The Excavation of a Bronze Age Cemetery on Knighton Heath, Dorset*. Oxford: British Archaeological Reports, British Series 98.

Pfaffenberger, B. 1988. Fetishised objects and humanised nature: towards an anthropology of technology. *Man* 23(2), 236–252.

Richards, J. 1990. *The Stonehenge Environs Project*. London: English Heritage Archaeological Report 16.

Seager Thomas, M. 1999. Stone finds in context: a contribution to the study of later prehistoric artefact assemblages. *Sussex Archaeological Collections* 137, 39–48.

Stanford, S. C. 1982. Bromfield, Shropshire – Neolithic, Beaker and Bronze Age sites, 1966–79. *Proceedings of the Prehistoric Society* 48, 279–320.

Stevanovic, M. 1997. The age of clay: the social dynamics of house destruction. Journal of Anthropological Archaeology 16, 334–395.

Tilley, C. 1996. *An Ethnography of the Neolithic: Early Prehistoric Societies in Southern Scandinavia*. Cambridge: Cambridge University Press.

Turner, C. E. L. 1998. *A Re-interpretation of the Late Bronze Age Metalwork Hoards of Essex and Kent*. Unpublished Ph.D. thesis, Department of Archaeology, University of Glasgow.

Verlaeckt, K. 1998. Metalwork consumption in Late Bronze Age Denmark. In Mordant, C., Pernot, M. and Rychner, V. (eds), *L'Atelier du Bronzier en Europe du XXe au VIIIe Siècle avant notre Ère, Tome III: Production, Circulation et Consommation du bronze*, 259–271. Paris: Comités des Travaux Historiques et Scientifiques.

Welbourn, D. A. 1981. The role of blacksmiths in a tribal society. *Archaeological Review from Cambridge* 1, 30–41.

Worsaae, J. J. A. 1866–1871. Sur quelques trouvailles de l'Age du Bronze faites dans les tourbières. *Memoires de la Société Royale des Antiquaires du Nord*, 61–75.

Wymer, J. J. and Brown, N. 1995. *Excavations at North Shoebury: Settlement and Economy in South-East Essex 1500 BC–AD 1500*. Chelmsford: East Anglian Archaeology Monograph 75.

15   A time and a place for bronze

Martyn Barber

Introduction

Personal experience has made it clear that the phrase 'Bronze Age metalwork' is one that can clear rooms, or at least prompt a quick change of subject. Getting to grips with the typological minutiae that can seem to dominate the subject is a process whose lengthy and complicated nature can make avoidance seem the best option. Nonetheless, general developments in the way we consider the material culture of past societies as well as specific studies of Bronze Age metalwork by Richard Bradley, Stuart Needham and others all point towards the possibilities for metalwork to make a more useful and interesting contribution to the study of the Bronze Age (e.g. Levy 1982; Needham 1988; Bradley 1990; Budd and Taylor 1995; Bridgford 1997; Dickens 1997). New discoveries need not be regarded purely as cultural and chronological markers. However, rather than offering a comprehensive discussion of the subject, the aim of this paper is to highlight some of the ways in which metalwork deposition has been considered, underlining some important recent contributions, and to point out further potential approaches to interpreting prehistoric metalwork.

From the days of Christian Thomsen onwards, the Bronze Age has been viewed as a period of the prehistoric past when the principal tools and weapons were manufactured from copper or a copper alloy. Over the course of time, the relative importance of bronze to the ways in which we understand life in the Bronze Age has fluctuated considerably, but from an early stage, in the absence of little else beyond barrows and their contents, it was crucial to the reconstruction of the past. Perhaps the most important contribution of metalwork studies was towards the creation of chronological and cultural frameworks – the subdivision of the Bronze Age over time and space, and the recognition of links between different geographical regions. However, it also offered significant clues about the socio-economic character of the period. Social and cultural developments were closely linked to advances in technological capabilities. In addition to the functional potential of the objects concerned, metal has also been perceived as possessing particular forms of value, generally expressed through concerns with power and prestige. Of importance here are factors such as access to the raw material, to finished objects and to metalworking expertise itself. The ability to possess metal objects, to control their movement and restrict their possession have become important elements in understanding how Bronze Age societies functioned.

Today, of course, the Bronze Age is littered with an array of debris far more extensive and varied than anything available to previous generations of prehistorians, the generations that laid the foundations for the ways in which we discuss the Bronze Age today. To the enormous wealth of objects that once offered the principal medium for fleshing out the period has been added an impressive and diverse range of sites – physical evidence to complement the artefactual material on which reconstruction of the 'drama of prehistory' (Childe 1949, 2) once depended. Added to those material and physical remnants are myriad ways of looking at and thinking about the evidence. The impact of such developments becomes readily apparent when comparing general accounts of the Bronze Age published over the past thirty years or so. As recently as 1974, Colin Burgess, in Renfrew's ironically-titled 'British Prehistory: a New Outline', was still acknowledging the very real problem that, 'Study of the British bronze age has always been hampered by a lack of settlement evidence . . . Most of our knowledge of the period is derived from burial and ritual sites and unassociated artefacts'

(Burgess 1974, 165). This is no longer so, and consequently little of the interpretative content of Burgess's extremely detailed chapter remains relevant today. Subsequent accounts by Burgess (1980), Darvill (1987), Parker Pearson (1993) and Barrett (1994), among others, testify to the rapid changes in outlook inspired and demanded by new discoveries, fresh perspectives and reassessments of older material. However, with some notable exceptions, the impact of all this on the study of Bronze Age metalwork has been less dramatic, with much discussion continuing along traditional lines – typological analysis, distribution patterns, industrial traditions, inter-regional contact, chronology – with no real sense that this work, valuable as some of it undoubtedly is, contributes significantly to the broader picture. At the same time, there is insufficient acknowledgement of the very real problems concerning the theoretical foundations of these analytical approaches.

Bronze deposition past and present

Of greatest concern is the fact that much discussion of Bronze Age metalwork has taken place without a proper consideration of the depositional circumstances of the objects concerned (Bradley 1990). Deposition or disposal is generally presumed to have been deliberate but unproblematic, yet as Bradley and others have emphasised, bronze is a recyclable material and the available evidence suggests that recycling was a common feature of the British Bronze Age (e.g. Rohl and Needham 1998). Concerns increase when we realise that the metalwork available to us does not represent a random cross-section of the material manufactured and circulated during the Bronze Age (Needham and Burgess 1980; Barrett and Needham 1988). The artefacts that we possess today are actually the residues of a variety of depositional practices rather than a random reflection of routine domestic, economic and industrial activities.

A major reason why such issues have been neglected in the past is the simple fact that contextual information – the sort of detail that could help to shed a little light on the circumstances of deposition – is usually lacking. It is unfortunately the case that the overwhelming majority of Bronze Age metal artefacts available for study were neither found by archaeologists nor recovered in a careful and controlled manner. Until recently, nearly all were accidental discoveries during the course of agricultural or building work, railway or road construction, quarrying or dredging. More recently, the growing popularity of metal-detecting has added a more purposeful element to the search for metal objects, sometimes with spectacular results, but the majority of discoveries still occur outside of any informed research framework, while the archaeological investigation of findspots remains the exception rather than the rule. This last fact is particularly pertinent given the relative rarity of metal finds from settlement sites. Although pottery and stone objects are ubiquitous at such places, and bone common given the correct soil conditions, metal remains unusual although not unknown.

Such a lack of evidence for the circumstances of deposition should represent a major weakness in any attempt to understand the roles and significance of metalwork. If we cannot explain its deposition, how can we reliably make use of it for typological and chronological studies, let alone make assessments of its social and cultural value? In fact, these weaknesses have effectively been concealed by the early establishment and widespread acceptance of quite specific explanations for deposition and non-recovery.

Today, we have clear and unambiguous, although not universally acknowledged (e.g. Pendleton 1999) evidence that deposition in the Bronze Age could be non-random, selective and purposeful, with no intention to recover. Furthermore, it appears to have been motivated by factors other than security or economics. However, the more traditional explanations offer a rather limited and limiting set of choices that focus mainly on temporary storage or concealment of personal possessions. They revolve around the burial of so-called hoards – assemblages of bronze objects concealed, or at least found, together. Since the later nineteenth century, there have been clearly understood explanations of how these hoards came to be buried. Sir John Evans was not the first to present them, but his 1881 tome on ancient bronzes represents an important stage in British Bronze Age studies. The basic choices he presented remain familiar today: the founder's hoard, the merchant's hoard and the personal hoard. Evans did raise the matter of votive deposition, an explanation used by some foreign scholars to account for certain accumulations of material, but he felt that it had not really been the (ancient) British way of doing things. This reluctance to accept a religious or ritual motive for metalwork deposition outside explicitly funerary contexts proved remarkably long-lived in the British Isles (see Bradley 1990 and Taylor 1993 for discussion). A more recent shift in outlook owes as much to studies of depositional practices at certain Neolithic monuments, and to notions of structured deposition (Richards and Thomas 1984), as it does to the remarkable but so far unique discoveries at Flag Fen (Pryor 1991; 1992).

Depositional practices: the evidence

The uneasy relationship between traditional explanations of deposition and the available evidence have been best demonstrated by Stuart Needham in a study of depositional patterns in the Early Bronze Age of Britain and Ireland (Needham 1988). For example, he was able to demonstrate that clear distinctions existed between the types of object appropriate for use as grave goods and those that appeared in contemporary hoards. He also noted clear instances of uneven geographical distribution in the archaeological record: the mapping of hoard findspots, arranged by chronologically successive 'Metalwork Assemblages', indicated a trend throughout the course of the Early Bronze Age from a highland- and Ireland-dominated distribution towards a lowland concentration. As for the reasons for depositing those hoards, he argued that,

> None of the British hoards has any evidence connecting it explicitly to the process of metal-working; explanation of the broken objects in some hoards is ambiguous, and therefore they cannot necessarily be regarded as the unretrieved stock-piles of smiths, or indeed of merchants . . . Only rarely are the circumstances of hoards adequately recorded, but sometimes they give evidence of considerable care in the arrangement of objects, thus hinting that deposition was not only deliberate, but intended to be permanent . . . here is something beyond a purely functional requirement in their act of burial (Needham 1988, 232).

Arguably, this is equally applicable to the hoards of the Middle and Late Bronze Age, although these have not been subject to the same level of analysis, particularly at a national scale. Although this is not the place to discuss the evidence in detail, a few examples will suffice. An excellent recent example is a collection of bronzes from South Dumpton Down on the Isle of Thanet, Kent (D. Perkins, pers. comm.). A subrectangular enclosure associated with Deverel-Rimbury pottery contained a pit in its enclosing ditch. This pit had been dug into the ditch when the latter had already been substantially backfilled. Towards the base of the pit were four palstaves, lying together on their sides and arranged in an arc or fan-shape. The four palstaves were similar in form and were unused, broadly as cast although tidied up to a certain extent, but with blades unsharpened. Lying over them was a large slab of tabular flint. A little higher in the pit fill was another palstave, this time lying on its face, and with a bronze bracelet resting on top of it. The circumstances suggest an act of deposition late in the history of the enclosure, and clearly it was an act concerned with more than just storage or disposal.

An interesting comparison can be made with another broadly contemporary enclosure at South Lodge, on Cranborne Chase, just in Wiltshire (Barrett *et al.* 1991). This example also raises the issue of explaining the presence of single, or unassociated items in the archaeological record. Excavated in the late nineteenth century by Pitt Rivers and again more recently by John Barrett and Richard Bradley (*ibid.*), South Lodge has had a long and varied history in twentieth century archaeology, with changing interpretations of its nature and function as well as its date broadly reflecting developments in the understanding of the Bronze Age. Barrett and Bradley argued on the basis of their own work and re-analysis of Pitt Rivers's excavations that the enclosure phase occurred late in the history of the site. More recently, David McOmish (pers. comm.) has argued that the enclosure earthworks actually represent the final stage in the history of the settlement, the enclosing earthworks being constructed at or shortly after the settlement had been abandoned. This suggestion finds support in evidence provided by both excavation and survey, and has clear implications for the interpretation of finds recovered from the ditch fills. Particularly noteworthy are the fact that the enclosure ditch and bank on the northern side cut through a large spread of burnt flint that had accumulated during the life of the settlement, and the observation that the lynchet across the enclosure's main western entrance still survives as an earthwork even though 'heavy traffic through that entrance would surely have caused more erosion' (Barrett *et al.* 1991, 183). The enclosure ditch, once cut, had been rapidly backfilled; Barrett and Bradley (*ibid.*, 153) note that, 'the excavated profile [of the ditch]is steeper than we would expect from a chalk-cut ditch which had silted naturally'. The bottom three feet or so of ditch fill was composed entirely of chalk rubble, and above this was what Pitt Rivers had referred to as the 'mixed silting'. A bronze razor and a bronze awl were found on the bottom of the ditch, the former in the northeastern corner, the latter in the opposite southwestern corner. A razor, bracelet and some bronze wire were all found within a short distance of each other at the northern end of the eastern ditch, all at the base of the mixed silting. Finally, a side-looped spearhead came from high in the ditch on the southern side, near the southeastern corner and close to a break in the enclosure bank. The timing of the construction of the ditch and the nature of the backfilling, as well as other artefactual evidence from the ditch, all argue against the metalwork representing settlement debris accidentally incorporated in the ditch, as of course does the presence of an internal bank. It should also be noted that such circumstances are not even unusual on Cranborne Chase, let alone elsewhere in southern England (see Brück 1999a). This example also serves as a reminder that the reasons for constructing enclosing earthworks are equally problematical, and by no means restricted to the most obvious explanations, such as defence or stock management (e.g. Bowden and McOmish 1987; 1989).

The Late Bronze Age is perhaps most commonly associated, as far as metalwork is concerned, with two phenomena: deposition of single items in rivers and other wet places, and the large accumulations of whole and fragmentary items known as 'founder's hoards'. Recognition of the former has played a key role in the broader acceptance of ritual deposition as an explanation, although at the same time it has led to a potentially misleading distinction being drawn between 'wet' and 'dry' contexts. Needham's detailed analysis (1990) of the assemblage from Petters Sports Field has underlined the difficulties in interpreting Late Bronze Age 'dryland' hoards in simplistic terms as metalworking scrap or stock. Another good example is a hoard found at Withersfield, Suffolk, in 1993 (Anon. 1996), which like the Petters and Dumpton finds is another rare instance of an excavated hoard. Its existence was suggested by a small surface scatter of bronzes in a ploughed field. Excavation uncovered a remarkable arrangement of objects: a tightly packed mass of metal, comprising from the top,

> a layer of packed bronze-cake fragments . . . at a depth of 30cm, the whole mass being roughly circular, with a diameter of 25cm . . . the depth of this layer of fragments was 15cm. Below this level, five axes were visible, deliberately packed to the sides of the whole with cake fragments, all five axes being positioned vertically...; a small socketed chisel/gouge had been placed lying flat, together with five broken axe fragments, all lying centrally (Anon. 1996, 115–117).

Three of the axe blades pointed upwards, the other two were socket-upwards.

Turning to single items of Late Bronze Age date, an excellent example comes from Barford in Warwickshire (Oswald 1966/67). The site itself is a triple-ditched ceremonial and/or funerary monument of Late Neolithic/Early Bronze Age date, multi-phase in construction and owing something to both hengiform and round barrow traditions. In the early first millennium BC, a number of pits were dug into the monument. One in particular contained a complex sequence of fills, but it seems that after the pit had been dug and backfilled, it was dug into once more, this time for the purpose of depositing a bronze socketed chisel, which was accompanied by what the excavator described as a small fossil sponge, both objects being covered and concealed by a large potsherd.

Ritual intent

Such evidence for selective, formal and deliberate deposition of metalwork inevitably leads in the direction of a ritual or votive interpretation. These are concepts with a rather chequered history in archaeology, although the past twenty years or so have seen the recognition and understanding of ritual practices in the archaeological record placed on a rather more sound footing than had once been the case (Garwood *et al.* 1991; Barrett 1994, ch. 3; Brück 1999b). Previously, the term 'ritual' has been used to explain (or explain away) phenomena that are otherwise apparently inexplicable to us – things that seem illogical, uneconomic, or non-functional. Ritual behaviour is often associated with religious practices or performances, and the purpose of both has on occasion been depicted in quite crude terms, for example as a social mechanism by which certain groups or individuals might attain power over people and things. At the same time, the performance of rituals has been seen as something ultimately quite distinct from everyday life and consequently requiring little further attention once identified.

A persistent belief in a clear distinction between the sacred and the profane, and an assumption that such distinctions can be observed in the archaeological record, is a feature of archaeological analysis that has received much comment and criticism (Barrett 1991; 1994, 77–84; Brück 1999b). There is a growing awareness of the ongoing, if largely subconscious interaction between the mundane – the everyday social practices and subsistence activities of individuals and groups – and the broader cosmological concerns that help to shape social and economic relationships and activities. Effectively, what we might characterise as religious beliefs and ritual practices were an integral, if sometimes hidden element of everyday life. However, putting such awareness into practice is another matter entirely.

For British prehistory, there have been noteworthy studies of the orientation and internal workings of round houses and settlements (e.g. Hingley 1990; Parker Pearson and Richards 1994; Oswald 1997), while discussion of the use and symbolic potential of material culture, including its deposition, has been a marked feature of Neolithic and Early Bronze Age studies for some time now. By and large, metal has not figured in such discussions. Part of the problem appears to be a perception that it is an inherently utilitarian material used to create objects that serve a primarily practical purpose. At the same time, the landscape of the Middle Bronze Age and later periods is perceived to be more 'domestic' in nature, as the monuments characteristic of earlier millennia cease to be constructed or actively used (see Barrett *et al.* 1991, 143–144, 223–226). This decline in the archaeological visibility of ceremony and ritual is underlined by the apparent disappearance of funerary practices over the same period. The Neolithic and Early Bronze Age are characterised commonly by the physical presencing of ancestors in the landscape, and of rituals of social practice and interaction. These funerary and ceremonial aspects of social life served to establish links between people and with places. They were given monumental and, perhaps intentionally, permanent expression in a landscape still occupied by relatively mobile communities. By the Later Bronze Age, of course, the focus of ritual is less physically tangible. The archaeological record is instead dominated by the monuments of everyday life – settlements, enclosures, field systems and so on – accompanied by an increasingly broad range of artefacts. The latter are generally used to build a picture of the sort of activities occurring at these sites, and can provide invaluable dating evidence. The disappearance of material and monumental evidence of an overtly non-utilitarian nature has led to the Later Bronze Age being viewed primarily within a framework that highlights the economic, the technological and the subsistence-related aspects of life and only occasionally acknowledges the spiritual side (see also Brück 1999b). However, formal, stylistic and contextual analyses of those artefacts, metalwork included, highlight the continuance of ritual and ceremonial practices.

The significance of bronze

The social role of material culture has been a subject of keen debate in recent years. Our perceptions of prehistoric society arise from a conceptual framework grounded in our own interpretations of the material remains of the past. Likewise, to the original creators and users of those remains, they will not have been viewed solely as inert products of technology and labour with primarily utilitarian and economic value, but will have been seen to reflect and participate in social relationships. Phrases such as 'the social life of things' (Appadurai 1986) and references to 'artefacts with personalities' (Thomas 1996) neatly encapsulate the idea that objects may have identities or possess cultural values reflecting aspects of their origin, history of ownership and use. Different aspects of those identities may come to the fore in different social contexts. At the same time, the historical and ethnographic record serves to remind us that materials may be physically and culturally manipulated in many different ways, frequently ways that are totally alien to our own experiences. A good example here comes from the

work of Roy Larick (1985; 1986; 1991), who has studied the use of spears among groups of Maa-speaking pastoralists in East Africa. Among these groups, the seemingly ever-changing form of spears helps males to move through a sequence of age grades, where graduation to each new grade alters one's status and social networks. The form of an individual's spears communicates his economic, physical and social status to whomever he meets – his age and social position determine the range of spears he may possess. The males pass through age grades at regular intervals and spear styles identify them as members of a specific cohort and grade. Interestingly, it is the warriors who are responsible for innovation in spearhead form and style, bringing in new formal elements or innovations as each new generation consciously seeks to distinguish itself from the preceding one, something that can also involve the modification of jewellery, clothing and songs.

Moving from the products themselves towards the manner of their creation, Lahiri (1995) meanwhile has drawn attention to a preference for working with copper of high purity in Indian metalworking, particularly when creating objects for use in ritual contexts. Hosler (1994; 1995) has described the situation in pre-colonial and historic west Mexico, where the two properties of metal of most interest to metalworkers and the society in which they operated were sound and colour. According to Hosler, this example,

> strikingly demonstrates the ways in which symbolic and ideological factors can shape technologies. Ancient metallurgy emphasized certain physical properties, sound and color, which expressed fundamental religious beliefs, and . . . those beliefs were embedded in, and perpetuated through the technology and its products (1995, 113).

Similar ideas can be clearly observed in some recent ethnographic and historical studies of iron and copper working in sub-Saharan Africa (see for example Herbert 1984; 1993; Childs 1991; Rowlands and Warnier 1993; Schmidt 1996; 1997). African iron-working practices both contain and objectify much wider ideas about the cosmologies – the wider systems of belief – that help to provide organising frameworks within which social practices and relationships, including iron working, could take place and be understood. In mining, smelting and casting, from the perspective of those participating and those excluded, all associated activities contribute to a successful outcome. This includes the performance of rituals and the observance of taboos and other restrictions relating to the age and gender of those taking part in the various stages of the process, activities whose performance both reflect cosmological beliefs and help to shape and reinforce them as social norms. Thus, the apparently ritual aspects are essential production requirements; no distinction is made between technology and ritual (or 'magic') (see also Brück 1999b). Technology is firmly embedded within social contexts and within a broader conceptual framework that offers a means of understanding the world and structuring human behaviour.

With iron working, smelters and smiths often appear to have regarded themselves as participants in a natural process by which certain materials were transformed into something that could be adapted to culturally useful ends (Rowlands and Warnier 1993). The metalworkers served to facilitate this process, helping via taboos, rituals and technological expertise to remove likely impediments and protect against perceived sources of danger both to the participants and to the outcome of the process. Thus, 'technology must . . . be understood in a cosmological context. [It] is embedded in belief systems about social relationships and the natural world' (Goucher and Herbert 1996, 55). For Childs and Killick (1993, 325),

> All social behaviour, including technology, is grounded in a conceptual framework that imposes order on the world and lends structure to human existence. These beliefs guide the choices in all facets of life. In the context of technology, these choices include the organization of labour and the selection of resources, tools, and the sequence of acts that constitute a technological process.

For metalworking in prehistory, the significance of viewing this technology and its products can perhaps be taken even further, recalling Eliade's suggestion (1968, 76) that the discovery of the means of manipulating metals changed the whole world of meaning – that metals opened a 'new mythological and religious universe', although he felt that it had been a less radical change than that brought about by the earlier discovery and adoption of agriculture.

Naturally, we cannot simply transfer either the specifics of a particular ethnographic example, or cross-cultural generalisations, to the British Bronze Age. However, recent years have seen studies of prehistoric architecture, for example, that draw on the idea of cosmological principles being translated into social and cultural practices via the performance of everyday activities. Given the prominent position that metalworking, metalworkers and metal objects occupy in the myths of some African societies – the mythological tales that explain and contain the apparent basis for the contemporary organisation of society and its components – and in particular the creation myths, there is no reason why we should not also think in similar terms about metal and

metalworking, to see technological practices and their products as embodying not only personal meanings but also expressing, or allowing the expression of, and maintaining and reworking the ideology of a given society.

Richard Hingley (1997) has recently drawn on some of the ethnographic work noted above, particularly that of Eugenia Herbert (1993), in attempting to establish the existence in Iron Age Britain of a metaphorical link between iron working and regeneration, both human and agricultural. In discussing the ways that people in the Iron Age might have conceptualised iron, Hingley argued that,

> the life-cycle of objects was viewed in some contexts as reflecting and projecting the life-cycle of people and the crops and animals upon which they depended. Iron objects and the process by which they were made became increasingly powerful because of the association with regeneration and agricultural production. During the development of a relatively intensively occupied agricultural landscape in southern Britain from the Deverel-Rimbury period onward, the process of iron production and the objects which were produced became increasingly powerful symbols of regeneration and fertility (1997, 10).

However, in many of the African societies studied by Herbert and others, the situation is rather more complex. Rowlands and Warnier (1993) in particular have exercised a note of caution over the ways in which some have attempted to use the ethnographic accounts to link iron working with fertility, arguing that although iron making and other forms of production are not necessarily understood in different terms to human or agricultural fertility and reproduction, neither can the latter be regarded as simply providing a model for other forms of production, such as ironworking. Instead, conceptual links are often made between metalworking and other productive or procreative processes, such as human and agricultural production, pottery making and so on (Brück 1999a; this volume).

Metalwork in the British Bronze Age

Clearly, it is instructive to contrast the ways in which objects and productive processes are conceptualised in other societies with the ways in which they have traditionally been seen in archaeology – often simply as a means of placing material assemblages in time and space. But how successful have we been at achieving this? A recent radiocarbon dating programme suggests that the overall sequence of development for British Bronze Age metalwork, as established over the past 120 years or more, is broadly correct (Needham *et al.* 1997). However, at the same time, other forms of evidence suggest a far more complex, diverse and fluid situation than is apparent from the traditional explanations of deposition and the accompanying sequence of poorly explained 'industrial' phases (e.g. Taunton, Ewart Park, etc.). Indeed, given the lack of a clear link between distribution, deposition and production, these so-called industries appear more than ever as an interpretative straitjacket that does little to aid the understanding of the social context of Bronze Age metalwork.

Viewing metalworking and metal objects from a broader social and cultural perspective, acknowledging both cosmological frameworks and the broad range of meanings potentially possessed by artefacts, serves to clearly undermine the comparatively simplistic ways in which the use and deposition of Bronze Age metalwork have traditionally been discussed. Instead, a complex and changing web of meanings was drawn on at particular times and in particular places, allowing bronze objects to be incorporated in what appear to have been small scale, perhaps communal events serving to link people with places, myth with history. In many cases, they appear directly linked with the foundation or abandonment of houses or settlements. However, the precise reasons for depositional events are likely to have varied considerably across time and space, something perhaps evident in the variety of contexts in which metalwork occurs, the different 'rules' governing the selection of appropriate objects adopted in different times and places, and the clear discontinuities in deposition observable across time and space.

Furthermore, rather than treating metalwork deposition in isolation, it is essential to recognise that similar questions can be asked about the presence on settlements and other sites of other kinds of material (see Brück 1995; 1999a; this volume). In the Late Bronze Age, for example, Needham (1992, 60) has noted how 'the settlements themselves can contain, amidst the general domestic debris, occasional deposits of material goods, or the remains of food, animals or humans, in contexts which suggest their deliberate placing to non-utilitarian ends'. At Runnymede (*ibid.*), these deposits included a lamb and a ewe buried on either side of a roundhouse. To return to South Lodge, in the interior of the building designated Structure 1 was a single pit that had been cut through the clay fill of the house terrace and into the underlying chalk. The upper fill contained a cluster of flint nodules; at the bottom of the pit, against its northern edge, was the left half of the carcass of a cow. It is clear that only the left side of the animal had been buried (Barrett *et al.* 1991, 157, 161). Within Structure 2 was a mound of pottery with a quernstone placed on top (*ibid.*, 183). Mean-

while, in Hut N at Itford Hill in West Sussex,

> at the foot of the scoop on the north side of the platform was a large portion of the skeleton of an ox. It lay directly on the chalk floor and was covered with clean undisturbed chalky silt. It must have been coeval with the occupation or abandonment of the site (Burstow and Holleyman 1957, 188).

No limb bones were present. Similar examples are numerous, and point to episodes of deposition associated directly or indirectly with the foundation, use or abandonment of settlements or houses.

Acknowledgements

Particular thanks are due to Dave Perkins of the Trust for Thanet Archaeology for all the information provided over the past few years, including details of the Dumpton hoard; to Dave McOmish for allowing me to name and shame him with respect to South Lodge; to Jamie, whose arrival delayed completion of this paper; and to the editor for her comments and patience.

References

Anon. 1996. A Late Bronze Age hoard from Withersfield, Suffolk. *Journal of the Haverhill and District Archaeological Group* 6(2), 115–122.

Appadurai, A. (ed.) 1986. *The Social Life of Things*. Cambridge: Cambridge University Press.

Barrett, J. C. 1991. Towards an archaeology of ritual. In Garwood, P., Jennings, D., Skeates, R. and Toms, J. (eds) *Sacred and Profane: Proceedings of a Conference on Archaeology, Ritual and Religion, Oxford 1989*, 1–9. Oxford: Oxford University Committee for Archaeology Monograph 32.

Barrett, J. C. 1994. *Fragments from Antiquity: an Archaeology of Social Life in Britain, 2900–1200 BC*. Oxford: Blackwell.

Barrett, J. C., Bradley, R. and Green, M. 1991. *Landscape, Monuments and Society: the Prehistory of Cranborne Chase*. Cambridge: Cambridge University Press.

Barrett, J. C. and Needham, S. P. 1988. Production, circulation and exchange: problems in the interpretation of Bronze Age bronzework. In Barrett, J. C. and Kinnes, I. A. (eds) *The Archaeology of Context in the Neolithic and Bronze Age: Recent Trends*, 127–140. Sheffield: Dept. of Archaeology and Prehistory, University of Sheffield.

Bowden, M. and McOmish, D. 1987. The required barrier. *Scottish Archaeological Review* 4, 76–84.

Bowden, M. and McOmish, D. 1989. Little boxes: more about hillforts. *Scottish Archaeological Review* 6, 12–16.

Bradley, R. 1990. *The Passage of Arms: an Archaeological Analysis of Hoards and Votive Deposits*. Cambridge: Cambridge University Press.

Bridgford, S. 1997. Mightier than the pen? An edgewise look at Irish Bronze Age swords. In Carman, J. (ed.)

Material Harm: Archaeological Studies of War and Violence, 95–115. Glasgow: Cruithne Press.

Brück, J. 1995. A place for the dead: the role of human remains in Late Bronze Age Britain. *Proceedings of the Prehistoric Society* 61, 245–277.

Brück, J. 1999a. Houses, lifecycles and deposition on Middle Bronze Age settlements in southern England. *Proceedings of the Prehistoric Society* 65, 145–166.

Brück, J. 1999b. Ritual and rationality: some problems of interpretation in European archaeology. *European Journal of Archaeology* 2(3), 313–344.

Budd, P. and Taylor, T. 1995. The faerie smith meets the bronze industry: magic versus science in the interpretation of prehistoric metal-making. *World Archaeology* 27, 133–143.

Burgess, C. 1974. The Bronze Age. In Renfrew, C. (ed.) *British Prehistory: a New Outline*, 165–232. London: Duckworth.

Burgess, C. 1980. *The Age of Stonehenge*. London: J. M. Dent.

Burstow, G. P. and Holleyman, G. A. 1957. Late Bronze Age settlement on Itford Hill, Sussex. *Proceedings of the Prehistoric Society* 23, 167–212.

Childe, V. G. 1949. *Prehistoric Communities of the British Isles*, 3rd edition. London: W. and R. Chambers.

Childs, S. T. 1991. Style, technology and iron smelting furnaces in Bantu-speaking Africa. *Journal of Anthropological Archaeology* 10, 332–359.

Childs, S. T. and Killick, D. 1993. Indigenous African metallurgy: nature and culture. *Annual Review of Anthropology* 22, 317–337.

Darvill, T. 1987. *Prehistoric Britain*. London: Batsford.

Dickens, J. 1996. A remote analogy? From central Australian tjurunga to Irish Early Bronze Age axes. *Antiquity* 70, 161–167.

Eliade, M. 1968. The forge and the crucible: a postcript. *History of Religions* 8, 74–88.

Evans, J. 1881. *The Ancient Bronze Implements, Weapons and Ornaments of Great Britain and Ireland*. London: Longmans, Green and Co.

Garwood, P., Jennings, D., Skeates, R. and Toms, J. (eds) 1991. *Sacred and Profane: Proceedings of a Conference on Archaeology, Ritual and Religion, Oxford 1989*. Oxford: Oxford University Committee for Archaeology Monograph 32.

Goucher, C. L, and Herbert, E. W. 1996. The blooms of Banjeli: technology and gender in west African iron making. In Schmidt, P. R. (ed.) *The Culture and Technology of African Iron Production*, 40–57. Gainesville: University Press of Florida.

Herbert, E. W. 1984. *Red Gold of Africa: Copper in Precolonial History and Culture*. Wisconsin: University of Wisconsin Press.

Herbert, E. W. 1993. *Iron, Gender and Power: Rituals of Transformation in African Societies*. Indianapolis/Bloomington: Indiana University Press.

Hingley, R. 1990. Domestic organisation and gender relations in Iron Age and Romano-British households. In Samson, R. (ed.) *The Social Archaeology of Houses*, 125–147. Edinburgh: Edinburgh University Press.

Hingley, R. 1997. Iron, ironworking and regeneration: a study of the symbolic meaning of metalworking in Iron Age Britain. In Gwilt, A. and Haselgrove, C. (eds)

Reconstructing Iron Age Societies, 9–18. Oxford: Oxbow Monograph 71.

Hosler, D. 1994. *The Sounds and Colors of Power: the Sacred Metallurgical Technology of Ancient West Mexico*. Cambridge, MA: MIT Press.

Hosler, D. 1995. Sound, color and meaning in the metallurgy of ancient west Mexico. *World Archaeology* 27, 100–115.

Lahiri, N. 1995. Indian metal and metal-related artefacts as cultural signifiers. *World Archaeology* 27, 116–132.

Larick, R. 1985. Spears, style and time among Maa-speaking pastoralists. *Journal of Anthropological Archaeology* 4, 206–220.

Larick, R. 1986. Age grading and ethnicity in Loikop (Samburu) spears. *Journal of Anthropological Archaeology* 4, 269–283.

Larick, R. 1991. Warriors and blacksmiths: mediating ethnicity in East African spears. *Journal of Anthropological Archaeology* 10, 299–331.

Levy, J. 1982. *Social and Religious Organization in Bronze Age Denmark: an Analysis of Ritual Hoard Finds*. Oxford: British Archaeological Reports, International Series 124.

Needham, S. P. 1988. Selective deposition in the British Early Bronze Age. *World Archaeology* 20, 229–248.

Needham, S. P. 1990. *The Petters Late Bronze Age Metalwork: an Analytical Study of Thames Valley Metalworking in its Settlement Context*. London: British Museum Occasional Paper 70.

Needham, S. P. 1992. The structure of settlement and ritual in the Late Bronze Age of south east Britain. In Mordant, C. and Richard, A. (eds) *L'Habitat et l'Occupation du Sol à l'Âge du Bronze en Europe*, 49–69. Paris: Editions du Comité des Travaux Historiques et Scientifiques.

Needham, S. and Burgess, C. 1980. The Later Bronze Age in the lower Thames Valley: the metalwork evidence. In Barrett, J. and Bradley, R. (eds) *Settlement and Society in the British Later Bronze Age*, 437–69. Oxford: British Archaeological Reports, British Series 83.

Needham, S., Bronk Ramsay, C., Coombs, D., Cartwright, C. and Pettit, P. 1997. An independent chronology for British Bronze Age metalwork: the results of the Oxford Radiocarbon Accelerator Programme. *Archaeological Journal* 154, 55–107.

Oswald, A. 1966/1967. Excavations for the Avon/Severn Research Committee at Barford, Warwickshire. *Birmingham Archaeological Society Transactions and Proceedings* 83, 1–64.

Oswald, A. 1997. A doorway on the past: practical and mystic concerns in the orientation of roundhouse doorways. In Gwilt, A. and Haselgrove, C. (eds) *Reconstructing Iron Age Societies*, 87–95. Oxford: Oxbow Monograph 71.

Parker Pearson, M. 1993. *Bronze Age Britain*. London: Batsford/English Heritage.

Parker Pearson, M. and Richards, C. 1994. Architecture and order: spatial representation and archaeology. In Parker Pearson, M. and Richards, C. (eds) *Architecture and Order: Approaches to Social Space*, 38–72. London: Routledge.

Pendleton, C. F. 1999. *Bronze Age Metalwork in Northern East Anglia: a Study of its Distribution and Interpretation*.

Oxford: British Archaeological Reports, British Series 279.

Pryor, F. 1991. *Flag Fen: Prehistoric Fenland Centre*. London: Batsford/English Heritage.

Pryor, F. (ed.). 1992. Current research at Flag Fen. *Antiquity* 66, 439–531.

Richards, C. C. and Thomas, J. S. 1984. Ritual activity and structured deposition in later Neolithic Wessex. In Bradley, R. and Gardiner, J. (eds) *Neolithic Studies*, 189–218. Oxford: British Archaeological Reports, British Series 133.

Rohl, B. and Needham, S. 1998. *The Circulation of Metalwork in the British Bronze Age: the Application of Lead Isotope Analysis*. London: British Museum Occasional Paper 102.

Rowlands, M. and Warnier, J. P. 1993. The magical production of iron in the Cameroon Grassfields. In Shaw, T., Sinclair, P., Andah, B. and Okpoko, A. (eds) *The Archaeology of Africa: Food, Metals and Towns*, 512–550. London: Routledge.

Schmidt, P. R. (ed.) 1996. *The Culture and Technology of African Iron Production*. Gainesville: University Press of Florida.

Schmidt, P. R. 1997. *Iron Technology in East Africa: Symbolism, Science and Archaeology*. Oxford: James Currey.

Taylor, R. J. 1993. *Hoards of the Bronze Age in Southern Britain: Analysis and Interpretation*. Oxford: British Archaeological Reports, British Series 228.

Thomas, J. 1996. *Time, Culture and Identity: an Interpretive Archaeology*. London: Routledge.

16   Firstly, let's get rid of ritual

Colin Pendleton

Introduction

This short paper is based on part of a body of research carried out mainly between 1986 and 1992 (Pendleton 1999), which was primarily concerned with the interpretation of Bronze Age metalwork from northern East Anglia, (i.e. Norfolk, Suffolk and Cambridgeshire). As the area includes the former fenlands, as well as some major rivers, the problem of ritual deposition in wet places has been one of the major issues examined.

The subject is important. Most existing textbooks and many other publications continue to regard ritual or votive offerings as an explanation for many of the finer and more exciting artefacts from these so called 'wet' locations, and use this explanation to create a religious background for the Later Bronze Age.

In the space available I will initially define what I mean by ritual. I will then examine river finds, followed by wet fen finds, and finally come to a brief conclusion.

What is ritual?

Although it is obvious that religion must have formed an active part, both in life and death, of Bronze Age society, it is the identification of formalised acts, that is ritual, that presents one of the most problematic areas. Some forms can be witnessed, most notably in burial rites. As Pader (1982, 36) said, a funeral, 'by any definition, is a ritual activity'. This must be accepted, yet in most instances, even with burials, it is the degree of ritual that is important as 'ritual and non-ritual behaviour cannot be distinguished absolutely from one another' (*ibid.*). I have taken this to be the case and my main concern has been with the more highly formalised, indisputably 'ritual' behaviours.

River finds

Of the total of over 11,000 metal artefacts recorded from northern East Anglia, only 45 or 46 (or 0.4% of the total) were found in rivers. In addition, there are a minimum of 18 objects from meres, one from a medieval turbary, six from canals and five from beaches (Table 16.1). Only one concentration of river finds occurs, from the Little Ouse. This relates closely to a terrestrial assemblage, including metalwork and occupation debris, distributed in a band along the southeastern fen edges.

It is clear that many of the 'river finds' were not Bronze Age deposits. Most were actually from dredgings or bank materials that do not always derive from the rivers alone. Indeed, the use of imported soil and clay for embanking rivers was common practice from at least the seventeenth century. Only one object is actually known to have been found in a river. The finds from turbaries and canals demonstrate that material has been redeposited relatively frequently over recent times.

A wide variety of implement types are represented amongst the river finds (Tables 16.1 and 16.2). Although there is a greater incidence of larger bronzes, for example swords and spearheads, this is to be expected in these deposits (especially as dredging was the main means of discovery, cf. Bradley 1979, 3; Ehrenberg 1980, 1–7). Of the river finds, 25/26 (54/58%) are weapons, which compares to the 27–28% from a dry land situation, 60% of beach finds, and 33% of canal finds. From this it can be seen that the percentage of 'high-status' weaponry from rivers is not particularly meaningful. Indeed the second-rate condition of some of the sword castings suggest that they were unlikely to have been prestigious. Neither are weapons particularly rare. Of the four main implement types characteristic of the Late Bronze Age in East Anglia, socketed axes

Table 16.1 *Count of metalwork from bodies of water*

CAMBRIDGESHIRE	Rivers	Meres	Turbaries	Canals	Sea
swords					
rapiers	1				
dirks/dagger	1			1	
knives	3				
spearheads	1	2		1	
palstaves/flanged axes	4	2			
socketed axes	1	4			
hammers		1			
gouges		2			
SUBTOTAL	11	11		2	

NORFOLK	Rivers	Meres	Turbaries	Canals	Sea
swords	1	2+			
rapiers	1				?1
dirks/daggers	1				
knives				?1	
spearheads	3	1			?1
flat axes				1	
palstaves	1		1	1	
'celts'		1			?1
gouge	1				
hoard	1				
SUBTOTAL	9	4+	1	?3	?3

SUFFOLK	Rivers	Meres	Turbaries	Canals	Sea
swords	5				
rapiers/dirks/daggers	7-8				
knives	½				
spearheads	3	3+			?1
ferrules	1				
flat axes					?1
palstaves	2-3				
socketed axes	3				
chisels	1				
quoit-headed pin	1				
torc				?1	
other		Yes			
SUBTOTAL	24-26	3+(+?)		?1	?2

TOTAL	44-46	18+(+?)	1	?6	?5

account for 74.7%, pegged spearheads for 14.5%, swords for 8.6% and gouges for 2.2% of the total.

Nevertheless, this martial material is frequently seen as being significant in terms of 'special deposits'. In view of this, it can be pointed out that important metalwork of other periods is also found in rivers. White (1979), for example, examined finds from the River Witham. Although the finds of Bronze Age metalwork (three swords and a dagger) and Iron Age metalwork (the Witham shield, the Tattershall Ferry carnyx, four swords with three scabbards and a dagger) are often quoted, the Saxon artefacts (the Washingborough hanging bowl, the Fiskerton triple pins, two stirrup irons, a shield boss, two axes, a spearhead and two swords) and Medieval finds (a sample of which includes six candle-

Table 16.2 *Count of metalwork from rivers*

River	Cam	Nene	Gt. Ouse	Lt. Ouse	Lark	Wissey	Waveney	Yare	Gipping	Orwell	Stour	Alde	Box	TOTAL
swords			1	3	1					1				6
rapiers/dirks/daggers	1	1		5-6	1			1	1	1				11-12
knives	2		1	0-1			1							4-5
spearheads	1			2		3						1		7
ferrules				1										1
palstaves		2	2	2		1								7
socketed axes		1		1			1				1			4
chisels/gouges				2										2
pins													1	1
putative 'hoards'						1								1
TOTAL	4	4	4	17	2	5	2	1	1	2	1	1	1	45

Table 16.3 *Comparative proportions of fen/fen-edge metal finds (excluding hoards)*

FEN/FEN-EDGE FINDS		Bladed weapons	Spearheads	Total weapons	Ornaments	Tools	TOTAL
Cambridgeshire, Norfolk and Suffolk SMR	No.	22-23	27	49-50	4	94-97	147-151
	%	15-16	18	32-34	3	62-66	100
North-west Suffolk survey	No.	24	34	58	9	171	238
	%	10	14	24	4	72	100

SUFFOLK NON-FEN FINDS		Bladed weapons	Spearheads	Total weapons	Ornaments	Tools	TOTAL
Metal-detected finds	No.	7	10	17	4	51-52	72-73
	%	10	14	23-24	6	70-72	100

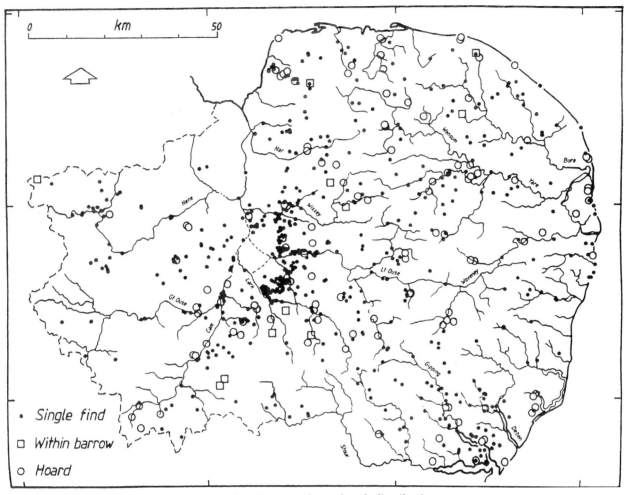

Fig. 16.1 *Rivers and metalwork distribution*

sticks, a set of chain mail, together with a spearhead and sword, a helmet, seven other swords, a knife and a dagger) are equally impressive and more numerous. Equally an examination of Saxon Christian period swords from Suffolk (when one would presume ritual was not a factor in their disposal) shows 40% occur in rivers (Pendleton 1999, 69). It has also been estimated (Ewart Oakshott, pers. comm.) that between 75% and 80% of Medieval swords from England with a known provenance come from rivers. It should be noted that none of the genuinely high-status Bronze Age material – the gold – has been found in a river.

Even if it is accepted that the East Anglian Bronze Age river finds were all originally deliberately deposited in rivers (as opposed to being redeposited in a riverine context as a result of postdepositional factors), the amount of material is so small as to be insignificant. It should also be remembered that river traffic existed in the Bronze Age. Of particular relevance is the river-related distribution of hoards in the Late Bronze Age and the possibility for conflict and/or loss in these situations. The similar distri-

bution of riverine and dry land finds in the area of the Little Ouse (Fig. 16.1) should be seen as supporting evidence for accidental, or at least secular/profane, deposition in East Anglian rivers.

Wet fen finds

In 1882, John Evans, while discussing the Wilburton hoard in Cambridgeshire, suggested that one possibility regarding the peat fen location of the objects, was 'that they may have been thrown into the water as precious offerings to the gods' (Evans 1884, 114). This theme has been periodically reiterated, especially in relation to finds of fine, complete, or so-called 'high status' material. However, it was only from the 1960s, following Coles's work on shields (Coles 1962) and Trump's limited research on rapier finds from the East Anglian fens (1968), that such claims came to gain momentum. Support was offered by new environmental studies that suggested climatic deterioration in the later prehistoric period. Burgess (1974, 195–197, 311) claimed this

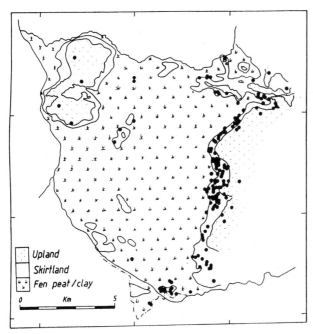

Fig. 16.2 *Wissey Embayment prehistoric 'scatters'*
(after Silvester 1991)

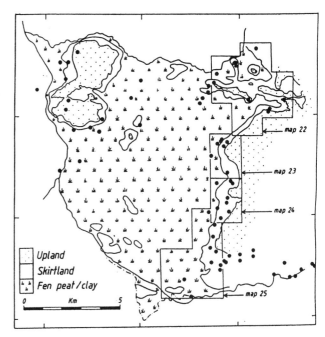

Fig. 16.3 *Wissey Embayment Bronze Age metalwork*
(Pendleton 1999)

was possibly the result of a catastrophe event leading to an Early/Middle Bronze Age hiatus and the rise of new water-based religious centres. 'Ritual deposition' had become broadly accepted as fact in the majority of publications discussing the Bronze Age during the 1970s.

Doubts soon came to be cast, for example by Rowlands (1976, 119), Pryor (1980, 490) and Chowne (1980, 300), although the general published consensus continued and continues to support ritual. Initially, I had no reason to doubt the popular belief in a change from a sun-based to a water-based religion, or an alternative view of an 'ostentatious disposal of wealth to maintain a prestige based economy' theory (as in Bradley 1984, 101–105), as acceptable explanations for the majority of the finds. However, when I began to look at the evidence more closely, a number of significant factors became apparent. With regard to the status of the objects it became clear that there was no difference between the types of finds from the fens and those from elsewhere in the region (Table 16.3). Their condition was also variable with the great majority being damaged or effectively worn-out. Regarding the contemporary value of bronzes, it also became clear that the metal, despite being imported into the region, was not particularly valuable in its own right (there are at least 11,000 bronzes known to survive in the three counties). Where associations could be shown, they consisted of waste pottery, worked flints and animal bone fragments. If the metal items were deliberate offerings, then it appears that domestic rubbish was as well.

Beside instances of stratigraphic association, the general background distribution of the metal finds was also invariably closely matched by evidence of settlement in the form of surface scatters of lithics, pottery, animal bone, quernstones etc. Although this was commonly labelled Neolithic, Early Bronze Age or Iron Age, it should be emphasised that lithics and pottery, in the vast majority of cases, are chronologically undiagnostic in northern East Anglia in later prehistory. Detailed examination shows that the precise dating of the bulk of finds to any one period is usually impossible and many of the sites are actually multi-period later prehistoric.

To demonstrate the correlation between the metalwork and this settlement debris we can use, for example, Silvester's work (1991) and Healy's work (1996) on the Wissey Embayment, Norfolk (Figs 16.2 and 16.3). From this it can be seen that the distribution of the majority of metal artefacts corresponds closely to the areas defined as scatters. Beside these scatters there is a more widespread background of material, worked flint in particular, only a haphazardly gathered sample of which was collected and analysed. An examination of the metalwork findspots that appeared to be in the fen peat deposits (as mapped by Silvester) also revealed, in the majority of cases, either lithic material or evidence of pre-peat subsoil deposits in the ploughsoil. Particularly significant was the distribution of 'pot-boiler' sites, often mapped as occurring some way into the peat (Silvester 1991, fig. 49). These must have been constructed on dry land, and in the same way as the metalwork, are misrepresented by the

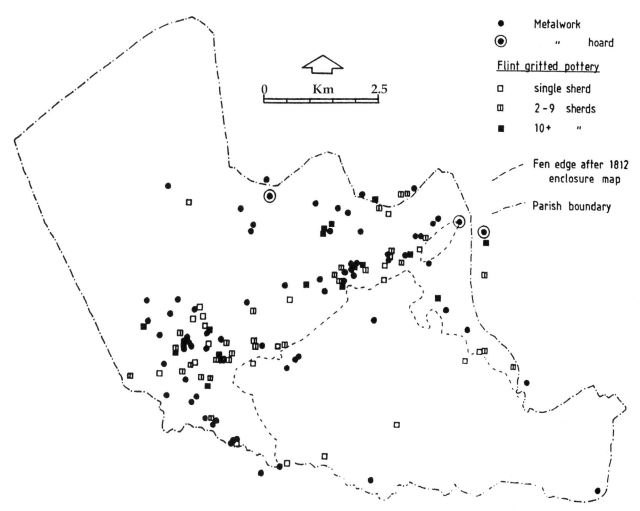

Fig. 16.4 *Flint-gritted pottery and Bronze Age metalwork in Mildenhall Parish, Suffolk (fenland to the northwest)*

generalised mapping so often employed. At a more detailed scale, the distribution of one of the non-metal artefact types common to Later Bronze Age assemblages in the region, namely 'flint-gritted' pottery, was compared to that of the metalwork in Mildenhall parish, Suffolk (Fig. 16.4). The visible correlation is again notable. Only one significant group of metal finds (one small hoard and four single objects) occurs that is not close to finds of pottery. These artefacts are from the north-central area of the parish in an area that had not been field-walked.

Finally, it was obvious from the historical and more recent accounts of the discovery of the objects that the overwhelming majority of the material, including the metalwork, came from below, not within the peat deposits. As most of the peat has now wasted away, we are mainly dependent on these earlier accounts. The details offered usually make it plain that the finds relate to the subsoils underlying the later wet deposits. A typical example was the shield from Sutton St Michael, Norfolk, said

to have been found 'under seven feet of peat lying on and partly covered by white sand' (Norfolk Sites and Monuments Record, number 8318). In 1923 Fox, discussing the archaeology of the Cambridge region, wrote that 'in Burwell Fen the stone (and bronze) implements are found lying on the clay below the peat, and it is on record that finds in other fens have been similarly situated' (Fox 1923, 7). For some reason, the significance of this seems to have been overlooked in recent years.

There are occasional accounts that sound more convincing as 'wet' finds, for instance finds made peat digging. However, even these are usually cases of redeposition. Management of the fenland landscape by an array of major and minor drainage works, most of the latter of which are invisible on the present land surface, has resulted in a substantial proportion of the subsoils being relocated, even if at only a localised scale. In addition to this, the fields have also been subjected to extensive 'claying' operations in the early/mid nineteenth century. Similarly, coprolite extraction, mainly in the late

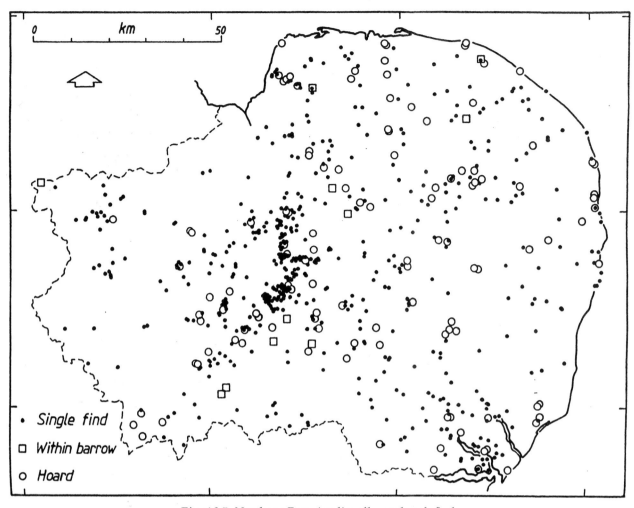

Fig. 16.5 Northern East Anglia: all metalwork finds

nineteenth century, also overturned vast areas of the Cambridgeshire fens (in a 30 year period nearly one-and-a-half million tons of phosphate was extracted from the coprolites: Grove 1976).

That some finds actually derive from the peat is not in doubt, for example the rapier from near Chatteris recorded by Evans (1881, 250) as being 'found at the bottom of an old canoe, between the peat and clay'. Similarly the palstave from Wood Walton, Cambridgeshire, was found, according to a 1952 account, 'stuck in a bog oak tree . . . subsequently covered by peat' (Garrood 1952). Nevertheless, of the 278 stray finds and 23 hoards listed (in 1987) from the fen zone, only a handful look reasonably convincing as cases of artefacts deriving from a Bronze Age wet deposit, and these are usually associated with cause-ways, skeletal remains or peat covered boats or trees. Apart from the skeletal associations being seen as possible 'grave' goods, none of the finds need suggest ritual deposition.

A number of more general factors also require consideration. The frequency and likely contempor-

ary low value of the metalwork has already been mentioned. It can also be seen that the distribution of metal artefacts (Fig. 16.5) is no longer restricted to the fenland area (where layers of peat protected the material evidence from up to 2000 years of arable agriculture). Metal detecting in particular is now demonstrating a widespread distribution of metal-work (Fig. 16.6) on all soil types. The fen-edge area is still of great importance in that the evidence survival there is far more complete than can be expected over the majority of the landscape. Indeed, it is this evidence, in the form of the settlement debris associated (even if only loosely) with the Bronze Age metalwork, that is crucial in our inter-pretation. We can therefore make a strong case for profane deposits (of rubbish?) rather than anything more complex.

Conclusions

The conclusions, resulting from detailed research,

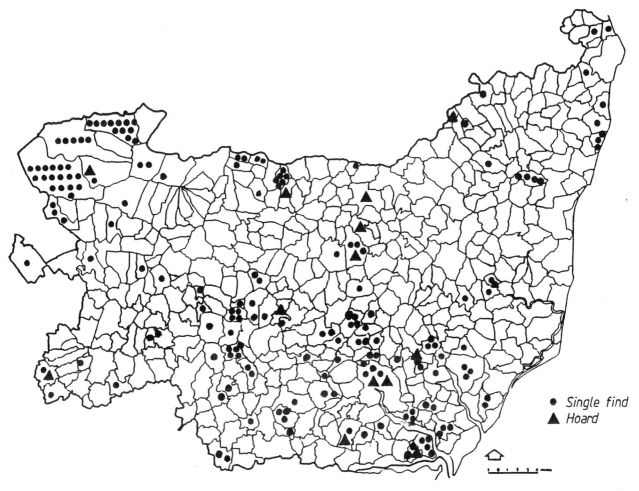

Fig. 16.6 *Bronze Age metalwork recovered from Suffolk parishes by metal detector*

are clear. There is no evidence to support ritual deposition of metalwork in northern East Anglia during the Later Bronze Age. Although I have not undertaken the necessary work for other areas, I would tentatively suggest that the same is likely to be the case in the rest of Britain. This work demands a more reasoned understanding of the period and I propose that we now revise any assertions of a heavily ritualised Bronze Age society.

References

Bradley, R. 1979. Interpretation of Later Bronze Age metalwork from British Rivers. *Journal of Nautical Archaeology* 8, 3–6.

Bradley, R. 1984. *The Social Foundations of Prehistoric Britain.* London: Longman.

Burgess, C. B. 1974. The Bronze Age. In Renfrew, C. (ed.) *British Prehistory: a New Outline,*165–232, 291–329. London: Duckworth.

Chowne, P. 1980. Bronze Age settlement in South Lincolnshire. In Barrett, J. and Bradley, R. (eds) *Settlement and Society in the British Later Bronze Age,* 295–305. Oxford: British Archaeological Reports, British Series 83.

Coles, J. M. 1962. European Bronze Age shields. *Proceedings of the Prehistoric Society* 28, 156–190.

Ehrenberg, M. R. 1980. The occurrence of Bronze Age metalwork in the Thames: an investigation. *Transactions of the London and Middlesex Archaeological Society* 31, 1–15.

Evans, J. 1881. *The Ancient Bronze Implements, Weapons and Ornaments of Great Britain and Ireland.* London: Longmans, Green and Co.

Evans, J. 1884. On a hoard of bronze objects found near Wilburton Fen near Ely. *Archaeologia* 48, 106–114.

Fox, C. 1923. *The Archaeology of the Cambridge Region.* Cambridge: Cambridge University Press.

Garrood, J. R. 1952. A palstave in 'Bog Oak' at Wood Walton. *Transactions of the Cambridgeshire and Huntingdonshire Archaeological Society* 7, 82.

Grove, R. 1976. *The Cambridgeshire Coprolite Mining Rush.* Cambridge: Oleander Press.

Healy, F. 1996. *The Fenland Project, Number 11, the Wissey Embayment: Evidence for Pre-Iron Age Occupation.* Chelmsford: East Anglian Archaeology Monograph 78.

Pader, E. J. 1982. *Symbolism, Social Relations and the*

Interpretation of Mortuary Remains. Oxford: British Archaeological Reports, International Series 130.

Pendleton, C. F. 1999. *Bronze Age Metalwork in Northern East Anglia: a Study of its Distribution and Interpretation*. Oxford: British Archaeological Reports, British Series 279.

Pryor, F. 1980. Will it all come out in the wash? Reflections at the end of eight years' digging. In Barrett, J. and Bradley, R. (eds) *Settlement and Society in the British Later Bronze Age*, 483–499. Oxford: British Archaeological Reports, British Series 83.

Rowlands, M. J. 1976. *The Production and Distribution of Metalwork in the Middle Bronze Age in Southern Britain*. Oxford: British Archaeological Reports, British Series 31.

Silvester, R. J. 1991. *Fenland Project 4: the Wissey Embayment and the Fen Causeway, Norfolk*. Chelmsford: East Anglian Archaeology Monograph 52.

Trump, B. A. V. 1968. Fenland Rapiers. In Coles, J. M. and Simpson, D. D. A. (eds) *Studies in Ancient Europe*, 213–251. Leicester: Leicester University Press.

White, A. 1979. Antiquities from the River Witham (parts 1, 2 and 3). In *Lincolnshire Museums Information Sheets*, 12–14. Lincoln: Lincolnshire County Council.

17   Mining and prospection for metals in Early Bronze Age Britain – making claims within the archaeological landscape

Simon Timberlake

Introduction

Investigations into flint mining and stone axe quarry sites prior to 1985 helped revolutionise perceptions of contemporary technology, trade and to some extent social organisation within the British Neolithic. Similarly, the discovery since 1986 of some of the earliest metal mines within these islands seems likely to make as important a contribution, perhaps even to provide a completely new direction for contemporary Bronze Age studies. Time will tell, but the quest to locate the sources of Bronze Age copper and the origins of metal production in this country is a subject already experiencing something of a renaissance (Budd *et al.* 1992; Budd 1993; Craddock 1995; Ixer and Budd 1998; Rohl and Needham 1998; Northover 1999).

Nevertheless, one is left with the distinct feeling of a conceptual gulf separating the positions of the field investigators/interpreters of the archaeological landscape and the archaeological scientists. Few outside the world of archaeo-metallurgy have entered the debate and examined the implications of all this data, most of which concerns the distribution and very nature of the mining sites themselves. Such sites are, after all, the *only* definitive evidence we have for the exploitation of any indigenous metal ore during this period. Much therefore has been left undiscussed, academic argument by and large centring on long-held ideas of technological process, metal composition and typology, and assumptions about source – all useful perhaps, but at the same time a quite mechanistic approach that has left little room for any speculation on the social context of prospection and mining. In contrast, Neolithic flint mining and stone axe quarrying has been much better studied with respect to both its place and space within the contemporary landscape (Cummins 1980; Bradley 1984; Healy 1984).

The field, excavation, and dating evidence

The basis for this timely reassessment has been the excavation of some ten Early Bronze Age mines or prospection trials within England and Wales, plus the probable identification of some 10–15 others based on field or documentary evidence for the distribution (Fig. 17.1a and b) of stone mining tools (O'Brien 1996; Timberlake 1998). Typically such tools were waterworn cobble stones that were carefully selected and brought to the sites (sometimes from some distance away) and then used, often without any prior modification, as hand-held or hafted implements for the purposes of rock breakage or ore crushing. The dating and functional evidence for the use of these tools is discussed comprehensively by Gale (1995) and Craddock and Craddock (1996).

The identification and dating of these mines has resulted from the joint collaboration of mining historians, cavers, archaeologists and geologists (for example the Early Mines Research Group (Timberlake 1994a; Craddock and Craddock 1997) plus others (Dutton and Fasham 1994; Lewis 1994)), the results of which have challenged many previously held assumptions concerning both the richness and accessibility of surface deposits, the survival of this evidence in the face of modern mining activity, plus the more traditionally held view of some archaeologists (Coghlan and Case 1957) that Irish or continental sources of copper were preferentially used during the British Bronze Age .

Although evidence for Bronze Age copper mining in southwest Ireland is considerable and well researched, only three sites, Mount Gabriel (Jackson 1968; O'Brien 1987; 1994), Canshanavoe (O'Brien 1996) and Ross Island (O'Brien 1995) have been excavated and dated, even though another eight or nine 'primitive' mines have been identified, pre-

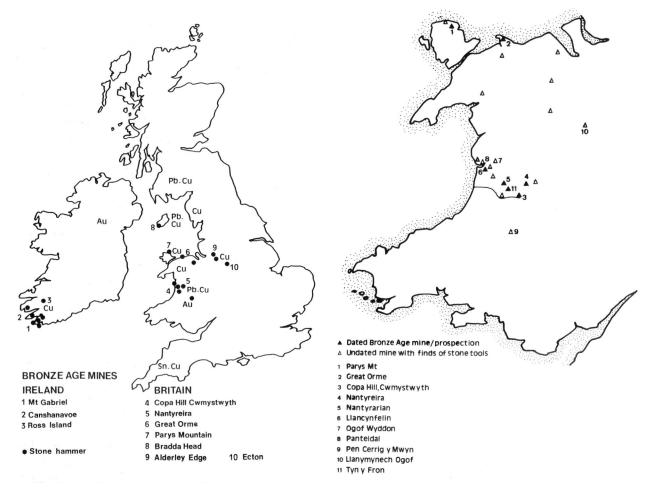

Fig. 17.1a *Stone hammers and Bronze Age copper mines within the British Isles*

Fig. 17.1b *Early Bronze Age mines and stone tools in Wales*

dominantly of the 'Mount Gabriel' type. The latter type of working exploited thin discontinuous beds of low grade ore (now mostly oxidised to malachite) within the Old Red Sandstone, usually as small mines or prospections worked by short fire-set drifts. At Mount Gabriel these workings have been dated to the latter part of the Early Bronze Age (c. 1800–1500 BC), roughly contemporary with the working of the mines on the British mainland. In marked contrast to this, the Ross Island mine located on the shores of Lough Killarney was already at work during the latter half of the third millennium BC. Associated with this earliest phase of mining (2400–2000 BC) was a Beaker work camp in which was found evidence for simple hut habitations (post hole groupings) with pottery scatters, layers of crushed mineral, and pits which had clearly been used for ore concentration as well as some form of roasting or smelting. Exploitation here of a rich, shallow deposit of chalcopyrite and arsenical copper (tennantite) seems to be the most likely explanation for the source of the earliest Irish metal type 'A' (Northover 1999).

The distribution of British mines, only two of which lie in England (Alderley Edge and Ecton in north Staffordshire), is heavily biased by the number of sites in mid-Wales, the majority of these being small trials or prospections carried out upon surface exposures of lead/zinc/copper sulphide veins. However, the two largest Bronze Age mines (Parys Mountain and the Great Orme) are both located on the north Wales coastline, and are almost exclusively associated with copper mineralisation. Yet it is only upon the Great Orme, where sufficient ore and good drainage allowed exploitation to continue to a depth of over 30m below ground (Lewis 1990), that we find some evidence for post-1500 BC mining (in fact this extended well into the Late Bronze Age/Iron Age: Lewis 1994; 1996). However, this is rather unusual. There are now more than sixty radiocarbon dates available from early mine excavations within Britain and Ireland (including from bone, antler, and wooden artefacts), the great majority of which confirm that the main period of mining and prospection activity during the Bronze Age was confined to a 300 year period between 1900 and 1600 BC.

Locations of prehistoric mines and the problem of the missing evidence

It is an interesting exercise to compare the distribution pattern for known or suspected Bronze Age mines in Britain with the main areas of copper mineralisation and for mining during the historic period. There is correspondence in many areas (one might expect the Bronze Age prospectors to be attracted to the richest near-surface deposits in preference to the others), but equally there are important omissions.

It is perhaps no surprise therefore that there is evidence for early exploitation on Parys Mountain within northeast Anglesey, one of the largest base metal deposits in Britain and an operation that nearly put all the mines in Cornwall out of business at one point during the eighteenth century. Similarly, the mines on the Great Orme's Head, Llandudno, were important during the nineteenth century, while both Alderley Edge and Ecton mines were among the biggest producers in central England. Even Bradda Head, a site on the southern coast of the Isle of Man where stone hammers have been found in mixed spoil and scree associated with the outcrop of a copper vein in the cliffs, was an important nineteenth century mine (Pickin and Worthington 1989).

Yet there are other areas of significant copper mineralisation where any such links with 'primitive' (probably prehistoric) mining appear quite tenuous. In historical times copper has been mined in southwest Scotland, northwest Yorkshire (Askrigg area), parts of northeast Wales and Shropshire, on the Welsh Borders and in Somerset (Quantocks and Exmoor), yet in none of these areas is there much suggestion of pre-Medieval activity. More importantly, in Cumbria, particularly around Coniston where copper has been mined from the sixteenth century onwards (and where stone for axe making was quarried nearby during the Neolithic), we have as yet been unable to forge any secure link between stray finds of hammer stones and Bronze Age mining. The situation is frustratingly similar in central and southern Snowdonia, historically one of the main areas of Welsh copper production.

Perhaps the greatest enigma of all is the almost complete lack of residual evidence for prehistoric copper mining from southwest England, in particular within those areas traditionally richest in copper and tin production, west Devon and Cornwall. These areas are thought to include some of the best preserved and perhaps some of the most intensively occupied and exploited Bronze Age landscapes in Britain.

Thus we have a distinct dichotomy existing between areas such as mid-Wales, a region that returned only 7000 tons of recorded copper concentrates throughout the whole of the nineteenth-early twentieth centuries, and Cornwall, a county that has produced many millions of tons of copper ores during historic times – yet that has provided us with barely any evidence for early mining and prospection. Such a situation is not easy to explain.

Nevertheless, it is worth reflecting for a minute or two on several possible scenarios. It would be wrong to consider purely economic criteria here, or even to assume that the positive or negative evidence as it appears now is accurately reflecting what went on in the past. Could it be that insufficient attention has been paid to the search for the evidence of stone implements at mining sites? Seven or eight years ago one might have argued this with more justification, but since then considerable attention has been paid to this anomaly (Sharpe 1997), and still no link has been made between any stray finds of hammer stones and Cornish copper mines. Topography has undoubtedly helped to preserve the remains of early mining on hilltops in areas such as mid-Wales, and it could be argued that the much more intensive mining activity which has since taken place within the flatter landscape of Cornwall has removed, either through burial or else as a result of reworking, a much larger proportion of the earliest evidence. That may be so, but such evidence was never eradicated in other areas of Britain where mining disturbance has been equally intense (e.g. Parys Mountain, Alderley Edge and Great Orme). At almost all of the latter sites some traces of this early activity still remains visible at the surface. However, this may not be the case where such sites of early extraction have since been completely buried or else removed by coastal erosion.

The degree of exposure of mineral veins within cliff outcrops around the Cornish coastline is considerable, and it is no secret that many of the earlier post-Medieval workings were worked inland from cliff exposures along openworks referred to locally as 'gunnisses' (such as we find near Wheal Coates, St. Agnes). Over a period of 3500 years it is perfectly possible that some of the earliest sites of sea-level working could have been removed by erosion, in which case their stone hammers would have been recycled and probably now lie unrecognisably amongst other beach cobbles (Timberlake 1992a). However, such scenarios do not explain the total absence of evidence relating to early mining. Nevertheless, it may still be easier to comprehend the loss of context where this relates to prehistoric tin working.

Penhallurick (1986) documents in exhaustive detail the discovery of prehistoric artefacts, human remains, and tools such as wooden shovels, antler picks, and stone implements (some of which may have been used during Earlier Bronze Age alluvial tin extraction) found amongst seventeenth-nineteenth century tin workings in the Carnon Valley and elsewhere. However, the survival of eluvial or alluvial copper ore in this environment is much rarer; indeed there is no record at all of this having been found or extracted from the valley tin gravels. Thus the only realistic scenario which remains for winning copper ore without the use of stone tools is in the collection of loose samples of rich oxidised minerals from gossan exposures. The alternative would be the use of *metal mining tools*. However, there seems to be no conceivable reason why tools made of copper or bronze (a prestige material but at the same time one relatively ineffectual against hard rocks) should have been used here and nowhere else. Indeed, evidence for the use of *stone mining tools* during the cultural and technological Early Bronze Age is overwhelming from across both the Old and New Worlds (Craddock 1995).

It would appear therefore that such technological or utilitarian explanations are insufficient in themselves to explain this apparent anomaly. Perhaps there were geo-political, cultural or other influences (belief systems) at play? Indeed, the importance of particular associations of paired metals as a resource within geographically separated areas could be seen as part of the reasoning behind this. For example, there is an association between copper and lead in mid-Wales, while in Cornwall, tin and gold (Penhallurick 1986) may have been the main metals of interest. In this latter location the two occur together within the alluvial gravels.

Perhaps it was *because* both tin and copper were equally valuable and essential resources for bronze that they were never worked together. Territorial control, agreements, trade considerations, perhaps even ritual, may have overridden purely practical factors of distribution. Some sort of protectionism or restriction of resources (particularly as it effects tin, a metal with an altogether more limited distribution in the Old World) may have been operating in the southwest.

As regards copper, it would appear that a much greater effort was paid to the finding of this metal in those areas where it was present in smaller quantities. Perhaps it was important for different tribal groups to locate their own supplies? Cornish copper, for one reason or another, may never have been readily available. Recent lead isotope data (Rohl and Needham 1998), although a little ambiguous, appears to support this idea. This concept of restriction and a different focus for land use in Cornwall was discussed by Herring (1997). The southwest was agriculturally rich, and thus cultivation rather than metals may have been the prime source of wealth and interest to its inhabitants. Although the demand for metal extraction most probably was there, all available human resources may well have been directed towards the extraction of tin and gold, the job of searching for copper being left to the pastoralist prospectors living in the uplands of England and Wales.

Looking for minerals in the prehistoric landscape – the identification of 'prospection areas' within mid-Wales

Within the distribution of Bronze Age mining sites scattered around the hinterland of Plynlimon (Fig. 17.2) can be seen the elements of a pattern that might provide us with some clue as to the methods and techniques of prehistoric prospection. Although most of these sites appear to be associated with small-scale copper mineralisation, it could equally be argued that an early interest in the lead and silver content of the veins may also have dictated the choice of locations (Bick 1999). However, geological controls and mineralogical factors aside, there may be other reasons why some deposits were discovered and worked yet others were not. Indeed, there are a number of richer and equally accessible copper veins (e.g. Pensarn, Esgair Hir, Dylife, Gwestyn and Geufron) that were apparently ignored.

It seems possible now to identify at least five distinct *prospection areas* within the mining region, evidence that would seem to favour the idea of a concerted approach to prospection during the Bronze Age, rather than this being a purely opportunistic response to chance discovery.

Concerted prospection activity

The most easterly identified prospection area lies immediately to the east of Plynlimon and includes, within a 3–4km radius, the mines of Nantyreira (Timberlake 1988) and Nantyrickets, both of which are located on the uppermost reaches of the River Severn and associated with riverbed exposures of mineral vein. Southwest of Plynlimon, within the watershed of the Ystwyth River, lie Grogwynion and Copa Hill (Timberlake 1990a; Timberlake and Mighall 1992). These latter mines are both to be found high on the northern slopes of the valley. To the north of here another group of mines, Tyn y fron (Timberlake 1996b), Nantyrarian (Timberlake 1992b; 1995b), and Twll-y-mwyn, associated with the Rheidol, Melindwr and Erfin valleys respectively, are all to be found within a 8–10km radius of each other. On the southern side of the Dovey Estuary, located on the edge of the upland/lowland margin encircling Borth Bog, appears a tight cluster of sites that includes the mines of Erglodd and Llancynfelin (Timberlake 1992b; 1995b). Facing these, on the opposite bank of the Dovey are a further two probable sites, Panteidal and Balkan Hill, Aberdovey

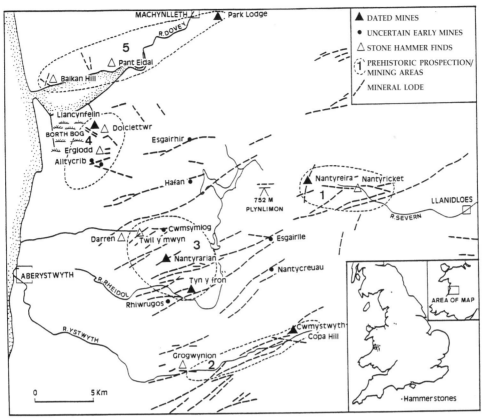

Fig. 17.2 Mineral veins and prospection areas in mid-Wales

(Pickin 1990), while out on a limb, but within the same valley some 2km to the east of Machynlleth, lies the small mine of Ogof Wyddon or Park Lodge (Timberlake and Mason 1997).

Locally, nucleation or radiation of prospection and exploitation sites might have occurred as mineral veins were located, then followed along outcropping faults. Some of these can be traced for several kilometres across country. An example may be seen at Llancynfelin, where the Bronze Age prospectors sampled the same vein at three different locations from the shoreline to the top of the former 'island', a peninsula now surrounded by reclaimed wetland (Timberlake 1992b). Still other factors may dictate the course and success of prospection. Although many of the east-west valley routes into the interior would still have been heavily forested at this time, some of these could have provided a useful means of access for prospectors. Observation and sampling of the river beds would reveal the presence and composition of any mineral veins, just as vein-rock cobbles (or 'shoad ore') washed down from tributary streams might suggest the locations of outcrops high on the valley sides. Powerful upstanding quartz veins, such as the type that typically carry mineral in the area, are at their most obvious when viewed from the valley floor, just as are the outcrops of the distinctly rusty-coloured ankerite (iron carbonate) lodes, so often a sure indi-

cator of the presence of copper (chalcopyrite) ore within mid-Wales (Bick 1991). Infertility and pollution in soils, as indicated by yellowing grass and natural tree clearings well might accompany the mineralisation, whilst spring lines at lode outcrops can sometimes provide indications of the metals present, usually in the form of the precipitates of malachite (green), lead oxide minerals (red and white), hydrozincite (white), manganese (black), and iron ochre (red-brown) – staining which in some circumstances could have been visible from more than a kilometre distance. It seems likely that such highly visual criteria would have provided the essential pointers leading to the discovery of these primitive mines, just as the grouping of sites at certain valley and side tributary locations suggests the existence of both access routes and focal points for prospection (Fig. 17.3).

In addition there is an important link to be made with the coast. The outlook of what must be the largest grouping(s) of sites is to the west over the Dovey Estuary – a probable access route for river traffic as well as coast-hopping seafaring boats, and once perhaps the route to north Wales and Ireland, a theory implied in earlier ideas of Beaker period trade (Childe 1930; Varley 1964) and also alluded to (perhaps rather comically) within Yalden's poem about ancient British miners (Williams 1866). Much less speculative is the evidence for the use of beach

Fig. 17.3 A view of Copa Hill from the floor of the Ystwyth Valley. The early opencast (A) on the brow of the hill appears much as it might have done 3500 years ago. At this point, the outcropping ankerite-quartz vein of the Comet Lode (C.L.) would have been highly visible to early prospectors

pebbles as hammer stones. In the case of Copa Hill (Cwmystwyth), many hundreds of these cobbles were brought some 25km to the site, most probably collected from the storm beaches located to the south of Aberystwyth (Timberlake 1990b), a factor which supports the idea of seasonal working by people who lived for at least part of the year on the coast.

Up till now it has not been possible to distinguish any meaningful differences or trends between radiocarbon dates obtained from the various mid-Wales mines. Such differences might suggest discreet phases of prospection or else confirm the idea of contemporary exploitation of mines within individual prospection areas. However, considerably more research, fieldwork and refinement of the dating evidence is first needed before any sort of meaningful pattern can be suggested.

Opportunistic mining and prospection – a cause and effect of other activities

Whether or not discoveries of ore were made through concerted searches or else purely by chance, the process of prospection may well have been a subsidiary activity of transhumance agriculture, and may thus have been linked with the role of pastoralists in the uplands. Yet if this model of Bronze Age metal discovery and production is to be seriously considered, then it bears little resemblance to the

more organised approach to mining and prospection typical of the early historic period in Europe. By this time, all such activities were considered a craft, with the individuals carrying it out afforded special privileges and, to some extent, separated from the rest of society (Agricola 1556; Davies 1935). Perhaps a closer parallel might be drawn between our prehistoric miners and subsistence pastoralists, tribal societies or caste groups, some of whom even today carry out prospection and small-scale opportunistic mining in parts of Africa, South America, and the Indian subcontinent (Craddock, P. T. pers. comm.). Furthermore, it is still commonplace for mountain shepherds, hunters and guides (certainly within the Himalayan zone) to regularly prospect and sometimes even mine veins for mineral specimens to sell. Such work is always independently initiated, locally organised, relatively unskilled, and invariably of low status.

Some useful comparisons could be made with Shennan's (1999) study of the social organisation and production of an Early Bronze Age mining camp and community at Klinglberg in the Mitterberg region of the Austrian Tyrol. However, in mid-Wales no such associated mining camps have been located and the organisational basis for any of this work is quite unknown. More importantly, the primitive nature of these mid-Wales workings, with little evidence for work areas outside of the mines themselves, suggests seasonal or occasional working, most likely by pastoralist miner/prospectors. This is an altogether less sophisticated model than that which has been proposed for the Mitterberg, yet we should also acknowledge the considerably lower level of production involved, perhaps carried out over a longer period, and possibly without the demands from any particular metal producing centre. Copper mining may have been carried out by these subsistence pastoralists purely as a means to enter the exchange economy, and thus prepared copper ore rather than smelted metal may have been the means for exchange with metal artefacts or prestige goods. In this respect, the work view and outlook of these upland miners may have differed considerably from that held by miners on the Great Orme, where mining may have been their main, but not necessarily their sole occupation.

By the end of the Early Bronze Age and beginning of the Middle Bronze Age many parts of the uplands above 350–400m OD in the Plynlimon area had been cleared or thinned, most probably as a result of transhumance agricultural activity (Moore 1968). This is suggested both by the siting of cairn cemeteries within the upland landscape and the interpretation of pollen evidence from both upland and lowland sites (Casseldine 1990). Such clearance and renewed clearances associated with the initial stages of pioneer transhumance would indirectly have provided those engaged in such work with the clearest observation and familiarity with landscape, rock outcrops and mineral occurrences. Overall rock exposure would have increased following burning, while the felling and uprooting of trees may also have resulted in additional run-off and rapid erosion of slopes, leading to still further exposure of bed rock. Such losses of tree cover and topsoil invariably opened up possibilities for prospection and the chance discovery of ore bodies.

Could we thus relate the conjectured period of maximum prospection activity in the uplands (estimated at between 1800–1700 BC) with a phase of elevated erosion and thus increased alluviation in the valley bottoms? Pollen and charcoal sequences in such sediments might help, and this data may be linked to charcoal (burning) horizons and pollen declines recorded within upland peat mires (Timberlake and Mighall 1992). Widespread tree clearance would also have provided a ready source of fuel for fire-setting, a situation which would have encouraged active prospection. In area such as mid-Wales, with more than a thousand known mineral veins, these prospection sites may once have been much commoner than present evidence suggests. Many of these may simply have been eroded away or become buried beneath rock tallus or peat. A lot more research is needed here, and comparisons

should also be sought within the Alpine and other Central European mining areas.

Mines and monuments in the Bronze Age landscape

It has long been recognised that geological controls are paramount in determining the location of mines, yet it may also be possible to detect some relationship between place in the landscape and the position or alignment of prehistoric trackways, boundaries, burial sites, standing stones, burnt mounds or other contemporary monuments. From first appearances, a desk-top/field-based study of the Plynlimon area did not reveal any sort of patterns, although there is a real problem here of establishing contemporaneity between monuments, many of which have neither been excavated nor dated.

The detection of trackways or approximate routes through the Cambrian Mountains was considered to be a good starting point. The course of some may have been influenced by pre-existing mine(s), while the discovery of new mines may have been hastened by their proximity to already established lines of communication. The original sampling routes of prospectors may once have been the floors of east-west valleys, but it is much more likely that a combination of valley, valley-head and ridge paths would have provided the quicker access into, as well as across the mountain divide, facilitating a general route from east to west. What may once have been markers for such a route (or perhaps even a boundary line between two designated areas) can still be followed from the coast up onto the Plynlimon plateau, an area of burial and possibly also of ritual importance during this period. The course of this 'route' is indicated by a loose alignment of several groups of standing stones that may be followed along the southern ridge of the Silo valley from west of Penrhyncoch to Disgwylfa, then northwards around the lower slopes of Plynlimon (Fig. 17.4). As well as its association with other probable Bronze Age monuments (cairns and tumuli), the line passes close to the large putative Early Bronze Age mine of Twll y mwyn and Darren, while a possible continuation of this route east of Plynlimon may well follow a descent from the plateau along the upper reaches of the River Severn past the mines of Nantyreira and Nantyrickets (Timberlake 1994a).

Burnt stone mounds appear to be common, yet are little studied within this area. According to conventional explanations most may be cooking mounds, but it is also interesting to speculate on other possible uses for these sites. Suggestions have been made of primary metal production or working uses for some (Lynch 1991; Timberlake 1994a), but none of these claims has yet been verified. Better researched local

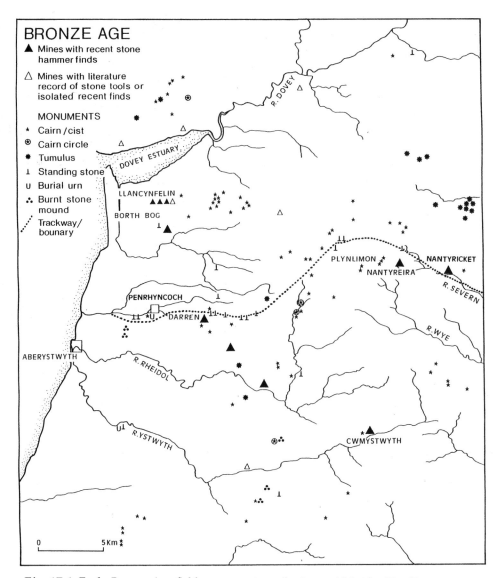

Fig. 17.4 *Early Bronze Age field monuments and mines within the Plynlimon area*

examples such as that of Troedrhiwgwinau (Caseldine and Murphy 1989) are contemporary with the mining period, yet are located on the coastal strip and appear quite unrelated to the distribution of mining sites. Although smelting seems an unlikely explanation, the true function of the latter sites remains as enigmatic as ever.

The amount of de-afforestation taking place post-2000 BC (Casseldine 1990) suggests the increased agricultural exploitation of the local landscape and the movement of new peoples into the area. Mining activity often appears to have been carried out on the very margins of the highest land at or below 400m OD, a wide marginal zone located between the ritual landscape dominated by the burial cairns of the Plynlimon plateau and the afforested or else cultivated and agriculturally rich valley bottoms and coastal lowlands.

The technology, ores and productivity of upland mines

Excavations for the purposes of dating have now been carried out at six of these primitive mines, but a comprehensive study has been undertaken of only one site, the Comet Lode opencast on Copa Hill, Cwmystwyth (Fig. 17.3), the subject of a ten-year programme of investigation, a report on which is currently in preparation.

It seems likely that Copa Hill was among the largest of the mid-Wales mines. On current dating evidence this appears to have been at work sometime between 2000 and 1600 BC or thereabouts, during which time some 5000 metric tonnes of rock were removed and deposited on the slope alongside, and for some 100m downhill of the base of this trench working (Timberlake 1990b). Above, the main chalcopyrite and galena vein has been followed into the hillside, leaving a cutting some 50m long by 15m wide (at the top) and in places 10–15m deep. The richest ore appears to have been won at the bunching or intersections of this vein with several smaller lead veins, some of which also appear to have been followed, and the lead extracted alongside the copper, leaving pillars of rock in between (much of this lead ore was apparently left in the mine). Over the thousands of years following its prehistoric abandonment, the interior landscape of the opencast has become gradually submerged beneath slumped-in spoil, silt and peat.

As mining continued after 1900 BC, the open-works got deeper and flooding became a problem (possibly within the first 100 years of working). As a result of this we find evidence for the use of some rather innovative solutions in tackling this problem – perhaps involving som of the earliest examples of mine drainage equipment known (Timberlake 1994). A channel or entrance was first cut to a depth of about 2m into the side of the working, excavation opened up lengthways along the direction of cleavage of the slate in order to ease the extraction of the rock with basic tools such as antler picks and stone hammers. Although this may have been cut to de-water the part-flooded mine, the trench probably also served as an additional working area. Several split and hollowed-out lengths of log (mostly alder) were subsequently laid end to end (6–7m) along the floor of this cutting, supported on branches and sloping slightly towards a point of exit onto the slope below. It appears that one of these front section(s) may have been cantilevered across part of the openwork to a fault in the side wall, in order to tap a source of seasonal or permanent water that had been leaking into the working. The longest section of this system of launders or guttering was found perfectly preserved and lying *in situ* when the mine was excavated (Fig. 17.5), the waterlogged deposits of mine sediment immediately beneath this containing masses of discarded debris such as broken antler picks and hammers, bits of withy (hazel) basketry, rope, handles for hammer stones, fragments of worked wooden stemples and the remains of brush-wood brought up to the site for use in the mine (Timberlake 1995a; 1996a). This fortuitous survival of organic debris has provided us with some of the best evidence of daily life and technology at work in a primitive mine – evidence which has yet to be interpreted fully.

Fire-setting of the quartz stringers and hardened wall-rocks surrounding the mineral vein appears to have been the main method of excavation, access into the individual trenches being by means of rock-cut steps and wooden stemples. From the sump of these interconnected workings, water may have been baled out using skin bags pulled up on rope and beam

Fig. 17.5 *An excavated wooden launder lying* in situ *within the entrance cutting to the Bronze Age mine on Copa Hill. In the foreground is one of the large Cu/Pb veins removed in prehistory. Indicated (Pb) is the course of one of the smaller lead (galena) veinlet(s) sampled by the earliest miners*

pulleys. This technology may also have been used for the removal of rock and ore. It would appear that much of this was removed in baskets, in all probability carried out on the miner's backs. The ore appears to have been crushed on hammerstone anvils, most of this work taking place on the surface of the tips, but also perhaps within the entrance cutting, where copper and/or lead ores may have been washed and separated within the wooden sluice, or possibly even within the hollows of the rock floor.

Although actual prospection activity may have been a single sex activity, I am inclined to believe that the seasonal or even an occasional work pattern of small scale mining may have involved both communal or family groups (an analysis of the archaeology of Copa Hill is beginning to suggest that there were also considerable periods of inactivity on-site). Recent experimental work has shown that hammerstone haftings require regular repair and renewal whilst in use (Craddock 1990), implying that children and women may well have been involved in this and other activities. Furthermore, the discovery of a few small and apparently unusable pebbles brought up to site (alongside the much larger beach cobbles) seems to indicate the presence of children, thus notionally supporting the idea of communal mining and mixed sex/age groups. A rather similar model has been suggested for underground mining on the Great Orme (Lewis 1994).

The nature and whereabouts of the smelting operations associated with these mines provides us with another enigma. Exhaustive searches looking for the evidence of this (Timberlake 1991) suggests that it is not to be found within the vicinity of the mines. The chance discovery of an Early Bronze Age smelting hearth at Pen Trwyn on the Great Orme (Chapman 1997; Gwynedd Archaeological Trust 1999) represents something of an exception, but even here the site lies more than 1.5km from the centre of mining within the Pyllau Valley. The use of an essentially non-slagging, poorly reducing smelting process (Craddock 1994; 1995), and the construction of simple bowl furnaces which leave little or no trace of themselves within the archaeological record (Timberlake 1994b), have been suggested as reasons why no evidence of smelting has yet been found. That aside, mining on Copa Hill may only ever have produced one small bag or basket of hand-selected/cobbed mineral per day, an amount that could easily have been carried down the hill on someone's back each evening to a settlement site, presumably one located in the valley bottom within a kilometre or two of the mine. A rather similar model of spatial separation between mines and settlements is suggested by the evidence from Klinglberg and the Mitterberg in the Austrian Tyrol, even though the scale of production there may have been many times larger (Shennan 1998).

Finally, when it comes to the question of ore production and the total mass of metal produced during the suggested 200 year operation of the mine on Copa Hill, we are still very much in the dark. It has not been possible to fully excavate this site; thus the number and dimension of the veins (as opposed to the rock removed in opening them up) is unknown. Where these have been revealed, we have been left with only negative evidence. Thus even if we were to assume that much of what was removed *did* contain chalcopyrite (copper ore), we still cannot be certain of its grade. Similarly, we have no reliable means of estimating the amount of lead ore extracted, even though it is abundantly clear that much of this (galena) was eventually discarded, either within the mine itself or else onto the tips. One also needs to consider the scale of losses at the hand picking, crushing and washing (concentration) stages of production, as well as those incurred during the actual reduction (smelting) of the ore. Of

the latter process, little is known, either of the techniques employed, or of the level of metal recovered. A maximum of 2–4 tons of copper metal has been suggested as a total figure for copper production (Timberlake 1990b). This was based on an estimate for the extraction of 48 tons of copper ore (chalcopyrite at 20–30% copper), calculated as a percentage (1%) of the known tonnage of spoil, and assuming a minimum recovery rate of 30–40% after processing and smelting. One might justifiably argue a case for multiplying or dividing this figure by a factor of two, but this guess is still as good as any that we might come up with now.

Based on such a calculation, it seems doubtful whether the whole of the mid-Wales mining and prospection area (these all being very similar sorts of deposits) could have produced much more than 6–10 tons of copper metal during the whole of the Early Bronze Age, perhaps it was considerably less (O'Brien (1996) has proposed a similarly modest production rate of 15–20kg of copper metal per annum over a 200 year period for the Mount Gabriel mines). Compare these figures then with the rather more optimistic estimate of between 175 and 238 tons of copper metal for the Great Orme (Lewis 1996), a sum which on the one hand seems perfectly plausible if one calculates the size of the Bronze Age workings and the probable volume and grade of workable ore, but makes no sense when comparing this with the known quantity of Early-Middle Bronze Age bronze artefacts recovered from the whole of the British Isles. No one has yet suggested that Welsh or indigenous British copper was being traded beyond these shores at this time – so *if* it really was being produced, then it should still be here, but where?

Perhaps instead we should be asking the following: How much copper or bronze went out of circulation during this period, presumably deposited as grave goods (from which context, after all, most of the known artefacts are derived)? And what percentage of this amount has already been recovered? Interestingly, these questions have already been asked of the Eneolithic (Copper Age) in central and southeastern Europe, where the possibility of recycling previously deposited metal has been offered as an explanation for the apparent hiatus in copper production (Taylor 1999). Perhaps then we should be asking ourselves how much Early Bronze Age copper continued in circulation throughout the Later Bronze Age and beyond? We might make a comparison with the present day. Some of the iron first smelted during the Victorian period is probably still in use today, recycled many times in between. At times of shortage, or increased demand, or when there were potential threats to the supply (such as during the 1940s), this was certainly the case.

Whatever the true figure is for Bronze Age

production, my hunch is that many of our current estimates for efficiency and metal recovery are way too high, and that these answers will only be forthcoming once the secondary processing, smelting and metal working sites to these mines have first been identified, excavated, and are better understood. Allied with experimental reconstructions, such knowledge will undoubtedly help us to reach a much more realistic expectation of production.

The end of mining – environmental change, exhaustion, or the opening up of new resources?

The apparently abrupt cessation to this earliest phase of mining and prospection within the British Isles may owe its origin to a number of different coinciding factors that appear to have culminated around 1500 BC, at the end of the Early Bronze Age.

Some of these may be linked to geo-political, cultural and demographic changes as represented by new burial and settlement practices, pottery styles, metalwork types and compositions (Northover 1980) which we first notice at the beginning of the Middle Bronze Age. Access to new and more plentiful supplies of copper from elsewhere may also have coincided with exhaustion of the richer surface-worked or easily accessible deposits as well as with increasing problems encountered with drainage at the mines (except within the limestone headland of the Great Orme, where underground mining appears to have continued, albeit at a much slower rate). Another factor may be the wholesale movement of people out of the uplands (where many of the mines and most of the mineral veins are located). For the latter two scenarios, climatic deterioration may have been in part responsible, deterioration leading to increased precipitation, and in some areas considerable encroachment of peat bog.

This appears to have been the fate of the mine on Copa Hill. Although much of the good ore had already been removed, the mine was probably only abandoned when it became flooded, the surrounding landscape having become wetter and wetter as first grassland, then blanket bog developed above the mine following peat initiation sometime between 1700–1500 BC (Timberlake and Mighall 1992). De-afforestation resulting from agricultural clearance, but perhaps also from the demands of mining, an activity that involved the consumption of large amounts of wood used in fire-setting (Mighall and Chambers 1993), may have been important contributory factors leading to local environmental decline. The environmental effects of mining may thus in part have been the cause of its abandonment.

Explanations for such changes in the use and exploitation of these deposits should be sought both at the local and regional level, examining all those interrelationships between place, environment, the economics of exchange and demand, territory, prestige and belief.

Supply, trade, and patterns of power

Up till now we have looked at these mines purely as sites of extraction rather than as one end of a chain of production linking the landscape of source material with that of the finished prestige object. In order to try and understand the nature of this link we need to pose questions that empirically may prove impossible to answer. For example, how important were these sources of metal at the beginning of the metalworking period? With what status were the sites or peoples who worked them held? And, how did these mines fit into the social and political map of Britain during the first half of the second millennium BC?

The process of analogy may prove helpful here. As a model, Bronze Age mines might be compared with Neolithic stone axe factories (Timberlake 1992a). Both types of site produced items of high utilitarian, symbolic (ritual or prestige) and economic value. Similarly, both were restricted to very specific, yet widely dispersed and exceedingly limited outcrops of rock or mineral, commonly located in quite isolated, mountainous locations. However, at the actual locations of these factories or mines, little now survives in the way of associated settlements, work places or well defined processing areas. There is also little to be found in the way of material culture – domestic or personal artefacts that might otherwise help to ascribe a sense of status or belonging to the workforce. Yet in both cases we possess some evidence (even if circumstantial) for the existence of complex distribution routes away from the sources.

The parallel between axe factory and Bronze Age mine seems to falter as soon as one looks for further evidence of regional importance through plotting the density or distribution pattern of different types of associated field monument. For instance, the grouping of henge monuments and stone circles during the Later Neolithic within north Wales and Cumbria has been linked to the economic, ritual or symbolic importance of major axe factory sites such as Graig Llwyd and Langdale (Burl 1976; Houlder 1976). The regional distribution of such monuments has also been shown to coincide with the principle distribution areas of stone axe groups (Bradley 1984). However, no good correlation has yet been made between Bronze Age mines and the distribution of

Bronze Age monuments. Southwest Ireland has many Bronze Age monuments, although the distribution bears no obvious relationship to that of the known mines (O'Brien 1990). However, mid-Wales, which has the greatest number of potential mining sites, has a rather moderate distribution of Bronze Age monuments, while the larger production centre based on the Great Orme appears to have an even less clear-cut relationship with contemporary sites. Nevertheless, it seems inconceivable that further links will not at some point be made between the location of Bronze Age mines and the occupation, use and status of their surrounding landscapes. For instance, it has been suggested that there may be some connection between the presence of Mount Gabriel-type mines in southwest Cork and the distribution of Irish wedge-shaped tombs and copper axes, although the case is still far from proven (O'Brien 1994).

Meanwhile, the contrast remains. Stone axe factory sites appear to have high status, whereas copper mining sites apparently do not. Although this could be something to do with those differences in time-span, as well as the peoples and cultures involved, it could also be something to do with the nature of the product. During the Later Neolithic, axes traded from different axe factory sites would have been instantly recognisable by discerning recipients and easily identifiable with their original sources. It seems possible therefore that such objects fabricated from natural stone, and possessing prestige, economic and perhaps even a magical value would confer similar status upon the sites and regions where they were produced.

Copper or bronze, on the other hand, being artificial products and of the same appearance in the processed state regardless of where their components originated, may not have engendered the same relationship with their sources. Although the finished alloy artefact would probably have possessed similar status to the stone axe (and perhaps greater still during the period in which both co-existed), the relationship that existed with the suppliers of unworked metal, even more so with the suppliers of ore, may have been strictly economic. Furthermore, the many stages of the distribution, smelting and remelting of both copper and tin may even have confused the bronzesmiths themselves as to the origin of the metal. As time progressed it seems likely that more and more mixing of metals was taking place, with contributions from many different ore sources alongside additions of recycled scrap. Bronze artefacts might then, as now, have been more readily identified with the 'industry' that produced them than with the original source(s) of metal. These may well have been at opposite ends of the country, as was almost certainly the case with the tin from southwest England and copper from north Wales.

Nevertheless, Bronze Age copper mines must still have commanded some economic importance, if only to the pastoralists/prospectors who worked them and the tribal groups who controlled the territories within which most were located. Yet how does the possession of mineral resources compare with the ownership of agricultural wealth? It seems questionable whether a few copper mines within an otherwise infertile mountain terrain could have commanded any greater political or economic importance than an equivalent sized area of productive and agriculturally rich lowland. In fact, quite the reverse may have been true. Unlike tin and gold, the sources of early copper were numerous and surface deposits could be easily worked and small amounts obtained, such that by the end of the Early Bronze Age there may actually have been a surfeit or overproduction of metal (one only has to recollect the tonnages of copper calculated for the Great Orme!). Of course this is speculation, but there are good reasons for suggesting it. Meanwhile, all the various possibilities need to be addressed. We can only guess as to how prehistoric mining was organised, how it affected land use and rights, and what it contributed to the economy of the upland and coastal areas of western Britain during the earlier part of the Bronze Age.

Summary and conclusions

This paper has presented a body of evidence which clearly demonstrates that copper mining and prospecting was widely undertaken during a 400 year period between 1900–1500 BC (Early Bronze Age) within certain areas of England and Wales. However, a policy of protectionism connected with the presence of gold and tin may explain why no such evidence has yet been found in southwest England. Elsewhere, opencast exploitation of near-surface deposits of chalcopyrite (together with malachite on the Great Orme) was carried out using stone tools. Lead ores may also have been extracted in mid-Wales. Within the latter region there appear a number of well defined prospection areas, and here there is evidence of a sense of 'place' for these sites in the landscape, independent of purely geological controls.

The role of pastoralist farmers has been examined and it has been suggested that transhumance agriculture, land clearance and erosion may all have a part to play in prospection. Similarly, there is evidence to suggest that the same groups were also involved in the seasonal working of upland mines, most of which appear to have been abandoned by the end of the Early Bronze Age.

Previous estimates for Early Bronze Age copper production probably require considerable downsizing. The mine on Copa Hill (Cwmystwyth), worked periodically for atleast 200 years, may never have produced no more than 2 tons of metal. The total for mid-Wales may therefore have been as little as 6 tons, while production from all British mines (including the Great Orme) may have amounted to no more than 50 tons for the whole of this period. Nevertheless, by the end of the Early Bronze Age we could still have been witnessing a net surfeit of copper metal.

Since much of this evidence for mining is still relatively new, there has been little inclusion of this data within regional archaeological studies, with many sites not even included within county SMR lists. Unlike Neolithic axe factories and flint mines, there has been little analysis carried out on the location and status of these sites, either/or their place within the contemporary archaeological landscape or their relationship (if any) with regional metalwork groups and distribution networks. Indeed, some useful comparisons have now been made of those links between stone axes and axe factory sites, and between bronze artefacts and copper mines. Many of the latter would have proved difficult to identify with a source, perhaps explaining why the mines may never have possessed a sense of place and status outside of their immediate locality.

Yet indirectly, the presence of these sites dotted around the uplands of Wales, on the Great Orme and elsewhere must have exerted a major, but still unrecognised influence upon the development of Bronze Age technology, and thus by inference the course of Bronze Age society in Britain.

Acknowledgements

I would like to acknowledge the considerable help provided by the members of the Early Mines Research Group excavation team in uncovering the *prima facie* evidence, in particular Brenda Craddock who also provided several of the illustrations used in this paper. I am grateful also to David Bick with whom discussions on such matters have always proved both stimulating and rewarding.

References

Agricola, G. 1556. *De Re Metallica* (trans. Hoover, H. C. and Hoover, L. H. 1950). New York: Dover Publications.

Bick, D. 1991. *The Old Metal Mines of Mid-Wales, Part 6: a Miscellany.* Newent, Glos.: Pound House.

Bick, D. 1999. Bronze Age copper mining in mid Wales – fact or fantasy? *Journal of Historical Metallurgy* 33(1), 7–12.

Bradley, R. 1984. *The Social Foundations of Prehistoric Britain.* London: Longman.

Budd, P. 1993. Recasting the Bronze Age. *New Scientist* 1896(Oct.), 33–37

Budd, P., Gale, D., Pollard, A. M., Thomas, R. G., and Williams, P. A. 1992. The early development of metallurgy in the British Isles. *Antiquity* 66(252), 677–686.

Burl, A. 1976   *The Stone Circles of the British Isles.* New Haven: Yale University Press.

Caseldine, A. E. 1990. *Environmental Archaeology in Wales.* Lampeter: Department of Archaeology, St. David's University College/CADW.

Caseldine, A. E. and Murphy, K. 1989. A Bronze Age burnt mound on Troedrhiwgwiniau Farm near Aberystwyth, Dyfed. *Archaeology in Wales* 29, 1–5.

Chapman, D. 1997. Great Orme smelting site, Llandudno. *Archaeology in Wales* 37, 56–57.

Childe, V. G. 1930. *The Bronze Age.* Cambridge: Cambridge University Press.

Coghlan, H. H. and Case, H. J. 1957. Early metallurgy of copper in Ireland and Britain. *Proceedings of the Prehistoric Society* 23, 91–123.

Craddock, B. R. 1990. The experimental hafting of stone mining hammers. In Crew, P. and Crew, S. (eds) *Early Mining in the British Isles*, 58. Maentwrog: Plas Tan y Bwlch Snowdonia National Park Study Centre.

Craddock, B. R. and Craddock, P. T. 1996. The beginnings of metallurgy in south-west Britain: hypotheses and evidence. In Newman, P. (ed.) *The Archaeology of Mining and Metallurgy in South-West Britain*, 52–62. *Mining History: Bulletin Peak District Mines Historical Society* 13(2).

Craddock, P. T. 1994. Recent progress in the study of early mining and metallurgy in the British Isles. *Journal of the Historical Metallurgy Society* 28(2), 69–85.

Craddock, P. T. 1995. *Early Metal Mining and Production.* Edinburgh: Edinburgh University Press.

Craddock, P. T. and Craddock, B. R. 1997. The inception of metallurgy in south-west Britain: hypotheses and evidence. In Budd, P. and Gale, D. (eds.) *Prehistoric Extractive Metallurgy in Cornwall*, 1–14. Truro: Cornwall Archaeological Unit.

Cummins, W. A. 1980. Stone axes as a guide to Neolithic communications and boundaries in England and Wales. *Proceedings of the Prehistoric Society* 46, 45–60.

Davies, O. 1935. *Roman Mines in Europe.* London: Macmillan.

Dutton, L. A. and Fasham, P. 1994. Prehistoric copper mining on the Great Orme, Llandudno, Gwynedd. *Proceedings of the Prehistoric Society* 60, 245–286.

Gale, D. 1995. *Stone Tools Employed in Prehistoric Mining.* Unpublished Ph.D. thesis, Department of Archaeological Sciences, University of Bradford.

Gwynedd Archaeological Trust 1999. Pentrwyn Metal working site, Great Orme. Gwynedd Archaeological Trust Report 321.

Healy, F. 1984. Farming and field monuments: the Neolithic in Norfolk. In Barringer, C. (ed.) *Aspects of East Anglian Prehistory*, 77–140. Norwich: Geobooks.

Herring, P. 1997. The prehistoric landscape of Cornwall and West Devon: economic and social contexts for metallurgy. In Budd, P. and Gale, D. (eds.) *Prehistoric Extractive Metallurgy in Cornwall*, 19–22. Truro: Cornwall Archaeological Unit.

Houlder, C. 1976. Stone axes and henge monuments. In Boon,G. and Lewis, J. M. (eds.) *Welsh Antiquity*, 55–62. Cardiff: National Museum of Wales.

Ixer, R. A. and Budd, P. 1998. The mineralogy of Bronze Age copper ores from the British Isles: implications for the composition of early metalwork. *Oxford Journal of Archaeology* 17, 15–41.

Jackson, J. S. 1968. Bronze Age copper mining on Mt. Gabriel, west Co.Cork, Ireland. *Archaeologia Austriaca* 43, 92–114.

Lewis, A. 1990. Underground exploration of the Great Orme copper mines. In Crew, P. and Crew, S. (eds) *Early Mining in the British Isles*, 5–10. Maentwrog: Plas Tan y Bwlch Snowdonia National Park Study Centre.

Lewis, A. 1994. Bronze Age mining on the Great Orme. In Ford, T. D. and Willies, L. (eds) Mining Before Powder, 31–36. *Bulletin of the Peak District Mines Historical Society* 12(3).

Lewis, A. 1996. *Prehistoric Mining at the Great Orme: Criteria for the Identification of Early Mining*. Unpublished Ph.D. thesis, University of Wales, Bangor.

Lynch, F. 1991. *Prehistoric Anglesey : the Archaeology of the Island to the Roman Conquest* (second edition). Llangefni: Anglesey Antiquarian Society.

Mighall, T. and Chambers, F. M. 1993. The environmental impact of prehistoric mining at Copa Hill, Cwmystwyth, Wales. *The Holocene* 3(3), 260–264.

Moore, P. D. 1968. Human influence upon vegetational history in north Cardiganshire. *Nature* 217, 1006–1007.

Northover, J. P. 1980. The analysis of Welsh Bronze Age metalwork. In Savory, H. N. *Guide Catalogue of the Bronze Age Collections*, 229–243. Cardiff: National Museum of Wales.

Northover, J. P. 1999. The earliest metalworking in southern Britain. In Hauptmann, A., Pernicka, E., Rehren, T. and Yalcin, U. (eds) The Beginnings of Metallurgy, 211–226. *Der Anschnitt 9*.

O'Brien, W. 1987. The dating of the Mt. Gabriel-type copper mines of West Cork. *Journal of the Cork Historical and Archaeological Soci*ety 92, 50–70.

O'Brien, W. 1990. Prehistoric copper mining in south-west Ireland. *Proceedings of the Prehistoric Society* 56, 269–290.

O'Brien, W. 1994. *Mount Gabriel: Bronze Age Mining in Ireland*. Galway: Galway University Press.

O'Brien, W. 1995. Ross Island and the origins of Irish-British metallurgy. In Waddell, J. and Shee Twohig, E. (eds) *Ireland in the Bronze Age*, 38–48. Dublin: The Stationary Office.

O'Brien, W. 1996. *Bronze Age Copper Mining in Britain and Ireland*. Princes Risborough: Shire Books no. 71.

Penhallurick, R. D. 1986. *Tin in Antiquity*. London: Institute of Metals.

Pickin, J. 1990. Stone tools and early metal mining in England and Wales. In Crew, P. and Crew, S. (eds) *Early Mining in the British Isles*, 39–42. Maentwrog: Plas Tan y Bwlch Snowdonia National Park Study Centre.

Pickin, J. and Worthington, T. 1989. Prehistoric mining hammers from Bradda Head, Isle of Man. *Bulletin of the Peak District Mines Historical Society* 10(5), 274–275.

Rohl, B. and Needham, S. 1998. *The Circulation of Metal in the British Bronze Age: the Application of Lead Isotope Analysis*. London: British Museum Occasional Paper 102.

Sharpe, A. 1997. Smoke but no fire, or the mysterious case of the missing miner. In Budd, P. and Gale, D. (eds) *Prehistoric Extractive Metallurgy in Cornwall*, 35–40. Truro: Cornwall Archaeological Unit.

Shennan, S. 1999. Cost, benefit and value in the organisation of early European copper production. *Antiquity* 73, 352–363.

Taylor, T. F. 1999. Envaluing metal: theorizing the Eneolithic 'hiatus'. In Young, S. M. M., Pollard, A. M., Budd, P. and Ixer, R. A. (eds) *Metals in Antiquity*, 22–23. Oxford: British Archaeological Reports, International Series 792.

Timberlake, S. 1988. Excavations at Parys Mountain and Nantyreira. *Archaeology in Wales* 28, 11–17.

Timberlake, S. 1990a. Excavations at an early mining site on Copa Hill, Cwmystwyth, Dyfed, 1989 and 1990. *Archaeology in Wales* 30, 7–13.

Timberlake, S. 1990b. Excavations and fieldwork on Copa Hill, Cwmystwyth, Dyfed, 1989. In Crew, P. and Crew, S. (eds) *Early Mining in the British Isles*, 22–29. Maentwrog: Plas Tan y Bwlch Snowdonia National Park Study Centre.

Timberlake, S. 1991. New evidence for early prehistoric mining in Wales – problems and potentials. In Budd, P., Chapman, B., Jackson, C., Janaway, R. and Ottaway, B. (eds) *Archaeological Sciences 1989: Proceedings of the Bradford Conference, September 1989*, 179–193. Oxford: Oxbow.

Timberlake, S. 1992a. Prehistoric copper mining in Britain. *Cornish Archaeology* 31, 15–34.

Timberlake, S. 1992b. Llancynfelin Mine. *Archaeology in Wales* 32, 90–91.

Timberlake, S. 1994a. Archaeological and circumstantial evidence for early mining in Wales. In Ford, T. D. and Willies, L. (eds) Mining Before Powder, 133–143. *Bulletin of the Peak District Mines Historical Society* 12(3).

Timberlake, S. 1994b. An experimental tin smelt at Flag Fen. *Journal of the Historical Metallurgy Society* 28(2), 122–129.

Timberlake, S. 1995a. Copa Hill, Cwmystwyth. *Archaeology in Wales* 35, 40–43.

Timberlake, S. 1995b Llancynfelin and Nantyrarian Mines. *Archaeology in Wales* 37, 62–65.

Timberlake, S. 1996a   Copa   Hill,   Cwmystwyth. *Archaeology in Wales* 36, 60–61.

Timberlake, S. 1996b. Tyn y fron Mine, Cwmrheidol. *Archaeology in Wales* 36, 61–63.

Timberlake, S. 1998. Survey of early metal mines within the Welsh Uplands. *Archaeology in Wales* 38, 79–81.

Timberlake, S. and Mason, J. 1997. Ogof Wyddon (Machynlleth Park Copper Mine). *Archaeology in Wales* 37, 62–65.

Timberlake, S. and Mighall, T. M. 1992. Historic and prehistoric mining on Copa Hill, Cwmystwyth. *Archaeology in Wales* 32, 38–44.

Varley, W. J. 1964. *Cheshire before the Romans*. Chester: Local History Committee of Cheshire Community Council.

Williams, J. G. 1866. *A Short Account of the British Encampments lying between the Rivers Rheidol and Lyfnant in the County of Cardigan and their Connection with the Mines*. Aberystwyth: Cambrian Press.

18   The times, they are a changin': experiencing continuity and development in the Early Bronze Age funerary rituals of southwestern Britain

Mary Ann Owoc

Introduction

As recently as ten years ago, an article concerned with Bronze Age funerary practice would have seemed out of place in a volume primarily concerned with landscape and settlement. Indeed, from initial appearances at least, the discussion of mortuary practices *per se* occupies but a small part of the current collection of papers. Although it is wholly reasonable to argue for reasons elaborated below that discussions of Earlier Bronze Age funerary/ ritual practices should play a larger role in investigations of Later Bronze Age domestic or settlement activity, recent work on the period has begun to belie even the categorical distinctions between 'ritual' and 'everyday', 'tomb' and 'house', and 'early' and 'middle' that have framed archaeological perceptions and practices concerned with the later third and second millennia BC (Barrett 1991; 1994; Bradley 1998; Brück 1999; 2000). Indeed, in light of these and other examinations, such distinctions have begun to appear increasingly fallacious and may well prove to be detrimental to our efforts to interpret and explain the material residues of this crucial period in prehistory. In a spirit then, not of division and difference, but of continuity and change, the following contribution is offered.

It is suggested below that current models that have used funerary evidence to interpret the transformations in traditions of knowledge and practical human realities during the second millennium BC do not address the full range of activities evidenced by the material record. In particular, the abundant evidence for solstial alignments, deliberately selected and used monument materials, and a rise in rituals and material culture related to cremation practices indicate that extending our interpretative umbrella to encompass the perceptual schemes, or practical taxonomies, that structured activities

relating to the burial of the dead may prove fruitful in augmenting our understanding of the links between the practices of the Earlier and Later Bronze Age. A close examination of a number of discrete funerary/ritual activities at monument locales in southwest Britain (Cornwall, Devon and Somerset) with this objective in mind reveals nuances in the funerary record that, when considered alongside current formulations, contribute to a more comprehensive view of the changes in temporality, human relations and activities during the period in question.

Finally, in light of the remarks above, it is important to stress that although the subject matter of this contribution is primarily the funerary activities of a number of later third and second millennium BC communities in southwest Britain, the traditions of knowledge that shaped and were reproduced by these practices stretched both backward and forward to encompass a far longer period of time, and a wide range of practical circumstances.

Reviewing the developmental sequence

A number of years ago, Barrett (1991, 120) suggested that an examination of the mortuary activities of the Earlier Bronze Age was crucial for understanding the development of settlement and agrarian practice in the second millennium BC. Engaging in efforts that supported this assertion, he and others charted a series of now fairly familiar trends in funerary practice (mainly in southern Britain) between the fifth and first millennium involving mound construction and corpse treatment. A critical review of the elements of this funerary sequence has served a primary inquiry into how funerary practices might have forwarded the ongoing development and negotiation of social relations from the third millennium onwards (Barrett 1988; 1989; 1991; 1994; Garwood 1991; Thomas 1991; Mizoguchi 1992). Moreover, as such negotiated relationships between the living, the living and the dead, and the past and present are seen in current archaeological formulations to be ultimately constitutive of societal reproduction, the funerary rituals of the Bronze Age are thus also argued to have facilitated the agrarian and tenurial transformations during the mid to later second millennium BC, particularly with respect to matters of inheritance, obligation, and affinity. At a larger scale, such transformations are seen to have involved changes in the long term ideological structures of temporality and subjectivity (being-becoming) that were aligned with more concrete changing relationships between communities and their landscapes (mobility to residential permanence, long to short fallow agriculture) (Barrett 1994).

Briefly reviewing some strands of the funerary sequence as currently read, it has been suggested that the end of the third and the early second millennium witnessed a variety of funerary practices in which particular social identities and relations of affinity or descent were highlighted and created by associational and contextual relationships established between both corpses and monuments/graves and through specific offerings to the dead. In this initial period (characterised by a number of Beaker and Early Bronze Age graves), the funerary rite appears focused on the body and burial (in contrast to Neolithic practices), while the importance of the monument lay less in its architectural form, than in its ability first to provide an associational framework for burials and second to exist in certain spatial relationships to other such monuments. This funerary 'topography' allowed particular community and familial histories to be constructed by connecting the past with a dynamic present in which obligations and relations between the living were under a constant process of negotiation. Importantly, although a variety of pre-mound structures, enclosures and revetted mounds existed, the kinds of practices that created and reproduced important community ideologies/traditions of knowledge or 'the order of things' (e.g. calendrical rituals involving restricted movement or other spatial techniques) are largely thought to have been carried out at other communal locales such as henges or stone circles.

Throughout the course of the second millennium BC, several important changes took place in the mortuary sequence, notably a shift of reference to the covering mounds through monumental enlargement via the addition of new burials. Additionally, the construction of some mounds may also have been part of an active strategy of monumental reproduction, as particular individuals and families actively copied nearby older forms thus creating important visible links with past ancestors, and related rights to resources. These temporal developments occurred alongside an increasing frequency in the practice of cremation, which became the dominant method of corpse treatment by the middle of the second millennium BC. Cremation shifted the moment of the deceased's transition to the pyre, and set up a situation whereby obligations to the deceased or mourners' rites of passage took the form of cremation deposits into or near established mounds. The monuments took on new importance, then, as places where generalised relations between living communities and the ancestral dead were established. Finally, towards the end of the sequence, the remains of the dead also came to be sited closer to and sometimes within the rapidly developing settlement compound or domestic walls, as the residence became the most important locale wherein society was reproduced.

Continuity and change in southwestern funerary practices

A detailed look at the kinds of activities undertaken by later third and second millennium BC communities in the Southwest in part confirms the existence of the general constructional and funerary trends cited above, yet also indicates that some augmentation of these various historical strands is required, as is a change of theoretical emphasis to encompass functions of the sites that go beyond the merely social. In particular, giving additional attention towards the built forms of the monuments throughout the period addressed, as well as the symbolic character and timing of particular activities in relation to them, indicates both greater continuity of practice from the third to the second millennium, and more nuanced funerary rituals that accomplished a number of crucial interrelated things for the communities that practiced them. The importance of these observations for enhancing our view of the changing temporalities and subjectivities during the course of the second millennium BC cannot be understated.

A number of well-excavated and reported single sites and barrow cemeteries in Cornwall, Devon and Somerset (Appendix 1) were analysed with the objective of delineating discrete activities, their role in particular funerary sequences, and changing local and regional mortuary practices over time (Owoc 2000). Results indicated that the earliest Beaker and Beaker/Food Vessel sites were just as likely to contain inhumed, as cremated remains.[1] Further, some graves were reopened and original burial deposits were removed, disturbed and/or added to (e.g. Try, Court Hill, Davidstow XXVI, Gwithian GM–V). Certain of these early graves may have been designed to be temporary resting places only, indicating the persistence of protracted funerary rituals and skeletal mobility from the earlier third millennium BC (e.g. Caerloggas Downs I and possibly the Longstone) (Williams 1988). Many of the cremations were the product of a careful selection of cooled and perhaps curated bones, sometimes accompanied by similarly selected animal parts (e.g. Cocksbarrow, Davidstow XIX and III, Tregulland, Chewton Plain 5). A number of these early sites were also characterised by pre-mound or pre-burial rituals involving the construction of special temporary enclosures (wooden circles and ring cairns of various sorts) that were altered, dismantled and/or that changed composition at significant times (e.g. Cocksbarrow, Tregulland, Carvinak, Trelen 2). Many of these enclosures were accompanied by other features (fires, pits, etc.). The creation and alignment of both enclosures and associated features were carefully timed and designed to coincide with one or more important solstial events during the yearly solar cycle or to highlight this cycle generally. The solar cycle itself was also more generally referenced (e.g. Davidstow Moor XXVI and III, Cocksbarrow, Trelen 2, Farway sites, White Cross Ring). This was accomplished through the use of entrances, post erections and grave alignments, and by the directed movement of mourners. Sequential timed mound construction was rare in these early sites, mound and enclosure form were observed to be both diminutive *and* monumental, and monuments and enclosures were also carefully constructed of deliberately chosen materials (see below).

These early trends are nicely illustrated by the site of Cocksbarrow, a probable Beaker site on the St. Austell granite in Cornwall (Miles and Miles 1971) (Fig. 18.1). The site was the repository for the cooled and probably bagged cremated skull, long-bones, metapodial and phalange fragments of an adult male accompanied by a horn ladle. These remains lay below a *c.* 21m diameter turf mound, capped with yellow kaolinised granite. The capping material was most likely obtained in a nearby stream valley where it lies exposed. However, before the cremation was deposited and the mound was constructed, mourners initially erected a double ring of posts, the earliest stakes of which flank the entrance and were opposed to the west/northwest by another group of early stakes and a pit. This pit and the earliest stakes are all located at or near equinoctial and solstial sunrise and sunset positions, indicating some liminal period during which the natural passage of the sun around the horizon was marked and noted (Owoc 2000). Mourners then replaced this enclosure with an inner and outer cairn circle, the

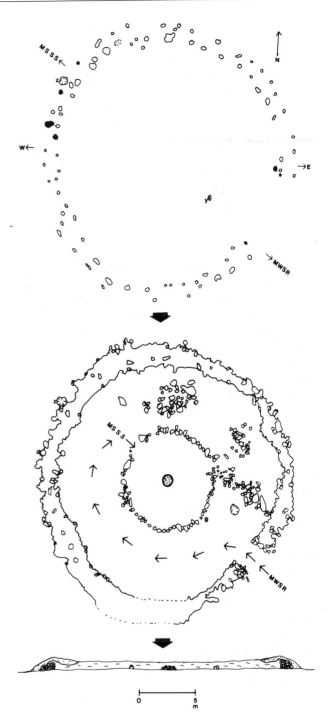

Fig. 18.1 *Cocksbarrow (after Miles 1975: 59)*

entrances of which aligned with the midsummer sunset and midwinter sunrise positions respectively when viewed from the site's center (Fig. 18.1). The arrangement of stones between the two rings indicated that mourners carrying the remains of the deceased took a clockwise course, entering the monument at the midwinter sunrise position (the shortest, darkest time of the year and the beginning of the sun's seasonal cycle) and depositing the deceased through a door aligned on the physically and temporally opposed midsummer sunset (the longest day of the year, at the end of the sun's seasonal cycle). Through ritual acknowledgement and manipulation of time and space, then, the life and funeral of the deceased could also be linked to a larger vision of the temporal order. Additionally, the form of the covering mound was probably not without significance as the stratigraphy of the mound itself served to invert and thus draw attention to the natural relationship between its two components. Through this particular construction technique, the mourners were able to contrast/highlight the brightness and hue of these materials, opposing both darkness with yellow brightness, and surface with subsurface context, paralleling the sun's passage above and below the horizon. At Cocksbarrow, then, the cooled, carefully selected and bagged remains of the deceased, the deliberately chosen alignments and entrances, the transition from wood to stone circles, and the form of the mound all point to a ceremony that employed principles of enclosure, alignment, stratigraphy, and time to create an overwhelmingly powerful view of the order of things and the place of the living and dead within it.

A similar set of activities involving structured movement, skeletal selection, solstial alignments and/or careful timing may be observed at other early Beaker/Food Vessel sites in the Southwest, as noted above. Although activity in many of these early sites tends, as at Cocksbarrow, to be restricted to activities prior to and surrounding the deposition of human remains (during which the living and the dead might be understood to be in a liminal state), the form of the mound or enclosure also appears to have been instrumental in constructing a particular sort of view, or reading of the funerary ritual. In particular, the enclosures divide living from dead and the covering mounds and enclosing banks were constructed of deliberately chosen and often carefully stratified materials employed with the intent of establishing very clear metaphorical relationships between the living, the deceased and the landscape, the progress of the funerary ritual itself and the perceived form and activity of the cosmos.[2]

During the period *c.* 2000–1700 BC, Collared, Biconical and Trevisker Urns, Enlarged Food Vessels and related ceramics gradually became the pots of choice in the funerary rituals of the Southwest (Tomalin 1982; 1983; Parker Pearson 1990; 1995). Some continuity in the use of pre-mound rituals involving solstial alignments and extended pre-burial rituals is apparent in these sites (e.g. Davidstow Moor I and V, Crig-a-Mennis, Watch Hill, Caerloggas Downs III), but changes are visible especially in a greater emphasis on mound construction. However, it is not always the case that the mounds on any of these sites consistently dwarf their

earlier neighbors. What distinguishes these monuments is not exclusively their size (indeed, some quite large monumental Beaker mounds also exist, for example Carvinak), but rather that their size is a product of a series of sometimes timed additions of caps/crusts. Although the addition of some of these caps involved the deposition of human remains (inferred at Trelen II), other caps were added during post-burial ritual activities related to the earlier burial of one or more individuals (e.g. Charmy Down 6, Davidstow Moor I, Colliford Reservoir II and IVC). Embellishments of this nature were sometimes accompanied by activities at the monuments' peripheries, in ditches or on their surfaces, that included the lighting of fires, feasting, the digging and filling of pits with earth and charcoal, and the manipulation and deposition of various items including wood, flints, pebbles, fruit and charcoal (e.g. Nancekuke, Watch Hill, Davidstow Moor V and I). Activities of this nature may also occur in the absence of monumental embellishment, and again may not always have involved the addition of further burials. This post barrow or post-burial activity contrasts with the finality of the mounds and enclosures at the Beaker and Beaker/Food Vessel sites, where ritualisation generally preceded mound/cairn construction. Notable also during this period is the growing popularity of cremation and the higher incidence of fires, charcoal deposits and hot or *in situ* cremations than that observed at the earlier sites. Therefore, although the pyre was often separate from the locus of burial, remnants from the pyre (cremated remains, hot ashes, urns) and actions and artifacts designed to elicit its image and accomplishments (fires, ash spreads, charcoal heaps, fired ceramics) were highly visible and played a major role in the funerary rituals on these sites. Less skeletal selection and careful bagging of remains appears to have taken place, as entire bodies or fragments only were carried to the monuments or cremated there (e.g. possibly Nancekuke). Ceramic vessels were often buried at these sites in the absence of human remains, or with token cremated fragments only (e.g. Crig-a-Mennis, Davidstow Moor V).

The Early Bronze Age site of Davidstow I, on Davidstow Moor in Cornwall (Christie 1988), clearly illustrates the changes noted above, as its builders combined a number of traditional constructional techniques and ritual practices with several post-burial rituals involving fire, feasting and the addition of layers to the mound. Activity on the site began between 2112 and 1645 BC when mourners created a yellow subsoil ring by stripping some of the site's turf, effectively creating a copy of two nearby circular banks. They also lit a variety of fires, deposited some cremated remains, created a small

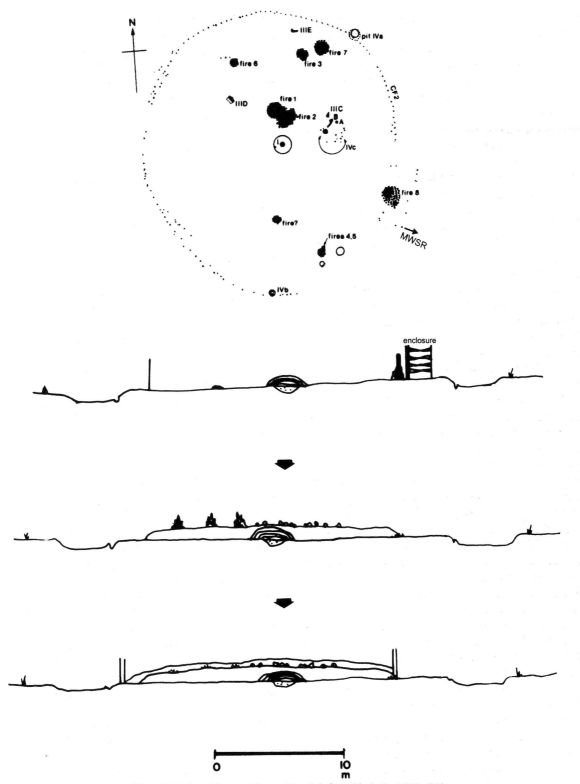

Fig. 18.2 Davidstow Moor, Site I (after Christie 1988: 32)

alternating light and dark stratified mound, deposited charcoal, and placed some wooden objects into the surface of the mound. All of these activities took place within, or were surrounded by a stake circle, or hurdle work fence (Fig. 18.2). The northern terminus of the entrance to this enclosure was aligned on the point of the midsummer sunrise, and mourners appear to have anticipated this event during burial rituals by the burning of a post in a wooden enclosure just to the north of this point (following a much older local practice). Additional stakes surrounding the position of the midsummer sunset attest to the probable anticipation and marking of this occurrence as well. After the central activities were complete, mourners raised a flat-topped turf mound over the site (Fig. 18.2). After its completion, they then lit a number of fires on its surface and participated in further activities resulting in the deposition of a large number of quartz stones, potsherds from at least two different vessels, a flint blade, and some flakes. They also consumed or burned some shellfish. After these activities were complete, mourners added a flat-topped layer of earth over the mound, which may have been revetted with a fence or stake ring.

The character of some of the later activities at sites such as Davidstow I are of interest, as is the material used to construct the various mound caps/layers. As noted above, various ceramics and lithics comprise some of the materials deposited at these sites, as do white quartz pebbles, grain rubbers, quern-stones, wood and fruit. Furthermore, fires and charcoal deposits were not uncommon. Although the timing, placement and specific character of these activities varies from act to act and from site to site, when placed in their specific temporal-spatial context, many actions appear to be the product of a particular way of perceiving the deceased, their life and death, and the passage of the funerary rite. In particular, it appears that analogous qualities of pots and persons were being highlighted, as were the similar transformations each undergoes when in contact with fire. Further, other analogies were clearly drawn between humans and wood and/or stone respectively, both in terms of their position in the landscape, their physical qualities living and dead, and their transformational response to fire. Finally, the presence of grain rubbers and quern-stones may be understood as very appropriate *significata* within a larger symbolic universe concerned with the transformational processes by which things go from wet and pliable, to dry and brittle.[3]

The often carefully timed addition of mound/bank/cap materials and offerings at these sites seem similarly designed to encourage reflection on the relative properties of living and deceased persons. When considered contextually in terms of their origin, artificial and natural stratigraphic positions, and temporal appearance on the sites, the sometimes alternating, colourful mound caps and crusts (and offerings) point to a variety of different conceptual schemes that both guided and were reproduced by the builders at the sites who drew on their potential polysemy.

Mound burial became generally uncommon in the Southwest between the fifteenth and fourteenth centuries BC. The funerary monuments that occur towards the end of this tradition continue to include abundant evidence for the lighting of fires, the spreading of charcoal and so on, and in many cases, they display the continuing practice of post-burial 'incorporative' activities, either in terms of monumental embellishment, or other deposits such as those noted above. The sites are often the repositories for a *number* of (comparatively-speaking) cremations, indicating familial relations and age grades, which are interred both urned and unurned. Some were transported hot to the site, or likely re-cremated on the site (e.g. Treligga 1 and 2, Upton Pyne, Chysauster). Little evidence for the sort of skeletal selection that characterised some Beaker/Food Vessel sites was noted, and although graves and urn groups were occasionally and variously aligned with respect to the passage of the sun, the sort of timed activities and impressive solstial geometry of the preceding centuries is absent. Whereas some of the earlier monuments previously discussed are noteworthy for their lack of significant amounts of human remains, a number of these later sites appear to have more of an unmistakable *burial* function. The mounds of this later period vary from simple to quite complex. Some were simple turf mounds or cairns, but others were carefully constructed of distinct materials that were often contrasted spatially and/or temporally in terms of their colour, natural stratigraphic position, texture and consistency.

Upton Pyne 284b, an unusual, stratified funerary mound in south Devon (Pollard and Russell 1969; 1976), exemplifies many of the above features of this group of later sites (Fig. 18.3). Mortuary activities took place on the site between 1749 and 1495 BC, beginning with the careful stripping of the turf, topsoil and some of the orange sandy subsoil, each of which was separately retained, including a leached A2 horizon. Mourners then placed a number of inverted and upright urns on this surface, some of which contained partial cremations or tiny fragments of calcined bones and charcoal deposits. A cist was also constructed that contained an inverted urn, and another pit contained some fragments of calcined bone and large pieces of charcoal. The identified remains were all infants. One of the inverted urns containing bone fragments was afterwards covered by a small sandy mound; this urn was probably deposited earlier (but by less than one year) than the others. Three urns lay on an east-west alignment. Soon after these activities were completed, mourners built a small mound over all the area, using the previously stripped sandy subsoil. Small amounts of calcined bone, charcoal lumps and dark earth were incorporated into this mound, and mourners threw handfuls of charcoal across it during construction. At some point they also spread small amounts of purple clay on the stripped surface. The builders then enlarged the site by the addition of a turf mound constructed of the turves

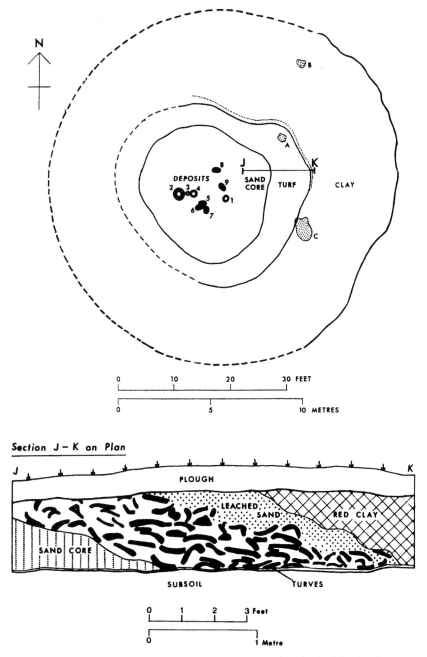

Fig. 18.3 *Upton Pyne 248b (© Devon Archaeological Society)*

removed during the initial site stripping. They heightened and capped the mound with the leached sandy A2 horizon. After this action, the mourners/builders waited while the leached cap hardened and weathered, after which they gradually finished the site, basket load by basket load, with an orange-red clay envelope. The material for this final layer was most likely obtained from a subsoil vein just uphill from the site. When completed, the site extended to 18m in diameter.

The builders and mourners of the emerging Later Bronze Age, then, continued to practice a variety of post-burial incorporative activities, and all evidence suggests that the same themes of transformation by fire resulting in hardening and drying both structured and were reproduced by their funerary rites of passage. The earlier liminality of the deceased before burial cannot be as easily demonstrated, and efforts by builders and funerary specialists to symbolically link the passage of the deceased with the repetitive physical and temporal passage of the sun are diminished or entirely absent in these sites.

It now remains to relate these general observations (drawn together in Tables 18.1 and 18.2) to the wider changes that took place in Bronze Age society between the third and first millennia BC.

Table 18.1 Southwestern Beaker/Bronze Age sites containing pre-mound structures, skeletal selection and grave re-opening, numerous fire featres and post-burial activity

Vessel/date	Pre-mound alignments, rings, "mound pits"	Skeletal selections, grave reopening	Hot or in situ cremations, multiple fires, charcoal deposits/pits, re-cremations	Timed mound enlargements, post mound activities/features
Beaker/3rd millennium	Trelen 2, Carvinak, Cocksbarrow, Davidstow III and XXVI, Farway sites, White Cross Ring	Try, Longstone, Cocksbarrow, Tregulland, ?Davidstow XIX, Davidstow III and XXVI, Chewton Plain 5		
Beaker/Food Vessel	Tregulland			
Food Vessel	Watch Hill			Watch Hill
Urn/Non-Beaker EBA	Crig-a-Mennis, Davidstow I	Treligga 1, ?Court Hill, ?Gwithian GM-V	Davidstow Moor I and V, Crig-a-Mennis, Cataclews, Colliford CRIVC and CRII, Treligga 1, 2 and 5, Stannon Downs 1, Shaugh Moor Cairns, Upton Pyne, Chysauster	Davidstow Moor I and V, Crig-a-Mennis, Nancekuke, Caerloggas Downs I and III, Colliford CRII and CRIVC, East Putford I, Charmy Down 6, Upton Pyne

Table 18.2 Funerary trends in southwest Britain

	2400	2200	2000	1800	1600	1400	1200	cal BC
Pre-mound alignments, circles		———————————						
Bone selection, grave opening		———————————						
Multiple fires, charcoal deposits/pits, re-cremations				————————				
Timed mound enlargement, post-barrow rituals				————————				
Urn burials, domestic burial								

-----------Beaker-----------

-------Food Vessel------

--------------------Urn--------------------⇒

An assessment of similarities and differences

From our earlier overview of Bronze Age funerary trends in southcentral Britain, it is clear that in order to come to terms with the changing temporalities and subjectivities of communities over the course of the second millennium BC, two important things must be addressed. They are first, the social significance of grave-site and cemetery topography, and second, the rise of cremation and its relationship to the changing role of the funerary monuments in the mourning practices of local communities (Barrett 1994). It would appear that a similar set of concerns to create identities, establish important kin relations, link past to present, and fulfil obligations to the dead were also acted upon in the funerary rituals of the Southwest during the course of the period under study. For instance, ample evidence indicates that graves, especially in the late third and early second millennium, were re-opened for the insertion of new burials or the removal of skeletal material. Some early sites were marked by no more than a ring-ditch, a bank, a small mound, a platform or a stone marker (e.g. Davidstow III and XXVI – Phase I, Try, Farway Rings, White Cross Ring, Burnt Common Ring). Additionally, the location of earlier graves and monuments was also an important factor structuring later burials and mounds (e.g. Charmy Down Cemetery, Davidstow XXVI). Finally, both the rise of cremation to dominance as a corpse treatment and the growing importance of the mound in later funerary rituals has also been demonstrated.

At this point, it becomes necessary to situate alongside these observations and their significance several points that have emerged from the above overview of southwestern funerary practices. One is the presence, continuity and disappearance of the pre-mound solar rituals during the late third and early second millennium BC. Another is the tendency for some early mourners to practice skeletal curation, selection and mobility. Lastly, the introduction between 2000 and 1700 BC of sequential post-burial mound enlargement and related incorporative activities and their continuity into the Middle Bronze Age must also be attended to.

Temporalities and transformations in southwest Britain

The extent to which knowledge of all of these funerary activities may enhance our grasp of the changing routines of practice and perception between the third and first millennium BC depends on the particular correspondence between them and other activities taking place elsewhere. The nature of this correspondence may be appreciated by placing the observed changes in southwestern funerary practice alongside the record of settlement development for the period in question. Again, general similarities exist between southwestern and southcentral Britain (as outlined in Barrett, Bradley, and Green 1991; Barrett 1994; and Brück 1999) in terms of the presence and absence of field systems, settlement enclosures and a clearly defined 'domestic' component in the later and earlier periods respectively. Specifically, evidence for southwestern Beaker and Early Bronze Age settlement residues occurs at a number of locales, and consists mainly of sherds, isolated postholes, scatters of lithic material and a few short-term structural traces (Mercer 1968; ApSimon and Greenfield 1972; Megaw 1976; Mercer and Dimbleby 1978; Brisbane and Clews 1979; Fleming 1979; 1980; 1983; 1987; 1988; Wainwright and Smith 1980; Fordham and Mould 1982; Gibson 1982; Maguire, Ralph, and Fleming 1983; Smith 1987; Todd 1987; Bell 1990; Nowakowski 1991). This, combined with evidence for hoe cultivation in the Beaker and Early Bronze Age levels at Brean Down (Bell 1990), and the absence of substantial lynchets associated with these early settlement residues, indicates the presence of short-term, perhaps seasonal habitation sites, with fluctuating and impermanent grazing, stock rearing and agricultural activity. Furthermore, evidence for earlier occupation scatters at a number of Middle Bronze Age settlement sites, and some conformity between

earlier monumental and later agrarian landscape divisions on Dartmoor, suggests that a partially structured system of residential mobility probably existed that was tied both spatially and temporally to the ceremonial use of the landscape (Barnatt 1989; Owoc 2000; A. Fleming, pers. comm.). Such evidence is consistent with what Barrett (1994, 144) has described as 'long fallow' systems for southcentral Britain. During this early period, the funerary rituals of the Southwest were sometimes characterised by long periods of liminality for the deceased, which included skeletal movement, manipulation and curation. The funerary rituals during this liminal period and surrounding the burial of a corpse marked and celebrated the repetitive, cyclical patterns of the observed cosmos, and defined the deceased not only in terms of his or her relationship to others, but also in terms of the physical landscape as perceived.

The formalisation of the settlement and residential patterns noted above began with the construction of unenclosed structures, small settlement systems and larger field boundaries perhaps as early as 2000–1700 BC. Examples include sites on Dartmoor (Saddlesborough Reave, Shaugh Moor settlement and other structures and enclosure walls) and Brean Down (Structure 57/Layer 6a) (Wainwright and Smith 1980; Smith *et al.* 1981; Balaam, Smith and Wainwright 1982; Bell 1990). Interestingly, it is during this period that significant changes are first apparent in the funerary rituals of the Southwest, evidenced by the rise of extensive post-burial/incorporative activities, during which relatives likely fulfilled ritual obligations to the deceased, and marked their joint staged journeys through the mortuary rite of passage. The increasing occurrence of cremation and of fire features, and the appearance and wider adoption of cinerary urns and related vessels, attest both to the increased emphasis on the mourners' rites of passage (Barrett 1994, 123), and the development of various metaphorical constructions related to the theme of transformation.

The centuries between 1700 and 1400 BC in the Southwest witnessed the establishment and growth of residential systems characterised by domestic compounds, substantial structures, agricultural and pastoral enclosures, manuring practices, multi-cropping, cereal production and domestic craft production at settlements such as Shaugh Moor, Holne Moor, Stannon Down, Brean Down, Trethellan, Poldowrain, Gwithian, Chysauster, and Trevisker (Thomas 1958; Megaw, Thomas, and Wailes 1960–61; ApSimon and Greenfield 1972; Merrifield and Moor 1974; Megaw 1976; Johnson 1980; Wainwright and Smith 1980; Smith *et al.* 1981; Smith and Harris 1982; Todd 1987; Fleming 1988; Nowakowski 1989; 1991; Bell 1990; Smith 1996).

Although continued exploitation of wild resources and variable forms of mobility most likely characterised these systems (Whittle 1997), they appear identical to the sorts of agrarian developments observed across southcentral Britain that Barrett (1994, 147) has referred to as 'short fallow'. On the basis of such similarities, we may extend the parallels between the two areas by further inferring that during this period the peninsula was also characterised by continued social definition and closure, as particular farming units (identified archaeologically across the uplands) developed within wider kinship links. The funerary activity accompanying the development of such agrarian and settlement practices indicates an increased emphasis on the burial *group*, and the continued performance of variable, likely appropriate actions that temporally and symbolically charted the mourners' and deceased's progress through the rite of passage.

The totality of the southwestern picture may now be integrated with the wider portrait of Bronze Age development put forth by Barrett (1994) and briefly outlined above. His model rests on an important premise that occupation practices and annual sequences of economic activity during the period influenced both the way time was measured (Leach 1966, 133; Brück 1999, 70) and the specific character and outcome of human interactions (Barrett, Bradley and Green 1991). Given the degree to which the funerary practices of the Bronze Age took place in highly charged situations of co-presence and were deliberately differentiated from other practices employing similar material culture,[4] it should also be possible in light of the above to appreciate how various temporalities and human relations may have been objectified and carried forward by the funerary rituals of the Southwest. Barrett's developmental overview of the Later Neolithic and Bronze Age outlines a gradual shift from an early period characterised by 'temporal structure[s] which harmonised the routines of life [involving movements through the landscape] with the natural cycles of the day and night and the passing of the seasons' (1994, 74) to a later one characterised by the labour of agriculture and the seasonal maintenance of particular portions of land. For these earlier communities, then, time was likely experienced as a series of repetitions, or repeated contrasts (Leach 1966), as days and nights grew shorter or longer, sunset followed sunrise, and the land became dark and light with the daily passage of the sun around the horizon. By focusing on these *timeless* cycles, the builders of southwestern funerary sites in the late third and early second millennium BC highlighted and reproduced this view of time, while simultaneously (and effectively) denying the sorts of irreversible or non-repetitive notions of time (Leach

1966, 125; Bloch and Parry 1982) that death would otherwise have forced upon them. This sense of timelessness may also have been reinforced in part by a continued tradition of elongated (and in some cases indeterminate) funerary liminal periods during which the remains of the deceased were curated, moved around, scattered and so on. It should not surprise us that practices reproducing a sense of timelessness via human remains persisted well into the Early Bronze Age alongside other, newer practices that focused on the burial of the deceased. Ample evidence for variable forms of mobility among agrarian societies exists (Whittle 1997), and passage tombs, stone circles and henge monuments (all of which could be argued to have reproduced a similar form of temporality) continued in use throughout the Early Bronze Age in the region (Todd 1987; Barnatt 1989). Furthermore, this sense of timeless repetition was echoed in the form of the monuments themselves, which often metaphorically referenced similar symbolic principles to those highlighted in the pre-mound structures and activities (Owoc 2000).

Although it appears that many funerary participants of the Earlier Bronze Age continued to be influenced by the sorts of temporalities and symbolic constructions that had guided the practices of their ancestors, the beginnings of a formalisation in human and landscape relations, and the ongoing development of genealogical reckoning between 2000 and 1700 BC clearly influenced and were undoubtedly perpetuated by new mortuary practices. In developing circumstances where the living and the dead increasingly belonged to communities in which the relationships of people to one another were being redefined and consolidated under new modes of production (Barrett 1994), and experiences of time and space were slowly changing, funerary rites began to involve local communities in ways that earlier ones did not. Increasingly, the mortuary order of things (encapsulated in the transition from human to ancestor, flesh to bone, or wet to dry) became dependent on the prescribed actions of kin. Beginning in the earlier second millennium BC, then, southwestern mound rituals with their sequential, drawn out incorporative mound caps, offerings, fires, meals and other acts, display a sense of 'directional time' (Barrett 1994, 136), or a *timely* nature, as mourners deliberately linked (physically and symbolically) the deceased's passage to their own proscription and obligations.

As these new systems of human and human-landscape relations became more structured, pre-mound solstial activity, which reflected different and earlier ways of being-in-the-world declined at the funerary sites of the Southwest, whereas practices reflecting the constitution of time according to familial obligations continued. Additionally, the burial of multiple individuals in a number of Middle Bronze Age sites celebrated and validated the social ties established through new tenurial circumstances. Finally, the increase in cremation, the continuity of rituals involving fire, and the persistent and frequent use during Middle Bronze mortuary practices of material symbols related to the broader theme of transformation all suggest that the funerary realm increasingly spoke of the day-to-day concerns, realities and practical taxonomies of the domestic, farming environment (Owoc 2000). Given these circumstances, the gradual movement of the rituals of death into the settlement and the eventual symbolic and physical replacement of the tomb by the house becomes much easier to conceptualise.[5]

Conclusions

Performing an in-depth analysis of discrete actions resulting in the construction of a number of southwestern Beaker/Bronze Age mortuary monuments reveals a number of parallels between the mortuary trends of this region and southcentral Britain, but also exposes elements in the funerary tradition meriting additional investigation. In particular, the presence of extensive solstial alignments, timed pre- and post-burial symbolic activities involving the deceased and the mourners, and the often complex architectural design of the mounds/cairns indicates that enlarging the interpretative framework through which we currently understand Bronze Age funerary practices may augment our understanding of the importance of these sites in facilitating the wider transformations that occurred during the second millennium BC.

Notable among the general conclusions arising from an investigation of these practices is the fact that considerable continuity in the ideologies that framed communities' views of themselves and the world around them existed from the Later Neolithic into the Bronze Age, so that well into the second millennium BC, the funerary rite of passage and the life of the deceased were metaphorically related to the passage of the sun, the cycle of the seasons and the composition of the landscape. Some continuity in the treatment of mortuary remains also existed, with extended liminal periods occurring alongside visible inhumation or cremation burial. Such practices reproduced a timeless reality consistent with continued structured mobility within the landscape despite the slowly changing relations between persons and kin groups.

Another important conclusion arising from a recognition of these particular practices is that the specific form of the monument and symbolic activities related

to it played a pivotal role in defining both the relative states of the deceased and the mourners. This was important during *both* earlier centuries and later ones, when changes to the sites became crucial for reproducing important ties within local groups and reinforcing a sense of directional time.

Finally, the increasing popularity of cremation was seen to have occurred within wider developments in the tradition of knowledge throughout the mid-second millennium that focused more and more on themes of transformation and analogous relations between pots, grain and people, ultimately making way for the culmination of a Later Bronze Age agrarian society.

Acknowledgements

Special thanks go to David Pedler for preparing Figures 1, 2, and 3.

Notes

1   Although the acidic character of many of the soils in the Southwest is certainly a contributing factor to the archaeological invisibility of inhumation burials, the large number of cremation burials in the early sites, as well as ample evidence indicating the former presence of inhumed corpses (graves, artifact positioning, and phosphate analyses), suggests that an approximate reflection of the ratio between cremated and inhumed remains may be achieved. Similar indications of multiple corpse treatments during the Early Bronze Age in other regions also exist (Peterson 1972; 1977).

2   It is apparent that the sites' builders and ritual specialists used simple associational techniques to create analogous relationships that generated metaphorical links between the landscape, the cosmos, the living and the dead. For a more extended and contextual study of the appearance, meanings and use of these alignments, and the ways in which mourners may have read the funerary rituals, see Owoc 2000.

3   For a more in-depth, contextual study of these activities, the materials they employed, and their meanings within the developing tradition of knowledge in the Southwest, see Owoc 2000.

4   I have argued elsewhere (Owoc in press) that the effectiveness of Earlier Bronze Age funerary practices in reproducing particular traditions of knowledge was in part the result of strategies of ritualisation and differentiation that distinguished mortuary practices from other activities.

5   Unfortunately, an expanded discussion of the ways in which the construction of the houses and settlement enclosures of the Later Bronze Age drew on a long term, developing tradition of knowledge is not possible here, but is addressed elsewhere (Bradley 1998; Owoc 2000).

Appendix 1: list of funerary/ritual sites and cemeteries referred to above

Caerloggas Downs I–III, Cocksbarrow, The Longstone, Trenance Downs, Watch Hill (Miles 1975; Miles and Miles 1971)
Carvinak (Dudley 1964)
Cataclews (Christie 1985)
Charmy Down sites (Grimes 1960; Williams 1950)
Chewton Plain sites (Williams 1947)
Chysauster (Smith 1996)
Colliford Reservoir sites (Griffith 1984)
Court Hill cairn (Green 1973)
Crig-A-Mennis (Christie 1960)
Davidstow Moor cemetery (Christie 1988)
East Putford I (Ralegh Radford and Rodgers 1947)
Farway sites/White Cross Ring/Burnt Common Ring (Pollard 1967; 1971)
Gwithian GM–V (Thomas 1958)
Lousey Barrow (Christie 1985)
Nancekuke (Christie 1985)
Shaugh Moor cairns (Wainwright, Fleming and Smith 1979)
Stannon Downs cemetery (Harris, Hooper and Trudgian 1984)
Tregulland (Ashbee 1958)
Trelen 2 (Smith 1984, 1988)
Treligga cemetery (Christie 1985)
Try (Russell and Pool 1964)
Upton Pyne 248b (Pollard and Russell 1969; 1976)

References

ApSimon, A. M. and Greenfield, E. 1972. The excavation of Bronze and Iron Age settlements at Trevisker, St. Ewal, Cornwall. *Proceedings of the Prehistoric Society* 38, 302–381.
Ashbee, P. 1958. The excavation of Tregulland barrow, Treneglos Parish, Cornwall. *Antiquaries Journal* 38, 174–193.
Balaam, N. D., Smith, K. and Wainwright, G. J. 1982. The Shaugh Moor project: fourth report – environment, context and conclusion. *Proceedings of the Prehistoric Society* 48, 203–278.
Barnatt, J. 1989. *Stone Circles of Britain*. Oxford: British Archaeological Reports, British series 215(i).
Barrett, J. C. 1988. The living, the dead, and the ancestors: Neolithic and Early Bronze Age mortuary practices. In Barrett, J. C. and Kinnes, I. (eds) *The Archaeology of Context in the Neolithic and Bronze Age: Recent Trends*, 30–41. Sheffield: John Collis Publications.
Barrett, J. C. 1989. Time and tradition: the rituals of everyday life. In H.-Å. Nordström and A. Knape (eds), *Bronze Age Studies: Transactions of the British-Scandinavian Colloquium in Stockholm, May 10–11, 1985*, 113–126. Stockholm: Museum of National Antiquities.
Barrett, J. C. 1994. *Fragments from Antiquity: an Archaeology of Social Life in Britain, 2900–1200 BC*. Oxford: Blackwell.

Barrett, J. C., Bradley, R. J. and Green, M. 1991. *Landscape, Monuments and Society: the Prehistory of Cranborne Chase*. Cambridge: Cambridge University Press.
Bell, M. 1990. *Brean Down Excavations 1983–1987*. London: English Heritage Archaeological Report 15.
Bloch, M. and Parry, J. 1982. *Death and the Regeneration of Life*. Cambridge: Cambridge University Press.
Bradley, R. 1998. *The Significance of Monuments: on the Shaping of Human Experience in Neolithic and Bronze Age Europe*. London: Routledge.
Brisbane, M. and Clews, S. 1979. The East Moor systems, Alternum and North Hill, Bodmin Moor. *Cornish Archaeology* 18, 33–60.
Brück, J. 1999. What's in a settlement? Domestic practice and residential mobility in Early Bronze Age southern England. In Brück, J. and Goodman, M. (eds) *Making Places in the Prehistoric World: Themes in Settlement Archaeology*, 52–75. London: UCL Press.
Brück, J. 2000. Settlement, landscape and social identity: the Early-Middle Bronze Age transition in Wessex, Sussex and the Thames Valley. *Oxford Journal of Archaeology* 19:3, 273–300.
Christie, P. 1960. Crig-a-Mennis: a Bronze Age barrow at Liskey, Perranzabuloe, Cornwall. *Proceedings of the Prehistoric Society* 26, 76–97.
Christie, P. 1985. Barrows on the north Cornish coast: wartime excavations by C. K. Croft-Andrew 1939–1944. *Cornish Archaeology* 24, 23–121.
Christie, P. 1988. A barrow cemetery on Davidstow Moor, Cornwall: wartime excavations by C. K. Croft-Andrew. *Cornish Archaeology* 27, 27–169.
Dudley, D. 1961. The excavation of the Carvinak barrow, Tregavethan, near Truro, Cornwall. *Journal of the Royal Institute of Cornwall* 2.44, 414–451.
Fleming, A. 1979. The Dartmoor reaves: boundary patterns and behavior patterns in the second millennium BC. *Proceedings of the Prehistoric Society* 49, 195–241.
Fleming, A. 1980. The cairnfields of north-west Dartmoor. *Proceedings of the Devon Archaeological Society* 38, 9–12.
Fleming, A. 1983. The prehistoric landscape of Dartmoor. Part 2: north and east Dartmoor. *Proceedings of the Prehistoric Society* 49, 195–241.
Fleming, A. 1987. Bronze Age settlement in the southwestern moors. In Todd, M. (ed.) *The South-West to AD 1000*, 111–133. London: Batsford.
Fleming, A. 1988. *The Dartmoor Reaves*. London: Batsford.
Fordham, S. and Mould, Q. 1982. The South Hams survey. In Balaam, N. D., Smith, K. and Wainwright G. J. The Shaugh Moor project: fourth report – environment, context and conclusion. *Proceedings of the Prehistoric Society* 48, 261–266.
Garwood, P. 1991. Ritual tradition and the reconstitution of society. In Garwood, P., Jennings, D., Skeates, R. and Toms, J. (eds) *Sacred and profane: proceedings of a conference on archaeology, ritual and religion, Oxford, 1989*, 10–32. Oxford: Oxford Committee for Archaeology Monograph 32.
Gibson, A. M. 1982. *Beaker Domestic Sites: a Study of the Domestic Pottery of the Late Third and Early Second Millennium BC in the British Isles*. Oxford: British Archaeological Reports, British series 107.
Green, H. S. 1973. The excavation of a round cairn on

Court Hill, Tickenham, north Somerset, 1969. *Proceedings of the Somerset Archaeology and Natural History Society* 117, 33–45.

Griffith, F. M. 1984. Archaeological investigations at Colliford Reservoir, Bodmin Moor, 1977–78. *Cornish Archaeology* 23, 49–139.

Grimes, W. F. 1960. *Excavations on Defence Sites 1939–1945. I: Mainly Neolithic-Bronze Age.* London: HMSO.

Harris, D., Hooper, S. and Trudgian, P. 1984. Excavation of three cairns on Stannon Downs, St. Breward. *Cornish Archaeology* 23, 141–155.

Johnson, N. 1980. Later Bronze Age settlement in the South-West. In Barrett, J. C. and Bradley, R. J. (eds) *Settlement and Society in the British Later Bronze Age*, 141–180. Oxford: British Archaeological Reports, British series 83.

Leach, E. 1966. *Rethinking Anthropology.* London: Athlone Press.

Maguire, D., Ralph, N. and Fleming, A. 1983. Early land use on Dartmoor – palaeobotanical and pedeological investigations on Holne Moor. In Jones, M. (ed.) *Investigating the Subsistence Economy*, 57–105. Oxford: British Archaeological Reports, International series S181.

Megaw, J. V. S. 1976. Gwithian, Cornwall: some notes on the evidence for Neolithic and Bronze Age settlement. In Burgess, C. and Miket, R. (eds) *Settlement and Economy in the Third and Second Millennia BC*, 51–66. Oxford: British Archaeological Reports, British series 33.

Megaw, J. V. S., Thomas, A. C. and Wailes, B. 1960–61. The Bronze Age settlement at Gwithian, Cornwall. *Proceedings of the West Cornwall Field Club* 2.5, 200–215.

Mercer, R. 1968. The excavation of a Bronze Age hut circle settlement, Stannon Down, St. Breward, Cornwall, 1969. *Cornish Archaeology* 9, 17–46.

Mercer R. and Dimbleby, G. W. 1978. Pollen analysis and the hut circle settlement at Stannon Down, St. Breward, Cornwall, 1969. *Cornish Archaeology* 9, 17–46.

Merrifield, D. L., and Moore, P. D. 1974. Prehistoric human activity and blanket peat initiation on Exmoor. *Nature* 250, 439–441.

Miles, H. 1975. Barrows on the St. Austell granite. *Cornish Archaeology* 14, 5–81.

Miles, H. and Miles, T. J. 1971. Excavations on Longstone Downs, St. Stephen in Brannel and St. Mewan. *Cornish Archaeology* 10, 5–28.

Mizoguchi, K. 1992. A historiography of a linear barrow cemetery: a structurationist's point of view. *Archaeological Review from Cambridge* 11.1, 39–49.

Nowakowski, J. 1989. *Gwithian: an Assessment of the Bronze Age Excavations, 1954–1961.* Truro: Cornwall County Council.

Nowakowski, J. 1991. Trethellen Farm, Newquay: the excavation of a lowland Bronze Age settlement and Iron Age cemetery. *Cornish Archaeology* 30, 5–242.

Owoc, M. A. 2000. *Aspects of Ceremonial Burial in the Bronze Age of South-West Britain.* Unpublished Ph.D. thesis, University of Sheffield.

Owoc, M. A. In press. Bronze Age cosmologies: the construction of time and space in south-western funerary/ritual monuments. In Smith, A. and Brookes, A. (eds) *Holy Ground: Theoretical Issues Related to the Landscape and Material Culture of Ritual Space.* Oxford: British Archaeological Reports.

Parker Pearson, M. 1990. The production and distribution of Bronze Age pottery in south-western Britain. *Cornish Archaeology* 29, 5–32.

Parker Pearson, M. 1995. South-western Bronze Age pottery. In Kinnes, I. and Varndell, G. (eds) *'Unbaked Urns of Rudely Shape': Essays on British and Irish Pottery for Ian Longworth*, 89–100. Oxford: Oxbow Monograph 55.

Peterson, F. 1972. Traditions of multiple burial in later Neolithic and Early Bronze Age England. *Archaeological Journal* 129, 22–43.

Peterson, F. F. 1977. *Bronze Age Funerary Monuments in England and Wales.* Unpublished Ph.D. thesis, University of Edinburgh.

Pollard, S. H. M. 1967. Seven prehistoric sites near Honiton, Devon, Part I, a Beaker flint ring and three flint cairns. *Proceedings of the Devon Archaeological Society* 25, 19–39.

Pollard, S. H. M. 1971. Seven Prehistoric sites near Honiton, Devon, Part II, three flint rings. *Proceedings of the Devon Archaeological Society* 29, 162–180.

Pollard, S. H. M. and Russell, P. M. G. 1969. Excavation of round barrow 248b, Upton Pyne, Exeter. *Proceedings of the Devon Archaeological Society* 27, 49–78.

Pollard, S. H. M. and Russell, P. M. G. 1976. Radiocarbon dating. Excavation of round barrow 248b, Upton Pyne, Exeter. *Proceedings of the Devon Archaeological Society* 34, 95.

Ralegh Radford, C. A. and Rodgers, E. H. 1947. The excavation of two barrows at East Putford. *Proceedings of the Devon Archaeological Exploration Society* 3, 156–163.

Russell, V. and Pool, P. A. S. 1964. Excavation of a menhir at Try, Gulval. *Cornish Archaeology* 3, 15–27.

Smith, G. 1984. Excavations on Goonhilly Downs, the Lizard, 1981. *Cornish Archaeology* 23, 3–42.

Smith, G. 1987. The Lizard project: landscape survey, 1978–83. *Cornish Archaeology* 26, 13–68.

Smith, G. 1988. New radiocarbon dates from Medieval and Bronze Age monuments on Goonhilly Downs, the Lizard. *Cornish Archaeology* 27, 23–66.

Smith, G. 1996. Archaeology and environment of a Bronze Age cairn and prehistoric fieldsystem at Chysauster, Gulval, Cornwall. *Proceedings of the Prehistoric Society* 67, 170–219.

Smith, G. and Harris, D. 1982. The excavation of Mesolithic, Neolithic and Bronze Age settlements at Poldowrain, St. Keverne, 1980. *Cornish Archaeology* 21, 23–66.

Smith, K., Coppen, J., Wainwright, G. J. and Beckett, S. 1981. The Shaugh Moor project: third report – settlement and environmental investigations. *Proceedings of the Prehistoric Society* 47, 205–273.

Thomas, A. C. 1958. *Gwithian: Ten Years' Work (1949–1958).* Canbourne: Gwithian Excavation Staff.

Thomas, J. 1991. Reading the body: funerary practice in Britain. In Garwood, P., Jennings, D., Skeates, R. and Toms, J. (eds) *Sacred and profane: proceedings of a conference on archaeology, ritual and religion, Oxford, 1989*, 33–42. Oxford: Oxford Committee for Archaeology Monograph 32.

Tomalin, D. J. 1982. The formal and textural characteristics of the Biconical Urn assemblage from Shaugh Moor Enclosure 15 and their implications. In Balaam, N. D., Smith, K. and Wainwright G. J. The Shaugh Moor project: fourth report – environment, context and conclusion. *Proceedings of the Prehistoric Society* 48, 228–237.

Tomalin, D. J. 1983. *British Biconical Urns: their Character and Chronology and their Relationship with Indigenous Early Bronze Ceramics*. Unpublished Ph.D. thesis, University of Southampton.

Todd, M. (ed.) 1987. *The South-West to AD 1000*. London: Longman.

Wainwright, G. J., Fleming, A. and Smith, K. 1979. The Shaugh Moor Project: first report. *Proceedings of the Proceeding Society* 46, 65–122.

Wainwright, G. J. and Smith, K. 1980. The Shaugh Moor project: second report – the enclosure. *Proceedings of the Prehistoric Society* 46, 65–122.

Whittle, A. 1997. Moving on and moving around: Neolithic settlement mobility. In Topping, P. (ed.) *Neolithic Landscapes*, 15–22. Oxford: Oxbow Monograph 86.

Williams, A. 1947. Bronze Age barrows near Chewton Mendip, Somerset. *Proceedings of the Somerset Archaeology and Natural History Society* 93, 36–67.

Williams, A. 1950. Bronze Age barrows on Charmy Down, Lansdown, Somerset. *Antiquaries Journal* 30, 34–46.

Williams, G. 1988. *The Standing Stones of South-West England*. Oxford: British Archaeological Reports, British series 197.

19   Round barrows in a circular world: monumentalising landscapes in Early Bronze Age Wessex

Aaron Watson

Introduction

It has often been noted that Early Bronze Age round barrows were constructed in areas that already had a long history of monument use. In Wessex, large numbers of these mounds were built near to henges and were clearly intended to be seen from their interiors. While these barrows contained the dead and their accompanying artefacts, they should also be considered as places that had an unprecedented visual impact on the appearance of the landscape. Previous archaeological investigations of these sites have frequently been based on two different scales of analysis, some looking at individual sites or cemeteries (e.g. Fox 1942; Green and Rollo-Smith 1984), whereas others have examined regional distributions (e.g. Fleming 1971; Woodward and Woodward 1996). Round barrows have also been considered as an expression of social or territorial units (e.g. Renfrew 1973; Green 1974). In addition, the significance of the circle in the form of round mounds is increasingly being recognised, both in terms of their structure and their deployment across the landscape (Woodward and Woodward 1996, 288–289). With reference to the landscapes around Avebury, Stonehenge and the Frome Valley, this paper will suggest that Early Bronze Age round barrows not only related to circular geometry, but may also have reflected cosmological principles embedded within the architecture of nearby henge monuments.

Round barrows and henge monuments

From the time when people first began to 'alter the earth' with architecture, the appearance of the landscape and the meanings it held were transformed (Bradley 1993). The sheer size and perm-anence of many Neolithic structures ensured their survival into the Bronze Age, and some of these sites may have even remained in use at this time (e.g. Smith 1965, 204, 209–210; Thomas 1996, 229–232; Lawson 1997, 31–36). In addition, the association between round barrows and parts of the landscape dominated by Neolithic monuments would also seem to indicate their enduring importance. This association with pre-existing places may have been a form of legitimation or appropriation (e.g. Darvill 1997, 193; Bender 1998, 64–66). However, this does not address the specific patterning of round barrows in relation to earlier earthworks.

Bronze Age mounds were rarely placed in close proximity to henges, but instead stayed a specific distance from them (e.g. Woodward and Woodward 1996, figs 3 and 7). One explanation for this is that the space separating round mounds from henge monuments defined a special area or *cordon sanitaire* (Woodward and Woodward 1996, 288). This is most clearly illustrated at Stonehenge, which is situated within a basin surrounded by barrow cemeteries, most of which are over 500m from the henge. However, the presence of a small cemetery (G4–9/G10) within 300m of the southwest boundary of Stonehenge represents something of an exception (Darvill 1997, 193). The presence of this group of mounds may be better explained in terms of a *visual* rather than a spatial relationship with the older enclosure. The majority of cemeteries visible in other directions were placed on chalk ridges to be seen in profile, or even skylined from the henge. To the southwest there are no clearly defined ridges, and the horizon is close to the monument. This dictates that the mounds here *had* to be located immediately beyond the earthworks in order to be seen in this manner (Cleal *et al.* 1995, 37, 490). Similar allowance for the natural topography can also be seen in the close proximity of mounds to the

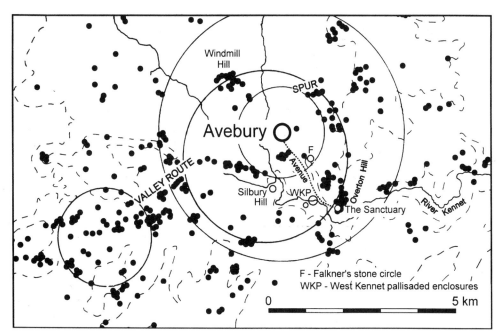

Fig. 19.1 *Map showing Bronze Age barrows around Avebury and places mentioned in the text. The analysis lines employed by Woodward and Woodward (1996) are included to highlight the broadly circular patterning of the mounds (after Woodward and Woodward 1996)*

Wyke Down henge on Cranborne Chase, and further afield at the Ring of Brodgar in Orkney. Rather than implying the existence of exclusion zones around these monuments, the pattern may be better understood as a conscious attempt to place barrows so that they are conspicuous to observers looking out from the henges. In short, they were constructed so that they appeared to completely surround these monuments.

Round barrows in a circular world

This pattern is important if we acknowledge that the architecture of many Later Neolithic henges was intended to orchestrate a particular view of the world (Watson 2000, 2001). Monuments were built to influence the ways in which people experienced the landscape around them. At one level, observers at their centres perceive themselves to be at the nucleus of a circular space defined by stones, timbers or earthworks. At another, the situation of many henges within valleys or basins contained by high ground creates the impression that the surrounding landscape is arranged *around* the monument (Richards 1996; Bradley 1998, ch. 8; Watson 2000, 2001). The ground plan of these monuments continued a theme of circularity that extended throughout much of later prehistory (Bradley 1998), and participants within perceived themselves to be at the focus of a 'circular' landscape. It was the positioning

and configuration of these monuments that served to structure the ways in which people understood time and space. Thus, Later Neolithic monuments may have served to symbolically represent the wider landscape within an architectural form. Perhaps these circular enclosures were believed to represent the centre of the world, or even the cosmos (Richards 1996).

If it is accepted that the structure of many henges embodied fundamental cosmological principles relating to a circular perception of the world, then the careful arrangement of barrows so that they appeared to surround Stonehenge acquires an added dimension. Perhaps people in the Earlier Bronze Age were not simply appropriating these sites, but were seeking to continue or reproduce these cosmological principles across the wider landscape. This possibility will be considered in three quite different regions of Wessex that contain both Later Neolithic monuments and large accumulations of Earlier Bronze Age barrows.

Avebury

There are a large number of round barrows in the vicinity of the henge monument at Avebury in Wiltshire. Woodward and Woodward (1996, 280) describe their distribution as a series of offset circles and suggest that these mounds were not focussed solely on Avebury but rather on the general group

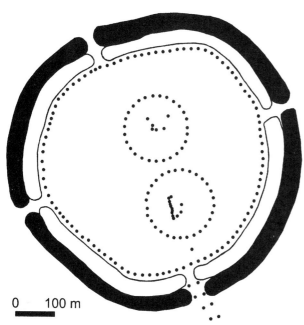

Fig. 19.2 *Plan showing a reconstruction of Avebury (after Smith 1965)*

0   100 m

of Later Neolithic monuments in this area (Fig. 19.1). However, these Neolithic sites seem to have been carefully placed to respond to the topography in particular ways, and may have reflected a cosmological understanding of the region. The landscape near Avebury is divided into a series of basins, each containing a Later Neolithic monument such as Silbury Hill, the West Kennet palisaded enclosures, and Avebury itself. Each of these sites gives the illusion of being situated at the centre of a circular basin, and the series of basins are collectively enclosed by high chalk downland. It is significant that an observer moving within the largest monument, Avebury, experiences a similar division of space (Fig. 19.2). Here, standing stones divide the interior into a series of circular areas, and moving through these areas effectively reproduces the experience of passing between monuments in the wider world. Just as the wider landscape is contained within an arc of high downland, so the participant at Avebury is bound within an earthen bank. Elements of the structure of this monument may have been created in the image of its hinterland, creating a microcosm of the world, which was at the same time the centre of the world (Watson 2001). Although it can be observed that Bronze Age round barrows were placed to overlook one or more of these monuments, the pattern of offset circles recognised by Woodward and Woodward could also be interpreted as an attempt to reflect the cosmological understanding of the environment as a series of circular spaces.

In this sense, it is interesting that not all of these

round barrows are intervisible with Later Neolithic monuments, as small groups of mounds appear to relate to movement around the wider region. There are strings of barrows overlooking the valley that approaches Avebury from the west, and observers moving along this route will encounter or see these mounds as they progress towards the henge. The axis of this pathway is even reproduced in some of the linear arrangements of barrows. To the east of Avebury, a line of mounds dominates a shallow spur extending from the ridgeway scarp. These are difficult to see from the henge, but are conspicuous when approaching Avebury from the east, north and south. Likewise, observers moving along the West Kennet Avenue will see a series of barrows that are prominently skylined along this route, but that cannot be seen so clearly from any other parts of the landscape.

Overton Hill is the focus for the only known ridge-top linear barrow cemetery in this area. The location is significant, as the line of barrows is set against the sky for anyone approaching along the Kennet Valley from the east. These mounds monumentalised a boundary between two different landscapes. There are no known Later Neolithic monuments in the valley between Overton Hill and Marlborough (see Whittle 1997, 169–170), but immediately to their west is the Sanctuary, a Later Neolithic circular monument connected to Avebury via the West Kennet Avenue. On reaching this elevated viewpoint, a vista dominated by large-scale Neolithic monuments is revealed, including two long barrows, Silbury Hill, and the West Kennet palisaded enclosures. The round barrows on Overton Hill are false-crested to be seen to best advantage by people approaching the region from outside, and are not visible from the Later Neolithic enclosures nearby. These mounds seem to emphasise a topographic threshold that separates the landscape of monuments from the wider world. The boundaries of this zone are marked elsewhere by clusters of mounds on Windmill Hill (see Whittle *et al.* 1999, 15–17) and the groups of mounds overlooking the approach from the west.

Stonehenge

In the vicinity of Stonehenge (Fig. 19.3), the topography and barrow groups are different to Avebury. Here, the henge occupies the centre of a wide chalkland basin, bordered by river valleys. This location may have been carefully chosen to orchestrate a distinctive relationship between the monument and the surrounding landscape. An observer standing within Stonehenge at the end of the Neolithic was contained within a concentric

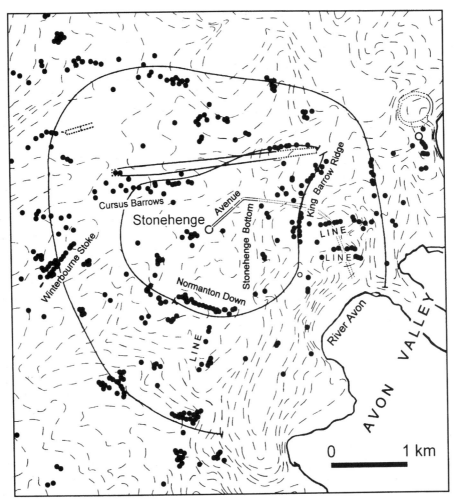

Fig. 19.3 *Map showing Bronze Age barrows around Stonehenge and places mentioned in the text. The analysis lines employed by Woodward and Woodward (1996) are included to highlight the concentric patterning of the mounds (after Woodward and Woodward 1996)*

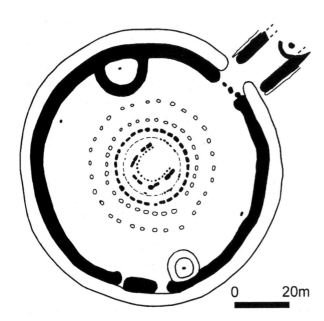

Fig. 19.4 *Plan of a late phase at Stonehenge (after Cleal et al. 1995)*

arrangement of earthworks and standing stones (Fig. 19.4). In turn, these architectural components appear to be at the focus of the natural topography. From the centre of Stonehenge, a series of concentric chalk ridges and valleys are seen to extend to the horizon. Thus, the participant is contained in a series of nested circular spaces where the monument and the wider world appear to operate on similar principles. It is within this context that the organisation of barrow cemeteries into concentric circular arrangements around Stonehenge may be better understood.

The large cemeteries that are intervisible with Stonehenge – Normanton Down, King Barrow Ridge and the Cursus barrows – are situated on ridge tops. This means that they are not only prominent from Stonehenge, but are also conspicuous to anyone approaching from *outside* the basin. For instance, the Normanton group is skylined from the south, and an observer walking from this direction will have to approach, and even pass between these barrows. Similarly, the Cursus barrows are highly conspicuous when approached from the north. To the east, the Old and New King barrows can be seen from large areas of the Avon Valley, and these particularly large barrows cut across the axis of movement formalised by the avenue. In each instance, the linear cemeteries mark a threshold from which Stonehenge can be clearly seen for the first time, with the stones being framed in the spaces between the mounds.

However, when walking through the Stonehenge landscape, it is apparent that the placing of round barrows does not simply reflect intervisibility with the henge. Many barrows are not visible from the stone circle, but *are* seen to best advantage from the Avenue. On the descent towards Stonehenge Bottom from King Barrow Ridge, the Avenue heads directly for G55, the 'Monarch of the Plain', which would have been skylined (Cleal *et al.* 1995, 40). In addition, there are strings of barrows immediately beyond the Stonehenge basin that are situated on subtle ridges or eminences that lead in the general direction of the central monument. Although most of these barrows are hidden from Stonehenge itself, it is possible that they were intended to be seen by observers approaching from outside this area. To the east, two approximate lines of barrows descend from King Barrow Ridge (Grinsell 1957), and a few examples across the River Avon suggest that they may once have continued in this direction. These alignments cut across the line of the Avenue and would have been passed by processions moving along this route. A small line of barrows also approaches the Normanton cemetery from the south.

Of particular interest are the organised cemeteries that contribute to the concentric arrangement around Stonehenge when viewed in plan (see Woodward and Woodward 1996, fig. 6), but that are not actually visible from the henge itself. For instance, the Winterbourne Stoke group recalls the Overton Hill barrows that are set close to Avebury and the West Kennet palisaded enclosures, but intervisible with neither. Although the placing of the Winterbourne Stoke mounds was influenced by a Neolithic long barrow, it is also crucial to recognise that they were situated to be highly conspicuous from the region to the west of the Stonehenge basin. As was the case at Overton Hill, observers approaching from outside the basin will see these barrows skylined, while the same mounds are not widely visible from within. Again, they seem to mark a boundary or threshold between two quite different landscapes. It seems that a visual relationship with the central henge was not essential, and that the importance of these and other cemeteries that lie out of sight from Stonehenge may have been to physically inscribe the overriding cosmic scheme across the wider landscape.

South Dorset

The henges of Maumbury Rings and Mount Pleasant are situated within a wide valley (the Frome Valley) bounded to the south by the South Dorset Ridgeway (Fig. 19.5). These henges were some of the later additions to a series of monuments constructed in a predominantly linear arrangement along the Alington Ridge above the River Frome (Fig. 19.6) throughout the Neolithic and into the Bronze Age (Bellamy 1991, 107–108, 129–130; Woodward 1991, 129–146; Sparey Green 1994). Linearity is also a characteristic of bank barrows and cursus monuments nearby, which themselves reproduce the linear aspect of the valley, nearby chalk ridges, and Chesil Beach to the south (Tilley 1999, ch. 6). This fundamental geometry also seems to have been reproduced in the extended arcs of Bronze Age round barrows on the Ridgeway (Fig. 19.5).

Maumbury Rings seems to have embodied a unique characteristic of the local area. It is set within a landscape that contains one of the densest concentrations of circular natural hollows, called dolines, in southern England (Sperling *et al.* 1977). These features formed throughout the Holocene, and result from the periodic collapse of sand and gravel deposits into cavities within the underlying chalk. The hollows vary widely in size, and many have a cone-like profile. Excavations at Maumbury Rings revealed that the interior was bounded by a ring of exceptionally deep artificial pits (Bradley 1975). These possess characteristics of the dolines in the wider landscape, and perhaps referenced these features in some way. Interest in the dolines continued into the Bronze Age. One of the densest groups of round barrows on the South Dorset Ridgeway was constructed among a remarkable concentration of dolines on Bronkham Hill (House 1991), and some of the larger barrows deliberately incorporated several of these features within their ditches (RCHME 1970, 466; Tilley 1999, 225–228). Relationships with natural features are unlikely to be fortuitous, illustrated by the excavation of an enormous, possibly natural shaft on Cranborne Chase. This has revealed a sequence of deliberate deposition extending from the Mesolithic to the Bronze Age (Green and Allen 1997). Similarly, swallets in the Mendip Hills have produced evidence for the structured deposition of both artefacts and human remains (Levitan *et al.* 1988).

The interior of Maumbury Rings may have created a space within which meaningful elements of the surrounding topography were referenced in combination with a tradition of circular geometry. The experience of moving *between* the monuments along the Alington Ridge may have related to a broader regime of movement through the topo-

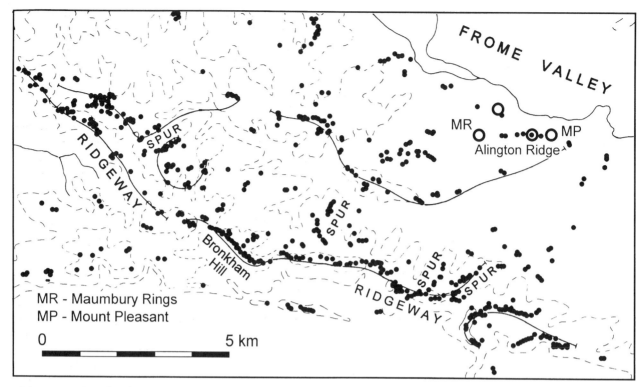

Fig. 19.5 *Map showing Bronze Age barrows near the Frome Valley and places mentioned in the text. The analysis lines employed by Woodward and Woodward (1996) are included to emphasize the linear patterning of the mounds (after Woodward and Woodward 1996)*

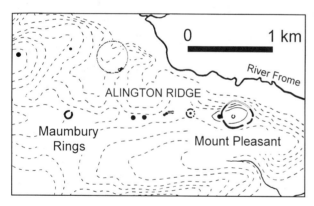

Fig. 19.6 *Monuments distributed along the Alington Ridge (after Sparey Green 1994)*

graphy of linear ridges and valleys. The arcs of round barrows reproduced this linearity but in a different place, and on a different scale. Here, each mound was a microcosm of the world, constructed in the image of the circle, but groups of barrows and the pathways between them also related to the wider world and natural places within it.

Many mounds on the South Dorset Ridgeway were not built to be seen solely from the Frome Valley sites. Their situation on the highest parts of the Ridgeway means that they are simultaneously seen and often skylined from *both* the north and

south (Tilley 1999, 216). To the south, these barrows overlook the Isle of Portland and the sea, and would be visible to seafarers as well as communities occupying the coastal plain. A similar pattern has been observed on the South Downs in southeast England (Field 1998, 321). In south Dorset, there are also arcs of barrows that occupy spurs extending from the northern side of the Ridgeway that are not false-crested from the henges, and thus comparatively inconspicuous. This could suggest that these mounds were not solely intended to be seen from these monuments, but were placed to overlook routeways or passes that link the coastal plain with the Frome Valley monuments. Similar to many barrows near Avebury and Stonehenge, it seems as if these mounds were placed to be seen or encountered by people who saw the landscape while they were moving through it, rather than simply from specific viewpoints.

Discussion

Overall, the evidence from the three study areas supports the suggestion that the placing of Early Bronze Age barrows reproduced the broad organisational principles of Later Neolithic henges in their vicinities. In part, barrows were concerned with intervisibility with these older sites, but they may also have been located with reference to cosmological beliefs that originated in the Neolithic. In all three regions, round barrows were placed on horizons that defined a 'circular' landscape around each henge. This is particularly apparent at Stonehenge, where some barrows had to be situated close to the enclosure in order to retain this relationship. Yet, it has also been noted that their distribution reproduced characteristics of the nearby henges *beyond* the viewsheds of these monuments. Major cemeteries such as the Winterbourne Stoke Crossroads group and Overton Hill seem to reflect a concern to influence the perceptions of people who were moving through the wider landscape. In this way, round mounds created thresholds between landscapes containing the henges and those beyond. With increasing distance from the henges, it seems that the patterning of barrows was influenced by routes of movement or significant places in the landscape, rather than circularity. These barrows were often placed to overlook routeways towards these monumental foci, or even to be seen from preordained paths or monumental avenues. The evident contrasts between the positioning of round barrows in the vicinity of Neolithic monuments, and those in regions where pre-existing monuments are absent, is an issue that remains to be fully investigated.

A continued adherence to cosmological principles in the Bronze Age need not indicate continuity in all aspects of society. The switch from the age of stone to the age of metal has traditionally been seen as a transition in terms of technological innovation, economic readjustment, and changing social relationships between people. Many Neolithic monuments have been interpreted as large-scale communal projects concerned with venerating the ancestors. In contrast, the funerary monuments of the Early Bronze Age are characterised by single articulated burials, rather than the collective disarticulated assemblages typical of Earlier Neolithic contexts (Braithwaite 1984, 112; Thomas 1991). In round barrows, particular individuals were accompanied by grave goods, including metalwork and new styles of ceramic vessel (Bradley 1984, 84–85). This could be indicative of a gradual decrease in the significance of the community and the development of a situation where individual status and social inequality were emphasised (see Shennan 1982; Braithwaite 1984; Thorpe and Richards 1984). Whereas single burials are consistently found, the treatment of the body, choice of grave goods, and appearance of the mound varied greatly, frequently confusing the interpretation of such burials. Even neighbouring mounds could possess complex and unique histories, and their appearance and contents could change over time, for example with the

insertion of additional graves (see Ashbee 1960; Peterson 1972; Barrett 1988). However, rather than seeing this as a problem, perhaps the distinctive qualities of each mound encapsulated the identity of the deceased. Each barrow may have held particular meanings relating to the human remains interred within, and by extension, cemeteries may have situated each individual within an historical framework that made visible relationships between people (Barrett 1994, 115). In this way, groups of mounds may have served to map genealogical relationships between deceased individuals over extended periods of time (Garwood 1991; Mizoguchi 1992; 1993; Last 1998), perpetuating the social order through the engagement of the living in the funerary rite (Barrett 1990).

Thus, there were distinct differences between monuments in the Neolithic and the Early Bronze Age that may reflect social change. Although round barrows may ultimately have their origin in the Neolithic (Kinnes 1979), their construction in the Bronze Age was quite different to anything that had gone before. It is interesting that in the face of this social change, people were continuing to refer to a cosmological order that they may have perceived to be eternal. Societies often seek to maintain a sense of continuity by incorporating references to the past in rituals (Shanks and Tilley 1987, 180–181). This may explain the increased activities at Neolithic henge monuments in the Earlier Bronze Age. For instance, burials were placed at Avebury (Smith 1965), ritual deposition occurred at Mount Pleasant (Thomas 1996), and circular arrangements of pits were excavated at Stonehenge (Cleal *et al.* 1995). These actions stressed continuity, but all were set against gradual social change that would ultimately lead to the final abandonment of these sites (Lawson 1997, 31–32; Bradley 1998, ch. 6). Round barrows embodied a contradiction between innovation and an archaic understanding of the world. The procession, the mourning, the acts of deposition, the placing of the body or the firing of the pyre, the construction of the mound and its subsequent reuse – all of these procedures stressed the importance of the deceased, as well as those involved in the funerary rite (Barrett 1990; Parker Pearson 1993). Society was becoming increasingly hierarchical with an emphasis on material value and social differentiation. While the dead were carefully fitted within a web of social relationships that existed across both space and time, such acts were simultaneously legitimated by the immersion of the mound within what was understood to be a timeless cosmological scheme that extended across entire landscapes.

Round barrows were not simply the physical expression of transformations occurring in wider society, but themselves played a role in this process.

Although their contents and form illustrate increasingly complex relationships between people, the monumentalisation of the landscape took place in relation to an ancient and established symbolic code. This can be seen at multiple levels, beginning with the basic circular ground plan of each mound (Bradley 1998). Collectively, these mounds perpetuated cosmological systems through the physical reworking of the topography itself. In this sense, it was not simply the relationships between people that were being rewritten, but also between people and the landscape. The potency of the natural world and the places within it have received considerable discussion (Bradley 1993; Tilley 1994). If the world was understood in terms of origin myths or ancestral forces during the Neolithic, then in the Earlier Bronze Age we may see a shift towards an emphasis on individuals, both living and dead (Barrett 1994, ch. 2). In part, this may be evidenced by the insertion of single burials at the base of some of the sarsen monoliths at Avebury (Smith 1965, 204, 209–210), suggesting that standing stones here may have become directly connected with particular people (Gillings and Pollard 1999, 185). In the wider landscape, it is possible that both individuals and the lineages to which they belonged were irreversibly becoming bound with the landscape (Barrett 1994, 147). Round barrows extended the tradition of monument building into new parts of the landscape, and in doing so created a new sense of space and time. Across Britain, the Earlier Bronze Age witnessed intensive exploitation, reuse and alteration of both pre-existing sites (Kinnes 1992, 116; Bradley 1998, ch. 9; Tilley 1999, 211–213) and natural places (Tilley 1996, 168–173). In Wessex, Bronze Age barrows sought to appropriate the ridges and folds of the downland itself. The association of mounds with topographic features such as chalk combes, springs and watercourses has been recognised in Wessex and beyond (e.g. Tomalin 1991; Field 1998; Tilley 1999, 216). These topographic features were likely to have been shrouded in mythology and meaning from earlier periods (Tilley 1994), and over time these meanings may have been repeatedly renegotiated (Tilley 1999, ch. 6).

In the Avebury, Stonehenge and Frome Valley regions, it seems that round barrows were fundamentally bound up within an understanding of the world that was already ancient. It is this emphasis on specific areas, often containing Neolithic monuments, that has been interpreted as evidence for the territorial division of the landscape (Renfrew 1973; Green 1974, 133–136). Yet, even if we set aside problems associated with the concept of territory (Ingold 1986, ch. 6; Chapman 1995), it is apparent that the subtle ways in which henges and round barrows were integrated with their surroundings represented rather more than simply the expression of territorial division. Rather, the very presence of these sites may have contributed to the processes by which such regimes may ultimately have come into being. Although there was intermittent cultivation during the Neolithic and Early Bronze Age in Wessex, it was not until the later second millennium BC that round barrows were ultimately superseded by bounded field systems, defined settlements, and hillforts (Bradley 1984, 91; 1998, ch. 10; Woodward 1991, 146–154; Gingell 1992, 151–158; Barrett 1994, ch. 6; Cleal et al. 1995, 339–342, 484).

Conclusions

The form and situation of round barrows seems to represent a compromise between architectural conventions, burial tradition, cosmology, the local topography and pre-existing monuments. Although the deployment of mounds could reflect territorial boundaries, a consideration of three regions in Wessex also seems to suggest that people were concerned to reference cosmological principles that were embodied in the architecture of nearby henge monuments. This may have been an attempt to legitimate changing social structures by referencing the past. Monuments were now being constructed, and rites conducted, in the interest of individuals or lineages, rather than the wider community. As the land was physically reworked, so its meanings became increasingly concerned with the interests of these individuals, rather than mythical ancestors. In this sense, round barrows may have marked a transformation in the social trajectory of prehistoric Britain that ultimately brought about the conditions under which land ownership and territorial division first became visible in the archaeological record (Barrett 1994). In the chalklands of Wessex, it seems possible that these monuments heralded a change that was to have tremendous repercussions into the future – a future made possible by the manipulation of a symbolic code that was already ancient when the construction of these mounds began.

Acknowledgements

An initial draft of this paper was presented at the Theoretical Archaeology Group conference 1998 in the session 'Remembering and Forgetting: Exploring the Past in the Past'. I would like to thank one of the organisers, Howard Williams, for his comments. The paper has also benefited from discussions with Richard Bradley, Andrew Fleming, Martin Green and Andy Jones.

References

Ashbee, P. 1960. *The Bronze Age Round Barrow in Britain*. London: Phoenix House.

Barrett, J. 1988. The living, the dead, and the ancestors: Neolithic and Early Bronze Age mortuary practices. In Barrett, J. C. and Kinnes, I. A. (eds) *The Archaeology of Context in the Neolithic and Bronze Age: Recent Trends*, 30–41. Sheffield: Dept. of Archaeology and Prehistory, University of Sheffield.

Barrett, J. 1990. The monumentality of death: the character of Early Bronze Age mortuary mounds in southern Britain. *World Archaeology* 22, 179–189.

Barrett, J. 1994. *Fragments from Antiquity: an Archaeology of Social Life in Britain, 2900–1200 BC*. Oxford: Blackwell.

Bellamy, P. S. 1991. The excavation of Fordington Farm round barrow. *Proceedings of the Dorset Natural History and Archaeological Society* 113, 107–132.

Bender, B. 1998. *Stonehenge: Making Space*. Oxford: Berg.

Bradley, R. 1975. Maumbury Rings, Dorchester: the excavations of 1908–13. *Archaeologia* 105, 1–97.

Bradley, R. 1984. *The Social Foundations of Prehistoric Britain*. London: Longman.

Bradley, R. 1993. *Altering the Earth*. Edinburgh: Society of Antiquaries of Scotland Monograph 8.

Bradley, R. 1998. *The Significance of Monuments*. London: Routledge.

Braithwaite, M. 1984. Ritual and prestige in the prehistory of Wessex, *c*.2200–1400 BC: a new dimension to the archaeological evidence. In Miller, D. and Tilley, C. (eds) *Ideology, Power and Prehistory*, 93–110. Cambridge: Cambridge University Press.

Chapman, R. 1995. Ten years after – megaliths, mortuary practices, and the territorial model. In Beck, L. A. (ed.) *Regional Approaches to Mortuary Analysis*, 29–51. New York: Plenum Press.

Cleal, R., Walker, K. and Montague, R. 1995. *Stonehenge in its Landscape: Twentieth Century Excavations*. London: English Heritage.

Darvill, T. 1997. Ever increasing circles: the sacred geographies of Stonehenge and its landscape. In Cunliffe, B. and Renfrew, C. (eds) *Science and Stonehenge*, 167–202. Oxford: Oxford University Press.

Field, D. 1998. Round barrows and the harmonious landscape: placing Early Bronze Age burial monuments in south-east England. *Oxford Journal of Archaeology* 17, 309–326.

Fleming, A. 1971. Territorial patterns in Bronze Age Wessex. *Proceedings of the Prehistoric Society* 37, 138–166.

Fox, C. F. 1942. A beaker barrow, enlarged in the Middle Bronze Age, at South Hill, Talbenny, Pembrokeshire. *Archaeological Journal* 99, 1–32.

Garwood, P. 1991. Ritual tradition and the reconstitution of society. In Garwood, P., Jennings, D., Skeates, R. and Toms, J. (eds) *Sacred and Profane: proceedings of a conference on archaeology, ritual and religion, Oxford, 1989*, 10–32. Oxford: Oxford University Committee for Archaeology Monograph 32.

Gillings, M. and Pollard, J. 1999. Non-portable stone artefacts and contexts of meaning: the tale of the Grey Wether (www.museums.ncl.ac.uk/Avebury/stone4.htm). *World Archaeology* 31, 179–193.

Gingell, C. 1992. *The Marlborough Downs: a Later Bronze Age Landscape and its Origins*. Devizes: Wiltshire Archaeological and Natural History Society.

Green, C. and Rollo-Smith, S. 1984. The excavation of eighteen round barrows near Shrewton, Wiltshire. *Proceedings of the Prehistoric Society* 50, 255–318.

Green, H. S. 1974. Early Bronze Age burial, territory, and population in Milton Keynes, Buckinghamshire, and the Great Ouse Valley. *Archaeological Journal* 131, 75–139.

Green, M. and Allen, M. J. 1997. An early prehistoric shaft on Cranborne Chase. *Oxford Journal of Archaeology* 16, 121–132.

Grinsell, L. V. 1957. Archaeological gazetteer. In Pugh, R. B. and Crittall, E. (eds) *Victoria County History of Wiltshire*, 21–272. London: Oxford University Press.

House, M. R. 1991. Dorset dolines: part 2, Bronkham Hill. *Proceedings of the Dorset Natural History and Archaeological Society* 113, 149–155.

Ingold, T. 1986. *The Appropriation of Nature*. Manchester: Manchester University Press.

Kinnes, I. 1979. *Round Barrows and Ring-Ditches in the British Neolithic*. London: British Museum Occasional Paper 7.

Kinnes, I. 1992. *Non-Megalithic Long Barrows and Allied Structures in the British Neolithic*. London: British Museum Occasional Paper 52.

Last, J. 1998. Books of life: biography and memory in a Bronze Age barrow. *Oxford Journal of Archaeology* 17, 43–53.

Lawson, A. J. 1997. The structural history of Stonehenge. In Cunliffe, B. and Renfrew, C. (eds) *Science and Stonehenge*, 15–37. Oxford: Oxford University Press.

Levitan, B. M., Audsley, A., Hawkes, C. J., Moody, A., Moody, P., Smart, P. L. and Thomas, J. S. 1988. Charterhouse Warren Farm swallet, Mendip, Somerset: exploration, geomorphology, taphonomy and archaeology. *Proceedings of the University of Bristol Spelaeological Society* 18, 171–239.

Mizoguchi, K. 1992. A historiography of a linear barrow cemetery: a structurationist's point of view. *Archaeological Review from Cambridge* 11, 39–49.

Mizoguchi, K. 1993. Time in the reproduction of mortuary practices. *World Archaeology* 25, 223–235.

Parker Pearson, M. 1993. The powerful dead: archaeological relationships between the living and the dead. *Cambridge Archaeological Journal* 3, 203–229.

Peterson, F. 1972. Traditions of multiple burial in Later Neolithic and Early Bronze Age England. *Archaeological Journal* 129, 22–55.

RCHME (Royal Commission on Historical Monuments, England) 1970. *An Inventory of Historical Monuments in the County of Dorset, Vol. 2: South-East*. London: HMSO.

Renfrew, C. 1973. Monuments, mobilization and social organisation in Neolithic Wessex. In Renfrew, C. (ed.) *The Explanation of Culture Change: Models in Prehistory*, 539–558. London: Duckworth.

Richards, C. 1996. Monuments as landscape: creating the centre of the world in late Neolithic Orkney. *World Archaeology* 28, 190–208.

Shanks, M. and Tilley, C. 1987. *Social Theory and Archaeology*. Cambridge: Polity.

Shennan, S. 1982. Ideology, change and the European Early Bronze Age In Hodder, I. (ed.) *Symbolic and Structural Archaeology*, 155–161. Cambridge: Cambridge University Press.

Smith, I. 1965. *Windmill Hill and Avebury: Excavations by Alexander Keiller 1925–1939*. Oxford: Clarendon Press.

Sparey Green, C. 1994. Observations on the site of the 'Two Barrows', Fordington Farm, Dorchester, with a note on the 'Conquer Barrow'. *Proceedings of the Dorset Natural History and Archaeological Society* 116, 45–54.

Sperling, C. H. B., Goudie, A. S., Stoddart, D. R. and Poole, G. G. 1977. Dolines of the Dorset chalklands and other areas of southern Britain. *Transactions of the Institute of British Geographers* 2, 205–223.

Thomas, J. 1991. Reading the body: beaker funerary practice in Britain. In Garwood, P., Jennings, D., Skeates, R. and Toms, J. (eds) *Sacred and Profane: proceedings of a conference on archaeology, ritual and religion, Oxford, 1989*, 33–42. Oxford: Oxford University Committee for Archaeology Monograph 32.

Thomas, J. 1996. *Time, Culture and Identity*. London: Routledge.

Thorpe, I. J. and Richards, C. 1984. The decline of ritual authority and the introduction of Beakers into Britain. In Bradley, R. and Gardiner, J. (eds) *Neolithic Studies: a review of some recent work*, 67–84. Oxford: British Archaeological Reports, British Series 133.

Tilley, C. 1994. *A Phenomenology of Landscape*. Oxford: Berg.

Tilley, C. 1996. The power of rocks: topography and monument construction on Bodmin Moor. *World Archaeology* 28, 161–176.

Tilley, C. 1999. *Metaphor and Material Culture*. Oxford: Blackwell.

Tomalin, D. J. 1991. Combe-cluster barrow cemeteries in the Isle of Wight: a locational prediction model. *Proceedings of the Isle of Wight Natural History and Archaeological Society* 11, 85–96.

Watson, A. 1998. *Circles of Earth and Stone: Monuments, Landscape and Prehistoric Cosmology*. Paper presented at the Theoretical Archaeology Group conference, Birmingham, Dec. 1998.

Watson, A. 2000. *Encircled Space: the Experience of Stone Circles and Henges in the British Neolithic*. Unpublished Ph.D. thesis, Dept. of Archaeology, University of Reading.

Watson, A. 2001. Composing Avebury, *World Archaeology* 33, 296–314.

Whittle, A. 1997. *Sacred Mound, Holy Rings*. Oxford: Oxbow Monograph 74.

Whittle, A., Pollard, J. and Grigson, C. 1999. *The Harmony of Symbols: the Windmill Hill Causewayed Enclosure*. Oxford: Oxbow Books.

Woodward, A. B. and Woodward, P. J. 1996. The topography of some barrow cemeteries in Bronze Age Wessex. *Proceedings of the Prehistoric Society* 62, 275–291.

Woodward, P. 1991. *The South Dorset Ridgeway: Survey and Excavations 1977–84*. Dorchester: Dorset Natural History and Archaeological Society Monograph 8.

20   Enduring images? Image production and memory in Earlier Bronze Age Scotland

Andrew Jones

Introduction

In this paper, I will discuss the construction and constitution of memory in the Earlier Bronze Age. I argue that an appreciation of the significance of memory is critical to our understanding of a whole series of Bronze Age cultural practices, including the production of rock art, the construction of mortuary monuments and the production and deposition of artefacts. In order to emphasise the importance of understanding the distinctive nature of memory during the Earlier Bronze Age, I want to begin by contrasting Bronze Age memory systems with systems that make use of the written word.

Why do we need to consider the issue of memory in either the past or present? Memory is of course crucial to our ability to act knowledgeably in the world; memories allow us to draw on past events in order to model those of the future. But where do memories come from? Memories are formed in the first instance through our access to knowledge. It is the construction of knowledge and its relationship to memory that is worth considering here.

Let's begin by considering how we formulate our knowledge of the Bronze Age in the present. Our libraries are full of volumes presenting distinct features of Bronze Age archaeology. We find corpora of metalwork and pottery, and volumes detailing mortuary contexts and rock art. Volumes are devoted to specific classes of artefacts such as Collared Urns (Longworth 1984), Beakers (Clarke 1970), goldwork (Taylor 1980), and so on. The presentation of artefacts in this way enables us to compare, contrast and group artefacts in a manner that we feel is both productive and meaningful to our understanding of prehistoric societies. The production of a corpus or catalogue involves the collation of numerous metrical and graphic data on a whole series of disparate artefacts that are then presented in a single volume as a cohesive whole. We tend to overlook the fact that the production of a corpus is a highly specific kind of cultural practice. The visual representation of knowledge in this way, in printed books associated with texts, illustrations and diagrams, is characteristic of a very specific technology of remembrance. Rather than holding knowledge at the individual level in the form of visual memory, printed books allow us to retain memory in a static form. Through the medium of the printed page, knowledge is separated from the knower (Fentress and Wickham 1992, 15–16).

One of the further crucial points concerning the technology of the printed page is that knowledge may be derived from multiple locations and re-ordered on the page in a quite different fashion. Rather than knowledge being related to experience of a single place or time, knowledge is in effect disembodied and may be held in perpetuity at some distance from the place in which it was initially generated (see Latour 1987; Gow 1995). This is precisely what we observe as a consequence of the production of corpora of Bronze Age artefacts. Artefacts are removed from their distinct geographical regions and placed in juxtaposition on the page with morphologically similar artefacts. This procedure allows us to gain an overview of particular classes of artefact and enables us to define our typologies and construct more refined chronologies for the period (e.g. Burgess 1980; Needham 1996).

Due to the specific form of our cultural practices, we arrive at a characterisation of memory as a form of template, an *aide mémoire* that is available to be drawn from the 'pages of the mind' at any particular time in the future. We occasionally forget that the practice of constructing monuments and depositing artefacts in their particular settings relates to quite different memory systems.

If we wish to understand how artefacts are

constructed and reconstructed in memory in local-ised settings during the Bronze Age, then we need to remind ourselves that our ability to compare and contrast disparate artefacts from distinct regions is a condition of modern book-based technologies of remembrance. In contrast, during the Bronze Age, we need to emphasise the critical importance of memory systems based on the materiality of the lived world, such as material culture and landscape.

Memories are therefore constructed and trans-ferred in different mediums and through particular kinds of cultural practice. If we want to examine how memory was constituted in the Earlier Bronze Age, we are required to attend to Bronze Age cultural practices. We need to assess how it is that the practices peculiar to the Bronze Age both construct and constitute a quite different process of memory production. When we come to examine the depositional contexts of artefacts during the Bronze Age, we find that in the Earlier Bronze Age artefacts are found in one of two places: either as components of mortuary contexts, or deposited singly or in hoards in inaccessible locations in the ground or in watery places (bogs or rivers). One of the important consequences of these practices is that there is a contrast with our modern approach to the mass production of artefacts in which we are able to draw template-like on a plethora of extant material objects. During the Earlier Bronze Age, many artefacts were committed to the ground, to rivers and to mortuary contexts. They no longer took part in the material world and were thus consigned to a place in mem-ory.

Art, artefacts, agency and amnesia

A consideration of agency is essential before we examine the nature of memory in Earlier Bronze Age Scotland. The notion of agency embodies the point that people, in both the past and present, draw knowledgeably on the world in order to carry forward their lives. The trajectories of their lives are framed by the conditions of the world that they inhabit. However, at the same time, these trajectories are reworked by the consequences of their actions. People act within and act on the world. But what is the world made up of? The world consists of both people and the material conditions that they inhabit. It is made up of both people and things. At this point, I do not want to enter into discussion of the ontological distinction between people and things (see for example Thomas 1998). Rather, I want to note that things may constitute one means by which social relations between people are conducted. They are an external means by which people carry forth their lives. Indeed, some commentators have sug-

gested that it is this relationship between people and things that allow societies to maintain themselves (Latour 1999).

It is important to consider the notion of externality in more detail. Here, we may consider the proposal that things act as repositories for the storage of human intentions (see papers in Renfrew and Scarre 1998). Gell (1992; 1998) considers precisely this point in relation to the production and subsequent effects of art. In effect, Gell proposes that art objects extend the intentions of the individual artist, in short the intention to affect and engage with the viewer, outwards into the world. Art objects achieve this effect by virtue of their ability to ensnare or trap the viewer. For Gell (1996), art objects are literally attractive; their technical and visual complexity attracts the viewer and thereby the intentions of the artist are conveyed to this viewer. Moreover, since art objects are external to the artist, the artist's intentions are distributed outwards across time and space. Art objects are therefore one means by which people (in this instance the artist) may carry forward their social intentions.

How does the production of art relate to memory? We need to consider the relationship between memory and the practices of artistic production in some detail (see Melion and Küchler 1991). Here, I am making an assumption that the production of images is one way in which memories are transmit-ted from one generation to the next. Images are one means of externalising memories. When considering the relationship between images and memory on the printed page, we tend to view memory as a template that is drawn on in the production of images. According to this formulation, image production is actualised by memory. However, we may equally consider memory to be actualised by image pro-duction. Memories are shaped or created by the active production of images. If this is the case, then rather than thinking of memory as a static store of images, we might consider that memory *is* the process of production and transmission. Human memory is therefore defined, in part, by the require-ment to reproduce visual information. If this is so, then maybe we need to reconsider the proposal that things act as repositories of human intentions and evaluate the possibility that the production and transmission of artefacts actually *embody* memories.

We need to shift away from our traditional view of the relationship between memory and images as amnesiac, to one that concedes that images are an active component of the process of remembrance. Although image production is critical to my dis-cussion, I feel that we need to extend the argument concerning images to encompass the production of other forms of material culture (see Connerton 1989). If we are to consider this as a possibility, then we are

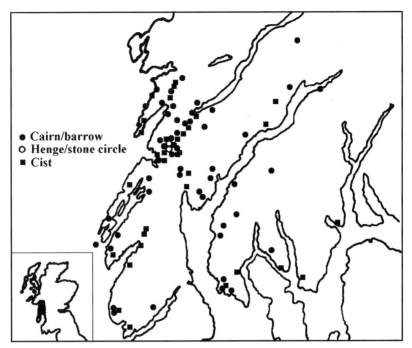

Fig. 20.1 *Map indicating distribution of monuments in Mid-Argyll; the concentration of monuments indicates the location of Kilmartin Valley*

required to attend to the specific kinds of cultural practices that relate to the transmission of material culture (see Strathern 1998). How do practices such as deposition, the construction of monuments and the decoration of rock surfaces relate to the cultural transmission of memories?

To recap, image production is involved in the production and transmission of memory, while images are also one means by which people extend their intentions outward into the material world. The two concepts are, of course, related, and with this qualification, I now want to consider them in relation to the 'technologies of remembrance' of Earlier Bronze Age Scotland.

Specifically, I will examine the relationship between the memories created by the execution of rock art and those related to the construction of mortuary monuments and the deposition of artefacts in the context of a series of burials located in the Kilmartin Valley, Mid-Argyll, Scotland. I will treat each of these practices individually before examining how they relate to each other prior to a concluding discussion of memory and image in the Earlier Bronze Age.

Iconography and imagery in the Kilmartin Valley

The Kilmartin Valley, Mid-Argyll, is situated on the west coast of Scotland. The valley runs between Loch Crinan and Loch Craignish to the southwest and

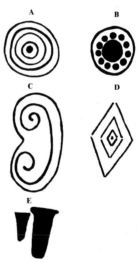

Fig. 20.2 *Some of the motifs found on different media in Mid-Argyll. A: cup-and-ring mark (from Poltalloch); B: rosette (from Ormaig); C: double horned spiral (from Achnabreck); D: lozenge (from Badden cist slab); E: axe motifs (from Nether Large North cist slab)*

Loch Awe to the northeast. It forms an important land route between the Irish Sea and mainland Scotland. The steep-sided, flat-bottomed valley has a remarkable concentration of prehistoric monuments, including chambered cairns, cairns, cists, timber circles, henges, standing stones and a proliferation of rock art (see Fig. 20.1).

I want to begin by describing the art found on different media in this area (Fig. 20.2) before describing the location and significance of the monumental features. At this point, I do not wish to consider the problematic nature of images in relation to chronology; rather, I simply propose to describe the nature and location of different kinds of motifs. Most of the motifs we observe are highly abstract. Firstly, we find pecked dots and circles. These 'cup-and-ring' motifs range from simple motifs with a single cup-mark, or a cup-mark with a ring, to complex motifs with multiple rings (see Morris 1977). These motifs are commonly found on rock surfaces in the open landscape, although several cup-marks and ring-marks are found on stones used for cists such as those at Barsloisnoch, Glennan, Nether Largie Mid and North, and Poltalloch. Cups and rings are also found on the standing stones at Ballymeanoch (RCAHMS [1988] 1999).

We also find a series of motifs with a wider currency that are commonly associated with passage grave art (Simpson and Thawley 1972); these include 'rosettes' (Van Hoek 1990), stars, ringed stars and horned spiral motifs. These are found both on open air rock surfaces, as at Ormaig and Achnabreck, and on upstanding monuments, such as on the southern stone circle at Temple Wood (Scott 1989; Frodsham 1996).

Lozenge motifs are found in several contexts. They can be seen on cist slabs, such as at Badden and Cairnbaan (RCAHMS [1988] 1999). They are also found on the upper sections of a number of Food Vessels, and on the upper sections of the Poltalloch jet necklace.

More general linear motifs are found on Beakers and Food Vessels. Here, they are comprised of cord or comb impressions. Linear motifs are also found in association with cup-and-ring motifs on open-air rock surfaces. Several impressed zigzag and triangular motifs are also found; these appear to be confined to the surface of Food Vessels.

Finally, we also observe a number of more representational motifs. These motifs, executed by pecking, comprise representations of metalwork, especially axes, on stone slabs. These are exclusively confined to cist slabs at Nether Largie Mid and North, and Ri Cruin, with a possible further example at Kilbride. Another possible metalwork motif is the pennanted halberd/boat motif from Ri Cruin.

How are we to approach these motifs? There are obviously chronological distinctions between different images. For example, the passage grave motifs are most likely to be earlier in date (Simpson and Thawley 1972; Bradley 1997, 107–113; RCAHMS [1988] 1999). However, since we are dealing with such abstract motifs, I feel that it is important to make few *a priori* distinctions between the media on which these images are inscribed. Rather than treating the production of images as examples of distinct and divisive

phenomena, related to either artefacts or rock surfaces, a more fruitful approach is to consider them as components of a continuum of iconographic images. This iconography consists of certain motifs articulated together on different media at certain times and in certain places. The aim then becomes to examine the grammatical and contextual relationship between motifs within this iconography (see Munn 1973; Morphy 1991; Bradley 1997, 10–11).

Images in the landscape

Having described the range of motifs found on rock surfaces, I want to describe the location of these features within the valley in more detail. In doing this, I want to consider not only what motifs are found in different regions of the landscape, but also how these images operate in terms of Gell's conception of agency. I will start with an examination of art in open-air settings.

At a general level, Bradley (1997) makes some interesting points concerning the execution of abstract motifs as components of rock art. He notes that these motifs are essentially communicative due to their visible location in the open air and their proximity to routeways and views (possibly overlooking and defining territories and rights of access). Their purpose was to create links of communication between distinct groups of people using a landscape whose lives intersected at different times. In terms of agency, these motifs extended the intentions of their authors in time, since the motifs provide the medium for communication to others members of the social group who may not have been co-present. However, due to their location on fixed rock surfaces, these images are static. At first glance, they do not appear to carry the intentions of their authors forward in space. However, as we shall see, each individual rock surface is intervisible and therefore connected. This has an important effect on how rock art is experienced spatially.

The rock art in Mid-Argyll is located at the head of the Kilmartin Valley in the area closest to the Crinan and Craignish Lochs. The rock art clusters around the upland valleys leading into this zone and within the upland area of the valley itself (Fig. 20.3). Bradley's recent analysis of this complex of rock art (1997; see also Gaffney *et al.* 1995) notes a number of important features. First, there is a distinction between simple and complex panels of carving on rocks: some panels only have single cup-mark motifs, whereas other rock surfaces have complex panels with numerous motifs, including earlier passage grave art motifs.

According to Bradley's analysis (1997, 120–126), the rock art in the Kilmartin Valley operates as part

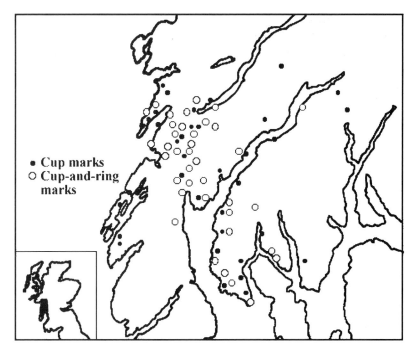

Fig. 20.3 *Map indicating the distribution of cup-marks and cup-and-ring marks in Mid-Argyll*

of a wider system in which one decorated rock surface is intervisible with others. The complex of decorated rock surfaces is located at the entrance to the Kilmartin Valley, and due to their intervisibility, the observer is led *in sequence* from one decorated rock to another, from the entrance of the valley into its interior. Crucially, it is those rock surfaces that are carved with the *most complex* motifs that are intervisible with other rock surfaces with complex motifs, and in turn these are intervisible with decorated upstanding monuments at Ballymeanoch and Temple Wood located on the valley floor. It is the complexity of motifs that draws in or ensnares the observer, since it is the most complex rock surfaces that are more visually arresting and carry the most information. Individual rock surfaces therefore extend the intentions of their authors forward in time and also in space, since they activate movement between rock surfaces and the monuments in the Kilmartin Valley.

What is more, the creation of images on rock surfaces is closely related to the production of memory. The execution of rock art appears to be *incremental* (Bradley 1991), with a sequence of motifs being produced, each of which interlocks and interrelates with former motifs. For instance, the four rock surfaces that compose the complex at Achnabreck are likely to have seen several episodes of image production, with each surface displaying interlocking and juxtaposed motifs (RCAHMS [1988] 1999, 8). Although there are differences between motifs on each surface at Achnabreck, and indeed

between distinct rock surfaces throughout the Kilmartin complex, there are also similarities, and we need to realise that the images on rock surfaces are inter-related both spatially and temporally.

If we take on board the possibility that these images were executed over a considerable period of time, then we might argue that it is the significance of place that promotes the decoration of rock surfaces, and that the decoration of rock surfaces gives additional significance to that place. Memories are activated through the repeated production of images related to significant places. This process of memorialisation is dynamic and the production of one set of images will condition the production of further images.

Furthermore, although the greater number of images carved on rock surfaces relates to the increased significance of place, this in turn relates to the increased amount of information conveyed by the images. Finally, this process leads to an increased complexity of images, which serves to attract attention. Each of these aspects of image production is mutually related. Crucially, these images have agency precisely because they are visible; they are located in open-air settings that remain available for reference and re-working a considerable time after their production. It is the distinction between the memorialisation process obtained by the production of visible images and the nature of the memorialisation process engendered by less visible images that concerns us here. It is to these less visible images that I will turn to now.

Graven images

I now want to consider the nature and chronological relationship of images on cist slabs. As noted above, there is a distinction between the kinds of iconographic motifs executed on cist slabs and those found in the open air. Cist slabs appear to have a predominance of linear or lozenge motifs and representations of metalwork. What is the status of these images in relation to those in the open air? There is a crucial link between cist slab, or single-grave art, and open-air art. This link takes the form of the simplest motif, the cup-mark. This is found in both contexts, suggesting that cist slabs form significant elements appropriated from open-air art sites (Bradley 1997, 136–150). In the case of the Nether Largie cist slab, the representation of axes appears to be superimposed on a series of cup-marks. Bradley (1993, 91–93) suggests that on this slab, there are at least four phases of image production. It would appear, then, that the incorporation of the cist slab into the cairn at Nether Largie involves a process of reuse. This process of re-use involves a visible element of the landscape that was reworked, through the creation of a quite different set of images, and placed in a non-visible location in the interior of the cairn. If we turn to the other examples of single grave art in Kilmartin, we note similar instances of reuse. For example, we note that the Badden cist slab, initially decorated with lozenge motifs, was reworked by cutting grooves on either side of the slab cut (Campbell *et al.* 1960). Again, the use of the cist slab indicates the reworking of motifs employed on an earlier structure, which were now hidden within the interior of a mortuary monument.

Are there any other instances of re-use in mortuary architecture? A number of cists in the linear cemetery in the centre of the valley, and those in the Polltaloch cemetery to the west of the valley, have grooved and battered edges. At this point, it is worth noting that the provision of cist slabs with grooved and battered edges is peculiar to Kilmartin (Campbell *et al.* 1960). The grooving of cists at the ends allows the close insertion of the end slabs, while battered edges provide a closer fitting joint. While this is the case, it is worth pointing out that although these architectural features allow the cist to be fitted together more closely, such features also afford two further things. Firstly, they allow the cist to be architecturally stable or free-standing with the minimum of support from cairn material, and secondly, since the cist slabs are constructed in such a way that they may be easily slotted together, these construction techniques allow cists to be equally easily dismantled. These features are only of importance if we entertain the possibility that cists underwent a considerable degree of re-working and

re-use prior to their final burial beneath cairns. There are several mutually related issues here: do cists have considerable histories of reuse, what do these phases of reuse constitute, and are cists available for reworking and redecoration prior to their final burial beneath cairns?

If we are to answer these questions, then we need to consider the empirical evidence more closely. Apart from the architecture of the cists themselves, there are three possible strands to our enquiry in this context.

1   First, I have noted above that the superimposition of art suggests a degree of reuse. Bradley's proposed four-phase sequence of image production at Nether Largie suggests repeated episodes of reworking prior to the use of the cist slab in a mortuary context. Although certain motifs, such as lozenges and cup-marks, may have prior significance, the critical thing to point out here is that they are incorporated into these highly specific Earlier Bronze Age contexts.

2   Our second line of argument depends on whether it is possible to demonstrate episodes of reworking. Here, it is notable that the interpretation of Greenwell's excavation of Kilmartin Glebe by the Royal Commission ([1988] 1999, 28–29) suggests a two-phase construction with the earlier phase represented by a boulder ring and slab-built cist and the later phase by a further boulder-built cist and cairn enlargement. Similarly, Scott's excavations at Temple Wood (1989) attest to processes of reworking. At the southern circle of stones, we note the construction of two earlier cists outside the stone circle that were encompassed by later phases of enlargement with the construction of a 'kerb' between the uprights of the stone circle. Further activity within the centre of the stone circle is indicated by the construction of two cairns, one of which covers a cist. It would seem, then, that there is evidence for a considerable time lag between the construction of cists and their burial beneath cairns.

3   A more general piece of evidence that suggests the possibility of considerable episodes of re-use prior to burial is that, overall, the burial monuments within the Kilmartin Valley are made up of flat cist burials and cist burials beneath cairns. Both of these classes of monument appear to contain the same form of material culture, especially Food Vessels. This suggests that we are not observing chronological changes in mortuary practices; rather, the two forms of mortuary architecture are part of the same tradition. This is a tradition in which we can observe a temporal sequence initiated by the construction of cists in

the first instance and finalised by the burial of these cists beneath cairns in the second instance.

Having rehearsed the evidence for these sequences of re-use and re-working prior to burial, we now need to assess what this evidence means in terms of processes of memorialisation. The cist architecture might be characterised as a very specific kind of technology of remembrance, a technology that allows the deposits within the cist to be re-memorialised at periodic intervals. Similarly, it is a technology that involves the transfer of already significant materials from one context to another, whether from the surrounding landscape or from previous sites of burial. Importantly, the critical aspect of this activity is that it involves a process of *incorporation* in which materials with prior significance are appropriated from elsewhere for use in the mortuary context. Ultimately, this process of incorporation is commemorative since it invokes, through the medium of material culture, the memories associated with other times and places. It is also *reiterative*, in that it involves reworking architectural elements and art that had prior significance. This process of incorporation is not isolated and there are a few Earlier Bronze Age sites in Scotland where evidence of reuse is also attested (Petersen *et al.* 1974; Dalland 1999).

While the processes of incorporation and reiteration operate in relation to the construction and decoration of cists, certain cist sites were chosen for elaboration and ultimate sealing through the construction of stone cairns. This act, to some extent, arrests the process of reworking and emphasises the process of incorporation, as certain places become the focus for monumentalisation. However, even this process involves incorporation, as cairn construction is in part determined by the construction of previous monuments, such that cairns become part of systems, most strikingly observed with the construction of the linear cemetery on the Kilmartin Valley floor. Similar processes of incorporation can be observed in relation to the standing stones at Ballymeanoch decorated with cup-and-ring motifs that refer to the art on open-air rock surfaces, while at the southern stone circle at Templewood, the double spiral motif refers to prior Neolithic systems of representation that are also found in juxtaposition with cup-and-ring motifs on open-air rock surfaces. Just as the construction of cairns over decorated rock surfaces arrests the process of re-working, so the incorporation of both previous and contemporary decorative motifs into upstanding monuments arrests the flow of memorialisation and reworking that is associated with the incremental production of open-air rock surfaces. With regard to monument construction, the process of incorporation in effect extends the notion of incorporation outwards into the wider landscape, as cairns and standing stones not only embody fragments from the surrounding landscape, but also actively transforms that landscape. Before assessing the implications of this particular technology of remembrance, I want to examine the nature of the artefact record.

Artefacts, images and deposition

In reviewing the evidence of artefacts and imagery, I again do not wish to discuss artefacts in terms of rigid typologies; rather, I want to examine the nature of images on artefacts and the depositional record for those artefacts.

Beakers are found in a number of different contexts in the Kilmartin Valley. One vessel was placed with two inhumations in a cist built inside the Crinan Ferry Cave (RCAHMS [1988] 1999, 108), while another was deposited in the chambered tomb at Nether Largie South (Henshall 1963). A Beaker was associated with three inhumations in a cist at Ballymeanoch henge, while a another was deposited with three barbed-and-tanged arrowheads and a flint scraper in a cist at Temple Wood (Scott 1989, 101). Finally, a Beaker was deposited with a crouched inhumation in a cist in the cist cemetery at Poltalloch.

There are at least fourteen certain Food Vessels from the Kilmartin Valley. They were almost exclusively deposited in cists or in cists beneath cairns, and they are associated with both cremations and inhumations. Their depositional contexts are therefore more restricted than those of Beakers. Whereas Beakers appear to have been deposited in some contexts that allowed a level of access, such as caves or chambered tombs, Food Vessels were placed in contexts that were more often sealed. Although there are significant overlaps in the kinds of contexts in which Beakers and Food Vessels were deposited, for example both are found in cists, and sometimes in the same cist cemetery, as at Poltalloch, there are also differences. It is these similarities and differences that I want to draw out.

Overall, I want to emphasise two points of difference and similarity. Although we observe contextual similarities in the deposition of Beakers and Food Vessels, we also observe similarities in the decorative techniques applied to these two broad classes of pottery. Both Beakers and Food Vessels in Kilmartin were decorated with a series of linear horizontal and vertical designs comprised of cord and comb impressions. The important difference between Beakers and Food Vessels in relation to decoration is that although similar decorative techniques were used, the combination of techniques was quite different. Moreover, the decoration of Food Vessels is of a greater order of complexity than that of Beakers in this area. Food Vessels were decorated all over with complex designs that visually are not easily divided into distinctive motifs, whereas the decoration of Beakers is simpler, and distinct motifs are visually easier to ascertain.

Another important difference lies with the fact that certain motifs on Food Vessels are also related to those found on other artefacts. For example, lozenge motifs are found on the upper zones of the jet spacer-plate necklace from Poltalloch and on the upper area of the Food Vessel from Barsloisnoch. Indeed, the jet necklace was found in the same cist cemetery as a number of Food Vessels. Moreover, the same motif is found repeated on cist slabs from Badden and Cairnbaan. There appears to be a contextual relationship between certain kinds of design and certain kinds of context.

Art, incorporation and memory

On the face of it, the re-use of cist slabs and the deposition of decorated artefacts have little in common. On the contrary, I want to suggest that not only do these practices have certain commonalties, but that both are associated with a related process of memorialisation. As I argued above, some level of re-use and re-working can be discerned in relation to cists. The practices associated with reiteration also involve a process of *incorporation*, since they actively include elements from previously significant contexts.

I want to argue that the incorporation of structural elements in mortuary contexts and the execution of art are, in terms of memory, two sides of the same coin. I have already argued that the production of art is an essentially commemorative process since memories are activated by images. However, we may go one step further and note that the production of an image also involves a process of incorporation since, at the cognitive level, the representation of the image is incorporated in material form. Images in effect *incorporate* some of the properties of that which they are imitating. It is due to the ability of images to re-present in this way that images provide a conduit for memories since they create an *imitation* of the memory of a given object. It is precisely because images, however abstract, have the power to re-present that the circulation of images is carefully guarded in both contemporary and traditional societies (Morphy 1991; Taussig 1993). Due to the property of similarity (the ability that images have to incorporate, within their form, elements of other images), certain images are imbued with qualities of agency (Gell 1998, 99–104).

Let's consider for a moment the images of bronze axes on the cist slabs at Nether Largie Mid and North, Kilbride and Ri Cruin. Many commentators have seen these as *representations* of bronze axes (Simpson and Thawley 1972) that act as substitutes for the presence of metalwork (Needham 1988; Bradley 1997). This view is fundamentally correct, but let us consider these images in terms of the agency instantiated through their production. Firstly, it is important to observe that the production of these images by pecking is analogous to the production of the pecked stone moulds required for the production of bronze flat axes. A metaphorical link is established due to their execution using the same techniques. In many ways, then, the images of bronze axes have agency since technologically by their very form they are able to generate further bronze axes. The images of flat bronze axes stand for flat bronze axes in a very active way; they presence and signify the memory associated with the production of axes and they incorporate the properties of axes. In this instance, then, the production of art is closely allied to the production of memory.

We have seen that the production of images on cist slabs is related to processes of incorporation, but how can we consider the practice of incorporation in relation to artefacts? As noted above, there are both similarities and differences between Beaker and Food Vessel decoration and context. This is to be expected since as, Mizoguchi (1993) recognises, depositional practices are partly constrained by their relation to previous depositional practices, while also providing the medium for transforming contemporary practice. We observe this transformation as we see a shift over time from pots with less complex decoration that are deposited in more accessible contexts, to pots with complex decoration deposited in inaccessible contexts. In the case of both context and decoration, over time Food Vessels actively incorporate elements of the funerary practices associated with Beakers. The periodic deposition of pots in mortuary contexts is similarly an act of incorporation that promotes the active production of memories. This process of incorporation goes further, since we also find the same motifs, especially the lozenge, employed on jet necklaces, Food Vessels and cist slabs.

Images of death

So far, we have seen that images occur in two main contexts in the Kilmartin Valley. Firstly, they are found on rock surfaces in the open air or on upstanding monuments; secondly, they are found on cist slabs, pottery and other artefacts in mortuary contexts. There are relationships between the two:

cup-marks are found in both contexts, and we may argue, following Bradley (1997, 136–150), that the carved rocks in mortuary contexts represent re-used components from the surrounding landscape. However, the kinds of motifs found in mortuary contexts are quite different to those in the open air, suggesting a significant act of transformation, with one set of images appropriate to visible settings, and another set of images related to less visible mortuary contexts (see also Simpson and Thawley 1972).

I want to retain this contrast, but I also want to consider these two sets of images with regard to the issues of memorialisation discussed at the outset. As argued above, images not only activate memory, but because of their ability to visually engage, they participate in the active transmission of memories. Due to its visibility, rock art served to communicate the intentions of its authors both temporally and spatially, enabling territories and rights of access to be defined, and drawing the observer from surface to surface into the ceremonial landscape at the heart of Kilmartin.

How do the images associated with mortuary contexts operate? We have already noted that the process of memorialisation associated with artefacts and cist slab construction is related to processes of incorporation and repetition. I have also argued that the production of images is an active part of the process of incorporation. To begin with, we need to be aware when considering the deposition of arte-facts in mortuary contexts that these objects are deposited with the human body, either in the form of a cremated or inhumed individual. As Last (1998) observes, the human body is not only a symbolic resource around which objects are placed (see Thomas 1991), but is also 'an emotive trace of an embodied subject' (Last 1998, 44). The body in the grave does not simply represent the corpse of an unknown faceless individual; rather, it represents the corporeal remains of an individual who intervened in the life of others. As such, it is a focus for bereavement and remembrance.

I now want to shift the emphasis from the corpse to the objects placed alongside the corpse, and I want to suggest that we focus on an aspect of mortuary practices that remains implicit to mortuary studies. Although archaeologists often use grave goods to determine the status of the deceased, there is little recognition of one of the primary relationships between grave goods and memory, that is their role in objectifying the experience of loss (see Maschio 1993). The active disposal of grave goods is a culturally important material metaphor for the expression of the emotion of loss (see Tarlow 1999, 20–50 for discussion of the primacy of metaphor and emotion in mortuary rituals). I concur with Fowler (2000) that we face considerable problems in at-

tempting to relate to emotion cross-culturally; nevertheless, I contend that the practice of depositing artefacts in the grave has the effect of temporalising or breaking emotive ties as artefacts are lost from view. Artefacts stand as visible reminders of the dead, and as the corpse is buried, so are the artefacts that crystallise memories of the individual.

Given this point, we need to ask the following question: why are images of any nature related to mortuary contexts? As Barrett (1990, 111–116; 1994) notes, the proliferation of distinct classes of pottery in mortuary contexts during the Earlier Bronze Age relates to the increased interest in the classification of the individual. Similarly, Boast's analysis (1996) of the distinction between Beakers from settlement and mortuary contexts indicates the predominance of fine ware Beakers in mortuary contexts. He attributes this pattern to the biographical status of the Beaker; since it is associated with the individual in life, it is buried with that person on death. However, he also notes that Beakers in burial contexts tend to bear the most complex decorative motifs. To some extent, these two observations may be reiterated with regard to Food Vessels. There is a singular lack of Food Vessels in settlement contexts, while the majority of Food Vessels in burials are decorated with complex visual designs.

The distinctiveness of the artefacts associated with the corpse is critical, and indeed we may observe that in the Kilmartin Valley, as more generally, each of the Food Vessels and Beakers placed in mortuary contexts is decorated in an individually distinctive manner. The images associated with the artefacts in the grave therefore serve a defining function: they provide a means of *fixing* memories. Due to the complex and distinctive nature of these artefacts, they effectively serve to entangle or retain memories otherwise related to the memory of the deceased: they provide a site or focus for memories (Maschio 1993; Hoskins 1998). In many ways, the materiality of the performance of deposition is constitutive of memory, and we may consider subjectivities to be created through this intense process of memorialisation. Just as the physical image of the deceased is removed from the gaze of the living in the form of the corporeal body by inhumation or more fully by cremation, this process is both objectified and intensified by the deposition of an image-bearing object. In the case of the Earlier Bronze Age, this object is a highly decorated pot or jet necklace.

We may extend this observation to the decoration and placement of cist slabs in the mortuary context. Just as the deposition of highly decorated artefacts both captures memories of the deceased and chan-nels feelings of loss through deposition, so the carving of bronze axes serves to emphasise the notion of loss. Axes are objects normally associated with the living; they are a rare component of mortuary assemblages (Needham 1988). Meanwhile, as noted above, the images of axes are active, since technologically they are related to the production of axes in stone moulds. Therefore, by placing these empty carvings in a mortuary context, they evoke the presence of something once productive that is now absent.

Both artefacts and single grave art are therefore related to the notion of loss. It is for this reason that these images are placed in an inward-facing position, facing the dead, whereas less complex images, such as cup-marks, associated with the art of the wider landscape, face outwards (Bradley 1992; 1997, 136–150). Just as both artefacts and the image of axes are associated with the living, so too are the lozenge motifs that adorn both jet necklace and cist slab. We may note, then, that images on artefacts and on cist slabs define a series of relationships between the adornment of the deceased, the artefacts placed with the deceased, and the cist slabs surrounding the deceased. We may think of images being located on a series of *nested surfaces* surrounding the body. These are related to successive levels of bodily intimacy: the body's internal sustenance in the case of pottery, the body's surface in the case of jet necklaces, and enclosing the body in the case of cist slabs.

Conclusion: images, memory and landscape in the Earlier Bronze Age

In this section, I want to draw together the discrete strands of Earlier Bronze Age commemorative practices in order to assess the distinct nature of both commemoration in the Kilmartin Valley and more generally during the Earlier Bronze Age.

I want to begin this task by taking up a concept discussed in the previous section. I noted that the placement of images in relation to the corpse was nested according to distinct levels of intimacy. However, we may extend the notion of nesting out from the mortuary context, and note that due to the organisation of monuments and rock art in the Kilmartin Valley, the landscape is also nested. We observe cairns containing artefacts and engraved cist slabs aligned in the centre of the valley, monuments carved with open-air art motifs situated closer to the head of the valley, while the upper reaches of the river valleys entering Kilmartin are defined by art on natural rock surfaces. This underlines the point that different kinds of image-based commemorative practices are related to different places within the

valley. In essence, we can note that we observe three distinct, but related technologies of remembrance:

1 Rock art is executed on natural rock surfaces. These images in effect are defined by the fact that they alter and simultaneously define immutable features of the landscape. They are a way of fixing memory in place that relates to the apparently unchanging character of that place. This is underlined by the ambiguity of the motifs; their meaning may be reinscribed over a considerable period of time.

2 This is by way of contrast with artefacts and art in mortuary contexts. As argued above, the images on artefacts and cist slabs are also a means of fixing memory, but that memory is transient in that it is related to the loss of a member of the living community. The incorporation of artefacts and decorated cists in the grave is related to the human life span, and these memories are reworked by periodic deposition or the re-use of cist slabs. Memories here are episodic.

3 Finally, the construction of monuments on the site of cist graves is a means of creating permanence, of overcoming the transience of the human life span.

These different technologies of remembrance are related to overlapping and interrelated notions of memory in which the expression of memory is mediated either in the form of the landscape or in the form of images.

In the light of this, I now want to assess more generally the nature of Earlier Bronze Age memory systems. In general, it is critical to point out that image production is an important component of Bronze Age memorial systems. However, we need to note that a critical aspect of images relates not only to their production, but also to their continual re-working. While the creation of images relates to the production of memory, the periodic deposition and re-working of images in the form of artefacts, cist slabs or rock art animates memory. This contrasts strongly with memory systems based on written documentation in which image-based memories require little reproduction in order to persist; in contrast, in the Bronze Age, the persistence of image-based memory required continual action. A disassociation of Bronze Age artefacts, rock art and mortuary architecture from their contexts is essential in order to pursue the refinement of chronologies and typologies. However, we need to remember that we must also recontextualise these components of Bronze Age archaeology in relation to their historically specific technologies of remembrance if we are to fully understand how art, artefacts and monuments came into being during the Earlier Bronze Age.

Acknowledgements

I am grateful to Richard Bradley, Jenny Rose and Hannah Sackett for discussing some of the ideas in this paper. I would also like to thank Jo Brück for her invitation to publish in this volume.

References

Barrett, J. C. 1990. Early Bronze Age mortuary archaeology. In Barrett, J. C., Bradley, R., and Green, M. *Landscape, Monuments and Society: the Prehistory of Cranborne Chase*, 120–124. Cambridge: Cambridge University Press.

Barrett, J. C. 1994. *Fragments from Antiquity: an Archaeology of Social Life in Britain, 2900–1200 BC*. Oxford: Blackwell.

Boast, R. 1996. Fine pots, pure pots, Beaker pots. In Kinnes, I. and Varndell, G. (eds) *Unbaked Urns of Rudely Shape: Essays on British and Irish Pottery for Ian Longworth*, 69–81. Oxford: Oxbow Monograph 55.

Bradley, R. 1991. Rock art and the perception of landscape. *Cambridge Archaeological Journal* 1, 77–101.

Bradley, R. 1992. Turning the world: rock carvings and the archaeology of death. In Sharples, N. and Sheridan, A. (eds) *Vessels for the Ancestors: Essays on the Neolithic of Britain and Ireland in Honour of Audrey Henshall*, 168–176. Edinburgh: Edinburgh University Press.

Bradley, R. 1993. *Altering the Earth: the Origins of Monuments in Britain and Continental Europe*. Edinburgh: Society of Antiquaries of Scotland Monograph 8.

Bradley, R. 1997. *Rock Art and the Prehistory of Atlantic Europe: Signing the Land*. London: Routledge.

Burgess, C. 1980. *The Age of Stonehenge*. London: Dent.

Campbell, M., Scott, J. and Piggott, S. 1960. The Badden cist slab. *Proceedings Society of Antiquaries of Scotland* 94, 46–61.

Clarke, D. L. 1970. *Beaker Pottery of Great Britain and Ireland*. Cambridge University Press. Cambridge.

Connerton, P. 1989. *How Societies Remember*. Cambridge: Cambridge University Press.

Dalland, M. 1999. Sand Field: the excavation of an exceptional cist in Orkney. *Proceedings of the Prehistoric Society* 65, 373–415.

Fentress, J. and Wickham, C. 1992. *Social Memory*. Oxford: Blackwell.

Fowler, C. 2000. The individual, the subject and archaeological interpretation: reading Luce Irigaray and Judith Butler. In Holtorf, C. and Karlsson, H. (eds) *Philosophy and Archaeological Practice: Perspectives for the 21st Century*, 107–135. Göteborg: Bricoleur Press.

Frodsham, P. 1996. Spirals in time: Morwick Mill and the spiral motif in the British Neolithic. *Northern Archaeology* 13/14, 101–139.

Gaffney, V., Stancic, Z. and Watson, H. 1995. Moving from catchments to cognition: tentative steps towards a larger archaeological context. *Scottish Archaeological Review* 9/10, 41–64.

Gell, A. 1992. The technology of enchantment and the enchantment of technology. In Coote, J. and Shelton, A. (eds) *Anthropology, Art and Aesthetics*, 40–67. Oxford: Clarendon.

Gell, A. 1996. Vogels net: traps as artworks and artworks as traps. *Journal of Material Culture* 1(1), 15–38.

Gell, A. 1998. *Art and Agency: an Anthropological Theory*. Oxford: Clarendon.

Gow, P. 1995. Land, people and paper in western Amazonia. In Hirsch, E. and O'Hanlon, M. (eds) *The Anthropology of Landscape: Perspectives on Place and Space*, 43–63. Oxford: Oxford University Press.

Henshall, A. S. 1963. *The Chambered Tombs of Scotland*, vol. 1. Edinburgh: Edinburgh University Press.

Hoskins, J. 1998. *Biographical Objects: How Things Tell the Stories of People's Lives*. London: Routledge.

Last, J. 1998. Books of life: biography and memory in a Bronze Age barrow. *Oxford Journal of Archaeology* 17(1), 43–53.

Latour, B. 1987. *Science in Action: How to Follow Scientists and Engineers through Society*. Milton Keynes: Open University Press.

Latour, B. 1999. *Pandora's Hope: Essays on the Reality of Science Studies*. Cambridge, MA: Harvard University Press.

Longworth, I. 1984. *Collared Urns of the Bronze Age in Great Britain and Ireland*. Cambridge: Cambridge University Press.

Maschio, T. 1993. *To Remember the Faces of the Dead*. Madison, WI: University of Wisconsin Press.

Melion, W. and Küchler, S. 1991. Introduction: memory, cognition, and image production. In Melion, W. and Küchler, S. (eds) *Images of Memory: on Remembering and Representation*, 1–47. Washington: Smithsonian Institute Press.

Mizoguchi, K. 1993. Time in the reproduction of mortuary practices. *World Archaeology* 25(2), 223–235.

Morphy, H. 1991. *Ancestral Connections: Art and an Aboriginal System of Knowledge*. Chicago: Chicago University Press.

Morris, R. 1977. *The Prehistoric Rock Art of Argyll*. Poole: Dolphin Press.

Munn, N. 1973. *Walbiri Iconography: Graphic Representation and Cultural Symbolism in a Central Australian Society*. Ithaca: Cornell University Press.

Needham, S. 1988. Selective deposition in the British Early Bronze Age. *World Archaeology* 20, 229–248.

Needham, S. 1996. Chronology and periodisation in the British Bronze Age. *Acta Archaeologica* 67, 121–140.

Petersen, F., Shepherd, I. A. G. and Tuckwell, A. N. 1974. A short cist at Horsbrugh Castle Farm, Peebelshire. *Proceedings Society of Antiquaries of Scotland* 105, 43–62.

RCAHMS [1988] 1999. *Kilmartin Prehistoric and Early Historic Monuments*. Edinburgh: HMSO.

Renfrew, C. and Scarre, C. (eds) 1998. *Cognition and Material Culture: the Archaeology of Symbolic Storage*. Cambridge: McDonald Institute.

Scott, J. 1989. The stone circles at Temple Wood, Kilmartin, Argyll. *Glasgow Archaeological Journal* 15, 53–124.

Simpson, D. and Thawley, J. 1972. Single grave art in Britain. *Scottish Archaeological Forum* 4, 81–104.

Strathern, M. 1998. Social relations and the idea of externality. In Renfrew, C. and Scarre, C. (eds) *Cognition and Material Culture: the Archaeology of Symbolic Storage*, 135–147. Cambridge: McDonald Institute.

Tarlow, S. 1999. *Bereavement and Commemoration: an Archaeology of Mortality*. Oxford: Blackwell.

Taussig, M. 1993. *Mimesis and Alterity: a Particular History of the Senses*. London: Routledge.

Taylor, J. 1980. *Bronze Age goldwork of the British Isles*. Cambridge: Cambridge University Press.

Thomas, J. 1991. Reading the body: Beaker funerary practice in Britain. In Garwood, P., Jennings, D., Skeates, R. and Toms. J. (eds) *Sacred and Profane: Proceedings of a Conference on Archaeology, Ritual and Religion, Oxford 1989*, 33–43. Oxford: Oxbow Monograph 32.

Thomas, J. 1998. Some problems with the notion of external symbolic storage, and the case of Neolithic material culture in Britain. In Renfrew, C. and Scarre, C. (eds) *Cognition and Material Culture: the Archaeology of Symbolic Storage*, 149–157. Cambridge: McDonald Institute.

Van Hoek, M. 1990 The rosette in British and Irish rock art. *Glasgow Archaeological Journal* 16, 39–54.

Afterword: Back to the Bronze Age

Richard Bradley

The Three Age Model has taken on new life in recent years, but it has done so in an unexpected way. It was originally devised to organise the material culture of prehistory according to the prevailing technology, stone, bronze or iron, but now it defines three groups of period specialists each with an agenda of its own. Over the past twenty years, work on these different periods has made remarkable progress, and yet it seems as if only one of these divisions could be studied at a time. First, there was a renewal of Bronze Age studies, then came a new assessment of the Neolithic period. There followed major changes in the character of Iron Age research. Each group of specialists set the agenda for a while, before the initiative passed to those working on another period. What is quite remarkable is how often the same body of ideas was transmitted from one chronological phase to another. Thus the 'new' Iron Age grew out of studies of the Neolithic, and the same may be true of some of Bronze Age research reported here.

This cycle has run for over two decades, and now there are signs that it may be beginning again. This volume comes twenty years after the proceedings of another conference, published as *Settlement and Society in the British Later Bronze Age*. As one of the editors of that collection, I have been asked to contribute to what is surely its successor. But I do not want to cast myself in the role of 'discussant', for this would be quite inappropriate; I have no intention of judging the separate papers, as they can stand on their own merits. Rather, it may be useful to characterise this volume by comparing it with its predecessor. In that way, it should be possible to define what is really new in Bronze Age studies. It may also help us to identify the problems that still need investigating.

It may seem an artificial exercise to compare one collection that is limited to the *Later* Bronze Age with another that considers the Bronze Age as a whole, but that is not the case. Well under half the contents of the present volume concern the first part of this period, and in some cases it is considered only in passing. The Later Bronze Age is analysed in considerable detail, yet I still find it difficult to pin down the distinctive character of the Early Bronze Age or to account for the contrast between these two phases. Generally speaking, individual studies are concerned with different kinds of evidence from these separate periods: with barrows, cairns and rock carvings in the Early Bronze Age rather than settlements, hoards and fields.

For all the theoretical advances of the past twenty years, it is easier to account for the archaeology of the Middle and Late Bronze Ages, and this is clear from the contents of the book. That is curious, for some of the major developments in our understanding of later prehistory have been inspired by work on much earlier periods. For example, there is a new emphasis on structured deposition, which grows directly from research on the Neolithic. Again, there is a growing concern with the symbolic dimensions of Later Bronze Age houses and field systems that bears the imprint of studies already conducted in Neolithic archaeology. But if that provides a source of inspiration, it seems strange that it has had so little influence over research on the *Early* Bronze Age. As matters stand, it is easier to contrast the ideas expressed in this volume with those in *Settlement and Society* than it is to compare them with the account of Early Bronze Age archaeology in Burgess's The Age of Stonehenge.

The contributors to *Settlement and Society* showed a predilection for general models that is less apparent here. From Rowlands's introductory chapter to Ellison's accounts of cemeteries and exchange systems, there was a willingness to work on the regional scale. Some of those models have fared better than others. A number seem unsatisfactory for purely empirical reasons: the pace of discovery has increased and more relevant material has been found. Others, my own included, do not do justice to the subtleties of the evidence that is now available; to some extent they are also vulnerable to changes of chronology. Only Rowlands's model, which was conceived on a European scale, still has the power to influence current work, and this is surely evident from Yates's contribution to the present collection. That is not to say that *Settlement and Society* was without studies conceived at a more local scale, but these were essentially descriptive and lacked the detailed appreciation of the field evidence that has been possible in more recent work. Put simply, there was no equivalent to Nowakowski's discussion of house abandonment or Barber's of metalwork deposition. New projects were certainly reported in the 1980 collection but only rarely were they discussed in detail or related to an explicit theoretical position. One exception was Drewett's innovative account of spatial organisation inside the Middle Bronze Age settlement at Blackpatch. His evidence can be interpreted in other ways, but the paper helped to set an agenda for more imaginative studies of Bronze Age settlements.

More recent field projects have been conducted at very different scales from those considered in 1980. There are very large excavated settlements like Reading Business Park or some of those considered in Yates's paper. There are extensive investigations of large tracts of the Bronze Age landscape, like the projects summarised by Malim and Ashmore, and there has also been a new generation of earthwork surveys like those described by Field. At the same time, greater attention has been paid to the full variety of sites, so that the smaller or more unusual examples described by Ashwin, Hinman and Locock represent something that is entirely new. The same is true of Jones's study of Bronze Age rock carvings and Timberlake's work on ancient mines.

Some of the projects described here offer a new integration between the separate elements in Bronze Age archaeology. Thus Brossler's account of Reading Business Park integrates field systems, houses and burnt mounds, just as Barber is able to consider the relationship between occupation sites and deposits of metalwork. Several of the contributors are also able to link the settlements of the living with the remains of the dead, and Yates can even suggest how land division on a regional scale was related to the distributions of ringworks and metal finds. Again, this evidence is overwhelmingly linked to the Later Bronze Age. A similar integration between the different parts of the Early Bronze Age landscape is still a task for the future.

In 1980, the range of theories applied to Bronze Age studies was really rather limited. Most derived from structural Marxism, with a particularly strong emphasis on core-periphery relations. Twenty years on, this approach has gone out of favour, although its assumptions have rarely been discussed. The emphasis on contrasting cores and peripheries has certainly been weakened by the more uniform distribution of fieldwork carried out as part of the planning process, but the truth is that small scale studies have simply become more fashionable. That is no bad thing, as the chapters by Jones, Brück, Nowakowski and Watson make clear. All are genuinely new and exciting, and none of them would have been easy to assimilate into the Bronze Age archaeology of twenty years ago. It remains to consider this work within a larger framework, and this is one of the challenges that still remain for the future. It may be necessary to build models on the scale of those offered in the 1980 collection in order to see this work in a wider perspective.

There are some topics that seem to have gone out of favour. There is very little here on ceramics or artefact chronology, although Ashmore's paper does provide a salutary message for those who employ radiocarbon dating. There is less on the deposition of metalwork, although the two papers that do consider this subject, those by Barber and by Pendleton, take radically different lines. Instead, an exciting new approach is provided by Timberlake's work at the metal sources themselves: an initiative that runs in parallel with new research on the axe quarries of the Neolithic period. In the same way, the study of the dead, which for many years seemed synonymous with Bronze Age archaeology, plays a very limited part in this collection. The same is also true of the origins of hillforts, for this was another of the main topics of discussion in Bronze Age archaeology a generation ago. Again, these omissions result from changes of fashion. The problems that were addressed in 1980 still need to be considered now.

Another area that is under-represented is the natural environment, which played a rather stronger role in the 1980 collection. This deserves more attention, for it may provide one way of unlocking the problems associated with the Early-Middle Bronze Age transition. At present, there seems to be something of a contradiction between the evidence from excavation and that provided by molluscan and pollen analysis. Despite the wealth of excavated material summarised by Yates, there is little to suggest that systems of regular land divisions existed in most parts of Britain before about 1500 BC. That might well point to the intensification of agriculture part way through the Bronze Age, but the environmental evidence suggests a rather different picture. Although the number of new clearings may have increased, there is evidence for a much more gradual intake of settled land extending back to at least the Late Neolithic. It seems as if the process of clearance and colonisation proceeded more evenly than the formal demarcation of farmland. It is important to consider how land holding was organised, for other changes happened at roughly the same time. It is surely no coincidence that the sites of deserted houses were more often respected from the Middle Bronze Age onwards and that their abandonment might have been marked by rituals of the kind discussed by Nowakowski. Like the field systems, their remains become visible to the archaeologist from the mid second millennium BC, but it would be unwise to take this evidence at face value. Kitchen's chapter also raises the question of settlement mobility, another issue that may have a direct relevance to this problem of perception. To investigate these questions further, it will be essential to pay more attention to Early Bronze Age settlement and landuse in future research.

There remain two crucial problems that must also be considered. They are not among the topics treated here, although both are implicit in some of these discussions.

There is the geographical scope of these papers, which is biased towards southern England. That is almost inevitable, for it is here that most new research has taken place. It is certainly the area that has seen the most sustained campaigns of rescue excavation. This volume summarises some of the results of that work. Although they have provided many insights, this is one way in which they may also distort our understanding of the Bronze Age as a whole.

Ashmore's contribution stands out from most of the other chapters in this book. That is not only because of his explicit emphasis on dating but because the chronological and cultural scheme in vogue in southern England simply does not apply to Scottish archaeology. Although the same types of metalwork may have been in use, the landscape evolved in a quite distinctive manner and many of the monuments conventionally assigned to the Late Neolithic or Early Bronze Age period have a much longer currency there. A similar problem affects a wider area. Kitchen's paper is especially interesting because it concerns the North of England where some of the houses and field systems originally considered to characterise the Early Bronze Age landscape appear to be later in date. That observation is important for again it serves to show how the conventional contrasts between the two halves of this period may not have the same significance outside southern England. By extension, there is yet another sequence in Ireland where ostensibly 'early' monuments like stone circles may extend into the Late Bronze Age in parallel with many of the hillforts that had previously been dated to the Iron Age. In each case the moral is clear. A scheme that works in an intensively researched lowland area need not have any relevance for other parts of these islands.

That carries a further implication. There are monuments in the North of Scotland that are dated to the Early Bronze Age by radiocarbon even though their closest equivalents are found in the 'Late Neolithic'. Irish hillforts have only been redated to the Late Bronze Age since it became apparent that the local Iron Age was aceramic. In the same way, there are difficulties of terminology. How should we talk about Bell Beaker pottery – should it be described as Late Neolithic or Early Bronze Age? – and in many areas, including parts of southern England, there is no obvious difference between Late Bronze Age and Early Iron Age ceramics. On both sides of the Irish Sea the conventional scheme is in trouble. Technological distinctions can be misleading; flint was used throughout the Bronze Age and into the Iron Age, while metal of any kind is rarely found in settlements prior to 400 BC. Faced with so many difficulties, it is becoming harder to use the language of the Three Age Model at all.

Should we go back to the 'Bronze Age'? I think not. Over a century after those period divisions were devised, it is time to work out a scheme better suited to the needs of archaeology.